MANAGING CULTURAL SYNERGY

THE INTERNATIONAL MANAGEMENT PRODUCTIVITY SERIES

A Complete Learning System

Robert T. Moran and Philip R. Harris

Volume 1:

Managing Cultural Differences

Volume 2:

Managing Cultural Synergy

Video Tapes:

Part 1. The Cosmopolitan Manager
Part 2. Transnational Managers as Cultural Change Agents
Part 3. Transnational Managers as Intercultural Communicators
Part 4. Understanding Cultural Differences
Part 5. Family Relocation Coping Skills
Part 6. Improving the Productivity of International Managers

Gulf Publishing Company
Book Division
Houston, London, Paris, Tokyo

THE INTERNATIONAL MANAGEMENT PRODUCTIVITY SERIES

Volume 2

MANAGING CULTURAL SYNERGY

Robert T. Moran
Philip R. Harris

Managing Cultural Synergy

Library of Congress Cataloging in Publication Data

Moran, Robert T., 1938-
    Managing cultural synergy.
    (Building blocks of human potential) (The International management productivity series ; v. 2)
    Bibliography: p.
    Includes indexes.
    1. International business enterprises—Management. 2. Comparative management. 3. Organizational change. I. Harris, Philip, 1926-   . II. Title. III. Title: Cultural synergy. IV. Series. V. Series: International management productivity series ; v. 2.
HD62.4.M67   658.1'8   81-13310
ISBN 0-87201-827-X   AACR2

Building Blocks of Human Potential / Leonard Nadler, Series Editor

The Adult Learner: A Neglected Species
Malcolm Knowles

The Adult Educator—A Handbook for Staff Development
Harry G. Miller and John R. Verduin

Managing Cultural Differences
Philip R. Harris and Robert T. Moran

Managing Cultural Synergy
Robert T. Moran and Philip R. Harris

The Conference Book
Leonard Nadler and Zeace Nadler

The Client—Consultant Handbook
Chip R. Bell and Leonard Nadler

Human Resource Development: The European Approach
H. Eric Frank

Leadership Development for Public Service
Barry A. Passett

People, Evaluation, and Achievement
George Nixon

The NOW Employee
David Nadler

Handbook of Creative Learning Exercises
Herbert Engel

Acknowledgments

Writing a book on any topic requires the cooperative efforts of many people. This book was no exception. The diversity of the themes and the geographic areas of the world which were covered also required the support and sharing of material from friends and professional colleagues. We thank, especially, Len Nadler, the series editor of Gulf Publishing Company's Building Blocks of Human Potential. Other colleagues who made significant synergistic contributions were George Renwick, V. Lynn Tyler, Nancy Adler, and Krishna Kumar.

We are grateful to Orville Freeman, president of Business International Corporation for his insightful foreword.

We also want to thank all those who permitted us to incorporate some of their ideas and materials in this volume. We have attempted to give credit to these persons and publications in both the text and chapter references.

Dedication

To all persons who behave synergistically, and thereby contribute to the fulfillment of individual and organizational potential.

About the Authors

Robert T. Moran, who received his M.A. and Ph.D. from the University of Minnesota, is a psychologist and an organizational management consultant whose specialties include cross-cultural training, program development and global human resource development. As an international consultant, he has worked with more than 1000 families moving overseas and many more managers who travel abroad. Dr. Moran has designed and conducted programs and seminars for the American Management Associations, Control Data Corporation, Chase Manhattan Bank, N.A. Esso Eastern, Inc., J.I. Case, and more than 100 other business organizations. Dr. Moran is now director of the program in cross-cultural communication and professor of international studies at the American Graduate School of International Management, Glendale, Arizona.

Philip R. Harris received his M.S. and Ph.D. from Fordham University. President of Harris International in LaJolla, California, he is a licensed management and organizational psychologist. As an international management consultant, he has successfully served over 150 multinational corporations, government agencies, associations, and educational institutions. His clients include Westinghouse Electric, Control Data Corporation, N.A.S.A., and the U.S. Department of Labor and Navy. A former college dean and vice-president, Dr. Harris was a Fulbright professor to India, as well as visiting professor at Pennsylvania State University, Temple University, and Sophia University, Tokyo. He is a member of the International Division Board for the American Society for Training and Development, which bestowed upon him its Torch Award for outstanding contributions to human resource development. Dr. Harris is author/editor of numerous articles and books in the fields of education and management.

Contents

Unit 1—Cultural Synergy in the Management Process

Unit 2—Fostering Synergy in Organizational Development

Unit 3—Cultural Specifics and Synergy

Foreword

A leading industrial statesman in Japan recently observed that U.S. and Japanese companies are 95% alike in their approaches and operations, but the 5% difference is what really matters. The observation conforms to our current fascination with the successful Japanese model of development, but is, I believe, overdrawn. What is true, however, is that we have concentrated hard and effectively on the 95% and have shared the knowledge and achievements contained in that 95% package with the rest of the world. And we have *not* paid enough attention, and certainly have developed no systematic approach, to that 5% that can indeed make a vital difference.

The authors of this book address themselves, in a way that is both sound and thought-provoking, to that neglected and important 5%. They proceed on a set of assumptions which my own observations during four decades in politics, government, and international business have compelled me to share:

● Interdependence—global interdependence—is no longer a matter of belief, preference or choice. It is an inescapable reality.

● The cultural synergies that are required as a corollary call not for compromise but for comprehension. As the authors put it: "In true synergy, nothing is given up or lost. . . Cultural synergy is like a successful marriage. Two people, two organizations, or two nations come together for mutual benefit to develop a relationship that is different in quantity and quality, and in productivity and reward, from the sum of their individual contributions."

● Cultural synergy, therefore, like sound economic development, is not a zero sum game.

● Multinational corporations have a special role not only in building cross-cultural bridges but in *innovating* synergies through their practical knowledge of putting together human and natural resources with the knowhow of managing both in the most effective way.

● Cross-cultural synergies have to be created not only abroad but at home as well. The United States especially, with its deliberately chosen heterogeneity and its commitment to both political and cultural pluralism, has, and will continue to have, minorities that have to be induced to contribute to the dynamic of our society, economically and culturally.

What makes this book particularly appealing is that the authors document their assumptions with meaningful case histories of companies and countries and distill useful checklists for hands-on management from a combination of theory and practice.

They also offer some provocative ideas pointing to where we are going, or should be going, and how these directions can be managed with a reasonable hope of success. Thus, they distinguish between "world-shapers" and "earth-squatters," and argue that, in administrating our global village, we must move, and indeed are moving, from bureaucracy to "ad hocracy," a process that managers will recognize as getting new or necessary things done through the mechanism of a task force.

They also produce a fundamental conclusion with which I concur: "Man is not a victim of fate; he can create history. In an epoch of nuclear power, technology, cybernetics, and bio-chemical advances, the opportunities to plot and navigate human evolution have never been greater. The choices that we make will largely determine the degree of control we exercise over changes, and in turn, the beneficial effects of them."

I would like to share with the readers of this intriguing volume, two contiguous comments.

At Business International we have found in the course of 27 years of working intimately with multinational corporations wherever based (the U.S. and Canada, all of Western Europe, Japan and, in recent years, companies with corporate headquarters in India, Brazil, Mexico, and Korea) that each multinational company has a culture of its own, in the full sense of that word, and that a successful cultural synergy therefore requires a fusion not only of home and host country cultures but of the corporate culture as well. For multinational corporations, cultural synergy is a trilateral process.

My other comment is purely personal. In my lifetime, I have moved in both awareness and action from being a concerned citizen of my native city, Minneapolis, to becoming a concerned citizen of my state of Minnesota, to becoming a concerned citizen of the United States, to becoming a concerned citizen of the world. I would like to testify that I found the process not seamless, but compelling; not easy, but inescapable. The authors of this book make a convincing case that all of us have to travel this route. I can only agree.

Orville L. Freeman
President and Chief Executive Officer—Business International Corporation
(Former U.S. Secretary of Agriculture and Governor of Minnesota)
June 1981

Preface

Our International Management Productivity Series ties together two concepts on cultural differences and synergy which we hope are "ideas whose time has come." Modern managers have only recently considered the cultural aspects of the management process, and the cost of this gap in the international manager's repertoire of skills has been significant. Our parallel themes have addressed (a) the realities of cultural *differences* in people, and how better to cope with them for improved interaction and commerce within the world marketplace; and (b) the challenge for *synergy* when we move beyond our cultural conditioning through cooperation and collaboration with others who are different from us.

In this second volume, we have reviewed many definitions, examples, and opportunities for synergy within the general practice of management; for organization development or renewal; and for doing business in geographic regions with unique cultural approaches.

Throughout the ages, it is remarkable how people have crossed beyond their own borders in the pursuit of trade relations, thereby creating mutually beneficial commercial and social transactions. The human drive to buy, sell, and exchange does not respect cultural boundaries, and has lead to numerous pioneering explorations and cultural interchanges. Marco Polo, Christopher Columbus, and the old China traders have something in common with today's global energy searchers, multinational managers, and traders in the People's Republic of China. They all moved beyond their home cultures to interact with a variety of host cultures in the hope of improved international business. Perhaps where missionaries, politicians, and the military have failed in promoting peace and prosperity by cooperation among nations, the 21st century cosmopolitan managers and technicians may succeed. Certainly, economic and community development on a plantetary scale can only occur when the human family learns to work together by capitalizing on its very divergences. As we grow in synergistic understanding and skills, we are in a better position to utilize effectively the resources of our own planet.

Cultural synergy can occur in the micro-management of a single enterprise or it can take place between and among human systems. The disappearing industrial paradigm of Western culture placed labor, management, and even government in competition and, often, in opposition to each other. The success of Japan demonstrated the obsolescence of that approach, because in that Eastern culture industry and employees cooperate for the good of the whole country. We propose that a synergistic "partnership" between the public and private sectors, involving managers, workers and consumers, is necessary for future survival. Certainly, collaboration is the key to creating a new organization in the developing metaindustrial culture.

High-synergy environments are supportive and result in cooperative actions and behaviors. Low-synergy environments are competitive and result in individualistic, "dog-eat-dog" behaviors. The greatest challenge in the future will be for all peoples to live together cooperatively on a planet of limited resources and unequal distribution. It is our hope that some of the ideas presented in this series will be instrumental in helping international managers in the improvement of the human condition.

For the reader's convenience we have divided the book into three units. Unit 1 considers synergy within the global management process. Unit 2 examines this key theme in terms of the organization and its development. Unit 3 discusses examples of synergy within specific regional cultures, and ends by challenging transnational managers. We hope that readers and colleagues will expand and develop the insights in these culture management volumes and accompanying videotapes.

Robert T. Moran
Phoenix, Arizona
Philip R. Harris
La Jolla, California
September 1981

Cultural Synergy in the Management Process

1.
Synergy in International Management

The crow imitating the cormorant drowns in the water.
—Japanese proverb

In a superb presentation of journalism, NBC* asked the question "If Japan Can . . . Why Can't We?" This documentary, which showed the viewers Japanese workers' quality circles, made it obvious that there is a high degree of cooperation between the workers and the managers. The success of Japan in a business context is indisputable.

> Two Chrysler assembly workers put a 13-hour stranglehold on the company's huge Jefferson Avenue plant Tuesday idling some 5,000 employees. The two men scaled over a 10-foot-high wire crib and pushed the control button, cutting off the electricity . . . Workers gave them a wire cable which they used to secure the crib. More workers gave them heavy chains and locks to further secure their positions. When the men finally came out at 7:11 p.m., they were given a hero's ride out of the plant.
>
> *Detroit Free Press*[1]
> July 25-26, 1973

The NBC production examined very carefully some of the similarities and differences in the Japanese and U.S. management systems. The program posed a question: Can the United States, which has been on the top for so long, borrow from another business system?

---

*Shown on NBC National Television June 24, 1980.

2

It is our conviction that all persons and organizations can learn from others and adapt aspects of those systems to fit their own. Here is an example of what we might learn from the Japanese. It was originally taken from the experience of one of the authors (Moran):

> I'd like to tell you how I first learned about Japanese management techniques. Between 1965 and 1968, I was the playing coach of the Seibu Railroad Ice Hockey Team, the best team in Japan. The owner of the team and president of the company, Yoshiaki Tsutsumi, decided to devote some of his time to developing ice hockey in Japan in preparation for the 1972 Winter Olympics, which had just been awarded to the city of Sapporo in northern Japan . . .
>
> In October 1968, shortly before leaving with a group of 25 Japanese hockey players for a one-month, 17-game match against Canadian amateur and semi-professional hockey teams throughout Canada, I was asked to attend a meeting with Mr. Tsutsumi. I was told the purpose of the meeting was to decide on the wardrobe for the players during their tour of Canada, which was to take place in January (Canada's coldest month).
>
> There were six persons at the meeting, including the owner/president, his secretary, three other staff persons, and myself. After exchanging pleasantries, we began the serious business of selecting what would go into each player's luggage bag.
>
> Department managers from the Seibu Department Store were waiting in an adjoining room with samples of the various possibilities. The meeting lasted over four hours. First, we decided on the outerwear—coats, hats, gloves, and overshoes. Then the formal and informal suits and sweaters, and finally the *underwear*. Yes, we even decided on the kind and number of undershorts that each player would be allocated. The person making these decisions was the president himself, Mr. Tsutsumi. Of course, many hundreds of hours were spent planning other aspects of the tour.
>
> Of the 17 games played in Canada, the Japanese team won 11, and from both Canadian and Japanese perspectives, the tour was a total success. On several occasions, during the pregame discussions and between-period pep talks, the fact that the company president was concerned about them to the extent of assisting with the selection of their wardrobe was mentioned. He also telephoned before and after each game and spoke to several of the players a number of times. In my opinion, this was an example of Japanese management in its purest form.
>
> What is the moral of this story? Is it that the owners of amateur and professional hockey teams (and perhaps baseball, football, and other teams as well) should select the underwear for their players? No, it isn't. But having worked and conducted communication and team-building workshops for a professional hockey team in the National Hockey League, I certainly believe that a

little more care on the part of the owners in *communicating* and working with the players might have done wonders for their morale and have had a positive impact on their ability to win hockey games.[2]

Can the crow learn to imitate the cormorant? Can any management system borrow from another? In some cases, yes, and in others, no.

BEYOND AWARENESS

Almost everything that appears in management literature is *comparative* in nature. A book compares, for example, managerial processes and interdepartmental relations in the United States and Germany. Or an article compares the career paths of Japanese and American managers. These kinds of cross-cultural studies are useful, and an excellent example is the work of Bernard Bass and his colleagues, who studied the attitudes and behavior of corporate executives in twelve nations.[3] First, however, because our world is becoming more pluralistic and interdependent, it is vital, though difficult to study *interactions* between managers from more than one country.

Second, we should not assume that the U.S. management techniques are necessarily the best for American managers or for managers of other countries. American management techniques are based on American values and assumptions (for example, that we can influence and control the future to a high degree). Managers from other countries do not necessarily have such values and assumptions—at least they do not place as much emphasis or importance on them.

Third, improved individual and organizational performance is the purpose of most organizational change. This is generally accepted by managers. In attempting to implement changes that facilitate individual and organizational performance, one strategy that has not been sufficiently employed in the United States with any degree of consistency is that of studying other nations' management systems—and asking what we can learn from them.

Many managers feel that there's no need to do this. After all, they ask, "Hasn't the United States developed the most highly sophisticated system of management in the world? And don't the managers of the best foreign companies come to U.S. business schools for MBA degrees and executive management courses?" Yes, it may be true that many foreign managers come to the U.S. for training, but Americans can still learn from and borrow aspects of foreign management systems.

What Is Cultural Synergy?

Throughout this book, the authors have provided many definitions and illustrations of synergy. The following phrases, which have been taken from many sources, describe the essence of cultural synergy:

1. It represents a dynamic process.
2. It involves two, often opposing, views.
3. It involves empathy and sensitivity.
4. It means interpreting signals sent by others.
5. It involves adapting and learning.
6. It means combined action and working together.
7. Synergy involves joint action of discrete agencies in which the total effect is greater than the sum of their effects when acting independently.
8. It has the goal of creating an integrated solution.
9. It is sometimes related by the analogy that $2 + 2 = 5$ instead of 4, but given the various cross-cultural barriers, cultural synergy may be the equation $2 + 2 = 3$. If the cultural synergy sum is not negative, progress has been made.
10. For two prospective synergists to synergize effectively, true and complete understanding of the other organization and especially of the culture is necessary.
11. Cultural synergy does not signify compromise, yet in true synergy nothing is given up or lost.
12. Cultural synergy is not something people do, rather it is something that happens while people are doing something else that often has little to do with culture.
13. Cultural synergy exists only in relation to a practical set of circumstances, and it takes place by necessity when two or possibly more culturally different groups come to the mutual conclusion that they need to unite their efforts in order to achieve their respective goals.

Cultural synergy can be approached in two different ways. One could be called the "Ugly Foreigner Approach." (We do not use "American" as Americans do not have exclusive rights to "ugliness.") This corresponds to Nancy J. Adler's "cultural dominance model" of management.

The organization or nation providing the technology, capital, or resources has the power to impose its business or management system on another system. Previous and current histories of multinational corporations are replete with examples of the "Ugly Foreigner" approach.

At the other extreme is the "When in Rome, do as the Romans" management approach. Basic to this strategy is the parent organization's concern for the culture or business system in which it is operating. Every attempt is made to use local labor, management and organizational style; it is a polycentric approach. As Lee Camarigg states:

> The process of developing cultural synergy can be compared to the process two individuals go through when they marry. Though raised in unique cultures with unique values, they come together and develop their own new envi-

ronment. This involves discussions about such things as housing and furniture (plant and facility), when meals will be served (scheduling), and how much money will be spent for what (budgeting). Besides the quantitatively measureable aspects of this new environment, there develops a style of living, relating, which is mutually agreed upon. Aspects of this new environment are composed of (1) consciously accepted values and mores that are part of each individual's previous environment; (2) consciously agreed upon values and mores, which require discussion and compromise either by one or both; (3) unconsciously agreed upon values and mores, which are aspects of one of the partners' environment and are accepted by the other without notice or compromise; and (4) unconsciously agreed upon values and mores that develop as one partner reacts to the other. These are the problematic aspects of a harmonious relationship.

The consciously accepted values and mores that were part of each individual's previous environment form the area of overlap. These are shared values and mores and are generally accepted mutually as valid. An example in the marriage scenario might be the religious practice of the couple. If both have been attending church regularly, in all probability, they will continue to do so. The same is true if they have not been attending regularly. It is doubtful that because of the marriage they will start.[4]

Examples of Cultural Synergy

The basis for studying managers is not through comparisons, but through *interactions*. Aspects of North American or European managerial systems are not necessarily appropriate for managers of other geographic areas and may not even be the best for their own managers. Let's look at a few examples from both a practical and a theoretical perspective.

Example One: The Type Z Hybrid
William G. Ouchi and Alfred M. Jaeger,[5] identify characteristics of typical American organizations (Type A):

1. Short-term employment
2. Individual decision-making
3. Individual responsibility
4. Rapid evaluation and promotion
5. Explicit, formalized control
6. Specialized career path
7. Segmented concern

and characteristics of typical Japanese (Type J) organizations:

1. Lifetime employment
2. Consensual decision-making
3. Collective responsibility

4. Slow evaluation and promotion
5. Implicit, formal control
6. Nonspecialized career path
7. Holistic concern

They then compare these organizations and relate them to their sociocultural roots. They conclude by presenting a hybrid organizational form (Type Z), which they suggest may be useful in the United States.

Each of the two types of organizational structures (American and Japanese) represent a natural outflow and adaptation to the environments to which they belong. However, a number of U.S. companies are now using aspects of Japanese management with great success.[6]

Ouchi and Jaeger suggest the following characteristics for Type Z organization (modified American):

1. Long-term employment
2. Consensual decision-making
3. Individual responsibility
4. Slow evaluation and promotion
5. Implicit, informal control with explicit formalized measures
6. Moderately specialized career path
7. Holistic concern for individuals

Example Two: The GM Experience

In the early 1970s, a 55-year-old General Motors factory in Tarrytown, New York, was infamous for having one of the worst labor-relations and poorest quality records at GM.[7] A turnaround grew out of the realization by local managers and union officials that disharmony threatened the plant's continued operation. Employees worried they'd lose their jobs so they began to work together to find better ways to build cars. Before this decision to work together, 7% of the workers were absent regularly and there were 2,000 outstanding employee grievances against management. The change came after GM management showed workers proposed changes at model changeover time in 1972 and asked for their comments. Many good ideas were presented. The plant supervisors also began holding regular meetings with workers to discuss employee complaints and ideas to improve efficiency. The benefits of these changes resulted in high-quality products, less than 30 workers' grievances outstanding, a less than 2.5% absentee rate, and declining worker turnover.

Such changes were all integral parts of the Japanese management system, but they fit for the U.S. workers at Tarrytown. They are also in harmony with American management theory of more participative leadership.

Example Three: Adler's Dominance, Compromise, and Synergy Models

Nancy J. Adler theoretically distinguishes between a cultural dominance model of management, a cultural compromise model of management, and a cultural synergistic model.[8] The cultural dominance model, described earlier as an "ugly foreigner" approach, is used when a company chooses to have one culture's style of management superimposed on the employees and clients of another culture. This model of management does not recognize or acknowledge the specific business or management styles of the nondominant culture. An example of the cultural dominance model, would be a U.S. organization that attempts to conduct business (marketing, advertising, or organizational structure) in the same way in Paris as in Los Angeles.

The cultural compromise model uses management policies and practices that are similar between the cultures involved in the business association. The new international organization culture that is created using this model is limited to those areas in which the national cultures are similar, as might be the case in North America.

Concerning her third model, Adler states:

> The cultural synergy model is designed to create new international management policies and practices. The cultural synergy model recognizes the similarities and differences between the two or more nationalitites that make up the international organization. The cultural synergy model builds a new international organization culture that is based on the national cultures of both employees and clients.[8]

Example Four: MNC Orientations

David Heenan and Howard Perlmutter, in *Multinational Organizational Development*, do not use the word "synergy," but list ethnocentric, polycentric, regiocentric, and geocentric as four orientations toward the subsidiaries in a multinational enterprise. *Ethnocentric* organizations use home-country personnel in key positions everywhere in the world, believing they are more intelligent and capable than foreign managers. *Polycentric* organizations leave the foreign managers alone (as long as the organization is profitable), because those managers know what is going on better than anyone else. *Regiocentric* organizations assign managers on a regional basis, such as a regional advertising campaign by French, British, and German managers with a European orientation. *Geocentric* organizations attempt to intergrate diverse viewpoints through a global systems approach to decision-making. In this case, superiority is not equal to nationality, and all groups can contribute to the organization's effectiveness.

Heenan and Perlmutter observe:

> Multinational corporate planners are evidencing renewed interest in environmental scanning and assessing outside forces. External stakeholders, particularly government and labor, are given major attention in charting the future worldwide course of the firm. What emerges from this review is a transformed MNC—an institution prepared to modify policies which may be outdated (such as insistence on wholly owned foreign subsidiaries) in favor of

strategies more compatible with the realities of the times. Consequently, mixed strategies on key decisions regarding ownership, staffing, and product development are adopted to accommodate varying stakeholder interests. . . .

The social architectural view of multinational organization development is based on the premise that the MNC is a purposeful system with its viability and legitimacy codetermined by internal and external stakeholders. As a rule, our suggested approach involves identifying the key stakeholders, examining the quality of relationships between stakeholders, and mobilizing their commitment to greater multi-nationalism. Our objective: to understand existing institutions and to help in some way to design new ones that can keep pace with the fundamental value changes that now influence the global industrial system.[9]

Example Five: Vectors Approach

In a paper prepared for a seminar taught by one of the authors, a graduate student from Switzerland, Anton Stauffer, described cultural synergy:

> Cultural synergy occurs when there is overlap of cultural beliefs and values to achieve more than the sum of each component. It is like the function of vectors—each vector alone drives with a certain force in a certain direction. Acting together, the resultant vector is the geometric sum of the individual vectors pointing in a certain direction (Figure 1-1).
>
> A multinational organization can thus be seen as a population of vectors each one having a slightly different direction and force depending on the values and skills of an individual. The geometric sum of these vectors is the

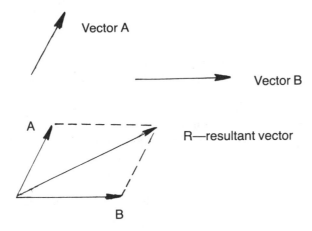

Figure 1-1. Cultural synergy is here represented by the resultant vector, R, the sum of the vectors (cultures) A and B. After Stauffer.

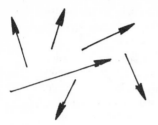

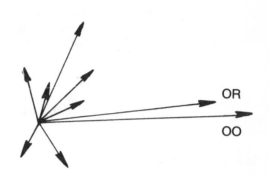

Figure 1-2. The "organizational resultant" (OR), or sum of individual values and skills, should as closely as possible reflect the organization's objectives (OO). After Stauffer.

"organizational resultant" (OR), which should be as close as possible to the organizational objectives (OO) (Figure 1-2).

The art of management is to find individual vectors so that they compare closely to the objectives established by the management, realizing that not all vectors can and should be equal in strength and force. This gets much more difficult in a cross-cultural situation, where the home country wants to implement objectives and policies which may run, at the worst, 180 degrees in the opposite direction of the "visiting" country's objectives and policies. In such a situation collaboration may be very difficult, if not infeasible.

In such a situation where you have some basic agreement, such as employment security, through mutual education and discussion both parties may come closer to agreed-upon objectives, and beneficial collaboration may ensue.

Figure 1-3 illustrates the group belief *before* education and discussion. Figure 1-4 shows the group belief *after* education and discussion and the resulting synergy.

Communication and discussion have brought both parties closer together, ending with a greater result. Cultural differences continue to exist, but mutual understanding is improved, and a better collaboration is possible.

However, the simple mathematical model of vectors cannot show all the nuances that usually prevail in a cross-cultural situation because no dynamic factor has yet been introduced. In this vector model time has not been considered, and human behavior simply cannot be expressed by an arrow pointing in some direction. Behavior changes over time, even from one day to another.

An example of cultural synergy experienced by me [Anton Stauffer], was in Brazil where more than 10 nationalities worked together on a green field project. This project was started and completed on time, and was producing

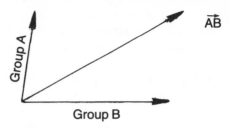

Figure 1-3. Vector A$\vec{B}$ represents the group belief *before* education and discussion. After Stauffer.

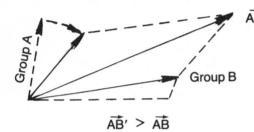

Figure 1-4. Vector A$\vec{B}'$ represents the group belief *after* education and discussion and shows the resulting synergy, because A$\vec{B}'$>A$\vec{B}$. After Stauffer.

afterwards at full capacity, something that is rare even in highly developed countries. How did it happen? Luck was probably on our side, but the real factor was management's understanding of the different cultural factors at work. But the understanding and awareness is only part of the solution. Making relevant decisions then implementing them to get the desired results is an art, requiring an understanding of different values and a very effective management of human resources in order to achieve such an organizational goal.

The slower moving Brazilian mentality normally prevailed, and had to be managed by the faster work mentality of the Europeans and Americans. Pressure had to be applied to reach the targets, but the question was how much pressure to apply and how to communicate it so as not to get a negative reaction. Whom can you delegate to do a particular job—and with whom— in order to get the best results? This is a difficult management task because even if the target is achieved, the cost may be extremely high. When cultural synergy works, the cost will be low, and future operations can be productive. In addition, the return for all sides involved is better; it is not a zero sum game, that is, when one wins the other loses. Both sides can reap benefits, even if certain cultural differences exist.

The Beginning or the End of Cooperation

With international trade and foreign investments on a steady increase, particularly with Third World countries that have strong nationalistic tendencies, deep understanding of forces at work and skills to manage these forces will be keys to successful international management. Thus, organizational strategy of the future will account for differences in vector strength and direction. Human resources will be used to contribute the maximum to the organizational objectives, emphasizing the individual's special skills or values. The criteria applied in decision-making will increasingly consider differences of the cultural values, while at the same time will also make maximum use of them. Thus, the manager's task is recognizing these differences and combining them in an optimal way. This must be accomplished within the contexts of the indigeneous national and organizational cultures if synergy is to be achieved. The case for this position is well stated by Gary Wederspahn:

> A heightened awareness of each other's cultural values enables coworkers of different nationalities to develop management strategies and plans to minimize potential conflicts and stress. But most importantly, it offers the possibility of helping them see differences as a source of *positive diversity* and enrichment of the management team that can enhance its overall effectiveness by turning cross-cultural stress into synergy. [10]

Cultural synergy is like a successful marriage. Two people, two organizations, or two nations come together for mutual benefit to develop a relationship that is different in quantity and quality and in productivity and reward, from the sum of their individual contributions. The skill of managing this synergistic relationship is the thrust of this book. Even naïve interpreters of world events and varied groups' relationships realize that short-term solutions and problems result from the dominance model of management or the ugly foreigner approach.

According to a Chinese proverb: "You cannot pluck a flower without disturbing the stars." All relationships are about interactions that influence each other. It is expected this volume will provide a framework and strategies for solving problems and building relationships that are in the best sense of the word "synergistic." George W. Renwick, in examining Australian and American differences, concludes:

> If these two people who differ on such fundamental points are to get on better with one another and work together with more satisfaction they can no longer assume they are similar to one another. they must begin to investigate their differences as well as their similarities and train themselves to recognize and *take advantage* of both. [11]

We call the "training" Renwick refers to as the ability to manage cultural synergy.

Cultural synergy can occur in the micro-management of a single enterprise or it can occur between and among human systems. The disappearing industrial paradigm in North America placed labor, management, and even government in competition and, often, in opposition to each other. The success of Japan has demonstrated the obsolescence of that approach, because in Japan government and industry cooperate for the good of the whole country. We propose that a synergistic ''partnership'' is necessary for survival in the future between the public and private sectors among managers, workers, and consumers.

Perhaps we can best end this chapter by referring to the research of Professor James O'Toole, University of Southern California's Center for Futures Research. In a study of 39 influential American leaders relative to the future of business-government relationships, he made a case for synergy when he concluded:

> For a century the key words used to describe the American political economy have been discord, disjunction, paradox, irony, conundrum, and contradiction. . . .But it is nevertheless essential to recognize that the dream of the free market remains enticing for most Americans. [12]

That dream may only be achievable through cultural synergy.

References

1. Quoted in *Work, Mobility and Participation,* by R. E. Cole, Los Angeles: University of California Press, 1979.
2. Moran, R. T. "Japanese Participative Management or How Ringi Seido Can Work For you," *Advanced Management Journal*, Summer 1979.
3. Bass, B. M., Burger, P.C., Doktor, R. and Barrett, G.V. *Assessment of Managers: An International Comparison.* New York: The Free Press, 1979.
4. Camarigg, L. Paper written at the American Graduate School of International Management, Spring, 1980.
5. Ouchi, W.G. and Jaeger, A.M. "Type Z Organization: A Better Match for a Mobile Society," *Academy of Management Review*, July 1978.
6. Ouchi, W.G. and Jaeger, A.M. "Made in America Under Japanese Management," *Harvard Business Review*, Vol. 52, no. 5, pp. 61-69, 1974.
7. "Stunning Turnaround at Tarrytown," *Time*, May 5, 1980.
8. Adler, N.J. "Cultural Synergy: The Management of Cross-Cultural Organizations." In: *Trends and Issues in O.D.: Current Theory and Practice,* Chapter 8. W. Burke and L. D. Goodstein (eds.), San Diego, CA, University Associates, 1980.
9. Heenan, D.A. and Perlmutter, H.V. *Multinational Organizational Development.* Reading, Mass.: Addison-Wesley Publishing Company, 1979.
10. Wederspahn, G.M. "Cultural Awareness for Managers," *The Bridge,* Vol. 6, no. 1, Spring 1981.
11. Renwick, G.W. "If Australians Are Arrogant, Are Americans Boring?" *The Bridge,* Summer 1980.
12. O'Toole, J. "What's Ahead for the Business-Government Relationship," *Harvard Business Review,* March-April 1979.

2.
Global Management in the Cultural Context

MANAGEMENT FUNCTIONS AND SYNERGY

Comparative studies of managers and management strategies and philosophies during the past few years have demonstrated the impact of national cultures on the values of administrators and their organizations. This chapter reviews some management functions from a cross-cultural perspective. The material and research cited are based on the premise that management practices are intimately bound to culture. The home culture of an executive or a multinational corporation impacts on business behavior. Opponents of this viewpoint believe that effective management is based to a large extent on universal principles that can be used in any country. The perspective of the authors of this book is that management is not based on such universal assumptions, though management theory and practice can be adapted appropriately across cultures. This perspective is reflected in the following quotations:

> The strategies and principles used by a society and all its organizations for dealing with disagreements and conflict reflect the basic values and philosophy of that society.
>
> R. Likert, 1976[1]

> . . . there are certainly differences and the French on the evidence do not perform as well as the Germans. The reason is that the French do not do enough planning. It is difficult to keep tight control, or, in other words, to have a clear idea of where you are in relation to your objectives if those objectives have not been clearly defined. The second factor is that in France, or at least in my

14

sample, company chiefs are more in favor of informal systems and central-ized decision-making than a formal system of procedures such as the Ger-mans and British have. . . . .I have tried to consider what the British and French could take from the Germans without altering their own basic philoso-phies and vice versa.

If we take for example the German method of budgeting for production costs and the centralization of their power structure, I would say that they could not be "exported" on to the British scene for one very simple reason; the British philosophy is based on decentralization of decision-making and maximum possible autonomy. On the other hand, there is nothing to stop Brit-ish firms adopting the German style 12 monthly plan. It does not pose any threat to their decentralized approach.

Introduction of a German style budgetary system, however, with costings on the basis of groups of 10, would require computers, a special headquarters team to run it, and a chain of command tightly controlled from the top—ex-actly what the British want to avoid. But, in the production field, on the other hand, there is nothing to stop the British copying the German way of requiring each operating unit to draw up its own 12 monthly program, including details of the improvements in performance expected from it.

J. Horovitz, 1979[2]

Many Americans are aware of the success of individual Japanese products. Japanese textiles, produced with cheap labor, were already inundating the United States in the 1950's. Since then, Japan's labor costs have risen until they are on a par with ours, but Japanese companies have raised productivity and expanded their ability to produce quality products at competitive prices. . . .Japanese steel plants have a capacity roughly the same as the United States or almost as much as the entire European economic community; but their capacity is the most modern and sophisticated in the world as we are belatedly acknowledging by using Japanese standards as the base measure for determining the "trigger" price. In motorcycles, the dominant four com-panies in the American market (Honda, Yamaha, Suzuki, and Kawasaki) are all Japanese. The United States reigned over the automobile industry, but last year Japan produced about 10 million cars, about the same as the United States, over 100 times the cars it produced 20 years ago. . . .In pianos, hard-ly a traditional Japanese instrument, in bicycles, tennis and ski equip-ment, snowmobiles, pottery, glass, machine tools, Japan is a strong competitor. . . .In banking, by 1978, of the world's largest 30 banks, 4 were American and 1 Japanese; of the top 300, 58 were American, 61 Japanese. . . .In the international market place, the chronic American trade deficits and continuing Japanese trade surpluses suggest that Japanese com-petitive superiority cannot be explained entirely by Japanese trade barriers which have been reduced rapidly since the late 1960's.

E. F. Vogel, 1980[3]

We are analyzed, inspected, and examined, usually very flatteringly, to determine how in 35 years we built a pile of rubble into a nation with the second largest gross national product in the non-communist world. . . .The key element in our economic growth is Japanese society itself. . . .Instead of the samurai warrior swearing fealty to his lord, the newly industrialized worker gave his loyalty to the employing corporation. In return, the corporation gave the worker the assurance of lifetime employment. . . .These two national characteristics—austerity and total loyalty to the company—have been the basis of the spectacular rise of our economy. They have given us a highly motivated, team-spirited work force that identifies with the fortunes of the company. . . .If you are married for life to the company, you have to feel that you have an impact on its operation and financial health.

K. Ibe, Chairman of Sumitome Bank, 1980[4]

The multinational corporation, long regarded by its opponents as the unique instrument of capitalist oppression against the impoverished world could prove to be the tool by which the impoverished world builds prosperity. . . .Third World multinationalism, only yesterday an apparent contradiction in terms, is now a serious force in the development process.

D. Hennan and W. J. Keegan, 1979[5]

The dilemma for the organization operating abroad is whether to adapt to the local culture or to try to change. There are examples of companies that have successfully changed local habits, such as the introduction of matrix organization in France. Many Third World countries want to transfer new technologies from more economically advanced countries. In order to work at all, these technologies presuppose values that may run counter to local traditions, such as a certain discretion of subordinates versus superiors (lower power distance) or of individuals versus in-groups (more individualism). In this case, the local culture has to be changed; but this is a difficult task which should not be taken lightly, and which calls for a conscious strategy based on insight into the local culture, in which accultured locals should be involved. Often, the original policy will have to be adapted to fit the local culture and to lead to the desired effect; we saw above how in the case of Management by Objectives this has succeeded in Germany but mostly failed in France."

G. Hofstede, 1980[6]

These observations illustrate the problem that international managers face as they work in a business environment with other leaders whose political, economic, technological, and cultural environment is different from theirs.

Any new management development can be studied for its cross-cultural implications, either in macro-or microcultures. For example, one could study how different cultures might react to matrix management. But within organizational culture, for instance in North America, this strategy represents cross-cultural or comparative management. Using Hughes Tool Company in California as the organizational culture, Baugh found that the type of managerial process employed in decision-making differed according to the team members' managerial responsibilities and professional background.[7] While many of the matrix managers made planning, staffing and directing decisions, Baugh found that virtually none reported making controlling or organizing decisions. Are cultural factors or bias involved in these findings? Among the six decision-making processes identified in his research, Baugh reported that the consensus approach was used because it shares risk and provides a common means to achieve an objective. The authors (Moran and Harris) contend that matrix management and consensus decision-making are examples of synergy, as well as indicators of meta-industrial organizational practices.

The same issues are also present in any technology transfer, especially between East and West or First and Third Worlds. In the foreword to Silvère Seurat's *Technology Transfer: A Realistic Approach*, John Humble capsulizes Seurat's synergistic approach for sensitive multicultural technicians and managers:

1. The insight that technology transfer above all is the capacity to store and transmit to people the accumulated experience and understanding of others.
2. The meticulous analysis of every facet of knowledge, skills, and perception that make for success in any task and operation. Then the use of advanced methods of motivation and reinforcement to transfer the knowledge and skills.
3. Sensitive adjustment to different cultural and work values.
4. Accelerated development of local managers and instructors so that dependence on expatriates can be reduced.
5. Close links with the educational systems of a community. Indeed, Seurat's method has itself been used with striking success to improve national systems of technical education.
6. Early planning of human and managerial aspects of new projects so that expensive and wasteful "crash programs" are avoided.
7. A systems approach that embraces all aspects of task analysis, organization design, recruitment, training, control, feedback, and dynamic development.
8. A proven capacity to deal with very large scale projects. The needs of the poor world are mind-boggling in their sheer numbers and urgency.
9. A dedication to the most cost-effective way to get results on every project.[8]

Culture and Managers

Few researchers have conducted the kind of studies on international managers that Bernard Bass and his colleagues have, in terms of the number of managers in the sample and the length of time the managers were studied. In *Assessment of*

Managers they profile managers from 12 nations to demonstrate how different cultural values and social characteristics result in different kinds of management behavior and objectives.[9] They studied managers from these countries to determine similarities and differences in attitudes, values and beliefs, and to see how they cope with the same kind of organizational problems.

The research results cover many areas too comprehensive to summarize. However, the U.S. managers were found to have a much slower rate of advancement than the average of those in other countries surveyed. U.S. managers were also found to have different life goals from managers in Britain, the Netherlands, Belgium, German/Austria, Scandinavia, France, Italy, Iberia, Latin America, India, and Japan (the countries in the study).

Managers from the United States were found to have individual self-realization, leadership and wealth as important self goals. U.S. managers had the highest tolerance for risk and conflict and the greatest preference for group participation in decision-making. In addition, they were seemingly faster and more effective in one-way and two-way communications than managers from the other countries, and they put a premium on maturity, logic, and adaptability.

It is important to know which management techniques work in different cultures and this can be determined by knowing the values and attitudes of managers from these countries. For example, participative decision-making seems to create satisfaction among managers in the United States. However, a more direct, authoritarian approach may be as effective, in other societies because participative approaches have to be more fully legitimized to be accepted by workers or managers from certain cultures. The level of cultural and industrial development may be a factor in preferring authoritarian to participative leadership.

A paradigm developed by anthropologists to help understand different orientations or approaches to important issues is presented in Table 2-1. This table illustrates the relativity of the management functions to be discussed, and from it we will suggest how each function might significantly influence what managers do.

From the cultural influences cited in Table 2-1, although they are highly generalized (e.g., man is evil), there follow many implications concerning the specific management functions of authority, leadership and one's place in a group. These are presented on page 20.

Robert Fillol in his book, *Social Factors in Economic Development*, suggested that development in Argentina will remain a problem because the Argentine "value-orientation profile" is inimical to the nation's economic growth.[10] He maintains the viewpoint that the passive value orientation profile of the Argentine society is the critical or fundamental factor that prevents the nation from accomplishing steady economic growth. This "profile" he refers to is a lack of "cooperation-mindedness" of "community spirit" in industrial relations.

Although our cultural heritage provides us with a unique guide to management practice, we can learn from the differences in other international managers.

Table 2-1*
Cultural Influences on Life Issues

	A	B	C
What is the character of human nature?	Man is evil†	Man is a mixture of good and evil†	Man is good†
What is the relationship of man to nature?	Man is subject to nature	Man is in harmony with nature	Man is master of nature
What is the temporal focus of life?	To the past	To the present	To the future
What is the modality of man's activities?	A spontaneous expression in impulse and desires	Activity that emphasizes as a goal the development of all aspects of the self	Activity that is motivated primarily toward measurable accomplishments
What is the relationship of man to other men?	Lineal—group goals are primary and an important goal is continuity through time	Collateral—group goals are primary. Well-regulated continuity of group relationships through time are not critical	Individual—the individual goals are most important

* Adapted from F. R. Kluckhohn and F. L. Strodtbeck's Variations in Value Orientations. Evanston, Ill.: Row, Peterson and Company, 1961, p. 11.
† This assumes that human nature is either mutable or immutable.

Some cultures are more synergistic than others, so it stands to reason that this impacts on management practice. For example, French culture is perceived to be more individualistic and less synergistic than other cultures. Thus, a French person's initial reaction to matrix management is to resist it, because of the requirements for shared authority and cooperation. Yet, even the French can learn to move beyond their cultural conditioning toward team management.

To understand how some of these factors might influence at a very practical level, one of the authors (Moran) developed an "Analysis of a Problem from Two Perspectives" worksheet. To complete the worksheet, the manager must describe a problem, analyze the problem from at least two perspectives, identify the basis of the problem in the values of a society, determine a problem-solving strategy that will work for both societies, and then assess how the implementation is working. This approach to problem-solving attempts to mold the different perspectives of the two cultures into a synergistic, or win-win situation for both cultures. An example of this approach is presented on pages 21-23.

Implications of Cultural Influences on Management Functions*

From the *Character of Human Nature* issue stem:

- Ability to compromise.
- Problem-solving approaches.
- Moral judgements.
- Guilt and punishment.
- Preoccupation with principles.
- Relationship between leaders and followers.
- Personalistic loyalties.

From the *Relationship of Man to Nature* Issue stem:
- Recognition of social conflict.
- Ideas on fatalism.
- Use of preliminaries and intermediaries.
- Resolution of conflict by restoration of harmony.

From the *Temporal Focus of Life* issue stem:
- The nature and value of social change
- The commitment to tradition.
- Orientation to the future.
- The value of efficiency.
- Risk taking.

From the *Modality of Man's Activities* issue stem:
- Activity separate from the individual is the standard of achievement that is external to the individual.
- Practicality.
- Spontaneous and integrated activity versus activity planned and divided into smaller units.
- Reflective, intellectual and creative activity; single role versus multirole performance; purpose of groups and memberships.

From the *Relationship of Man to Other Men* issue stem:
- The way people are socialized.
- Nature of groups.
- Peer groups relationship and relationship to inferiors and superiors.
- Status differentiation between leaders and followers.
- Formality and informality of relationships.
- Accorded and achieved status.
- Class and status consciousness.
- Egalitarian relationships.

*Modified from an unpublished paper by J. A. Mestenhauser.   ∎

Synergy Prospects:

In *English Culture and the Decline of the Industrial Spirit, 1850-1980,* Dr. Martin J. Wiener views the British as a culture in conflict. After a series of success stories— the bloodless establishment of democracy, the development of a world empire, triumphs in two world wars, evolution of a welfare state, and enlightened

(text continued on page 23)

Analysis of a Problem from Two Perspectives*

Description of the Problem

Perhaps one of the most difficult problems encountered by American businessmen and their respective families while conducting business and residing in Great Britain, is the apparent inability of the British to accomplish anything with speed or efficiency. Some foreigners in the U.K. believe this problem is inherent within British society and also manifests itself in the management structure of an English firm. Some American businessmen are continually frustrated by the seemingly slow and inhibited method of business procedure in Great Britain. Many examples can be cited whereby the newly arrived American executive has rushed into his British colleague's office in London full of zestful ambition to get the project underway, only to be quickly stumped by the tranquility, self-restraint, and perhaps, a seeming indifferent nature of the British associate.

American families living in Britain complain of the inordinate amount of time required by various service industries to respond to a request to perform the task at hand. For instance, should one require a plumber or an electrician, it is quite likely that the customer may have to wait twenty-four hours, and when the expert finally does arrive, he typically takes a longer time than one would deem necessary in the U.S. to carry out the job.

Analysis of the Problem

From the U.S. Perspective

From the American perspective, the British are criticized as being too soft and gentlemanly, lacking in aggression and self-discipline. Further, they are too comfortable with their heritage and current situation. Thus, they do not have an appetite for change and innovation.

Americans sometimes feel that the British do not have enough formal business education and that they are business amateurs in a specialist's world. Consequently, Americans may believe the British do not have either the capability to fully engage in rugged competition, nor do they have enough dedication to the profit motive.

As a result, Americans may conclude that the average British worker is basically lazy, unmotivated and ineffectual. Some British employees have an external image of incompetence and unenthusiasm.

From the British Perspective

The British worker, does not understand the constant need for rush that is so typical of his American counterpart. He or she views the American as being impatient, brash, overly aggressive, and forever striving to prove himself to his superiors.

The Britisher lives in a more relaxed and slow-paced environment, a characteristic that is attractive to foreigners. With centuries of European civilization behind them English people take life in stride. They do not see an overwhelming necessity to attack immediately a management problem or service call in the same way that his American peers do. While the British realize they must become more efficient and productive if they are to promote a healthier economy, they do not feel it is necessary to sacrifice their more casual and restrained nature, or quality of life, in

*This worksheet was completed by Christine Reddy, an English graduate student of the American Graduate School of International Management, September 1980.

Therefore, Americans perceive the British laborer as apathetic relative to how quickly he tackles a job, or indeed, whether it is accomplished at all between the necessary breaks for tea.

Identification of Basis of the Problem (Analysis of values, etc.)

From the U.S. Perspective

An American executive would, perhaps, summarize the basis of the problem of doing business with Great Britain as being a lack of aggression on the part of his British associate. An amusing comparison between the more assertive American attitude and the rather quiet and comfortable English approach is demonstrated by the anecdote of the American shoe salesman who was sent to Africa to sell shoes. A British salesman was also sent by his company in order to survey the potential market. Upon the arrival of the Englishman, he immediately sent a wire back to his home office in Northampton and said, "Coming back at once. Nobody wears shoes here." The American sent a telegram saying, "Send two million shoes. Nobody wears shoes here."

The American has been raised on the values of hard work, individual achievement, and success and evidence abounds of his constant quest to do better. Children are raised to believe that through applied effort and determination, one can climb further up the social ladder, get a better education, make more money, and marry someone successful. Consequently, it is imbedded in the American spirit to take every advantage for opportunity and achievement, and devote oneself to the classic American dream— to earn a small fortune through hard work and a determination, to succeed, and then retire and live comfortably from the profits.

Directly related to the American value of success is the belief that a person is in

favor of improved service and competitiveness.

From the British Perspective

Perhaps the most interesting contrast from the British point of view is the difference between how the two parties view business in general. In American society the industrialists were often admired for their wealth and power, whereas in Great Britain the industrialist lacked status. One must remember that because of the rigid class structure and restricted system of education, work did not inspire the same ambitions, social mobility, or status paths that it did in America. Work was previously disdained by all classes. There was a tendency for members of the upper elite to live a leisured life and they often looked upon the concept of work as being "beneath them." And the lower class, or the laborers, worked because of their economic and social dependence. Thus, because the British labor force was polarized by those people who had to work and those who did not, the educational system was not concerned with promoting management or business education.

Another virtue of the British that is closely allied to work, but that is at odds with the American view, is that of competitiveness. In England, the competitive spirit is traditionally more likely to be on behalf of one's group, team, or nation against another. The difference between the American individualistic spirit of competitiveness and the British communal orientation also points to the basis of the problem encountered by American executives operating overseas.

While the British are characterized by their lack of aggression, they feel that it stems from a rational need to keep things dividually responsible for one's own fate and has to rely on one's own resourcefulness. Consequently, in order to survive, flourish, and achieve, the American spirit is full of drive and competitiveness. These two factors of the American character have been paramount to the success of American industry.

under control. As a result, the British are well-known for affecting a certain docility and appearing aloof.

The British belief in self-restraint and the unflappable spirit is in direct opposition to the American brand of aggressiveness, but they believe these characteristics, rather than being deterimental to Great Britain, have been greatly responsible for peace and order within that country.

Problem-Solving

The expatriate managers should be aware, prior to their arrival in England of the different customs and traditions, beliefs and values systems of their host nation so they may understand what problems they can expect to encounter beforehand. Perhaps, by emphasizing the myriad differences found between the two cultures, the visitor would use more patience and understanding in dealing with their hosts. Many Americans believe that because the two countries share a common language, they also share a common culture. However, the problem described is a perfect example of how two cultures may operate in opposition to each other. Therefore, it is imperative that an American executive preparing to do business in Great Britain be made aware of the cultural nuances of the British in order that he may operate effectively within that environment.

Assessment of Implementation

Again, because the problem described does not relate to a specific confrontation, but is rather a direct result of the differences between two cultural groups, this step would be difficult to oversee. The American expatriate who has been, we hope, well-versed in the ways and mores of his British hosts, would be responsible for employing cultural sensitivity in all of his or her actions and should refrain from attempting to use an American ethnocentric approach in dealing with the British.

To determine the effects of a foreign deployment or cross-cultural indoctrination program, after a few months onsite survey, the feelings and attitudes of the American expatriate and his British colleagues to see whether or not they are both satisfied with their cross-cultural dealings with each other. Although good trade relations might indicate that the American and British executives are communicating effectively, oftentimes one must look much deeper, because in many cases cultural misunderstandings are not verbally stated, but rather remain under the surface where they do the most harm.   ■

relinquishment of an empire—this history professor maintains that the British are ill at ease with progress, and long for rural tranquility even at the expense of industrial progress. Economic behavior does not take place in a cultural vacuum, but there is a tribal character in work relationships and discipline. The development process of any nation and its commercial enterprises are affected by culture, society, and ideology. Research studies of the modernization process in societies emphasize the impact on a people of national character, values, and attitudes in the economic transformation of societies. The social and economic development of each people is unique. It influences how industrialists view their word and their role in it.

To enable Americans working abroad make the most of their foreign experience, pre-departure training in general and specific cultural aspects is proposed. American managers who are exposed to such cross-cultural orientations would be less likely to impose U.S. management mind-sets on British colleagues, and more likely to study British work practices that are encouraged in the U.K. and applicable in the States. Beyond that, while in the British Isles, they would search out means to foster collaboration with their British peers, as was done successfully in two World Wars.

CULTURE, ORGANIZATION, AND MANAGEMENT RESEARCH

Business schools in the United States offer many courses in organizational and human behavior in systems. Most of these courses deal with the formal and informal structure of the organization and its effect upon the organization's performance. Other offerings deal with motivational aspects of people and the dynamics in the system. For comparison some of the research involves multinational organizations and domestic organizations in other countries.

George W. England, Anant Negandhi, and Berhard Wilpert in their book, *Organizational Functioning in a Cross-Cultural Perspective*, have collected papers examining organizations across cultures.[11] Some of these studies are summarized here as they are relevant to our theme. England and others suggest four major reasons for studying organizational functioning in different countries. First, the studies should seek to establish certain hypotheses that apply universally across time and space. Second, they should determine if general cultural or national attitudes found in readings lead to observed differences in the organizational functioning. Third, the studies should seek to identify differences that are large and meaningful enough to warrant further research. And fourth, they should be used to identify practices, techniques, and relationships that can be used between countries and/or cultures.

F. A. Heller and B. Wilpert researched the influence and power-sharing found among senior level management in successful business organizations.[12] Their study comprised more than 1,500 senior managers in 129 large companies from 8 countries—France, Germany, the Netherlands, Israel, Spain, Sweden, the United Kingdom, and the U.S.A.—within 13 industrial sectors. Their paper dealt with the findings related to job performance requirements, skill acquisition time, specific decision, general decision, lateral decision, and formal skill qualifications.

Their findings illustrated that there is considerable support for the theory of human resources model thinking in that managers seem to adjust their decision-making processes to their perception of subordinates' skills. Where skills prove to be greater, participation in the decision-making process is significantly higher. Another indication of these findings is that presuming that participation in decision-making is indeed a function of skill resources, then increasing those skills will naturally increase participation. The link between skills and participation in decision-making seems to point out more strongly that managers in the countries studied tend to be more motivated by their sense of competence and their need to feel effective.

S. G. Redding and T. A. Martyn-Jones (in another study reported in England's book) examined the ways in which people in Southeast Asia think differently and the possible effects of this on managerial behavior.[13] They presented five areas of myths, or beliefs, generally held by the Orientals and then related them to five areas of managerial operations; causality, probability, time, self, and morality.

Causality—Is it possible that Asians do not get "organized" because the process of abstract thinking necessary to an organizational structure does not come naturally? Their study showed that Oriental cultures' businesses tend to be on a small scale, (not including Japan) and that most of these businesses operate without any organized planning system, formalized information, or allocation of responsibilities.

Probability—Oriental cultures tend to be described as fatalistic, with a close relationship between man and nature. Events occur in a cycle and explanations are given in terms of the inevitability of things.

Time—In Asia time has no beginning and no end, it is closely related to probability in that it is circular, things continuously follow one another. Orientals seem to have a lesser sense of urgency, because they do not conceptualize time in the same way that Westerners do. Because the future is regarded as being somewhat predetermined by elements beyond self, planning and forecasting do not come easily.

Self—Oriental cultures see the individual as being bound up into the social context, where individualism is less relevant. As a result, managerial beliefs in Asia shift towards the autocratic end, while still showing a greater expressed respect for subordinates than in the West.

Morality—Conformity to socially acceptable behaviors in the West is done through morality based on guilt, whereas the Orientals achieve the same result through a painful sense of shame or wounded pride within the individual. In a shame culture, the person produces behavior acceptable to others, and thereby creates greater restraint on at least interpersonal behavior.

From this study Redding and Martyn-Johns developed several hypotheses to indicate the relationship of these beliefs to managerial operations:

1. Oriental companies utilize less formal planning systems than the West.
2. Formal organization is less.
3. Staffing is less programmed and contains less formal training, while promotion decisions are less objective than in the West.

4. Oriental managers rely less on interpersonal confrontations, and control is facilitated using different social structures and norms.
5. Managerial decisions in Oriental companies consider the effects on other people more often than in Western companies.
6. Control of performance is less formal, and Oriental managers show less precision and urgency in such matters as timekeeping, scheduling, and completion dates.

The focus of another study by James Miller and others was the way in which culture influences the effectiveness and structure of organizations.[14] The authors presented three propositions, which were verified by data taken from the National Longitudinal Survey working age population. Proposition one stated that culture—whether it be the ecological and demographic environment, the social (which includes organizational) environment, or personal circumstances—influences an individual's perception and pattern of behavior. Proposition two stated that the behavior of a member of an organization results from the interaction of the three areas of culture mentioned above. Proposition three stated that an individual's behavior influences an organization, either through a singular contribution to the structure, through changes in other members' behavior, or through contributions to the overall behavior patterns.

The following conclusions emerged from the data used in this investigation:

1. Work values of Americans can be traced back to the work values of their Europeans ancestry, when wealth was to be valued only insofar as it reflected an individual's performance. Emphasis was also to be placed on a life of good deeds, ideas that were based on the religious background of most Europeans.
2. In contrast, black African groups, for example, raised large animals and grain and utilized the land. The size of the herd indicated a man's wealth. African groups tended to live in harmony with their environment, working it only for what they needed, based on the value system established by a communal relationship between family and tribe. As a result, black African groups would tend to transmit to future generations the utilitarian idea of work.
3. Data also showed that white men and women were more likely to view work as intrinsically valuable, whereas black men and women are more apt to view work in terms of wages.

Miller and his colleagues concluded that because of the influence of culture on the individual, there cannot be any one single management style or organizational structure. Organizations must be designed in order to accommodate shifting cultural patterns, in the environment. A second conclusion was that managers cannot assume that this study suggested wide cultural differences are based on how individuals perceive why they work. Managers will need to understand more about the cultural composition of the work force in order to motivate employees. Other aspects of individual interaction with an organization, such as authority and ability for independent action, may also be culturally influenced.

In an article in *Culture and Management*, H.C. de Bettignies and P. Lee Evans deal with the question of how different environments affect the men at the top in American and European firms, since the modernization of management in Europe will greatly depend on the organization and direction of the firm's chief executive.[15] Five specific areas of personal characteristics were discussed: social origins, education, and career development factors—age, "the climb to the top," and job mobility.

Regarding *social origins*, two conclusions were apparent: firstly, with regard to upper class managerial occupations, social origins did not play as major a role in the U.S. as in Europe and there is no clear indication that Europe is beginning to follow a more open social structure; secondly, it appeared that top management in Europe is predominately of upper-class origins, whereas it is an increasing middle-class domain in the United States.

Education is more highly emphasized in the U.S. than in Europe. This is due mainly to the value attached to on-the-job experience in most European countries, and to the high prestige given to careers outside commerce and industry.

Regarding *career development factors*, European companies tend to stress promotion and tenure more than American companies. This is seen in that many U.S. executives retire early or leave for another job. Job mobility, however is viewed equally among European and American executives, although there are distinct variations from country to country within Europe. Europeans present an ideal executive background as being a "generalist," with experiences in many departments and in general administration.

Bettignies and Lee concluded that distinct European characteristics do exist, although there is no prototype "European chief executive" as such. Differences do exist in attitudes and values, but these seem to result more from environmental and personal climates than from demographic or career characteristics.

Frank A. Heller conducted research that was designed to test the impact on leadership of managerial attitudes, such as the experience of managers, their perceptions of what goes on at work, their role expectations, and the organizational structure in which they must work.[16] Results indicated that managerial skills and job requirements were not easily definable. However, managers on different levels do seem to agree on responsibility, intelligence, and knowledge of technical matters. Differences appear most often in relation to leadership. Heller's research showed that most managers use different leadership styles in different situations. For example, Americans use a somewhat more "democratic" leadership style than the British, but both groups feel that if upper level management believes that lower level jobs require little skill, then leadership participation is kept at a minimum.

Heller's research concluded that it is undesirable to train managers in general principles, but more useful if people are made more sensitive to the situational factors that require different kinds of behavior. Even democratic methods in certain situations are not practical, and might lead to a credibiltiy gap between different managerial levels.

In another study reported in Weinshall, David J. Hickson and others investigated the effect of size of managerial structure.[17] They questioned the effect upon an organization of cultural factors that vary between societies, as opposed to the effects of "contextual" factors of a noncultural kind, such as size, ownership, technology, and field operation. Hickson et al, developed the following hypothesis: "Relationships between the structural characteristics of work organizations and variables of organization context will be stable across societies."

Basing their findings on fourteen organizations, they presumed that in all countries, size is the overwhelming factor in structure of activities, and size seems to be the fundamental ingredient of the organization. For example, when more people are brought together, more functions become specialized to develop more efficiency from personal skills and control of behavior. A result of bringing more people together is that problems of control stimulate development of control specialization, and the knowledge of what is happening in the organization held by any one person becomes continually smaller in comparison to the whole organizaiton. Therefore, more documentation of what ought to be done and is done is required. Although the level of these ingredients may differ between countries, the pressure exerted by the size is the same in each country. The ratio between these contextual variables of size or dependence and structural features will be of similar magnitudes and flow in the same direction. Interestingly, some cultures seem to favor complex macroorganizations, while others prefer family microorganizations.

Case Study in Cross-Cultural Technology Transfer

The world of engineering and technology is replete with examples of international management overcoming and utilizing cultural differences. Silvère Seurat, president of Eurequip, a French industrial consulting firm, has summarized one such experience in Africa that accomplished impressive results:

> Establishing a huge company in the middle of a desert poses huge technical and sociological problems; the Mauritanian people were not prepared for such industrial expansion. Personnel must be found, teaching organized, locals trained, jobs and organization adapted to local conditions in such a way that the supervisors can take over without disturbing plant running. This is an example of a technology transfer success.[18]

And in examining how a company should approach technology transfer, Seurat observes that bridging the cultural gap requires more than merely overcoming language and behavioral obstacles:

> The meaning of words in any language is colored by the emotional interpretations of those who use them. Such a "word drift" involves wide differences

from one nation to another. Where words relating to action are concerned (plan, objectives, management) Anglo-Saxons seem to color the words with ideas borrowed from economics and technology. Latins seem to modify the meaning of action words with ideas from politics or sociology.

In a political sense the word "plan" evokes ideas of *dirigisme,* state planning, antiliberalism, and will even be described as a left-wing idea. The word "strategy" is strongly associated for some people with militarism.

Many mental blocks can thus be thrown up by the use of certain words. On top of those individual blockages we find collective blockages: in a company that has unsuccessfully tried to apply management by objectives we must beware of negative reactions to the word "objectives."

And yet we must use words. In the plan's initial stages—even if it seems a waste of time—it is a good idea to organize an open debate to arrive at a consensus of the vocabulary to be used.

These are even more serious than language obstacles and less quickly solved. Without going into an exhaustive analysis of undesirable attitudes and behavior found in companies, we will center on three characteristics that tend to develop among employees in some companies as a result of the protective company cocoon:

1. A tendency to shy away from risk-taking and to prefer routine activities.
2. A tendency to shy away from conflict and to remain passive and dependent.
3. A tendency not to face up to unclear situations and to make superficial, intellectual analyses of situations rather than identify at any cost opportunities for action and to vigorously exploit them.

However, these three tendencies are the three major inhibitors when it comes to adopting positive attitudes to planning and above all, strategic planning. Planning in fact makes us look at the future in order to decide today's actions. In this leap into the future we will be led in a clear, open, and formalized way to:

1. Make choices despite much uncertainty; and as each choice means other choices must be abandoned, it leads to frustration and is demotivating.
2. Analyze not only strengths, but also weaknesses—and people do not like admitting weaknesses.
3. Take risks, demonstrate aggressiveness, which presages the future conflicts we try to avoid.
4. Face up to the problem of personal capacity (Will I be capable of successfully managing all that?) when we are not certain that God is on our side and success assured. That uncertainty is the most daunting of all. (Part of this analysis is borrowed from a lecture by Ed Bartee, Nashville Graduate School of Management and suggestions from Dr. M. Filiu of Eurequip.)

These attitudes, which seem widespread and valid on both sides of the Atlantic, are complemented in Latin countries by a particular attitude that goes by the name of "system D"—"D" standing for *debrouillardise,* resourcefulness. All formalized preparation for the future is rejected and choices are made on the spur of the moment. The flexibility, speed, and efficiency of such an approach is frequently mentioned, together with its successes and we must acknowledge that such a view is not totally unfounded.

How do we bridge that cultural gap?

What management information will bridge it? Among the majority of companies the answer to that question is pretty useless. "All you have to do is send top management on a planning course or on a training seminar. . . "

It's not so simple. Take the example of a group of top managers sent by their company to a planning seminar. In most cases rather than reducing undesirable attitudes it reinforces them, as the following illustrates:

1. We want them to accept conflict; but they find security in the return to the classroom, and the comforting dependence on the tutor leads to passivity.
2. We want them to leave routine behind and accept risk and the anxiety of the head-on-the-block decision. They'll attend the classes and, at best, study case histories that do not commit them. Without underestimating the value of business games, we must recognize that the impact of a game failure is far less impressive than the long-lasting consequences of wrong decisions in real life.
3. We want them to face up to unclear situations creatively, constructively, and positively; but the seminar will immerse them more in learning than in action. The brevity of the seminar demands that much of the information dealt with, even in case histories, is theoretical.

But before anything else we want them to change their behavior. Are they motivated to do so? And is not the seminar seen as a manipulation by management?

Evidently another method must be found—and our criticism suggests it. A learning period must be introduced into the organization. But because what must be learned touches behavior in action, the learning must be based on real problems facing the company. The knowledge and behavior acquired will be driven home by analyzing the consequences of actions following the first learning phase.

Yet, because we cannot learn everything at once, we must proceed by stages with a gradual build up. From that follows the concept of permanent training dealing with real planning problems as opposed to theoretical training. . .

When it is a question of training through action, and thus of inducing new behavior, we believe that the only really efficient approach is one in which the trainees solve real problems. That recommendation applies not only to individuals, but to groups too.

The approach starts with an evaluation of the group's educational level and seeks to raise this level by increasingly complex stages. Each stage starts from real situations understood and mastered by the group; these situations are presented in the form of a model easily understood by everyone. Working with the model one develops a degree of abstract objectivity and this new understanding is immediately applied to real situations.

Methods using deductive and inductive logic must be closely married. It is also necessary to include behavior (involving the group, motivation) and not to stop at intellectual advances. [18]

Synergistic Implications

We can learn a great amount from comparisons of U.S. and other organizations. The industry, size of the organization, and ownership pattern are variables that influence the factors that result in different kinds of corporate organizations. Organizational structures are often related to the economic performance of the firm.

Two fundamental questions are, how transferable are different kinds of organizations internationally, and, to what extent do different types of organizations affect transfer of mangement skills and technology? In other words, are some macrocultures more suitable for certain organizational microcultures?

It would appear that comparative management research in the world marketplace has focused on comparing differences in various cultures. Perhaps the time has come to direct investigations toward cross-cultural synergy. There are numerous examples of cooperation and collaboration in international management and community development and this book cites some of them. But what is needed is systematic research on how this is accomplished, and what the results are.

The same type of cross-cultural research should address the many examples of synergy present in the technology transfer of international corporations that have the responsibility for contracting, designing, and managing new plants and projects in the developing countries. They not only bring in a multicultural workforce, they also develop local talent in a pragmatic, synergistic system that bridges cultural gaps. Yet researchers have not directed attention to such macrotechnical efforts.

References

1. Likert, R. and Likert, J.G. *New Ways of Managing Conflict,* McGraw-Hill, 1976.
2. Horovitz, J. "The Frontiers of Management European Style," *Vision,* January 1979
3. Vogel, E.F. "Meeting the Japanese Challenge," *The Wall Street Journal,* May 19,1980.
4. Ibe, K. "People—Key to Japan's Success," *Business Week,* October 6, 1980.
5. Heenan, D. and Keegan, W.J. "The Rise of Third World Multinationals," *Harvard Business Review,* January-February, 1979.
6. Hofstede, G. *Motivation, Leadership, Organization: Do American Theories Apply Abroad?* European Institute for Advanced Studies in Management, AMACOM, 1980.

7. Baugh, J.G. *"A Study of Decision-Making Within a Matrix Organization,"* unpublished doctoral dissertation, United States International University, San Diego, CA, 1981. Available from University Microfilms International, 300 N. Zeeb Rd., Ann Arbor, MI 48016.

8. Humble, J. Quote from preface of *Technology Transfer: A Realistic Approach* by Silvère Seurat. Houston, Gulf Publishing Company, Inc., 1979.

9. Bass, B.M. et al. *Assessment of Managers: An International Comparison.* New York: Macmillan Publishing Company, Inc., 1979.

10. Fillol, T.R. *Social Factors in Economic Development: The Argentine Case.* Westport, Connecticut: Greenwood Press, 1961.

11. England, G.W., Megandhi, A.R., and Wilpert, B. *Organizational Functioning in a Cross-Cultural Perspective.* Kent, Ohio: Kent State University Press, 1979.

12. Heller, F.A. and Wilpert, B. "Managerial Decision-Making: An International Comparison." In: *Organizational Functioning in a Cross Cultural Perspective* by G.W. England et al. Kent, Ohio: Kent State University Press, 1979.

13. Redding, S.G. and Martyn-Johns, T.A. "Paradigm Differences and Their Relation to Management." In: *Organizational Functioning in a Cross Cultural Perspective* by G.W. England et al. Kent, Ohio: Kent State University Press, 1979.

14. Miller, J. et al. "Studies on Values, Goals, and Decision-Making: A Critical Evaluation." In: *Organizational Functioning in a Cross Cultural Perspective* by G.W. England et al. Kent, Ohio; Kent State University Press, 1979.

15. Bettignies de,H.C. and Evans, L. "The Cultural Dimensions of Top Executives' Careers." In: *Culture and Management* by T.O. Weinshall (ed.) Middlesex, England: Penguin Books, Ltd., 1977.

16. Heller, F.A. and "Comparing American and British Managerial Attitudes to Skills and Leadership." In: *Culture and Management* by T. D. Weinshall (ed.) Middlesex, England: Penguin Books, Ltd., 1977.

17. Hickson, D.J., Hinings, C.R., McMillan, C.J., and Schwitter, J.P. "The Culture-Free Context of Organization Structure: A Tri-National Comparison." In: *Culture and Management* by T. O. Weinshall (ed.) Middlesex, England: Penguin Books, Ltd., 1977.

18. Seurat, S. *Technology Transfer: A Realistic Approach.* Houston: Gulf Publishing Company, Inc., 1979.

3.
Motivation and
Decision-Making Across Cultures

Underlying all cultural influences are the value orientations of people. Therefore, our comments focus on the identification of personal, organizational, and cultural values, and the ability to create organizational environments that reflect more than one culture's values.

Organizational synergy is achieved when cultural influences are recognized, and cultural differences and similarities are used to create new organizational structures and management strategies. Figure 3-1 provides a model for how this might be accomplished. This book focuses on the problem-solving skills of the international manager. By applying the concept of synergy, it is possible to increase the number of viable alternative courses of action or intervention in any situation. Because we cannot analyze the cultural differences regarding motivation and decision-making of all the world's cultures in this chapter, we have presented an in-depth contrast of two representative ones: American and Japanese.

Although managers' daily activities—decision-making, problem-solving, organizing, etc.—are basically the same at all levels of an organization, the approaches to these activities certainly are not. The international manager must be aware that managers may plan, negotiate, communicate, evaluate, etc. in different ways. He or she must understand that the "what" of management is culturally oriented; and the "how" of management is embodied in motivation and decision-making. Therefore, we will first consider what U.S managers learn about motivation, and, by means of examples, suggest what some other business systems have taught their managers about it. Then, we will suggest ways that managers might borrow from another system (Japanese) to integrate aspects of both systems into new organizational structures or ways of relating to people, thus enhancing managerial performance and synergy.

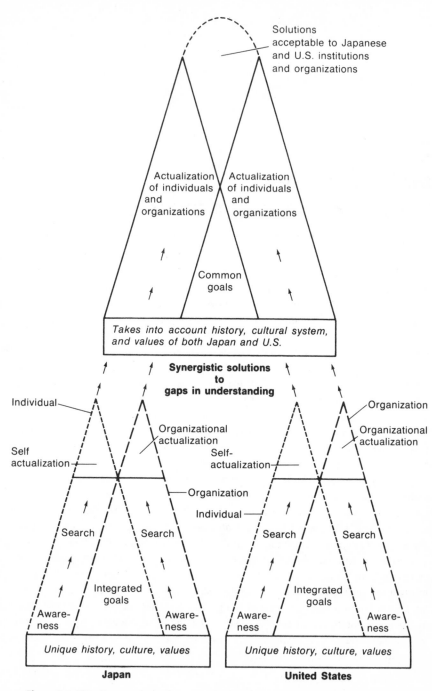

Figure 3-1. This diagram shows how organizational synergy can generate new management strategies and organizational structures (Japan and U.S. are used as examples).

MOTIVATION

Summary of Motivation Theories in the U.S.

Paul Illman in *Developing Overseas Managers and Managers Overseas* asks:

> Is there any major difference between motivating people at home and motivating them in a developing country? Basically, no. People are much the same everywhere and generally respond to the same stimuli. Peripherally there are some differences. . . Do the current concepts of motivation work in a society just moving into industrialization? Yes they do, though there are a few exceptions.[1]

It is the authors' belief that Illman's remarks are oversimplified and misleading.

One fundamental requirement for managers is that they understand themselves and the people they work with, whether they be superiors, colleagues, or subordinates. Realizing that different people are motivated by different things is important, understanding *what* motivates people is critical to effective management.

The growth of any organization greatly depends on its success in motivating its employees to direct their energies towards the accomplishment of organizational objectives. In management schools in the United States many theories of motivation are proposed and taught. No one explanation of human behavior is absolute, and some explanations conflict with others. At one extreme, there are theories that explain motivation as responses to external or unconscious forces. These approaches assume the worker or manager can be easily programmed. At the other extreme, people are seen as rational and predictable. In *Management Essentials,* William F. Glueck outlines these theories and we will draw on his work.[2] He states that "motivation is the process of factors that influence people to act." Motivation, therefore, arouses behavior, sustains behavior, channels behavior into a specific course. The following is a synopsis of contemporary institutional concepts used in American management.

Behavior Modification

This was one of the first systematic attempts to try to explain motivation. Its principal theorist, B. F. Skinner, believed basically that behavior is motivated by drive, and that drives were seen as deprivations of basic needs such as food and sex.[3] He did not believe that drives totally determine behavior, but that the probability of one drive rather than another determining behavior was thought to be a function of the drive times the incentive times the habit reinforcement.

Behavior modification experimentation began with animals, then was successfully transferred to mentally disturbed and retarded persons. The approach of positive reinforcement of acceptable behavior was also used with prisoners, alcoholics, drug addicts, and those who wanted to give up smoking. Eventually, it was applied to workers to increase their productivity and sales, reduce absenteeism and tardiness, and promote improved work behavior. Of all motivational theories, this system has worked consistently and is sometimes referred to as behavior management.

Psychoanalytic Motivation Theory

This theory argues that we behave in response to conflicting motives. In the unconscious there is a pool of repressed energies that are distorted by frustration and exert a stress on conscious reasons. These shape the patterns of daily life and behavior. The psychoanalytic school contends that the crucial motives for one's behavior are deep in the unconscious, tied to the past, and that the conscious motives are less important.

Herzberg's Two-Factor Theory

Herzberg developed his theory after asking engineers and accountants what factors at work satisfied them the most.[4] He then classified their responses as either motivators or hygenic factors. Hygenic factors, such as interpersonal relations, salary, personnel policies, physical working conditions, and job security, he maintained, must be present and "satisfied" before motivation can be accomplished. These factors alone, according to Herzberg, do not motivate people to greater productivity. People are motivated only when job satisfiers are present in the work situation. These motivators, according to Herzberg, are the nature of the work itself, the achievement of an important task, responsibility at work, recognition of work, and opportunity for advancement. The question here is, although this may be valid in American culture, will these same theories also apply overseas?

Maslow's Need Theory

Perhaps the most popular of all motivational theories was developed by Abraham Maslow.[5,6] His theory basically argues that there are two kinds of needs, innate needs and acquired needs. He theorized that human beings strive to satisfy their needs in a specific order, that is, one set of needs must be satisfied before moving to the next need level to further motivate behavior. When needs are not fulfilled, this is referred to as a state of deprivation. The order of needs indicated by Maslow are the physiological and psychological needs for food, water, rest, exercise, shelter, and sex; safety needs, which include the freedom from bodily harm; social needs, which are the needs for friendship, affection, and interaction; ego-esteem needs which include the needs for self-respect and self-confidence; and self-actualization, which is the need to realize one's potential in its fullest sense. Maslow argued that these needs are universal and form a hierarchy from lowest to highest.

McClelland-Atkinson Need Theory

McClelland and Atkinson studied how the basic needs—achievement, power, affiliation, and the minimization of pain—are conditioned by early childhood experiences.[7] They maintained that when a society has a high need for achievement, the themes of childhood stories and fairytales are not fatalistic, instead the children learn to read about heroes and heroines, where actions lead to success. According to this theory, which focuses basically on the need for achievement, the likelihood that a person would perform a task successfully depends on the strength of the motive times the subjective probability of success at the task and the strength of the incentive value of success. They have used this theory to increase job performance by adjusting conditions so that the achievement motive is actuated. Because American culture is highly achievement oriented, this approach is popular among U.S. behavioral scientists.

Theory X and Theory Y

Douglas McGregor developed what he called Theory X and Theory Y to explain management styles and worker motivation.[8] His premise is that every manager has certain beliefs and makes certain assumptions about the people who manage him and whom he manages. These basic assumptions, according to McGregor, can be categorized under Theory X or Theory Y.

The assumptions the manager makes under Theory X are that people have an inborn dislike of work, whether it is physical or mental, and they will do whatever they can to avoid it. The traditional approach, Theory X, also assumes that because of the inherent dislike of work, people will do just enough to keep their jobs, but not more. Therefore, they must be motivated through threats and force to meet even minimum requirements. Theory X maintains most people want security and therefore avoid responsibility because of the risk that this poses to their security. Responsibility implies the freedom to decide and to be independent, but given this freedom a person could make the wrong decision and this might threaten his security in the organization.

Theory Y, on the other hand, assumes that work is not alien to man's nature and it is just as natural as rest and play. Theory Y, the more participative approach, also assumes external pressures and controls do cause people to produce, but they are not the motivating influences. Theory Y holds that people are not reluctant to accept responsibility and that they will not only accept it, but will seek increasing amounts of it.

Since people are an organization's most important resource, understanding how people are motivated, how they behave, is an important part of any manager's responsibilities. Without studying and considering carefully the factors that are associated with productivity and worker motivation, the manager can easily fall into the habit of stereotyping or over-simplifying peoples attitudes and behaviors.

Human beings are a mixture of rational and emotional, and each human being develops a unique personality that directs his or her thinking, learning and actions within a cultural context. The factors that influence the development of the personality are of an environmental and hereditary nature. People behave in diverse ways because of differences in how they see the world around them. These perspectives result from attitudinal, value, and personality differences. They also behave differently because of differences in motivation. The international manager working overseas must comprehend what motivates persons in the host culture and avoid transplanting too easily home culture concepts of human behavior.

PRODUCTIVITY—JAPANESE-AMERICAN CONTRAST

From the preceding summary, it is clear that the theories of motivation that have been developed and applied in the United States are far from conclusive and that motivating individuals is a difficult task for all managers. A few examples of problems with U.S. productivity will illustrate this.

John Boothe, the president of the American Productivity Institute (1980) outlined the seriousness of this problem by stating that "from 1948 to 1968 productivity in the United States grew at a 3.3% compounded annual rate. From 1968 to 1978 it was 1.5%. In 1979, it was a minus 0.9%."

Claudia Deutsch illustrated the problem of productivity from another perspective when she observed that the word "productivity" itself is generally misused and that real productivity is often confused with conditions influencing it, the methods of raising it, and with the positive or negative attitudes toward it.[9] To economists, the definition of productivity is simple, it is basic output divided by basic labor input. But behaviorists, who deal in such immeasurable factors as job satisfaction and motivation, seem to confuse productivity numbers with the sentiment a person expresses when he says he has or has not had a productive day.

Deutsch also states there is widespread confusion between productivity and performance. Assembly-line workers can be rated in terms of productivity, while chief executive officers and other top level managers can only be rated in the performance category. For the educated white collar employees who fill the bulk of managerial and professional ranks, the distinction between productivity and performance is a shade of gray. Deutsch ends by quoting a psychologist who states that "You simply cannot boil everything down to Theory X versus Theory Y in management or the like."[9]

Productivity in Japan

Japan has somehow come to terms with an effective way of motivating employees and increasing productivity. An Example:

> Motorola Inc. couldn't figure out a way to make its Franklin Park, Illinois television plant profitable, so it was sold to a Japanese firm. Within two years the new management made the plant a model for productivity. How did they do it? By insisting on quality, participative management, and a close working relationship between engineering and manufacturing. The manager for pro-

ductivity of the Government Electronics Division of Motorola told members of the Planning Executives Institute that "the Japanese management had a dramatic effect on improving quality in that plant . . . before they took over the defect rate was 60%. By 1979 it was 1%." The most startling indicator of increased productivity was that the number of sets being turned out increased from 1,000 to 2,000 per day with virtually the same workforce. [10]

In 1979, Japan's productivity increased 8%. The Japanese learned from and borrowed aspects of U.S. quality control methods and applied these to Japanese industry and management in a unique way—now American managers are adopting that approach. Formerly, the phrase "made in Japan" was once synonymous with poor quality and cheap goods, but now it is usually a sign of excellent quality. The secret of Japan's phenomenal success in upgrading product standards can partly be attributed to the quality control circles.

In the 1950s groups of Japanese industrialists came to the United States and their purpose was to learn how American companies achieved quality control and efficient production rates. When they returned to Japan, they set up the Japan Union of Scientists and Engineers (JUSE). By the early 1970s Japanese firms had improved on American quality control methods. The American belief is that 90% of total quality control potentiality lay with managers and engineers, while the maximum contribution of the plant workers was estimated at 10%. But the Japanese experiences proved that blue collar workers can play a significant role in improving product quality and increasing production.

Quality circles are kept small with three or four to a maximum of twelve members who work in the same shop or in the same production line. The circle members meet regularly to exchange ideas for improving their job performance and results, and the circle leader takes the proposals to the meeting attended by managerial supervisors, who accept, modify, or reject these ideas. For example, in Japan in 1979, Samuel Electric, a leading home appliance manufacturer reported that it saved $180 million through company-wide management improvement campaigns. One third of this saving was directly due to suggestions by blue collar workers.

Motivation in Japan

There is no doubt about Japan's postwar economic success. Japan, a series of islands smaller than California, had risen from an isolated fuedal society in 1868 to politically challenge the world's major powers in the 1930s and '40s. Although it was left in shambles after World War II, Japan rekindled its economic growth by devising a system of industrial and economic development that basically aimed at two national objectives; economic growth and the rebuilding of national prosperity. This system was based on fundamental values within Japanese society; namely, the harmony between sometimes conflicting interests in the society to permit a maximum degree of cooperation between government, labor, finance, and industry. The national economic policy was established by a strong and highly respected centralized government. Many Western observers now wonder what the "secret" elements of the Japanese success might be. Perhaps it is the Japanese society or culture itself.

In the United States most American workers and managers place a high value on their professional accomplishments and promotions, and social status in the organization derives largely from these accomplishments. The fulfillment of the individual worker and manager is often attained through achievement, which motivates Americans and gives this society its quality of industriousness. The accomplishments of the American must be visible, personal, and measurable, because this society provides its major enforcement to its members by means of performance, attainment and achievement.

In Japan, however, there is a very different way of thinking. The Japanese society and company come first, then comes the individual. This difference in loyalty and emphasis is inherent in the Japanese culture. The dedication of Japanese managers and workers to their organization is unique among the industrialized countries of the world. Such commitment has its roots in history, when the Samurai expressed loyalties to their lords. With the changes in Japanese society in the late nineteenth century, the feudal ties of loyalty were not eroded, but were transferred to the organization of industry. As previously stated, instead of the Samurai warrior swearing fealty to his lord, the newly industrialized worker gave his loyalty to the employing company. In return, the corporation gave the worker assurance of lifetime employment and security.

The following are contributing factors associated with the productivity and motivation of Japanese employees.

Permanent or Lifetime Employment

The practice of lifetime employment is perhaps unique in Japan when compared with any other industrial country and seems to be a powerful motivation for their workers. Lifetime employment refers to the practice whereby an individual enters the company after graduation from high school or university and receives in-company training. This person remains an employee of the same company until the mandatory retirement age of 55. In the United States, worker freedom and mobility are a way of life. The typical U.S. employee changes jobs several times in his career. When business is poor and there are economic slowdowns, people are temporarily laid off from their work.

Japanese and American scholars have written a great deal about lifetime employment in Japan. Some see this practice growing out of traditional social relations, however a number of recent writings on this subject have concluded that it was institutionalized as part of Japanese employment-management practice only after WWI when it resulted from the employees' desires to stabilize labor relations in large organizations by cutting high labor turnover. After WWI this practice of permanent employment only applied to a minority of employees, and it was not until the late 1930s and the events following WWII that lifetime employment applied to a wide range of full-time employees and became institutionalized as part of Japan's employment practices. It still does not apply to the many part-time or temporary workers.

In a system of lifetime employment it is generally agreed that only under extreme circumstances, such as bankruptcy, will an organization terminate an employee. Terminating an employee under any other circumstances would be like "firing a son or daughter." It is very unusual for Japanese managers and workers to change employment and seek another position, although this practice is slowly changing. The resulting mutual loyalty is the basis for the spectacular rise of the Japanese economy. It has provided Japan with a highly motivated, team-spirited workforce that is highly loyal to the organization and identifies its fortunes with the fortunes of the organization. A question that many foreign managers ask themselves is how can a manager or worker who is assured or guaranteed lifetime employment be motivated to work hard if promotion is based on seniority rather than merit? The answer to this question, as are many answers about Japan, is based on an understanding of Japanese society.

Japanese employees enter a company after graduation from high school or college. The procedures for entering a Japanese company are rigorous and time consuming, and much effort is expended on the part of the organization determining whether or not this particular candidate will be an asset on a lifetime basis to the organization. Once this is determined, the Japanese employees are recognized as contributing an important ingredient to the success of the organization, and in identifying with the organization, the Japanese employee receives the feeling of integration into the company and society.

To leave a company in Japan would be very difficult for most Japanese employees, because it would mean a certain loss of identity and, therefore, of social recognition. Because of this, the Japanese workers and managers have very few alternatives to change companies and, therefore, are generally highly motivated to contribute to the organization's success because this person's own success is very much related to the success of the organization of which he is a large part. Psychologically, this implies that the Japanese employee tends not to think about potential failure in a very competitive market, but rather he is confident that hard work and diligence will somehow be rewarded in the long run.

Wages and Promotion

For a Japanese manager it is very important that he be graduated from a prestigious university—the more prestigious the university, the more eagerly he will be recruited by government agencies or important industries. Japanese universities are ranked according to their accomplishments into various categories, and the more successful corporations in Japan are able to recruit the better students from these institutions. Because of the entrance examination required of all Japanese students before entering a new level of education, the most intelligent students enter the most renowned schools.

To enter such schools means that the Japanese student has passed the very difficult and sophisticated examination. Preparations for these entrance examinations often take two or three years. Japanese students study hard in order to do well on these examinations, as they are aware that succeeding and entering a good university almost guarantees their future.

Recruitment in Japan basically takes place during the month of October, as the students graduate from their colleges in March. All persons entering receive approximately the same salary depending on the company and industry. These beginning salaries are not based on qualifications of the individual, but rather they are fixed by the organization. The salary in Japan has a number of components including a base salary, the job related salary, and a performance related salary. The salaries in Japan are based on education and on age. A person can usually predict his salary accurately after a certain period of time in that organization. (Table 3-1 shows the standard ranks in a typical Japanese company and their American equivalents).

When a Japanese manager enters the company, his or her training and education are undertaken by the personnel departments in the Japanese organizations. The training begins immediately and is the new manager's first experience in the corporate culture that the manager is entering. The training program covers wide areas and includes such things as how to speak with superiors, values and benefits of belonging to this company, and the philosophy of the organization. New employees rotate to several departments in order that they may be familiar with the total activities of the organization. This rotation usually takes many years until they are finally assigned to work for a specialized department. Because the Japanese employee works for the same company for a lifetime, it is not frustrating to change positions in the same company. In general, it could be said that Japanese education and training programs consist of orientation to the organization and on-the-job training through job rotation. A sense of belonging to the group becomes a great motivator and is constantly reinforced.

In Japanese organizations clear job descriptions are not generally provided, although the so-called "job analysis" has begun to be adopted by many of the organizations. For Japanese organizations and employees the detailed job descriptions are not necessary, because tasks are usually done collectively. Therefore, detailed job descriptions may be an obstacle in cooperating together for the mutual accomplishment of specific objectives. If each Japanese employee completely followed a job description, individualism would supersede collectivism which would not be significantly beneficial to the organization. Japanese employees help each other when they face new problems beyond the contents of their general job descriptions, and it is not unusual to find all the members of a department assisting a person when he is unable to finish a specific assignment because of illness or because of a very busy schedule.

Table 3-1
Comparison of Japanese and Western Job Titles

Rank	Direct Translation	English Equivalent*	Legal Status
Shachō	Company head	President	Director (representative)
Fukushachō	Deputy company head	Vice-president	Director
Senmu torishimariyaku	Special duty executive director	Senior managing director	Director
Jōmu torishimariyaku	Ordinary duty executive director	Managing director	Director
Torishimariyaku	Executive director	Director	Director
Buchō	Department head	Department head	Employee
Jichō	Deputy head	Deputy department head	Employee
Kachō	Section head	Section head	Employee
Kakarichō	Sub-section head	Sub-section head	Employee
Hanchō	Team head	Foreman	Employee
Hira-shain	Ordinary company member	Worker, executive	Employee

* The English equivalent is what Japanese of each rank customarily put on their English name-cards.
From *The Japanese Company* by Rodney Clark. Yale University Press, 1979.

The promotional system in Japan is based on age and seniority rather than on merit. The organization or company is like a large family, and within a family structure, collaboration and cooperation, rather than competition, are the norm. Therefore, persons are promoted in a highly predictable manner.

This promotion system generally has very little flexibility and for the Japanese employee who rises through the first step or rank rather automatically, his continued rise to the more important positions will depend on how he performs once he enters the supervisory level.

Bonus System in Japan

Another significant difference between Japanese and U.S. organizations that relates to motivation in Japan is the bonus system. Paid to employees twice each year this system depends on several factors, such as the person's monthly salary and the success of the organization during that particular time. Typically, individual members of the Japanese organization do not know what the other members specifically received, although guidelines in general are available. When an employee is aware that he or she has received a bonus above that received by the others in the department, this becomes a motivating force during the next six months to work even harder. If a company has had an extremely successful year, a bonus of six or eight times a monthly salary might be provided. If the company has had a particularly poor year economically, a bonus might not even be paid and this would be understood by the persons involved.

In addition to bonuses that are paid to each employee, other fringe benefits are offered, such as low cost, subsidized, or free housing, vacations in company-owned resorts or recreation areas, payment for transportation costs, free meals, and year-end parties are typical of the Japanese system of rewarding employees. All of these result in the feeling of belonging to the company, as expressed by a Japanese manager: "The company has given me everything, and therefore I'm going to work very hard for the success of my company."

DECISION-MAKING

Before reading this section on decision-making, we ask this quesiton: "What can we use from the Japanese system of motivating employees in our organizations?" The Japanese have successfully adapted it to American work environments in plants they operate in the U.S.

Domestic and international managers spend a large amount of time making decisions. Decision-making in many ways constitutes the foundation of the economic and political system in many countries. The organization of our environment exists the way it does because individuals (consumers, producers, voters, etc.) have the right of free choice. Decision-making is all pervasive—for not to make a decision is itself a decision.

Managers are often evaluated, promoted, and rewarded according to their effectiveness in making decisions. Most management courses at all levels in an organization include as part of the course content some material on decision-making. If the content is not directly on decision-making, it is discussed as part of problem-solving.

Decisions have impact and influence, and decision-making is performed by individuals who are influenced by their environment. Glueck identifies four stages in the decision-making process:[2]

1. Recognition and definition of the problem
2. Search for information and decision alternatives
3. Choice among alternatives
4. Implementation

He further states that a decision situation exists in a management context when "there is a gap between the desired level of achievement and the existing level, the gap is large enough to be noticeable, the decision-maker is motivated to reduce the gap, and the decision-maker believes he or she can do something about the gap."

Once a decision situation has been determined to exist, the manager begins to seek information and alternatives. Having identified the alternatives, a manager makes a choice, and implements the decision.

Many factors affect the decision-making process, including factors in the decision situation, such as the significance of the decision (the number of people affected, the amount of time and money involved, the amount of time the decision-maker has to make the decision) and the organizational culture. There are also factors in the decision environment (problems of environmental uncertainty) and factors in the decision-maker. The factors in the decision-maker that affect the decision making process include the decision mode, group versus individual decision-making, and the politics of the decision situation in a specific organizational environment.

Glueck identifies three kinds of decision-making modes:[2]

1. *Rational decision-maker.* In this mode the decision-maker is intelligent and rational, and makes choices to maximize his or her advantage. The decision-maker considers all alternatives, orders the consequences, and chooses the alternative that produces the maximum gain. People who accept this mode believe that individuals are careful in making decisions and that these decisions are directed in a conscious way to achieve a particular objective.

2. *Quasi-rational administrative satisfying decision-maker.* The proponents of this mode maintain that a manager has a general idea of the objectives, but does not rank them because they are multiple. The manager only investigates alternatives until a satisfactory solution is found. In this process, the manager knows only some of the advantages and disadvantages of the various alternatives and chooses the first alternative that is expected to meet the objectives. If no alternative satisfies minimal objectives, the manager reduces the level of the objective to be accomplished and accepts the first alternative to satisfy the new objective.

3. *Intuitive-heuristic decision-maker.* This mode assumes the manager makes decisions based on hunches and gut feelings, and other creative mechanisms. The method has sometimes been referred to as "heuristic" and includes thinking in analogies, concept association, and unfocused thought.

Other factors in the decision-making process include whether the decision is made by an individual alone, an individual in consultation with others, or made by those affected by the decision.

Don Koberg and Jim Bagnall present a model for creating problem-solving or the creative part of decision-making.[11] The model is a constant feedback system whereby a decision-maker never progresses without looping back to check on the outcome. The steps in the process as defined by Koberg and Bagnall are:

Accept situation—To accept the problem as a challenge; to give up our autonomy to the problem and allow the problem to become our process.
Analyze—To get to know about the ins and outs of the problem; to discover what the world of the problem looks like.
Define—To decide what we believe to be the main issues of the problem; to conceptualize and to clarify our major goals concerning the problem situation.

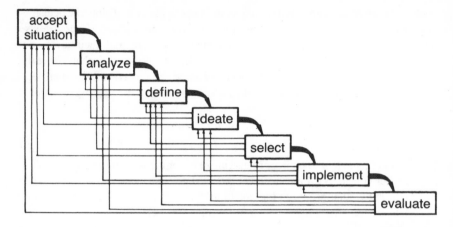

Figure 3-2. Schematic of Koberg and Bagnall's problem-solving model as a feedback system.

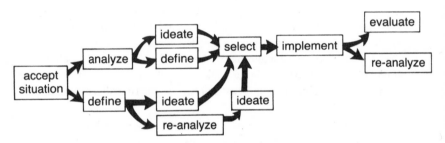

Figure 3-3. Schematic of Koberg and Bagnall's problem-solving model as a branching system.

Ideate—To search out all the ways of possibly getting to the major goals. Alternatives.

Select—To compare our goals as defined with our possible ways of getting there. Determine best ways to go.

Implement—To give action or physical form to our selected "best ways."

Evaluate—To determine the effects or ramifications as well as the degree of progress of our design activity.

Koberg and Bagnall illustrate these ideas as a feedback system, schematically shown in Figure 3-2, and as a branching system, as shown in Figure 3-3. Essentially, these are Western, specifically American, approaches to choice making. Synergy may occur by modifying different elements from the various decision strategies. Synergy may also occur when one uses ideas from other management systems. As a contrasting case in point, we turn again to an Eastern view of decision-making—the Japanese view.

DECISION-MAKING—JAPANESE-AMERICAN CONTRAST

In Japanese organizations decision-making is fundamentally different from that in most U.S. organizations. There are also many basic differences in management and business practices between Japan and the U.S.

In Japan the basic objective of the organization is harmony, there is a system of lifetime employment, and an employee is promoted through the seniority system. The organization is interested in long-term growth and market share. It is characterized as humanistic and paternalistic. Its employees are loyal and their private lives are intertwined with the company. Training is performance oriented.

In the United States, on the other hand, a basic objective of the organization is to maximize efficiency and profits. There is a high degree of job mobility, and promotion is based on merit. The organization is profit-oriented, and is characterized as materialistic and individualistic. Its employees are interested in themselves, and their private lives are *separate*. Training in the United States is *promotion oriented*.

In terms of *responsibility for origination*, Japanese decision-making is decentralized. It originates from the lowest management group affected by the decision, and its results—good or bad—are the responsibility of the entire enterprise. In the United States decision-making is more centralized, major decisions originate at top management levels (that is, at the level of the CEO, the executive committee, and so on), and top management is held responsible for the decision's results. Failures can effect the removal of the CEO or the firing of the management team.

Looking at the *route of decision*, in Japan a decision is debated by the originating group and passed horizontally or vertically to other groups as consensus of each group is reached. After all groups concerned have reached consensus, the decision document *(ringisho)* is passed to the highest authority level for his "stamp of approval." After the decision is approved, communication to those involved with implementation is simple, because action groups have all participated in formulating the decision.

In the United States a decision is debated and discussed by top management. Information pertinent to the decision is often provided by special groups or task forces. Certain types of major decisions may require board authorization and approval (for example, large capital expenditures, appointment of officers, sale of assets, mergers, and acquisitions). Communication with the implementing personnel regarding the final decision is often time consuming. The decision must not only be explained but often "sold" to the action group.

Approaches to decision-making also differ between the two countries. In Japan the first step is defining the question or the problem. Frequently, an intuitive approach is used in reaching a decision. An underlying consideration for all decisions is harmony—within the company, the market, the industry, and the economy. Another prime consideration is the decision's impact on the firm's employees. Frequently, a subjective approach is used (that is, strong personal relationships often outweigh profit considerations), and emphasis is on increased market share and corporate growth rather than on higher profits.

In the United States the first step is answering the question or solving the problem. Where possible, a logical, analytical approach is used and an attempt is made to quantify the answer. The underlying principle is producing the maximum economic benefit or contribution for the company. Of major consideration is the decision's impact—higher profitability and high rate of return on investment are of prime importance. Finally, decisions are objective and impersonal.

Ringi System of Decision-making

Since the end of WWII, beginning with the reconstruction of Japan, the influence of American management systems and business techniques on Japan has been significant. However, in all instances the adaptation of these American management concepts has been selective, and decision-making is one aspect of the Japanese business system that has not been influenced to any significant extent. It has remained unchanged because it is strongly rooted in the Japanese system.

In Japan an organization's decisions are arrived at by a collective decision-making process, which is called the *ringi* system. It describes the process of decision-making utilized by large Japanese corporations, and also refers to the formal decision-making process in Japanese government agencies. This ringi system represents a basic philosophy of management rooted in Japanese tradition and the word ringi consists of two parts: the "rin" means submitting a proposal to one's superior and receiving his approval, and the "gi" means the deliberation.

The person who makes the final decision on a proposal depends upon the importance of the subject being decided. Routine kinds of decisions are generally made by section chiefs *(Kacho)*. More important decisions are made by managers who are concerned with the subject. In the process of making a decision, meetings take place to insure that the decision is widely adopted. This system of having many meetings concerning a particular decision is often the approval-seeking process where a proposal, or the ringisho document that has been prepared by a lower functionary, works itself up the heirarchy of an organization in a slow, circuitous manner. At each step it is examined by the appropriate persons concerned, whose approval is indicated by placing a seal, and therefore a decision of approval, on the particular item being discussed. This group oriented, consensus-seeking process is characterized as bottom-up decision-making. There is much ambiguity in this system, whereby the group rather than the individual constitutes the basic unit of the enterprise. When a decision is made, all persons affected by the decision in the organization have had a chance to discuss it, modify it, and include their input.

When the formal ringisho has been prepared, it must be circulated among the various sections and departments that are affected and whose cooperation is necessary to implement this decision. Each manager evaluates the proposal, discusses it with his staff, and then indicates his approval by affixing his seal. The ringisho slowly works its way up to top management until finally the president reviews it.

When he sees that all other managers have affixed their seals, he puts his seal on the material, and the decision is final. The ringisho is then returned to the original proposer of the decision for implementation. The implementation phase is very quick, as the support of all the particular departments affected by the decision has already been given. During this time, there have been many formal and informal meetings, and it is not unusual for the managers of the various sections to have bargained heavily. Much of the discussion of the proposal takes place in an informal setting, perhaps in the evenings following work at a bar or cabaret when the managers gather to discuss their respective viewpoints on the various aspects of the proposal.

In order for the ringi system to operate effectively in Japan, a number of conditions are important. First, there is a great deal of emphasis on the informal, personal relations between the various managers, and therefore, there is much discussion, negotiation, persuasion that occurs at a variety of levels in the organization. Another condition is the strong pressure of shared understanding among the Japanese managers that they are all basically operating for the good of the organization or company as opposed to their individual good.

A Caution

Decision-making or problem-solving is more complex when the managers are multicultural than when all persons or organizations affected are from the same culture. Decision-making is also more complex when the decision-maker is from one culture and the problem involved is occurring in another culture. There are many asumptions underlying the process that are based on culture such as:

1. Is there really a problem? Whether or not there is a problem often depends on one's view of the world. Some cultures see life as a series of problems to which there are "solutions" (the U.S.), other cultures see life as a series of situations that are to be accepted.
2. Are problems to be solved or accepted?
3. To what extent should a manager attempt to influence the environment?
4. Can a manager determine the outcome or do other people and events have a greater significance?
5. Is the environment predictable or unpredictable?

SUMMARY

To sensitize international managers to cross-cultural factors in all management systems we have provided an overview of the ways motivation and decision-making are approached in U.S. organizations and in Japanese organizations. Can U.S. organizations use aspects of the Japanese decision-making process or other aspects of their management system? In adapting managerial strategies from other cultures the following steps are recommended for discussion and consideration:

1. Survey company practices that have been detrimental to the individual and the organization (for example, the implementation phase of a decision in U.S. organizations is time-consuming).
2. Identify aspects of foreign management (by study, discussion, and consultation with organizations that have utilized these aspects) that may be substituted for unsuccessful American techniques.
3. Determine a strategy cross-cultural implementation.
4. Set up an ongoing monitoring and evaluation process.

The future of our organizations and perhaps even nations will depend on the quality and process of the decisions made by responsible persons. Value systems and learned behavior guide individuals in the conceptualization of this process. The existence of many organizations will also depend on how people are motivated and rewarded for their contributions.[12]

In this chapter we have presented aspects of Japanese motivation and decision-making, perhaps, in a laudatory manner. In this our purpose has not been to be critical of the U.S. system, but to suggest that we can learn from others. We have only considered two cultures' approaches to motivation and decision-making. As international managers, we must also consider differences and synergistic opportunities available in many other countries, such as the Soviet Union, the People's Republic of China, or in regions, such as Africa and the Middle East.

References

1. Illman, P.E. *Developing Overseas Managers and Managers Overseas*. New York: AMACOM, 1979.
2. Glueck, W.F. *Management Essentials,* Hinsdale, Illinois: The Dryden Press, 1979.
3. Skinner, B.F. *Beyond Freedom and Dignity*. New York: Knopf, 1971.
4. Herzberg, F. *The Managerial Choice: To Be Efficient or To Be Human*. Homewood Ill.: Richard D. Irwin, Inc., 1977.
5. Maslow, A.H. *Eupsychian Management,* Homewood, Ill.: Richard D. Irwin, 1965
6. Maslow, A.H. *Motivation and Personality*. New York: Harper & Row, 1970.
7. McClelland, D. *The Achieving Society*. Princeton, N.J.: D. Van Nostrand, 1961.
8. McGregor, D. *The Professional Manager*. New York: McGraw-Hill, 1967.

9. Deutsch, C.H. "Productivity: The Difficulty of Even Defining the Problem," *Business Week,* June 9, 1980.
10. Nickell, N. *Arizona Republic,* May 29, 1980.
11. Koberg, D. and Bagnall, J. *The Universal Traveller.* Los Altos, California; William Kaufmann, Inc., 1976.
12. Steers, R.M. *Motivation and Work Behavior.* New York: McGraw-Hill, 1979.

4.
Leadership and Conflict in Management Synergy

LEADERSHIP PERSPECTIVES

No form of social or business organization has ever existed without leaders. Having someone in charge of the group is a cultural universal. Coordinating and using the power at their disposal is a part of all human systems. In the Western world, and in many other areas, the democratic system developed over centuries attempts to guard against the excessive use of power and corruption that may result. The Watergate phenomenon illustrated what happened to people in the executive branch of government who abused their power. Half-way around the world the issue was dealt with differently, when the "Gang of Four" were tried in the People's Republic of China.

The *Royal Bank Letter* cited these points on leadership from a Western perspective:

> It is the presence of a following that compels leaders to act responsibly. They occupy their positions only by others' consent. Responsibility is the lynchpin of leadership in a democratic society. A prime minister is responsible to the electorate; a general to the civil authority; a chief executive officer to the shareholders of his company. And every leader is responsible to those who follow him, no matter how many or how few.
>
> Yet if tyrants continue to carve out places for themselves in offices, on shop floors and elsewhere, they are no less vulnerable to overthrow than their counterparts in palaces. They may be mistaken for leaders, which they often believe themselves to be. But they are not, because they force people to go along with them instead of bringing them along with them. They bully and blackmail and manipulate; they do everything but lead.

Leaders are essentially politicians and must deal with political forces, wrote psychologist Harry Levinson in his excellent *Levinson Letter*.

Leading does not mean managing, wrote organizational expert Warren G. Bennis in his 1976 book *The Unconscious Conspiracy*. By definition, a leader's mission is to make progress; those who manage but do not lead are mired in the status quo.

In a study of the working days of five top U.S. executives, management scientist Henry Mintzberg found that they rarely had time to think about anything except the question immediately before them. Half of the activities they carried out lasted less than nine minutes, and only 10% lasted more than an hour. They "met a steady stream of callers and mail from the moment they arrived in the morning until they left in the evening, Mintzberg recorded. "Coffee breaks and lunches were inevitably work related, and everpresent subordinates seemed to usurp any free moment."

Nor was this frenetic regimen confined to the executive suite. A study of 160 British managers, mostly in the middle ranks, found that they were able to work for a half-hour or more without interruption only once every three days or so. The working lives of foremen were even more fragmented. A study of 56 foremen in the U.S. showed that they averaged an astonishing 583 activities, or one every 48 seconds, per 8-hour shift.

In the present setting, management scholar Douglas McGregor has suggested that "The essential task of management is to arrange organizational conditions and methods of operation so that people can achieve their own goals best by directing their own efforts toward organizational objectives." For the manager, this implies a thorough understanding of the individual personalities of the people he is called upon to lead. It also implies the exercise of some of the finest human values—respect for the individual, justice, consideration and understanding.[1]

Geert Hofstede, a Dutch social psychologist, posed the question "Motivation, Leadership, Organization: Do American Theories Apply Abroad?"[2] For more than 50 years, the management system in the United States has been exported to many areas of the world. However, successful management strategies and theories were also developed in other parts of the globe. Management systems evolve from the perspective of their culture. In the United States complex theories of leadership have developed, but do these theories apply elsewhere? Can Americans learn from the leadership theories or practice in other countries?

In his books *The Prince* and *The Discourses,* Machiavelli, the sixteenth century civil servant from Florence, described effective manipulation techniques for remaining in power. He also wrote about opportunism, deceit, bribery, and even murder. Machiavellian behavior is described by Arthur J. Kover,[3] professor of organizational theory at Cornell, as the strategy of acting dispassionately in one's own self-interest. Professor Kover teaches a course that is designed to equip students with the skills necessary to recognize Machiavellian behavior in others and to practice such techniques themselves to hasten their careers (murder excluded, of course). Thus, Machiavelli's ideas are still influencing management and training programs. However, in the United States the teaching of Machiavellian concepts is not one of the most popular approaches to leadership development.

The Center for Creative Leadership in Greensboro, North Carolina, has been conducting contemporary studies of leadership, largely from an American perspective. One of their reports reviews the connection of power, influence, and authority. The researcher, Morgan McCall, concludes that there are no definitive explanations of these interrelated terms, only trend indicators in the management literature relative to appropriate organizational behavior:

> *Leadership* is incremental influence over and above formal authority role, and may be a subset or facet of a larger function, power.
>
> *Power* is pervasive and complex, possessed by all in some degree. It is both a dynamic and neutral factor; and it is situational, being dependent on how it is used, for whom, and when appropriate. The methods for its use vary from obligation and expertise to manipulation and coercion. In any event, it is clearly lined to influence.
>
> *Influence* is moving other to action, or getting one's own way. There are many strategies for this purpose, such as assertion, bargaining, compromise, deceit, emotion, evasion, expertise, persistence, persuasion, reasoning, and threat.[4]

In another report on leaders and leadership, McCall concludes that leaders may have to work around existing roles and structures that are obsolete, and modify them or create new substitutes.[5] Effective leaders seem to involve flexibility in thoughts and actions as well as develop networks of people who cooperate to achieve the desired goals. McCall suggests the analogy of a manager as a leader who orchestrates a complex series of processes, events, and systems.

Perhaps the best known and most widely studied are the concepts of Douglas McGregor (Theory X and Theory Y), which were discussed in Chapter 3, and the leadership ideas of Robert R. Blake and Jane S. Mouton. Blake and Mouton describe their theory as follows:

> The heart of the Grid® approach to management is that these basic principles of behavioral science should be applied throughout an organization. They include fulfillment through contribution, open communication, conflict-solving by confrontation, responsibility for one's own actions, shared participation in problem-solving and decision-making, management by objectives, reward based on merit, critique for learning from experience, and norms and standards that support personal and organizational excellence.[6]

The "New Grid" developed by Blake and Mouton identifies five types of leadership basically distinguishing between the manager's concern for production or task versus a concern for people. (See Figure 4-1.)

The five leadership orientations as described by Blake and Mouton are:

9,1   In the lower right-hand corner of the Grid a maximum concern (9) for production is combined with a minimum concern (1) for people. A manager acting under these assumptions concentrates on maximizing production by exercising power and authority over people through compliance.

1,9   The 1,9 leadership style is in the top left corner. Here a minimum concern (1) for production is coupled with a maximum concern (9) for peo-

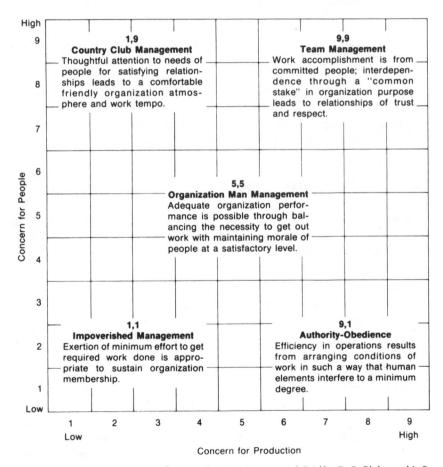

Figure 4-1. The Managerial Grid.® From *The New Managerial Grid* by R. R. Blake and J. S. Mouton, Gulf Publishing Co. 1978. Used with permission.

ple. Primary attention is placed on promoting good feelings among colleagues and subordinates.

1,1   A minimum concern for both production and people is represented by 1,1 in the lower left corner. The 1,1 oriented manager does only the minimum required to remain within the organization.

5,5   5,5 is in the center. This is the "middle of the road" theory or the "go-along-to-get-along" assumptions that are revealed in conformity to the status quo.

9,9   Production and people concerns are integrated at a high level in the upper right-hand corner representing the 9,9 style of managing. This is the team approach. It is goal-oriented and seeks to gain results of high quantity and quality through participation, involvement, commitment, and conflict solving.[6]

The Managerial Grid® theories and leadership strategies are promoted on a worldwide basis, with seminars held in Australia, New Zealand, Austria, Luxembourg, Brazil, Japan, Mexico, Venezuela, and many other countries. However, is it appropriate, as Blake and Mouton imply, to teach managers from other business systems to become leaders by "open communication, conflict-solving by confrontation, responsibility for one's own actions, . . . ,reward based on merit, . . . "? The theories of leadership as developed in the United States generally have those elements in common.

National Culture and Leadership Styles

Geert Hofstede in *Culture's Consequences* identifies four dimensions of national culture,* which suggest that a worldwide learning of U.S. concepts of leadership may be impossible.[7] These cultural dimensions are:

1. Power distance
2. Uncertainty avoidance
3. Individualism/collectivism
4. Masculinity/femininity

Power distance indicates "the extent to which a society accepts that power in institutions and organizations is distributed unequally."

The second dimension, *uncertainty avoidance,* indicates "the extent to which a society feels threatened by uncertain or ambiguous situations."

Individualism is the third dimension and refers to a "loosely knit social framework in a society in which people are supposed to take care of themselves and of their immediate families only." *Collectivism,* the opposite, occurs when there is a "tight social framework in which people distinguish between in-groups and out-

---

*See Chapter 13 of *Managing Cultural Differences,* Harris, P. and Moran, R., Houston: Gulf Publishing Company, 1979.

groups; they expect their in-group (relatives, clan, organizations) to look after them, and in exchange for that owe absolute loyalty to it."

The fourth dimension is *masculinity* with its opposite pole, *femininity*. This dimension expresses "the extent to which the dominant values in society are assertiveness, money and things, not caring for others, quality of life and people."

The most significant dimension related to leadership in Hofstede's study of 40 countries was the power dimension. On the basis of mean ratings of employees on a number of key questions he assigned an index value to each country.

Figure 4-2 shows the positions of the 40 countries on the power distance and uncertainity avoidance scales, and Figure 4-3 shows the countries' positions on the power distance and individualism scales.

The United States ranked fifteenth on power distance, ninth on uncertainty avoidance (both of these are below the average), fortieth on individualism (the most individualist country in the sample), and twenty-eighth on masculinity (above average).[8]

Therefore, do the leadership theories developed by Blake and Mouton, Likert, McClelland and others apply in other areas of the world? The assumption of those who conduct U.S.-developed leadership theory seminars in other areas of the world is that they do.

Let's look at a few examples and perhaps suggest the futility of trying to apply this assumption universally. In Hofstede's study the United States ranked fifteenth out of 40 on the power distance dimension. If this had been higher, then the theories of leadership taught in the United States might have been expected to be more "Machiavellian." We might also ask how U.S. leaders are selected. Most are selected on the basis of competence, and it is the position of the person that provides the authority in the United States, which is, theoretically at least, an egalitarian society. In France, there is a higher power distance index score, and little concern with participative management, but a great concern with who has the power.

Even today, French industry and the managers who run it are a mixture of the old and the new. Anthony Rowley said of the French, "Behind the glittering technological triumph of the Concorde and the insolent innovation of the Citroen motorcars, the backward and fragmented structure of many parts of French industry still survives unharmed." France is still an industry of family empires with many paternalistic traditions. There is also a remnant of a feudalistic heritage that is deeply rooted within the French spirit, which could account for the very conservative and autocratic nature of their business methodology.*

Hofstede has shown that in countries with lower power distance scores than the United States, such as Sweden and Germany, there is considerable acceptance of leadership styles and management models that are even more participative than presently exist. Industrial democracy and codetermination is a style that does not

(text continued on page 59)

---

*Specific aspects of the French national character are presented in detail in *Managing Cultural Differences*, Chapter 13.

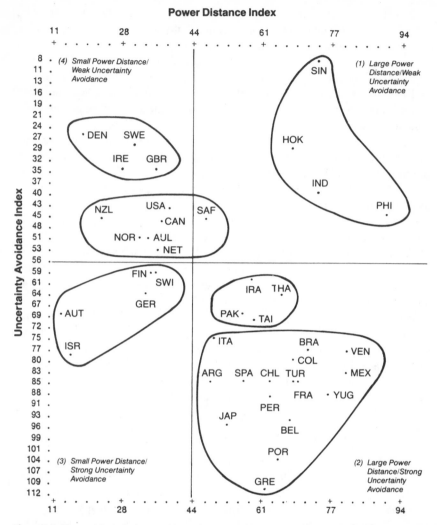

Figure 4-2. The position of 40 countries on the power distance and uncertainty avoidance scales. After Hofstede.

ARG	Argentina	FRA	France	JAP	Japan	SIN	Singapore
AUL	Australia	GBR	Great Britain	MEX	Mexico	SPA	Spain
AUT	Austria	GER	Germany (West)	NET	Netherlands	SWE	Sweden
BEL	Belgium	GRE	Greece	NOR	Norway	SWI	Switzerland
BRA	Brazil	HOK	Hong Kong	NZL	New Zealand	TAI	Taiwan
CAN	Canada	IND	India	PAK	Pakistan	THA	Thailand
CHL	Chile	IRA	Iran	PER	Peru	TUR	Turkey
COL	Colombia	IRE	Ireland	PHI	Philippines	USA	United States
DEN	Denmark	ISR	Israel	POR	Portugal	VEN	Venezuela
FIN	Finland	ITA	Italy	SAF	South Africa	YUG	Yugoslavia

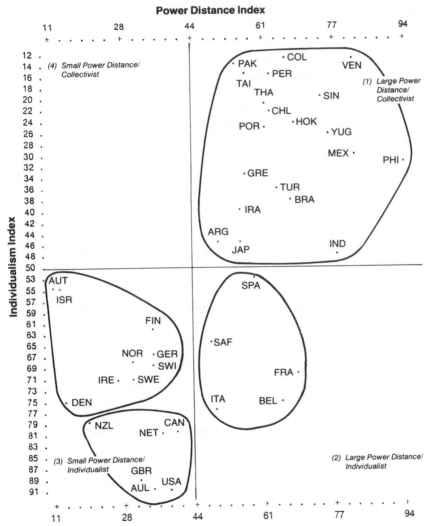

Figure 4-3. The position of 40 countries on the power distance and individualism scales. After Hofstede.

find much sympathy in the United States. Codetermination in Germany is relatively new, and in labor relations it is a revolutionary concept. It is also a large step towards greater worker participation in the decision-making and leadership roles of large corporations in that country. Some theorists suggest that it could be the beginning of a reordering of the capitalistic system as we know it today.

The German Codetermination Act of May 4, 1976 requires companies with more than 2,000 employees to include workers on the supervisory board (similar to a board of directors in the United States), with the extent of the worker representation on the supervisory boards depending on the number of employees in the corporation. If there are more than 2,000 employees, there are 20 members on the board, of whom 10 are representatives of the workers. Of these 10, six must come from the shop floor, three are elected by the unions, and one is to be a senior executive.

The German government, backed by labor, is a supporter of the Act, but must be careful not to alienate the powerful business community. Hofstede has demonstrated that in Germany there is high uncertainty avoidance and, therefore, industrial democracy is brought about first by legislation. In Sweden where uncertainty avoidance is low, industrial democracy was started with local experiments.

Hofstede continues,

> The crucial fact about leadership in any culture is that it is a complement to subordinateship. The Power Distance Index scores. . . are in fact based on the values of people as *subordinates,* not on the values of superiors. Whatever a naïve literature on leadership may try to make us believe, a leader cannot choose his style at will; what is feasible depends to a large extent on the cultural conditioning of his/her subordinates. I therefore show . . . a description of the type of subordinateship that, other things being equal, a leader can expect to meet in societies at three different levels of Power Distance, and to which his/her leadership has to respond. The middle level represents what most likely is found in the U.S. environment.
>
> Now neither McGregor, nor Likert, nor Blake and Mouton allow for this type of cultural proviso: all three tend to be prescriptive with regard to a leadership style which at best will work with U.S. subordinates and those in cultures with not-too-different Power Distance levels like Canada or Australia. In fact, my research shows that *subordinates* in larger Power Distance countries tend to agree more frequently with McGregor's Theory X while those in smaller Power Distance countries agree more frequently with Theory Y.
>
> The only U.S. theory of leadership that allows for a certain amount of cultural relativity, although indirectly, is Fred Fiedler's Contingency Theory of Leadership: Fiedler states that different leader personalities are needed for "difficult" and "easy" situations, and a cultural gap between superior and subordinates is one of the factors that makes a situation "difficult." However, this theory does not take the *kind* of cultural gap into account.
>
> In practice, the adaptation of managers to higher Power Distance environments does not seem to offer too many problems. Although this is an unpopular message and seldom professed in management development courses, managers moving to a higher Power Distance culture soon learn that they have to behave more autocratically in order to be effective.[7]

Where does this leave us as international managers? Perhaps we pick and choose, and adopt what is appropriate in the home culture. The matter is brought into focus as we examine a specific management system. The underlying assumptions regarding leadership in the United States are clearly seen in the practice of management by objectives. This assumes that a subordinate is independent enough to negotiate meaningfully with a superior (not too high of a power distance), that both the superior and the subordinate are willing to take risks (a low uncertainty avoidance) and that performance is important to both (high masculinity).

Hofstede continues to demonstrate the importance of cross-cultural research:

> Let us now take the case of Germany. This is also a below-average Power Distance country, so the dialogue element in MBO should present no problem. However, Germany scores considerably higher on Uncertainty Avoidance; consequently, the tendency towards accepting risk and ambiguity will not be present to the same extent. The idea of replacing the arbitrary authority of the boss by the impersonal authority of mutually agreed-upon objectives, however, fits the low Power Distance, high Uncertainty Avoidance cultural cluster very well. The objectives become the subordinates' "superego."
>
> In a book of case studies about MBO in Germany, Ferguson states that "MBO has acquired a different flavor in the German-speaking area, not least because in these countries the societal and political pressure towards increasing the value of man in the organization on the right to codetermination has become quite clear. Thence, MBO has been transposed into Management by Joint Goal Setting (Führung durch Zielvereinbarung)." According to him, MBO fits the idealogical needs of the German-speaking countries of the moment. The case studies in Ferguson's book show elaborate formal systems with extensive ideological justification; the stress on team objectives is quite strong, which is in line with the lower Individualism in these countries.
>
> The other case on which specific information is available is France. In France, MBO was first introduced in the early 1960s but it became extremely popular for a time after the 1968 students' revolt. People expected that this new technique would lead to the long overdue democratizing of organizations. Instead of DPO (Direction Par Objectifs), the French name for MBO became DPPO (Direction *Participative* Par Objectifs). So in France, too, societal developments affected the MBO system. However, DPPO remained in general as much a vain slogan as "Liberte, Egalite, Fraternite" (Freedom, Equality, Brotherhood) did after the 1789 revolt. Franck wrote in 1973 ". . .I think that the career of DPPO is terminated, or rather that is has never started, and it won't ever start as long as we continue in France our tendency to confound ideology and reality. . ." In a postscript to Franck's article, the editors of *Le Management* write: "French blue and white-collar workers, lower-level and higher-level managers, and 'patrons' all belong to the same cultural system which maintains dependency relations from level to level. Only the deviants really dislike this system. The hierarchical structure protects against anxiety; DPO, however, generates anxiety. . ."
>
> The reason for the anxiety in the French cultural context is that MBO presupposes a depersonalized authority in the form of internalized objectives;

but French people, from their early childhood onwards, are accustomed to large Power distances, to an authority that is highly personalized; in spite of all attempts to introduce Anglo-Saxon management methods, French superiors do not easily decentralize and do not stop short-circuiting intermediate hierarchical levels, and French subordinates do not expect them to. The development of the 1970s have severely discredited DPPO which probably does injustice to the cases where, starting from less exaggerated expectations, individual organizations or units in France have benefitted from it. [7]

The consequences of Hofstede's conclusions are significant. In this section we have discussed the problems of assuming that our management philosphies or strategies are exportable in their entirety. *They are not.* Leadership is learned and is based on assumptions about one's place in the world. Managers from other business systems are not "underdeveloped" American managers. Sometimes the cultures of host countries can be changed in part, but this is difficult and success depends on many variables. Considering seriously the dimensions of national culture, as identified by Geert Hofstede, will enable us to reduce costly mistakes.

Peter Drucker has aptly observed that there are no underdeveloped countries, only undermanaged ones. Yet, how much of this Austrian management theorist's concepts are globally applicable? Some hold there is a managerial subculture around the world in which many "Druckerisms" are appropriate. In this international microculture, pragmatism is the norm, and managers borrow and adapt administrative techniques from everywhere if it helps them to meet objectives.

The challenge for international managers is to develop a "management by synergy" style. Realizing the difficulty of imposing a culture-specific philosophy of management on another business culture is the first step. The next step is more difficult and involves developing management philosophies or practices that are compatible to most persons in the organization and viable in the host culture.

CONFLICT

Like leadership and power, conflict is a fascinating subject for research and discussion in organizations and family systems. Traditionally, the social scientists who have studied conflict have been keenly aware of its destructive element, which was observed in wars, strikes, family disruption, and disharmony whenever a conflict was observed. But in the past two or three decades the idea that conflict is only destructive and is therefore to be avoided at all costs has been replaced with the reality that conflict is present in most organizations and institutions and, if managed well, serves useful purposes. In this section we will identify some themes reflecting the U.S. viewpoint with regard to conflict and suggest ways that other societies resolve disputes. As Likert has stated: "The strategies and principles used by a society and all its institutions for dealing with disagreements reflect the basic values and philosophy in that society."[9]

Is Conflict Present in All Organizations?

Face it. Conflict is a reality of organizational life. Inevitable, often legitimate, and even necessary. A lack of conflict signals stagnancy; uncontrolled conflict threatens chaos.

Dramatic forces, released by rapid changes in technology, consumer demands, the increasing complexity of organizations, create confusion over goals and role expectations. The result? Conflict between managers and specialists, staff and line, causing breakdowns in both communication and coordination.

The results of these conflicts are all too familiar: performance problems, missed deadlines, ineffective leadership, and poor teamwork.

Needed: Executives who can diagnose and manage the conflict that saps your company's vitality, and who can provide constructive processes for conflict resolution.

Now there is a way for managers to overcome their aversion to conflict—and to systematically learn the delicate art of handling organizational conflict. It's called *Managing Organizational Conflict**

---

*From a 1977 Advanced Management Research, Inc., brochure on a seminar entitled "Managing Organization Conflict."   ∎

What is conflict? Like the word "culture" there is no single, agreed upon definition. Kenneth Thomas says: "Conflict is the process that begins when one party perceives that the other has frustrated, or is about to frustrate, some concern of his."[10] This frustration may result from actions that range from intellectual disagreement to physical violence. Another definition of conflict holds that it results when two or more persons or things attempt to occupy the same space at the same time. Regardless of which definition we accept in the United States, social scientists agree that the management of conflict is a major issue at the personal and organizational level and that ineffectively managed conflict decreases the effectiveness of the individuals involved and the ability of the organization to achieve its objectives.

Most managers in the United States are now viewing conflict as a healthy, natural, and inevitable part of relationships and organizations. This constructive approach to conflict views the positive attributes in any conflict situation. The idea of dissent is a strong tradition in American history from the beginning when the United States became a nation from a conflict, to the Civil War, the Civil Rights movement, and the Anti-Vietnam war movements.

The belief that conflict can be constructive requires that problems be addressed directly and that people can be motivated to search for solutions to these problems. Constructive disagreement may in fact be an integral part of American organizations. Edward Stewart states: "When faced with a problem, Americans like to get to its source. This means facing the facts, meeting the problem head on, putting the cards on the table, and getting information straight from the horse's mouth. It is also desirable to face people directly, to confront them intentionally."[11]

"The U.S. may be maturing in sophistication for dealing with conflicts when economic and military power alone will not result in an acceptable solution. This was demonstrated in the painful conflict with Iran over the hostage issue. It resulted in a *negotiated* settlement through third party intermediaries—the Algerians.

However, even in the United States conflict in organizations is perceived to have disadvantages when there are wide differences in viewpoints or perspective and these are carried to the extreme. In this case, conflict is perceived as destructive, as the conflict creates a high level of stress for the individuals involved which, in turn, affects their ability to perform. This undermines the cooperative dimension necessary in work groups, and results in much time and energy being devoted to discussing and settling differences among the various groups that should have been devoted to the accomplishing organizational objectives. Such a situation also thwarts the decision making process. Resolution of the conflict is often seen as a win-lose, when one side's gain depends on the other side's loss, rather than a win-win situation.

With the change in emphasis from the elimination of conflict to the management of conflict, Thomas identified two models of conflict between social units, which may be individuals, groups, or organizations. The process model attempts to understand the conflict phenomona by studying the dynamics of the conflict episodes. The process model, as conceptualized by Thomas, appears as:[10]

Frustration → Conceptualization → Behavior → Outcome → Frustration

Other's reactions

The frustration of one party leads to a conceptualization of the situation, to some behavior, to the reaction of the other party, and then to agreement or the lack of agreement. In the latter case, the conflict episode is continued with further frustration, a new conceptualization, etc. The process model is concerned with the influence of an event (e.g. some frustration) on the following events (e.g. the conceptualization of the problems, etc.). The structural model, according to Thomas, attempts to understand conflict by studying how underlying conditions shape events: "The structural model is concerned with identifying the pressures and constraints which bear upon the parties' behavior—for example, social pressures, personal pre-dispositions, established negotiation procedures and rules, incentives, and so on."[10] The structural model attempts to state the effect of these conditions on the behavior of the individuals involved in a conflict situation. Thomas maintains the two models complement each other.

Cross-Cultural Conflict

There has been a growing awareness on the part of international managers and behavioral scientists of the need to devise effective mechanisms for dealing with conflicts that are cross-cultural—that is, when the concerns of two parties who are from different cultures appear to be incompatible to one or both of the parties involved. In cross-cultural conflict the phases identified by Thomas have an added dimension of complexity. The frustration, which precipitates the conflict, may be based on a different perception of the situation, which could be culturally based, Examples of different perceptions of the problem on an international level include the problems in Northern Ireland, the continuing hostility between Israel and the Arab nations, and the tension between the U.S. and Iran. In an interesting experiment on the influence of culture on perception a group of Mexican and U.S. American children were shown a series of stereograms in which one eye was exposed to a scene of a bullfight and the other eye exposed to a scene of a baseball game. The researcher found that viewers predominately reported the scene appropriate to their culture. That is, the Mexican children tended to see the bullfight and the American children tended to see the baseball game even though they were simultaneously exposed to both scenes.

The conceptualization of intercultural conflict also adds a complex variable to the process. "Conceptualization" is the meaning that people give to what they perceive. When the participants in a conflict situation are from the same culture, they are more likely to perceive situations in basically the same way and organize their perceptions in similar ways. In examples of conflict resolution with persons from the same culture, though, there are many examples when the conceptualization of the problem is as different as the "bullfight" and the "baseball" game. The person involved in a cross-cultural conflict must be careful not to assume that the perception and values of the persons involved in the conflict are the same. Nancy Adler, suggests the following steps in conceptualizing a cross-cultural conflict, which in this case involves two Canadian microcultures:[12]

The process has three major components: perception, attribution, and decision.

Perception

Individuals perceive reality, including the situations that they are directly involved in, differently based on their culture.

One of the strongest sources of variance in perception is the difference in values across cultures. Differing values lead to different aspects of the same situation emerging as salient for members of different cultures. That culture influences perception—as well as the other steps in the process of conflict conceptualization and management—does not deny that individual differences, roles differences, and situation differences are also powerful forces. It strictly states that culture is an important force to understand in analyzing the conflict process.

Example: Francophone and Anglophone Canadians

An Anglophone manager of a Canadian firm notices that the Francophones are continually taking longer than one hour for lunch. As an Anglophone, the manager places a high value on efficiency in achieving organizational goals. The Francaphone employees tend to place a higher value on relationships and achieving organizational goals through relationships. Efficiency in goal achievement is not as important to many of the Francophones as it is to the Anglophone. The Francophone may not even notice that lunch has taken 1½-2 hours because relationships are not separate from work.

Values Contrast in Francophone/Anglophone Example

	Francophone	*Anglophone*
Values	Relationship	Achievement
Content	1½-hour lunch	1½-hour lunch
Context	Lunch seen as a part of work	Lunch not seen as a part of work
	1½-hour lunch is not salient	1½-hour lunch is salient
Conflict	No perceived conflict	Yes, perceived conflict

Attribution

How do we explain the situation to ourselves?

Casual attributions
Casual attributions answer the question: What led to this situation occuring?

Intentional attributions
Intentional attributions answer the question: Did this situation just happen or was it planned?

Decision

The choice of how I will behave is based on how I perceive the situation and how I explain the causes of the situation to myself. [12]

Cross-Cultural Management of Conflict

Earlier we reviewed changes in the attitude towards conflict in the United States. Hence, in American management literature there is an emphasis on the mechanisms for handling conflict. Ross A. Webber in *Management* suggests the following mechanisms for resolving conflict which take several forms: [13]

1. Dominance
   • Individual dominance
   • Coalition dominance
   • Majority dominance
2. Appeal procedures
   • Appeal to God or chance
   • Appeal to positional authority

- Due process and the right of appeal
- The ombudsman
3. System restructuring
   - Rotating personnel
   - Decoupling with a buffer
   - Buffering with a linking role
   - Decoupling by duplication
   - Unifying the work flow
4. Bargaining
   - Distributive bargaining (like dominance)
   - Integrative bargaining (making a larger pie)
   - Mediating
   - Internal organizational bargaining (for example, labor-management negotiations)

This outline represents one way of viewing methods of conflict resolution and the emphasis is on different structural tactics.

Kenneth Thomas and Ralph Kilmann suggest a two-dimensional scheme, with one dimension being the cooperative-uncooperative striving to satisfy the other's concern, and the second dimension being the degree to which one assertively pursues one's own concerns.[14] In this scheme (see Figure 4-4) the assertive style (4) is competitive and represents a desire to satisfy one's concern at the expense of the

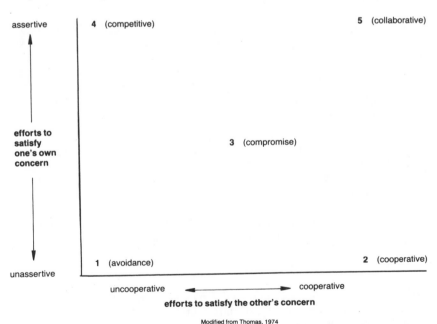

Modified from Thomas, 1974

Figure 4-4. A two-dimensional schematic showing the various "styles" of conflict resolution. After Killman and Thomas.

other. The cooperative style (2) attempts to satisfy the other but not one's own concern. A compromising style (3) is a preference for moderate, but incomplete, satisfaction of both parties. Labor-management disputes in the United States are characterized by this style. A collaborative style (5) attempts to fully satisfy the concerns of both parties (it is the most synergistic), and the avoidance style (1) is an indifference to the concerns of either party. The cooperative style as opposed to uncooperative is an Eastern mode of resolving conflict; the assertive style is more Western.

The effective international manager must be able to achieve a synergistic solution. This person will be able to diagnose a conflict accurately, and determine a strategy for managing the conflict. In describing the nature of the conflict, the facts, as perceived by both parties, and the values of the parties should be considered. Then, in determining a strategy for handling the conflict, the appropriate mode for the situation must be determined.

Now, let us contrast how conflict is managed in Middle Eastern and Oriental cultures. The following examples are from the Arab culture[15] and the People's Republic of China.[16] The material indicates alternative ways of resolving conflict and some of the basic values and underlying principles that give order to how members of the respective societies approach and deal with conflict in their personal and organizational lives.

Conflict Management in the Arab World

Raphael Patai portrays the Arabs as a conflict-prone people who have, out of social necessity and self-preservation, developed a particular mechanism for settling differences.

> In the Arab world, mediation on the tribal and village level has for centuries been the traditional method of settling disputes, and the same method has, in modern times, been adapted for settling political and military issues within and between Arab states. . .
>
> In every conflict, those involved tend to feel that their honor is at stake, and that to give in, even as little as an inch, would diminish their self-respect and dignity. Even to take the first step toward ending a conflict would be regarded as a sign of weakness, which, in turn, would greatly damage one's honor. Hence, it is almost impossible for an Arab to come to an agreement in direct confrontation with an opponent. Given the Arab tradition of invective and proclivity to boasting and verbal exaggeration, any face-to-face encounter between two adversaries is likely to aggravate the dispute rather than constitute a step toward its settlement.[17]

In the Arab world the task of the mediator is to separate and restrain the feuding parties. And the feuding parties often restrain themselves out of respect for the mediator. Thus, "the greater the prestige of the mediator and the deeper the respect he commands, the better the chances that his efforts at mediating a dispute will be successful."[17] In fact, some highly regarded families and groups carry an ascribed status as mediators. The mediator must be impartial and beyond pressures (including monetary ones) from either side in the dispute. The mediator will often promote compromise by appealing to the wishes of other respected parties; for example, "Do it for the sake of. . .your father/brother/etc." The ethical force of such an argument ("for the sake of") has three underlying assumptions, all of which remain unspoken but nonetheless understood by the disputants:

1. Each individual is obligated by ties of kinship to act in a manner that his kinsmen find gratifying.
2. The kinsmen, especially the older ones, are interested in the settlement of any conflict involving their kin group because every conflict represents a potential danger to the honor of the family.
3. By modifying his position, the disputant can manifest generosity which, in turn, redounds to the honor of his kin and Bedouin values.

According to Patai, reconciliation, not judgment of (legal) right and wrong, is the purpose of mediation. Even after a court of law has handed down a verdict, reconciliation is still viewed as necessary. According to Patai:

> . . .(mediators) are neither expressly interested in determining the guilt or innocence of any party in the dispute nor the rightness or wrongness of one claim over the other. They mediate. They do not arbitrate. They do not judge.
>
> . . .in order to restore peace in the community and to maintain the solidarity of the group, mediation must continue (even after a court verdict) until reconciliation is achieved.[17]

Edward T. Hall agrees with Patai on the importance of mediation in the Arab world but suggests that the volatile Arab temperament is a result (or luxury) of the mediation mechanism and not the cause of the mediation mechanism, as Patai has said.

> Hall: Arabs tend to depend upon outsiders to intervene in disputes, and we haven't always understood this. This is one case that Carter, and before him, Kissinger, did understand. The Arabs were depending on the U.S. to play the role of a strong interventionist in a dispute.
>
> Friedman (the interviewer): You mean something closer to a mediator. . .?
>
> Hall: I mean intervention. For instance, the law in the Middle East is: if there's a fight and somebody is injured, the crowd is guilty because the crowd didn't stop it. This means disinterested third parties who watch disputes going on share the blame for the disputes. When you grow up on an atmosphere of this type, you can tell people all kinds of things in public because you know there are others there who will stop you from hurting someone or getting hurt.

It makes for a very different kind of communication—more volatile but less risky.[18]

Hall's analysis of Arab mediation (or intervention) is somewhat different than Patai's. Hall seems to see the foundation of the mediation mechanism in the group-oriented nature of Arab society, whereas, Patai sees its foundation in the necessity of controlling the unstable personality of the Arabs. They both agree when compared with American methods of conflict resolution, the Arab prefers mediation to confrontation. In the broadest sense these respective methods of conflict resolution reflect one major aspect of a high-context versus a low-context culture.*

In the Arab world it is believed that mediation precluded a worsening of the conflict and, also, generally allowed for better mutual understanding than did confrontation. Arabs believe that the American win-at-all-cost attitude is not prevalent in their society, so compromise through mediation does not in itself represent for them a compromise of personal values. Arabs also believe that mediation, as opposed to confrontation, is rooted in a certain realism, namely: all problems do not have neat solutions; thus the need for compromise through mediation.

Patai states: (1) A mediator must be respected by both conflicting parties; (2) A mediator must "love" both parties equally; (3) No one will lose his temper in front of a respected mediator, for it would be an insult to the mediator; (4) The conflicting parties might make concessions solely because of their respect for the mediator (especially, if he is the father of the conflicting parties); (5) The mediator will quote extensively from the Koran in his attempts to resolve the dispute.[17] Mohammed states in the Sunna (commentaries on the Koran) that no dispute between friends should last more than three days; and the first of the disputing parties to say "Peace be with you" (the normal "hello" in Arabic) is the best person.

Conflict Management in the People's Republic of China

Up-to-date information on social relations in the People's Republic of China is scarce because the "How to Trade" books and reference manuals generally skip this important area of dealing with the customs between people.

In seeking to understand the Chinese way of dealing with conflict, there are two major areas to understand. First, the Confucian tradition, which is ancient, is still quoted and influential. The second is the modern Chinese ideology, particularly ideas implemented by Mao Zedung. To outsiders, there seem to be many similarities in Confucianism and the modern Chinese ideologies.

One theme present in both is that the Chinese tend to internalize conflict and avoid or ignore it as much as possible. For the Chinese, conflict is not good, desirable, or constructive for society or individuals. The absence of conflict is good.

---

*See *Managing Cultural Differences,* Chapter 2.

Ta-t'ung 大同 is the ideal "that may never work out in perfection." The Chinese characters themselves mean "great sameness" and other English translations include "harmony" and "great togetherness." But harmony implies differences that have accommodated one another and coexist tranquilly—rather like compromise. Sameness, on the other hand, suggests no differences. The ancient ideal, the Golden Age, was a time when there was a lack of conflict, there was nothing to divide the people. In popular usage this term connotes social unity and security. Actually, Confucian moderation or the Middle Way can really be seen as an extreme way in which there is a total lack of culturally sanctioned ways to deal with aggression and conflict, or to challenge established authority.

It is true that the dynastic cycle is a distinct feature in Chinese history. But dynasties fell only after they were so completely corrupt, debauched, and out of touch that all of the pent-up, internalized hostility came forth with a bang, and rebellions were always particularly long and bloody until a new authority asserted itself. In their search for new, strong authority the people even supported and legitimized invaders from beyond the Wall—the Mongols and Manchus. There is even room for speculation that if the Japanese invaders had used cultural traits to their own advantage, they might have won the support of the people.

Ta-t'ung, which remains a utopian ideal in modern China, means mutual assistance, and this means there will be no more conflict among the common people; there will be no difference between people. If everyone has received an education and everyone's point of view is the same, then there will be no disorder, there will be no war.

If everyone's opinions are not the same, it can lead to quarreling and confusion. *Hun-luan* 混乱 is the other side of the coin and prevents Ta-t'ung; it is what happens when things do not "work out in perfection." The first character means "mixed-up" and the second means "random" so that both point to a lack of order, chaos; it is usually translated as "confusion." Confusion is the result of conflict and release of aggression. It is, of course, totally undesirable and various, intricate ways to avoid confusion or conflict permeate Chinese culture.

The Chinese conceive of conflict in their everyday language by centering on ideas of oral gratification or dissatisfaction, and having enough food in a resource-poor society. Chinese internalize conflict and they do it literally by swallowing it and putting it in their stomachs. They eat loss, bitterness, and frustration—understandable when one thinks of the constant worry over having enough food. Only by putting away or swallowing individual hostilities, desires, and anger, could people function as part of a group for the benefit of all.

Babies are spoiled or "drowned in love" by giving them rich tidbits and feeding them until they are roly-poly. But, as a baby grows older, the child is disciplined by having food withheld and punished for fighting with siblings or neighbors. He is also told to swallow opinions and angers, as well as told how to think and what friends to have. If a child is not well brought up, he may be influenced by a "meat and wine" or a "meat and woman" friend, obviously someone without the best interests of the group or family at heart. Children or subordinates in the Confucian hierarchical system have never been expected to have opinions of their own but do only as instructed by a parent or authority figure. This is called "to listen to talk," meaning to say nothing and only obey.

Even today in the PRC this concept is prevalent. Professor Nien-Ching Yao, of the Beijing Institute for Foreign Trade, made interesting and relevant observations regarding this point while speaking about the Cultural Revolution. When asked what characteristics of the Chinese people might have led to the launching of the Cultural Revolution, he said,

> People, I think, the world over, tend to take existing values as values. You don't usually analyze according to a set of principles of your own. You accept what is considered a value. . . We can't expect everyone to analyze every question by a set of moral principles of their own because they simply don't have such a set of principles. People do have their different opinions, quite, but largely, in the overall picture, most of the people tend to accept existing value as value, as their own value. [19]

According to this reasoning, the Chinese do not have an internalized set of principles, but they do carry internalized conflict. No one wishes to risk an explosion of this hostility upon himself. Therefore, there are at least three culturally sanctioned ways to avoid Hun-luan and work towards Ta-t'ung. The first is *chiang jen-ch'ing* 講人情. The best English translation is "human-kind-ness" because then it can be understood as either "human kindness," particularly the showing of kindness by a superior, or as "humankind-ness," the ability to empathize.

These two ways of thinking about this concept also illustrate the two major ways of dealing with people. Four out of five Confucian relationships are hierarchical. Only one, between friend and friend, is equal. The Chinese tend to idealize friendship and value it greatly for the frankness and honesty it allows, but it is a tenous relationship. Because there is no clear order to it, the possibility of confusion and conflict hovers over it. In the friendship relationship friends empathize and can show their real feelings. On the other hand, any other relationship, even between husband and wife or parent and child, has a hierarchical order. In these relationships the subordinate hopes that the superior will have chiang jen-ch'ing, that he will show kindness and sensitivity.

In the Confucian idea only "cultivated" persons would be authority figures. Cultivated persons have the quality of chiang jen-ch'ing and they express it through what might be called etiquette, the second major way to avoid Hun-luan. *Ko-ch'i* 客氣, to be polite, implying a lack of aggressiveness or quarrelsome behavior, and *li-mao* 禮貌, good manners and propriety in one's social relations, are the major concepts. Trade negotiators' observations of Chinese etiquette in the formalized negotiation process, and that those who are sensitive to customs and etiquette make the deals, are examples of these concepts in practice. Also, they notice that the Chinese usually wish to know about the foreigners' backgrounds and intend to work towards a long-term friendship.

For the Chinese, the only way a face-to-face relationship can be conducted is by making the stranger or outsider a part of the family or of the existing social order. The creation of this relationship, in which the final outcome is a coming together and good feelings prevail, involves sensitivity to the others' feelings and situation as well as to his position or "face." This is again the concept of chiang jen-ch'ing and is accomplished through etiquette. Sincerity is included, but it is the sincerity of wanting to come to a harmonious point, to want to observe proper etiquette and keep proper order no matter what the real (or what Americans would term sincere) inner feelings of the people may be. Etiquette is a process towards a conflict-free relationship and it is also a buffer for avoiding conflict.

The third major way to avoid conflict and come to this point of harmony is through the use of an intermediary. Naturally, this person has good relations with and is well respected by both parties, and is usually an authority figure or superior in the social order. He or she understands chiang jen-ch'ing. Being sensitive to the "face" requirements of each party, he can reconcile the statuses of each side. This is what is important when people are judged by their position or status in relation to others, rather than by personal achievement or individual merit. The intermediary, associated with both groups, can act as a bridge to bring a member from one group into relation and harmony with a member of the other, the ultimate goal being to prevent Hun-luan. Once again, the only way to deal with another person is through a relationship established within the social order. Someone outside it must be brought into it either as an equal or hierarchically. In these ways, conflict is avoided.

A weakness in the Confucian system might be that it is too dependent on having good or "cultivated" people as leaders and that subordinates are personally tied to their leaders. Expected to follow blindly, they cannot disagree and have no recourse if the leader proves not to be cultivated or have human kindness. Eventually, unable to swallow any more, the peasants, the child, or the subordinate almost involuntarily unleash all pent-up frustrations and hostility. Then, indeed, chaos does reign; it is a fearsome time to live in; people do want to maintain social order and redouble their efforts to internalize anger so as to confine the horrors of aggression.

Modern China is still in a state of transition and search. The Communists, especially Mao Zedong, have wanted to rid society of the "Four Olds:" The Confucian customs, habits, culture, and social thought that they believed were greatly responsible for China's stagnation.

Before the Revolution, Mao instituted self-criticism groups, "release bitterness" meetings, and insisted that the Party should listen to the discussion and dissent of the people or the "mass line."

As the Communists won territory, they encouraged the peasants to "speak bitterness" and "to vomit bitter water" at the special meetings where the people could at last vent their real feelings against former landlords and bosses. Again, the same analogy to injestion is used, but this time the idea of expelling the bitterness was given positive connotation for the first time in Chinese society.

Mao's idea was to create a socially sanctioned, constructive method to deal with and resolve conflict for the Chinese. He was really looking for a middle way between complete avoidance and complete confusion and disruption. This idea can only exist, however, if people can and are expected to think for themselves and then not risk group ostracism for doing so.

Mao endorsed the positive aspects of conflict and competition, of having a cause and defending it:

> Conscientious practice of self-criticism is a hallmark distinguishing our Party from all other political parties. As we say, dust will accumulate if a room is not cleaned regularly. . . Our comrades' minds and our Party's work may also collect dust and also need sweeping and washing. The proverb "running water is never stale and a doorhinge is never worm-eaten" means that constant motion prevents the inroads of germs and other organisms. . . Fear neither criticism nor self-criticism. . .

Self-criticism with the use of cadre or neighborhood leader as intermediary is a part of modern China. Basically, the leader talks to each party separately and readies them, if possible, for a meeting and coming together before their peers. A commune leader has the all-around job of "mediating conflicts, punishing misdemeanors, and even persuading couples to have only one child." Until a problem becomes large enough to affect the harmony of the group or productivity, no action will be taken and sometimes people go to their leader on their own to find a solution to their quarrels.

Preparation by the leader for self-criticism is essential. It means to "make each person see what he has done wrong." Because everyone has been prepared, the actual self-criticism meeting can be expected to run smoothly. Usually things can be smoothed out in this manner, but sometimes things are only superficially smoothed out and resentment remains beneath. In fact, if one is sincere, one's "face" can be expanded in self-criticism.

Professor Yao stated: "Sometimes you have to talk to people more than ten times before they are prepared, it's a lot of work. That's called *ideological work* in our country." [19]

Mao wanted people to "dust the room." He fostered the Hundred Flowers Campaign and opened the Cultural Revolution, but each time he neglected to say that there was only one way to dust the room, only one ideological point to come to. Small differences are acceptable and, just as previously mentioned, no action will be taken, but there is no place for major differences. "To understand what one has done wrong" is to become ideologically correct and therefore socially acceptable. By doing so, one avoids or buries conflict and stays within the family, group, the social order.

If one does not see his faults, then very little can be done; he sacrifices his place and becomes an outsider. The trial of the Gang of Four is a case in point. At one time, their ideology was the correct line; now they are considered enemies of the people. An enemy is someone beyond the pale, completely outside the group. The Gang of Four deserve no sympathy; they brought punishment to themselves by being an enemy. The official Beijing newspaper stated: "Those who repeatedly commit injustices bring death to themselves." In this way of thinking, whoever is more powerful can avoid all discussion and working through of real differences by blaming the victim for his own punishment. The stronger can disengage himself from all responsibility and still avoid conflict by simply eliminating the enemy.

However, before someone is declared an enemy, that person usually has the chance to repent, to see where he or she was wrong. The case of the former foreign minister and his wife who were associated with the Gang of Four makes this point. They no longer hold office, of course, and have been criticized, but also have been given the chance to self-criticize and repent. There is no middle ground. They either completely accept what is considered right, or they are enemies and can be eliminated.

Until recently, people owed their allegiance to Mao personally and made his words their bible. Former Vice-Premier Deng said: "He acted as a patriarch. He never wanted to know the ideas of the others, no matter how right they could be; he never wanted to hear opinions different from his. . . If you don't understand this, you cannot understand why there was a Cultural Revolution." This admission seems to say that the Confucian social order remained, even in Mao's own personality. The "Four Olds" had not yet been eliminated. Now, the official pronouncement is that the Cultural Revolution was a national disaster, but at the time, people were simply doing what they have been conditioned to do for centuries—taking existing values as their values. They followed a strong authority figure, Mao. When he gave the cue to unleash hostility, they did.

In the 1980's, Party leaders in China seem to be trying to keep a lower profile, divide responsibility, and discontinue life-long tenure, led by the example of former Vice-Premier Deng. Mr. Deng also stated that Hua Guofeng could not be chairman for life, but only three terms at the most. People are generally dissatisfied with government since the arrest of the Gang of Four. They are tired of power struggles and drastic shifts in the Party line.

They have more of a wait-and-see attitude. If the leaders are working towards being competent managers rather than popular heroes and patriarchs, and if the people are no longer so ready to respond immediately to leaders' cures, then it may be possible for the Chinese to develop the middle way that Mao was so intent upon but could not live up to even in his own life.

Yuan Xianlu, foreign editor of the official *People's Daily,* said that China cannot blame everything on the Gang of Four. If the Gang is used as a scapegoat, no real progress can be made. The editors of *Time* assumed this meant that some disorder, temporary confusion, or conflict would be unavoidable while searching for new answers. The *Time* editors asked Yuan whether rising expectations and greater tolerance of criticism might hold long-term dangers for China. He answered:

> In the rural areas the farmers don't care about democracy. What they care about is good rulers. In the absence of democracy there are only two ways for people to show dissatisfaction—with silence or with rebellion. Now there is something in between. There is criticism, and that is healthier. [20]

The recent episode of Democracy Wall could be an example of the search for this middle way. Yet it was like a replay of the One Hundred Flowers Campaign. The wall was open for opinion posters and discussions took place for exactly one year. Since December 1979, all such expression has been forbidden, although a smaller substitute site was provided on the outskirts of Beijing.

It may be that each replay, each flowering, is practice in development of the middle way, but for the time being, it is well to remember the major points handed down in tradition. Conflict is not good and there has never been provision for criticism or individual opinion. Very sophisticated ways have been devised and are used in everyday life by all people to avoid conflict and confusion. The "great sameness" has not been achieved, but people still strive through etiquette, empathy, recognition of status, and use of intermediaries to avoid conflict and confusion as much as possible.

Conclusion

Tremendous amounts of money have been spent on developments that have made the material and physical lives of people from many nations more comfortable. However, we have not yet developed the mechanisms for problem-solving and resolving conflict on a nation-to-nation or individual-to-individual basis. One reason may be because we do not adequately understand the basic values and philosophy of the nations involved. Once we understand a people's culture, we might then be able to develop acceptable means for solving some of the cross-cultural problems that are created, in part, by our developments. By sharing international leadership and power, and cooperating in resolving intercultural conflicts, we take the first steps in promoting synergy. Perhaps transnational enterprises are the laboratories in which international personnel experiment with new behaviors that move beyond culture.

This chapter has focused on leadership and conflict in international management. For synergy to be developed, managers must appreciate the differences in cultural perspectives of these two key management dimensions. We have provided some examples of this relative to the concept of leadership, and an in-depth illustration of culture specifics on conflict. By examining this issue relative to China, one may be more subtle in dealing with conflict in another culture.

Although cultural differences exist in the global practice of leadership and coping with human conflict, the cosmopolitan manager is able to:

1. Understand the host culture's attitudes toward leadership and conflict.
2. Learn what can be adapted from this approach to one's learned style of leadership and conflict resolution.
3. Synergize the cross-cultural dimensions into a more global approach. Thus, when exercising power or dealing with conflict, a manager is more than eclectic, he or she is synergistic. Chapter 10 explores this further.

References

1. *Royal Bank Letter.* "Leadership at Work," Royal Bank of Canada, September/October 1980.
2. Hofstede, G. "Motivation, Leadership, and Organization: Do American Theories Apply Abroad?" *Organizational Dynamics,* Summer, 1980.
3. Kover, A.J. *Business Week,* "Machiavellian Tactics for B-school Students," *Business Week,* October 13, 1975.
4. McCall, M.W. *Power, Influence, and Authority: The Hazards of Carrying a Sword,* Technical Report No. 10. Greensboro, North Carolina: Center for Creative Leadership, 1978.
5. McCall, M.W. *Leaders and Leadership: Of Substance and Shadow,* Technical Report No. 2. Greensboro, North Carolina: Center for Creative Leadership, 1977.
6. Blake, R. and Mouton, J. *The New Managerial Grid.* Houston: Gulf Publishing Company, 1978.
7. Hofstede, G. *Culture's Consequences.* Beverly Hills, California: Sage Publications, 1980.
8. Rhenman, E., Stromberg, L. and Westerlund, G. *Conflict and Cooperation in Business Organizations.* New York: Wiley-Interscience, 1970.
9. Likert, R. and Likert, J.G. *New Ways of Managing Conflict.* New York: Mc-Graw-Hill, 1976.
10. Thomas, K.W. *Conflict and Conflict Management.* Los Angeles, University of California, Working Paper 74-3, 1974.
11. Stewart, E.C. *American Cultural Patterns: A Cross-Cultural Perspective,* LaGrange Park, Illinois: Intercultural Network, Inc., 1979.
12. Adler, N. *Cross-Cultural Conflict.* American Graduate School of International Management. Unpublished paper, 1978.
13. Webber, R.A. *Management: Basic Elements of Managing Organizations.* Homewood, Illinois: Richard D. Irwin, Inc., 1979.

14. Kilmann, R.H. and Thomas, K.W. *A Forced-Choice Measure of Conflict-Handling Behavior: The "Mode" Instrument.* Los Angeles Graduate School of Management, Working Paper 73-12, 1973.
15. Buttross, P. American Graduate School of International Management. Unpublished paper, 1980.
16. Siebert, H. American Graduate School of International Management. Unpublished paper, 1980.
17. Patai, R. *The Arab Mind.* New York: Charles Scribner & Sons, 1976.
18. Hall, E.T. Interview in *Psychology Today,* August, 1979, pp. 45-51.
19. Yao, N.C. From a lecture given at the American Graduate School of International Management, 1980.
20. Xianlu, Y. *Time,* November, 1980.

5.
Communication and Negotiation in World Management

Studies of what managers do each day indicate that 75% of their time is spent communicating. This includes writing, talking, and listening. In fact, all business ultimately comes down to transactions or interactions between individuals. The success of the transaction depends almost entirely on how well managers understand each other. Communication is the basis for negotiations.

International managers agree that communicating with foreign managers and clients is a primary responsibility and usually involves negotiating with others who are culturally different. The key problem for these managers is addressing such factors as different negotiating styles and contrasting cultural conditioning, which make each nation's negotiators behave and react in many different and unpredictable ways.

The first part of this chapter is on *communication,* and the second part examines *negotiating* in different business systems in the global marketplace.

The communication material contains portions of a five-day management training program used by a major U.S. multinational corporation in several areas of the world, including the Middle East.* It is followed by a critique of this material from the perspective of its application to learners from the Middle East.† By analyzing some of the questionable assumptions underlying this whole training strategy, we hope to provide international human resource specialists with insights that can lead to improved cross-cultural instruction.

---

*"Middle East" is a broad term and refers here to the Arab countries in the region generally referred to as the Middle East. However, this presentation does not reflect the cultural approach of Christian Arabs or Israelis.

†Written by R. Moran at the request of one of the trainers of the course.

INTERNATIONAL MANAGEMENT COMMUNICATION

This material is taken from management training materials prepared in the United States but used in other cultures.[††] As each section is considered, it is suggested that the reader identify the cultural factors, that are *assumed to be universal* in this material. The issue is how adequate or appropriate is this communication training for international managers. Critiques appear on pages 80, 89, and 91.

Section One: Performance Goals

On completing this section, participants will be able to:

1. Describe communication factors that influence work climate.
2. Identify and describe four key techniques for improving communications.
3. Identify their own communication strengths/weaknesses, relate these to management style, and utilize team feedback to plan for improvement.

As an example of some of the behaviors that impact organizational climate and communications, take a few minutes to look at the Managing Climate sheet, page 81. Some of these behaviors are subtle, and shape climate and the tone of interaction progressively, over time. Others are more direct and can trigger an immediate, but lasting, positive or negative response.

The important point to keep in mind is that the way we interact and communicate on a daily basis can impact short-term and long-term results and relationships. Results often depend on relationships.

Think back over relationships you've had with other managers. Focus on someone you've worked with or worked for who strikes you as a particularly effective communicator. What specific things did that person do in his/her daily verbal communications that were such a turn-on.

If these are "communication turn-ons," let's flip the coin and talk about managers you've known whose daily styles of communicating were a complete turn-off. What kinds of things did they do to make you feel that way?

Looking at these two lists, it's easy to see the black and white, good and bad of communicating. But in reality, communications are not so clear-cut, not so easily labeled positive or negative.

Critique of Section One—Performance Goals

The previous management instructions on communications are too provincial and ethnocentric for a multinational corporation. Having learned these lessons,

---

[††]Used with permission. Parts are omitted to preserve continuity. Shaded sections (this page, facing page, and pages 87-91) are the reprinted training materials.

Managing Climate

Behaviors that Help *Build* a Trust Climate

1. Express your doubts, concerns and feelings in an open, natural way. Encourage your subordinates to do so also.
2. When subordinates express their doubts, concerns and feelings, accept them supportively and discuss them thoroughly.
3. Set honesty as one standard that will not be compromised. Demand it from yourself and from your staff.
4. Be clear about your expectations when assigning work or eliciting opinions. Explain your reasons, wherever possible, behind requests and directions.
5. Encourage subordinates to look to you as a possible resource in accomplishing results, but develop and reinforce independence.
6. When something goes wrong, determine what happened, not "who did it."
7. Encourage active support and participation in corrective measures from those involved.
8. Share credit for successes; assume the bulk of responsibility for criticism of your unit.

Behaviors that Help *Preclude* a Trust Climate

1. Look on expressions of feelings and doubts as signs of weakness.
2. Be sarcastic, but cleverly so.
3. Let your subordinates know that you expect them to "stretch the truth" a little if it will make the organization look good.
4. Be secretive. Never let them really be sure what's on your mind. This keeps them on their toes.
5. Discourage subordinates from coming to you for help. After all, they should be "stem-winders" and "self-starters."
6. When something goes wrong, blow up, hit the ceiling, and look for the guilty party.
7. Gossip about and disparage others on the staff when they are not present. Overrespond to casual comments by others about your people.
8. Take credit for successes. Plan vendettas and other ploys to make other organizations look bad. Draw on subordinates for carrying these out. Always insist on plenty of documentation to protect yourself.

assume this company's representatives are assigned to an Arab culture in the Middle East. The following points are presented as they relate specifically to comments made in the critique* of the communicating section:

1. The person with whom a Middle Easterner is working is more important than the mission, product, or job.
2. Quiet strength is a greater value than an obvious use of power.
3. Patience is a virtue.
4. Friendship and trust are prerequisites for any social or business transactions, and are slowly developed.

---

*George W. Renwick assisted in the preparation of this critique, which was reviewed by five managers from the Middle East.

5. Confrontation or criticism in the presence of others should be avoided.
6. Middle Easterners love the spoken word, tend to ramble and don't get to the point quickly.
7. Middle Easterners are masters at flattery and appreciate compliments.
8. Middle Easterners find bluntness very disrespectful, which is why they usually respond in the most agreeable manner, regardless of truth.
9. Middle Easterners are very emotional people and are easily outraged by even slight provocations.
10. Middle Easterners are proud and their dignity is important to them.

In an attempt to systematically assess the content and approach of the training material, the following specific criteria have been determined:

Appropriateness of goals. The goals of the training are expressed only in terms of knowing and doing (knowledge and action). Increased ability to relate is reduced to increased ability to communicate; communication is, in turn, reduced to the taking of certain actions, which are to be taken only during the moments of direct contact, and are further limited to *saying* something.

Extremely heavy reliance is placed upon words. There is no attention given to nonverbal channels (of feedback, for example). This is inappropriate for any cross-cultural training materials, especially those to be used with (an by) people in the Middle East.

Role of trainer—clarity and appropriateness. There is no explanation of appropriate relationships with participants or effective means of establishing credibility, respect, confidence.

Directions to trainer—clarity and completeness. The directions regarding scheduling, procedure, and what to say are very detailed. No directions are given, however, regarding what the trainer should know about the training process and group process, nor are suggestions given regarding the trainer's attitudes and style or his appropriate expectations of participants; the latter will be especially important for an American trainer working in the Middle East.

Assumptions regarding participants' motivations and objectives. The communicating section assumes the purpose of communication is to get the job done. It further assumes that the participants also accept such an assumption. Middle Easterners do not make the same assumption.

The section assumes the participants place a very high value on *efficient* conversation. Middle Easterners do not place the same value on efficient conversation.

The "four techniques" assume the participants are primarily concerned, as they communicate, with the accurate transmission of facts (not with enjoyment, showing respect, building a relationship, etc.). Verbal accuracy is less important for Middle Easterners.

"Questioning skills" assume that the participants want information (not pleasure, rapport, trust, etc.). Middle Easterners are less apt than Americans to be intent upon simply gathering information.

The whole communicating section assumes that the participants are eager for more self-knowledge, self-awareness, self-understanding. Although a current preoccupation of Americans, self-analysis is not appealing for most Middle Easterners.

Appropriateness of rewards. The communicating section assumes participants will be adequately rewarded for their efforts by their learning and especially by the later benefits of their learning. Middle Easterners are likely to expect more tangible and more immediate rewards.

Degree of context provided for in design. The section is extremely low context (emphasis on words) in design. It allows for virtually no high context exchanges (emphasis on situations and internalization of meanings). Also, the unit is a decidedly linear design. Many Middle Easterners would find a such a low context, relentlessly linear design quite confining.

Basis of scheduling (clock vs. internal). The section is geared very closely to the clock; what happens when is determined largely by the machine. For Middle Easterners, on the other hand, issues are raised and actions taken only when the time is right—and the right time is determined not by reference to a mechanism but to a sense of the situation and the people involved.

Appropriateness of pace. The communication training session was to last five full hours without a break! It would be difficult for an American to keep attentive and stay at it for that long.

The tight structure, rapid pace, long hours would probably leave a Middle Easterner feeling regimented—something he definitely does not want to be.

Assumptions and provisions for relationships among participants. The section assumes only professional relationships among the participants, and these, it assumes, are quite clear and straightforward. A Middle Easterner is likely to feel this to be simplistic, naive, and restricting.

At no point does the section address the relationships among the participants; neither the goals of the training nor the directions to the trainer deal with the effect of the training—even the communications training—upon these relationships. A Middle Easterner who was involved and realized this would probably feel this to be negligent. He might resent it.

Modes of participation required of participants. The appropriateness of each mode of participation should be explored. For example, the degree of self-disclosure required. This needs to be determined and the Middle Easterner's reactions should be estimated.

Kind of feedback required. The section assumes that objective evidence presented by the trainer on group process and individual performance (style of management and communication skills) will be received and will be beneficial. It can, however, be counterproductive with Middle Easterners. Americans often want verbal feedback, sometimes they welcome it. Middle Easterners often do not want it, especially in the direct, professional, often negative way Americans tend to present it; such feedback is usually not the most effective way to increase the insight and ability of a Middle Easterner.

Few people like to discuss their problems, weaknesses, mistakes. Middle Easterners, especially, do not. For someone to point them out is quite uncomfortable. Middle Easterners, who can be very sensitive to the feelings of others, are themselves often sensitive to criticism, Feedback, in the limited sense in which Americans usually understand it, is therefore often felt by Middle Easterners to be blunt, harsh, lacking in finesse. A Middle Easterner will go to considerable lengths to avoid any direct encounter that will show himself or another in an unfavorable light; such a direct exchange would only be unpleasant and result in hurt feelings.

Sources of feedback required. The section requires that the participants receive feedback not only on two different qualities (their style of management and their communication skills), but also that they receive this from two different sources: both the trainer and their fellow participants. For a Middle Easterner, having his communication skills evaluated by each of the members of his group, one after another, would seem quite unnatural, contrived, tedious and superficial; the particular evaluations he was given might well be dismissed.

Mode of reasoning expected. The section assumes that the participants use a rational, inductive approach to persons and problems. Middle Easterners, however, are much more accustomed to an intuitive approach.

The section prescribes a cool, objective, clearly organized, predictable smoothly functioning business environment (see, for example, the desirable climate described). There is little room in the prescribed environment (as in the training program itself) for intense relationships and strong feelings, especially the expression of these. Such an environment would probably be both boring and frustrating for a Middle Easterner.

Degree of individual recognition. There is little acknowledgment of individuality in the design of the exercises or by the trainer. Where individual differences are identified, there is little affirmation of these, exploration of their origins, or explorations of means for making the differences complementary and productive.

Very little room is allowed for individual expression or contradictory input. This would probably be confining for a Middle Easterner.

The requirement to do so much work with others as a group would probably be unnatural and uncomfortable for Middle Easterners and resisted by them.

Number and variety of simultaneous demands. Middle Easterners, generally speaking, are not accustomed to doing several things simultaneously. Some parts of the section, however, require them to (asking the "right" kinds of questions, for example, and at the same time evaluating their questions, listening to feedback on their management styles, evaluating the feedback itself, evaluating the way in which the feedback is given, etc.).

Degree of standardization. The "four techniques" assume that all relationships on the job (as in the training program) are the same. No allowance is made for relationships of different duration or levels of trust, or for persons having different positions, ages or family ties. For a Middle Easterner, some of these techniques may be appropriate with some individuals under certain conditions, but with another individual other modes of initiating and responding (not mentioned in the unit) would be appropriate.

Similarly, "questioning skills" assumes every individual and every subject (social, business, personal, technical, etc.) is to be treated in the same way. A Middle Easterner does not assume this and certainly does not practice it.

Attention to detail required. Some of the exercises in the training program require prolonged attention to numerous details. A Middle Easterner is apt to feel many of the details are irrelevant and become impatient when required to keep focusing on them. "In basket" exercises, for example, are usually very inappropriate. (Case studies of models, for different reasons, are also inappropriate.)

Degree of reality. The techniques proposed to trainees assume a control over one's time that most Middle Easterners neither assume nor exercise.

The techniques further assume one-on-one communication situations when dealing with Middle Easterners (with a government official, for example), but the situation is often several-on-one with countless interruptions.

The techniques allow no room for using, and no means for interpreting, *silence*. For Middle Easterners, however, silence is an appropriate and expressive means of communication.

Summary of Section One Critique

The communication section is based on assumptions and priorities that are American and are often not compatible with the assumptions and priorities of many Middle Easterners. The section, therefore, would make demands upon Middle Eastern participants that would be distressing to them. The section prescribes a mold for the efficient communicator into which most Middle Easterners would not fit.

In the left-hand column of the "Managing Climate" instrument (page 81) there are behaviors suggested that help build a trust climate, and on the right-hand side, there are behaviors that can help preclude a trust climate. There are some problems with these:

1. It is stated that an expression of doubt and concern and feelings in an open and natural way would be a behavior which facilitates the building of a trust climate. This may be so from a Western perspective, however, this behavior might become a barrier to effective communication in the Middle East. Middle Easterners are sensitive, especially when it comes to the expression of doubt and concern in an open manner, in a non-familiar setting. Middle Easterners cherish honesty, but tact is extremely important when expressing doubt. This could be viewed as disagreement or disharmony that might cloud the trust climate between persons. Middle Easterners are generally very temperamental, and therefore they try to avoid arguments. Once there is an argument, it tends to be heated because each one in the discussion wants to be right.

2. The management style in the Middle East tends to be much more authoritative than in the United States. This is a cultural characteristic that can be explained by the following:

   • Governments in the Middle East generally are much more authoritative than governments in the west with the absolute authority being vested in the hands of the ruling class.
   • The social structure—Older persons are highly respected in the Middle East, and this stems from religious teachings.
   • The family structure—The father in a family in the Middle East is generally the most respected and authoritative person. He is the highest authority, and his children look up to him for guidance.
   • The manager in the Middle East enjoys his power and exercises his authority. Possessing power and authority in the Middle East is generally relished by those who possess it. To give into subordinates would be viewed by them as possessing weakness.

3. Honesty as a standard—Honesty is highly regarded in the Middle East, yet it is coupled with the concept of saving face and preserving one's honor. Middle Easterners are introverted and shy until a mutual trust is built, and at that time a person will share his concerns. The process of developing mutual trust takes a long time when compared with the establishment of relations in the United States. Honesty is also a word that has many meanings depending on the situation.

4. Clarity of expectations—Clarity in expectations is extremely important. It is very difficult to read another person's mind, but stating clearly what one wants is western. Another way would be to anticipate the needs or expectations of another (i.e. as Middle Easterners often do).

5. Encouragement of subordinates to look up to their superiors as a possible resource for accomplishing results. However, the people in the Middle East like to be independent, especially persons who are educated. If the superior is a foreigner, they probably would resent referring to him at all times for accomplishing tasks or results because it might make them feel inferior. The job might get done, but if not enough responsibility is given to the person from the Middle East, the trust climate would be stifled. They may also adapt the attitude of carelessness and simply do what is required from them without further incentive.

6. When things go wrong—It is sometimes necessary to tell someone that an error was made by someone in the organization, but this must be done very tactfully.

7. Active support and participation—This is a good point in helping subordinates realize and develop responsibility.

8. Sharing credit—This is considered generosity and would win the respect and support of persons one is working with.

All of the factors listed under the headings of behaviors that preclude a trust climate do in fact help preclude the development of trust in the Middle East. They are all unfavorable traits.

The next section of the management program is on active listening. The following are the instructions in the manual.

Section Two: Active Listening

What do we mean by *active* listening?

Active listening requires discipline and *concentration*. Sometimes it necessitates breaking the habit of planning what you would like to say next, rather than attending to what's being said to you now. Active listening requires *subject* involvement rather than *ego* involvement.

How do we know when people aren't actively listening to us?

1. When their responses have nothing to do with what was just said.
2. When they interrupt continuously.
3. When they're looking around the room.
4. When they're fidgeting.
5. When they take the first opportunity to change the subject.

Rate your listening abilities using the "Rate your Listening Abilities" instrument:

Rate Your Listening Abilities

	Almost Always	Usually	Occasionally	Seldom	Almost Never
Attitudes					
1. Do you like to listen to people talk?	5	4	3	2	1
2. Do you encourage other people to talk?	5	4	3	2	1
3. Do you listen even if you do not like the person who is talking?	5	4	3	2	1
4. Do you listen equally well whether the person talking is man or woman, young or old?	5	4	3	2	1
5. Do you listen equally well to friend, acquaintance, stranger?	5	4	3	2	1
Actions					
6. Do you put what you've been doing out of sight and out of mind?	5	4	3	2	1
7. Do you look at the speaker?	5	4	3	2	1
8. Do you ignore the distractions around you?	5	4	3	2	1
9. Do you smile, nod your head, and otherwise encourage the speaker to talk?	5	4	3	2	1
10. Do you think about what the speaker is saying?	5	4	3	2	1
11. Do you try to figure out what the speaker means?	5	4	3	2	1
12. Do you try to figure out why the speaker is saying it?	5	4	3	2	1
13. Do you let the speaker finish what he or she is trying to say?	5	4	3	2	1
14. If the speaker hesitates do you encourage him or her to go on?	5	4	3	2	1
15. Do you re-state what the speaker has said and ask if you got it right?	5	4	3	2	1

	Almost Always	Usually	Occasionally	Seldom	Almost Never
16. Do you withhold judgment about the speaker's idea until he or she has finished?	5	4	3	2	1
17. Do you listen regardless of the speaker's manner of speaking and choice of words?	5	4	3	2	1
18. Do you listen even though you anticipate what the speaker is going to say?	5	4	3	2	1
19. Do you question the speaker in order to get him or her to explain ideas more fully?	5	4	3	2	1
20. Do you ask the speaker what the words mean, imply?	5	4	3	2	1

Critique of Section Two—Listening

A few comments concerning the use of similar questionnaires across cultures, such as in some cultures. Instruments such as these ("Rate Your Listening Abilities") should be used with reservation in most instances. The reason is that it is an artificial way of gathering information in some cultures. It asks questions about personal things, and the participant from the Middle East might find this offensive. For example:

Question 1, "Do you like to listen to people talk?" People in the Middle East generally love to talk and to listen to people talk.

Question 3, "Do you listen even when you do not like the person who is talking?" Since relationships in the Middle East are of such importance, it is generally true that if a person does not like you or trust you, they will not listen to you as they would if they had a positive relationship with you.

Question 4, "Do you listen equally well if the person talking is a man or a woman, young or old?" From the Middle Eastern perspective, this answer would be different. If a man was listening to a woman, a man would not listen as intensely to a woman as he would to a man, and since respect is generally accorded more to an older person than to a younger person, more intent would be given when listening to an older person.

Question 5, "Do you listen equally well to friends, acquaintances or strangers?" Here again there is a very significant difference as a friend is listened to much more intensely than to an acquaintance or to a stranger.

Question 7, "Do you look at the speaker?" Here again there is a cultural dimension. Eye contact is culture specific in that we, in the Western world, are taught to look a person in the eye. Persons from the Middle East are also taught to look a person in the eye. However, when a superior is speaking, as a symbol or a demonstration of respect for this person, there would be less eye contact.

Question 9, "Do you smile, nod your head, or otherwise encourage the speaker to talk?" This is a very Western concept to demonstrate attention.

In addition, some of the factors that might influence the climate of communication in the Middle East are:

1. The situation itself.
2. The people involved in the situation or in the communication.
3. The age of the persons communicating.
4. The level of education of the people.
5. The social status of the person involved.
6. The amount of friendliness, sincerity, and honesty that are displayed by those that are communicating.

It is obvious that the specific points illustrated are based on American culture values and norms, and they do not take into account the unique history, socialization process, and cultural values of people in the Middle East.

Section Three: Questioning

Active listening and questioning skills support each other as techniques. Listening carefully enough to ask the right questions can help prevent entrapment in the communications hazard of making and acting on incorrect assumptions. People make assumptions all the time. Why does this happen so frequently and easily? Making assumptions so readily may occur because we each tend to view things from our own limited perspective, and that perspective is greatly influenced by our *experiences* and *expectations*.

Direct Questions

These questions require a specific, concise response. They usually can be answered by a single word or a simple phrase. They narrow the range of possible answers, usually focusing on a particular point. Direct questions:

1. Help gather specific information.
2. Save time by getting to the point.

3. Tell the other person exactly what you want to know.
4. Eliminate confusion.
5. Guide the discussion down the path you want it to follow.

Open Questions
To ask an "open" is to allow the person being questioned to give a variety of unstructured responses. He or she can express an opinion or state a point of view as part of the answer. Questions that ask for an explanation of events or the reasoning behind a particular decision are typically open questions.

Clarifying Questions
Sometimes even the correct use of direct and open questions isn't quite enough to get the information you need, or you might not be sure if your understanding of the information is the same as that of the person who's providing it. At times like these, you'll want to use clarifying questions: questions that ask for further explanation or examples of what's already been said.
These materials will give the reader a sense of the flow. Other topics in this section included feedback and exercises on message decay and questioning skills.

Critique of Section Three—Questioning

All people ask questions. However, it is an American cultural characteristic to gather information by asking a variety of questions. In the Middle East, in contrast to the American cultural norm, it is more important to listen and to observe the environment rather than to ask specific questions. It is also important to be aware of the kind of question that is appropriate. To whom is it appropriate to ask questions? When is it appropriate to ask questions? The implication in the questioning skills portion of the communicating section gives one the impression that the most important consideration concerning questioning skills is to be able to identify and to be able to use the three kinds of questions: the direct question, the open question, and the clarifying question.

In the Middle East, *direct questions* could very easily be interpreted as an invasion of privacy and result in a disharmonious relationship between the person who is asking the question and the person who has been asked the question. The concept of asking a direct question follows the Western concept of a low-context culture, which means that most of the information is contained in the words. The Middle East, in contrast, has been identified as a high-context culture whereby a great deal of the information is contained not in what is said, not in the words, but in the situation, the context, and in the person. It behooves the American manager working in the Middle East not to impose a norm or value of directness—yes, no—in response to a direct question, for example, but to be able to ask a question in such a way that he will be able to interpret accurately the response given the cultural characteristics of the person with whom he or she is interacting.

Persons from the Middle East agreed that *open questions* are a more appropriate method of asking questions and gathering information. This will allow the person to respond in a way in which the person being asked the question will be able to structure the response in such a way that there will not be created a defensiveness, and the person will have an input into the communication process.

Clarifying questions are also very useful in the Middle East, and these kinds of questions together with open questions are generally more appropriate and effective in communicating with persons from that area. The conclusion, therefore, is that in a training program in the Middle East, it would be more effective to train Americans and Middle Easterners to ask open and clarifying questions and to be able to interpret the responses.

Conclusion of Communication Section

It is evident from the foregoing comments, that the training material as presented is inappropriate, in general, for use in other cultures, in this case the Middle East. It is inappropriate because it is based on American cultural assumptions and values.

In conclusion we ask:

1. Is the communicating unit appropriate for international management training?
2. Is the unit appropriate for training Americans to communicate effectively with people in host cultures, such as in the Middle East?
3. Is the unit appropriate for training Middle Eastern personnel to communicate with Americans? *Yes, if we assume that the Middle Easterners are willing, in order to communicate with Americans, to communicate like Americans.* But this is not usually the case.

The application of this communicating section is therefore limited. It may be appropriate for training Americans to communicate with other Americans, but it is, in general, not realistic or acceptable from an intercultural, particularly Middle Eastern, perspective.

NEGOTIATING IN OTHER COUNTRIES

Economic interdependency among the nations of the world is a reality. No nation is completely self-sufficient and able to avoid trading with other nations for some of their required materials. Besides Canada, the major trading partner of the

United States is Japan. Another trading partner on a less grand scale is the Congo. The United States trades with almost every nation.

The business and government people who are engaged in this trade are negotiators and are involved in international negotiations. Dr. Glen Fisher in a paper prepared for the Foreign Service Institute of the Department of State asked, "Whether skill in international negotiation can be learned, or is it a product of personality and experience?"[1] It is our belief that negotiating is a skill and it can be improved. It is the purpose of this section to suggest some of the cultural variables and what specific skills are required. The basic problem of negotiating overseas has been stated by Fisher:

> The big problem is that people who find themselves negotiating at one level or another overseas, face the special task of taking into account the factors that make negotiation outside the United States different from negotiating at home. They face new negotiating styles, contrasting cultural conditioning and all the differing concerns and outlooks that make each country's negotiators behave and react in special ways.[1]

Pierre Casse, lecturer in the Economic Development Institute at the World Bank, stated that international negotiators need five skills.[2] We have changed some of the wording on his list, but accept the skills he identifies as being necessary for the international negotiator. The skills are:

1. To be able to see the world as other people see it and to understand others' behavior from their perspective.
2. To be able to demonstrate the advantages of what one's proposals offer so that the counterparts in the negotiation will be willing to change.
3. To be able to manage stress and cope with ambiguous situations as well as unpredictable demands.
4. To be able to express one's own ideas in such a way that people one negotiates with will accurately understand.
5. To be sensitive to the cultural background of the others and adjust the suggestions one makes to the existing constraints and limitations.

The following quotations are further suggestive of some of the difficulties in effectively negotiating in an international context.

> The secret of negotiations is to harmonize the real interests of the parties concerned. Thus, the great secret of negotiations is to bring out prominently the common advantage to both parties of any proposal, and to link these advantages that they may appear equally balanced to both parties.
> Francois de Collière

> Foreigners seldom understand what any controversy is about; they do not know what is being left unsaid because it is necessary to say it, or what is

behind the dazzling smiles, the hearty embraces, the damp kisses on stubby cheeks, the clasped hands, the compliments, the declarations of eternal friendship.

Luigi Barzini

The Americans will tell you that contracts were not lived up to. What do the Americans mean? They thought they had a meeting of minds once the clauses of contract were verbalized. They failed to realize that these declarations of intent were only the beginning—not the end—of the negotiations. They went ahead with their investments without having spent the time nailing down the fine points. They did not have their political operatives at work in Rome doing what they could to smooth the path for these investments. They did not tie themselves into the bureaucracy in Palermo. Thus, they lost out.

Douglas F. Lamont

We were psychologically wounded. We were not hurt financially. We got back all of our money with some interest. But I thought that the moment had come when chauvinism in the auto industry was a thing of the past. It is not. It taught us that, from now on, partnerships like that are out.

Giovanni Agnelli

The negotiator must be quick, resourceful, a good listener, courteous and agreeable. Above all, the good negotiator must possess enough self-control to resist the longing to speak before he has thought out what he intends to say. . . . Courage also is an essential quality, since no timid man can hope to bring a confidential negotiation to success.

Francois de Collière

It is not the most intellectual or the strongest species that survives, but the species that survives is the one that is able to adapt to or adjust best to the changing environment in which it finds itself.

Charles Darwin

Cultural Aspects of Negotiating

The "Negotiation Skills—Self-Assessment Exercise" at the end of this chapter (pages 99-103) gives feedback on a person's negotiating style, as well as information on how to recognize a style in one's negotiating counterparts and effective ways to respond to specific styles.

Negotiating, according to William Zartman,[3] is a dynamic process consisting of four important elements: the parties or sides, the values, the outcome, and the mutual movement.

The first element is the parties or sides that are engaged in the process, and they have their own internal dynamics. Second is the element of values or interests presented by the parties for the purpose of collective choice. Such values are "things" that matter to the parties and may be positive or negative, as benefits and cost. Third is the outcome, which may be successful or unsuccessful, depending on whether or not a single agreed value has been chosen as the result of the process. But successful or unsuccessful, all negotiations have outcomes in the sense of an agreed, jointly-determined value, even if that outcome is only the break-off of negotiation and the agreement to disagree. A final element is mutual movement, which is the beginning point in the process. Negotiation begins when some movement has taken place from the parties' initial positions, since merely stating positions does not constitute negotiation.

The Committee for the Judiciary of the United States Senate proposed the following definition of negotiation as it is used in the United States:

> To an American, negotiation is the least troublesome method of settling disputes. Negotiation may be exploratory and serve to formulate viewpoints and delineate areas of agreement or contention. Or it may aim at working out practical arrangements. The success of negotiation depends upon whether (a) the issue is negotiable, (that is, you can sell your car but not your child); (b) the negotiators interested not only in taking but also in giving are able to exchange value for value, and are willing to compromise; and (c) negotiating parties trust each other to some extent—if they didn't, a plethora of safety provisions would render the "agreement" unworkable.

Looking at the four elements of negotiating, Zartman suggests the United States' attitude influences each.

Selection of Negotiators

Depending on importance and complexity, the members are selected very carefully and only persons who have knowledge and experience, and who will conduct themselves in a manner beneficial to their sponsors' interests, are chosen. The team members might come from many different departments in an organization and the leader is the highest ranked person.

Values

In the exchanges that comprise negotiation, information is manipulated for the purpose of changing the other party's evaluation of the values involved, in order to bring about agreement at a point more favorable to one side or the other. One of the values and beliefs that exist in the American society that impacts the negotiation process is "time"; Americans are inclined to look to the present and the future more than to the past. This means, that in the negotiation process the Americans concentrate more on where they stand today and what more they can obtain from this basis in the future. They are not so concerned about what has happened in earlier contacts and meetings, and often take it for granted that the other part knows exactly what has happened in the past. Another factor concerning time is that the Americans are predisposed towards making concessions, and often make them early in the negotiations. If however, these concessions are not reciprocated, Americans have a tendency to become frustrated with the negotiation process.

American negotiators are interested in the "here and now" and the practical side of the negotiating process. Their goals are often short range, and the side effects that their actions are likely to produce in the future are not considered in great detail.

Americans also prefer "informality" (first name, casualiness, friendliness and the like). Such attitudes are likely to be transferred to the negotiation process. This might create an unhealthy atmosphere if this behavior is practiced in negotiations with, for instance, foreigners that have a more authoritarian system.

In negotiating, Americans often try to obtain "quantity instead of quality," and stress issues that have to do with speed, amount, and time, instead of concentrating on selectivity and details that might be important to the other party.

The Outcome

Zartman states there are seven "ways" of studying negotiations.[3]

1. Historical—a given outcome is explained through a particular set of ingredients or through one unique element.
2. Contextual—seeing outcomes determined by a particular phaseological interpretation of history, referring either to the history of the negotiation itself or to the larger phase of history into which it fits.
3. Structural—finding the explanation of outcomes in patterns of relationships between parties or their goals.
4. Strategic—focusing on the element of choice, as determined by the structure of the values at stake and also by the other party's patterns of selection.
5. Personality types—combining some of the insights of the structuralists with those of the behavioralists.
6. Behavioral skills—explaining outcomes as results from proper adherence to diplomatic codes of conduct.
7. Process variables—looking at negotiations as a challenge-and-response encounter in which the moves are the inputs, and negotiating is a learning process.

A dominant American way to look at the outcomes can be found in the structural approach. This explains negotiations as a function of the relative strength of the parties.

Mutual Movement

The beginning point in the process has taken place when there has been some movement from the parties' initial positions. This means, however, that if one side does not give in at all but forces the other side to make concessions, no negotiations have taken place.

In preparing for and analyzing a negotiation it will be useful to review these elements and by study and observation determine one's counterparts attitude and orientation towards the selection of the negotiators, the values or priorities present the outcome and the movement. The following examples of variations from a number of cultures are drawn from Fisher.[1]

There are many differences in the negotiation process from culture to culture and these differences could involve language, different cultural conditioning, different negotiating styles, different ways of thinking in problem solving, implicit assumptions, gestures and facial expressions, the role of ceremony and formality in negotiation process. These are some of the variables that may be operating in the negotiation process that negotiators should be aware of.

1. There may be a cultural conditioning with regard to the way negotiators view the nature of the negotiation process itself. American negotiators are often frustrated because their counterparts do not enter in the expected give-and-take, which they typically experience in domestic or labor-management negotiations in the United States. We are frustrated when we do not experience this overseas.

2. For many cultures, such as the Japanese, to openly disagree is not a pleasant experience and whenever there is a conflict in a negotiation situation, very often a go-between or a third person is used to assist in the negotiation process.

3. American negotiators usually begin a negotiating session by trusting the persons until proven otherwise. However for the French, they would be more inclined to mistrust until faith and trust is proven by their counterparts.

4. American negotiators view the process as a problem-solving exercise whereby a number of fallback positions are carefully discussed prior to a session. However, other cultures do not view it as a problem-solving exercise and their first position is the only position they have discussed and the one they wish to present and have accepted.

5. The role of protocol in negotiations is also very important in some cultures. For example, in the Mexican culture people seem to be selected as negotiators who are skilled at rhetoric and making distinguished performances. Negotiation is perceived from their perspective as a time to test Mexican honor and to determine the attitude of the American negotiators towards Mexicans.

6. Selection of the negotiation team may also differ by culture. In the United States, persons are selected primarily on the basis of technical competence. However, in other societies one may be negotiating with people who do not have a high degree of technical competence, because the members of a negotiation team are selected on the basis of personal power or authority.

7. The way the respective teams view the decision-making process has intercultural implications. In the United States, negotiators approach the

negotiation session and the decisions that result from it by essentially saying, "anything is O.K. unless it has been restricted." However, to their Soviet counterparts, they would approach the same situation with "nothing is permitted unless it is initiated by the state."

8. Decision-making in negotiations differ by culture. In Mexico, decisions are typically from a top-down position in an organization and these reflect the personalities of the individuals. And when Mexican negotiators work overseas, they prefer to work with high-level people and typically link issues with trade-offs (for example, conceding a point on narcotics control in exchange for freer vegetable importation into the United States.)

For international negotiations to produce long-term synergy, and not just short-term solutions, managers and their representatives, such as attorneys, should be aware of the multicultural facets in the process underway. The negotiator must enter into the private world or cultural space of the other, while at the same time sharing his or her own perceptual field.

Conclusion on Human Interactions

Those who would exercise synergistic leadership, whether as international trainers or managers, need an understanding of comparative management. That includes how peoples of other cultures with whom they interface are motivated, make decisions, exercise power, and deal with conflict. Futhermore, such cosmopolitan personnel are well advised to improve their skills in cross-cultural communications and negotiations. (The negotiation exercise that follows at the end of this chapter is helpful in this regard.)

In concluding our ideas on communicating and negotiating within the world marketplace the following quotations seem to summarize our thoughts best:

In all negotiations of difficulty, a man may not look to sow and reap at once, but must prepare business and so ripen it by degrees.

Francis Bacon

All good people agree,
and all good people say,
All nice people like US are We
and everyone else is THEY;
But if you cross over the sea
instead of over the way,
You may end up (think of it)
as a sort of (THEY).

Rudyard Kipling

Negotiation Skills
A Self-Assessment Exercise*

Please respond to this list of questions in terms of what you believe you do *when interacting with others*. Base your answers on your typical day-to-day activities. Be as frank as you can.

For each statement, please enter on the Score Sheet the number corresponding to your choice of the five possible responses given below:

1. If you have never (or very rarely) observed yourself doing what is described in the statement.
2. If you have observed yourself doing what is described in the statement *occasionally, but infrequently:* that is, less often than most other people who are involved in similar situations.
3. If you have observed yourself doing what is described in the statement about *an average amount:* that is, about as often as most other people who are involved in similar situations.
4. If you have observed yourself doing what is described in the statement *fairly frequently:* that is, somewhat more often than most other people who are involved in similar situations.
5. If you have observed yourself doing what is described in the statement *very frequently:* that is, considerably more than most other people who are involved in similar situations.

Please answer each question.

1. I focus on the entire situation or problem.
2. I evaluate the facts according to a set of personal values.
3. I am relatively unemotional.
4. I think that the facts speak for themselves in most situations.
5. I enjoy working on new problems.
6. I focus on what is going on between people when interacting.
7. I tend to analyze things very carefully.
8. I am neutral when arguing.
9. I work in bursts of energy with slack periods in between.
10. I am sensitive to other people's needs and feelings.
11. I hurt people's feelings without knowing it.
12. I am good at keeping track of what has been said in a discussion.
13. I put two and two together quickly.
14. I look for common ground and compromise.
15. I use logic to solve problems.
16. I know most of the details when discussing an issue.
17. I follow my inspirations of the moment.
18. I take strong stands on matters of principle.
19. I am good at using a step-by-step approach.
20. I clarify information for others.

---

*Adapted by Pierre Casse from Interactive Style Questionnaire (Situation Management Systems, Inc.) in *Training for the Cross-Cultural Mind*, SIETAR, Washington, D.C., 1979. Used with permission.

(continued on next page)

21. I get my facts a bit wrong.
22. I try to please people.
23. I am very systematic when making a point.
24. I relate facts to experience.
25. I am good at pinpointing essentials.
26. I enjoy harmony.
27. I weigh the pros and cons.
28. I am patient.
29. I project myself into the future.
30. I let my decisions be influenced by my personal likes and wishes.
31. I look for cause and effect.
32. I focus on what needs attention now.
33. When others become uncertain or discouraged, my enthusiasm carries them along.
34. I am sensitive to praise.
35. I make logical statements.
36. I rely on well tested ways to solve problems.
37. I keep switching from one idea to another.
38. I offer bargains.
39. I have my ideas very well thought out.
40. I am precise in my arguments.
41. I bring others to see the exciting possibilities in a situation.
42. I appeal to emotions and feelings to reach a "fair" deal.
43. I present well articulated arguments for the proposals I favor.
44. I do not trust inspiration.
45. I speak in a way which conveys a sense of excitement to others.
46. I communicate what I am willing to give in return for what I get.
47. I put forward proposals or suggestions which make sense even if they are unpopular.
48. I am pragmatic.
49. I am imaginative and creative in analyzing a situation.
50. I put together very well-reasoned arguments.
51. I actively solicit others' opinions and suggestions.
52. I document my statements.
53. My enthusiasm is contagious.
54. I build upon others' ideas.
55. My proposals command the attention of others.
56. I like to use the inductive method (from facts to theories).
57. I can be emotional at times.
58. I use veiled or open threats to get others to comply.
59. When I disagree with someone, I skillfully point out the flaws in the others' arguments.
60. I am low-key in my reactions.
61. In trying to persuade others. I appeal to their need for sensations and novelty.
62. I make other people feel that they have something of value to contribute.
63. I put forth ideas which are incisive.
64. I face difficulties with realism.
65. I point out the positive potential in discouraging or difficult situations.

66. I show tolerance and understanding of others' feelings.
67. I use arguments relevant to the problem at hand.
68. I am perceived as a down-to-earth person.
69. I go beyond the facts.
70. I give people credit for their ideas and contributions.
71. I like to organize and plan.
72. I am skillful at bringing up pertinent facts.
73. I have a charismatic tone.
74. When disputes arise, I search for the areas of agreement.
75. I am consistent in my reactions.
76. I quickly notice what needs attention.
77. I withdraw when the excitement is over.
78. I appeal for harmony and cooperation.
79. I am cool when negotiating.
80. I work all the way through to reach a conclusion.

Score Sheet

Enter the score you assign each question (1, 2, 3, 4, or 5) in the space provided. *Please note:* The item numbers progress across the page from left to right. When you have all your scores, add them up *vertically* to attain four totals. Insert a "3" in any number space left blank.

1. _____	2. _____	3. _____	4. _____
5. _____	6. _____	7. _____	8. _____
9. _____	10. _____	11. _____	12. _____
13. _____	14. _____	15. _____	16. _____
17. _____	18. _____	19. _____	20. _____
21. _____	22. _____	23. _____	24. _____
25. _____	26. _____	27. _____	28. _____
29. _____	30. _____	31. _____	32. _____
33. _____	34. _____	35. _____	36. _____
37. _____	38. _____	39. _____	40. _____
41. _____	42. _____	43. _____	44. _____
45. _____	46. _____	47. _____	48. _____
49. _____	50. _____	51. _____	52. _____
53. _____	54. _____	55. _____	56. _____
57. _____	58. _____	59. _____	60. _____
61. _____	62. _____	63. _____	64. _____
65. _____	66. _____	67. _____	68. _____
69. _____	70. _____	71. _____	72. _____
73. _____	74. _____	75. _____	76. _____
77. _____	78. _____	79. _____	80. _____
IN: _____	NR: _____	AN: _____	FA: _____

Negotiation Style Profile

Enter now your four scores on the bar chart below. Construct your profile by connecting the four data points.

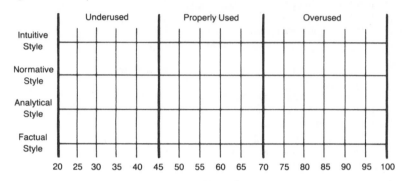

Description of Styles

Factual

Basic Assumption: "The facts speak for themselves."

Behavior: Pointing out facts in neutral way, keeping track of what has been said, reminding people of their statements, knowing most of the details of the discussed issue and sharing them with others, clarifying, relating facts to experience, being low-key in their reactions, looking for proof, documenting their statements.

Key Words: Meaning, define, explain, clarify, facts.

Intuitive

Basic Assumption: "Imagination can solve any problem."

Behavior: Making warm and enthusiastic statements, focusing on the entire situation or problem, pinpointing essentials, making projections into the future, being imaginative and creative in analyzing the situation, keeping switching from one subject to another, going beyond the facts, coming up with new ideas all the time, pushing and withdrawing from time to time, putting two and two together quickly, getting their facts a bit wrong sometimes, being deductive.

Key Words: Principles, essential, tomorrow, creative, idea.

Normative

Basic Assumption: "Negotiating is bargaining."

Behavior: Judging assessing and evaluating the facts according to a set of personal values, approving and disapproving, agreeing and disagreeing, using loaded works, offering bargains, proposing rewards, incentives, appealing to feelings and emotions to reach a "fair" deal, demanding, requiring, threatening, involving power, using status, authority, correlating, looking for compromise, making effective statements, focusing on people, their reactions, judging, attention to communication and group processes.

Key Words: Wrong, right, good, bad, like.

Analytical

Basic Assumption: "Logic leads to the right conclusions."

Behavior: Forming reasons, drawing conclusions and applying them to the case in negotiation, arguing in favor or against one's own or others' position, directing, breaking down, dividing, analyzing each situation for cause and effect, identifying relationships of the parts, putting things into logical order, organizing, weighing the pros and cons thoroughly, making identical statements, using linear reckoning.

Key Words: Because, then, consequently, therefore, in order to.

Guidelines for Negotiating with People Having Different Styles

1. Negotiating with someone having a *factual* style—
   - Be *precise* in presenting your facts.
   - Refer to the *past* (what has already been tried out, what has worked, what has been shown from past experiences . . .).
   - Be *indicative* (go from the facts to the principles.
   - Know your dossier (including the details).
   - Document what you say.
2. Negotiating with someone having an *intuitive* style—
   - Focus on the situation as a whole.
   - Project yourself into the future (look for opportunities).
   - Tap the imagination and creativity of your partner.
   - Be quick in reacting (jump from one idea to another).
   - Build upon the reaction of the other person.
3. Negotiating with someone having an *analytical* style—
   - Use logic when arguing.
   - Look for causes and effects.
   - Analyze the relationships between the various elements of the situation or problem at stake.
   - Be patient.
   - Analyze various options with their respective pros and cons.
4. Negotiating with someone having a *normative* style—
   - Establish a sound relationship right at the outset of the negotiation.
   - Show your interest in what the other person is saying.
   - Identify his or her values and adjust to them accordingly.
   - Be ready to compromise.
   - Appeal to your partner's feelings.   ■

References

1. Fisher, G. *The Cross-Cultural Dimension in International Negotiation.* Chicago: Intercultural Press, Inc., 1981.
2. Casse, P. *Training for the Cross-Cultural Mind,* SIETAR, Washington, D.C., 1979.
3. Zartman, W. *The 50% Solution.* New York: Anchor Press, 1976.

Unit 2

Fostering Synergy in Organizational Development

6.
Synergy in Organizational Culture

Imagine these scenarios:

▶ The chief executive officer of a large multinational corporation visits the facilities of a newly acquired subsidiary corporation to determine which of the parent company's policies, procedures, and personnel should be utilized in the merged firm, and which approaches or strategies should be retained. The assessment process will begin at lunch with the president of the acquired organization.

▶ A New England plant is being relocated to Alabama. Its employees have been given the opportunity to move to the South and join an enlarged workforce of local southerners. The plant manager is a technocrat from England who immigrated to the United States five years ago.

▶ A major retailer is in the midst of profound organizational change. A traditional enterprise with branches throughout the country, it is proud of its seventy-five years of customer service and the long employment records of its faithful employees. Declining sales, fierce competition, inflation impact, and like factors led to the election of a new chairman of the board. This administrator has brought in some very competent, modern managers, and together they have begun to shake up the whole "empire."

▶ A European conglomerate has purchased controlling rights of an American steel manufacturer. Key management positions have been filled with French, Italian, and German managers, and most of the competent American management has been retained. Plans are underway to improve operations and turn the company into a profitable venture.

▶ The management information systems specialist (MIS) is a relatively new position, surrounded by seeming magic and myth. But general managers are becoming less dependent upon the computer professionals in the data processing department. Now their own managers are more sophisticated at information processing, and all have access to their own microcomputers.

▶ Common Market partners are involved in a joint venture to produce an innovative airplane. It began with three major companies from three different countries, and eventually a fourth company/country entered into the agreement.

▶ A Canadian consulting firm agreed to assist a Mexican corporation in the use of advanced technology. It is part of a larger deal between the governments of both countries in which Mexican energy is to be supplied in return for Canadian expertise and equipment.

The common element in each of these scenarios is the opportunity to exercise leadership in cultural synergy. Differences in organizational cultures in these seven situations can either undermine the intended actions, or can be used to enhance goal achievement. Each cultural challenge will be addressed later in this chapter. But first, some further amplification of the words that describe this chapter seem to be in order.

DEFINITIONS AND DIMENSIONS OF ORGANIZATIONAL CULTURE

Synergy, the dictionary assures us, is cooperative or combined action. It can occur when diverse or disparate groups of people work together. The objective is to increase effectiveness by sharing perceptions, insights, and knowledge. The complexity and shrinking of today's world literally forces people to *capitalize* on their differences. For example in each of the opening scenarios, the participants can either impose "their way" or organizational culture, upon the others, often to their mutual detriment; or they can be aware of each other's cultural strengths and biases, in terms of their national and organizational characters. But a better approach is to objectively evaluate what is of "value" in each of the existing enterprises, and build upon such foundations. The synergistic agents are sensitive to cultural differences and opportunities for *mutual* growth and development.

An *organization* serves some human need—comfort or camaraderie, products or services, inspiration or education—through people who perform some function or work. The organization has been described as a collection of human objectives, expectations, and obligations. It structures human roles and relationships to attain its ends. (Reorganization, on the other hand, involves the severing of existing relationships, dissolution of existing structure, and the changing of organizational goals.)

Essentially, the organization is an energy exchange system. It transforms the input of natural or material energy, as well as human psychic and physical energy, into an output. To accomplish this, a system of feedback control is used, such as organizational communication: management information about budgets, productivity, human assets or personnel, and other facets of administration. The organization can be a government agency, a corporation, a trade or professional association, or a nonprofit entity. Whatever form this human enterprise takes, it acts as a lens to focus the energies of its people toward predetermined goals and objectives.

Culture is the way of living developed and transmitted by a group of human beings, consciously or unconsciously, to subsequent generations. More precisely, ideas, habits, attitudes, customs, and traditions become accepted and somewhat standardized in a particular group as an attempt to meet continuing needs. Culture is overt and covert coping ways or mechanisms that make a people unique in their adaptation to their environment and its changing conditions.

Organizations are actually *microcultures* that operate within the larger context of a national macroculture. Thus, an organizational culture may be the Mexican government, an American multinational or foundation, a British university or trust, the Roman Catholic Church, the Russian airline, Swedish Employers Federation, or the Association of Venezuelan Executives. Other transcultural organizations are synergistic in their structural make-up, such as UNESCO, International Red Cross, Diebold Europe, Management Centre Europe, or OPEC.

Figure 6-1 illustrates many of the aspects of organizational culture. Some prefer to view culture in terms of a human system. For example, Dr. Raymond Forbes defines an organization as an open, purposive, social, and technological system that achieves its objectives by focusing energy extracted from its environment. He describes its characteristics as:

1. Purpose (mission or goal).
2. Structure (formal/informal allocation of responsibility/power).
3. Internal systems (support services of people/technology).
4. Human interchange (organizational communications).
5. Culture (known body of policy, rituals, rules, regulations, and procedures).
6. Human knowledge (the know-how of manufacturing, marketing, administration, rendering services).
7. Work itself (job content and performance).
8. Results (outcome or affects produced by organization).[1]

However, it can be argued that many of these elements are actually part of the organizational culture. Forbes also provides useful explanations of related terms: "a system is a combination of component elements in dynamic interaction."[1] He views the characteristics of an "open system" as (a) input and output flow of energy and matter; (b) development and maintenance of a steady state for input of new energy and matter that does not disturb the system's structure and order; (c) increased controls to meet increased complexity and differentiation of compon-

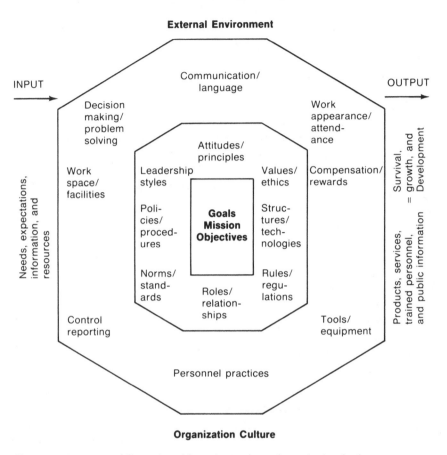

Figure 6-1. A conceptual illustration of the various aspects of organizational culture.

ment elements; and (d) extensive transactions with the surrounding environment. In the post-industrial scene organizational cultures should be open systems in which synergistic leadership will ensure ultrastability in the system and sensitivity to the macroculture in which the microculture operates.

In this period of transition from industrial to metaindustrial organizations, the traditional corporate cultures are challenged to adapt and change to meet the realities of the new information society. "High tech" or "gen tech" companies of today are prototypes of tomorrow's organizational cultures.

There are many methods for studying a macro- or microculture. Anthropologist Edward T. Hall, for instance, maps a particular culture by examining such dimensions as its message systems and interactions, associations and social roles, subsistence provisions by work and occupations, bisexuality practices (clan, sibling, marriage, and family groupings and customs, as well as sex roles), sense of territoriality and space, temporality (time, cycles, calendar, holidays), learning provisions and processes (child rearing, education, training, learning methods/aids/facilities), play and recreation (arts, sports, entertainment, exercise), ego and physical defenses (community structures, defense groups, military/industrial complex, the what, when, where, why and how of defense and social protection or satisfaction of security needs), and its exploitation or use of natural and human resources, (communication networks and groupings, food/agricultural industries and distributions, use of property and materials, technological systems). In any event, it helps to have some conceptual model that provides benchmarks for classifying or analyzing either a macro- or microculture.

The following are dimensions for understanding and analyzing organizational culture:

1. Communication, language
2. Dress, appearance
3. Food, feeding habits
4. Time, time consciousness
5. Rewards, recognitions
6. Relationships, sexuality
7. Values, norms
8. Sense of self, space
9. Organizational processes, learning
10. Beliefs, attitudes

Now as to synergy in organizational culture, our understanding may be facilitated by anthropologist Ruth Benedict. She maintained that some societies were synergistic and others were nonsynergistic or individualistic. We sense this ourselves as visitors to a strange land—some people we immediately like because we sense that generally the "host nationals" are nice, helpful, friendly, cooperative and secure in themselves; we perceive others as "foreigners," who are surly, unaffectionate or unfriendly, unhelpful or uncooperative, insecure, and low in morale. Benedict began to differentiate cultural groups in terms of the functions of their behavior—*how* they behaved with one another and strangers, rather than *why* they behaved as they did.

Using such insights, we can better comprehend organizational culture within a government agency or transnational enterprise. For example, a "high synergy corporation" would be one in which employees cooperated together for mutual advantage because the customs and traditions of that entity supported such behavior. In such a noncompetitive atmosphere the individual serves or works toward his/her own advantage and that of the group. Social and corporate obligations and responsibilities are put above personal desires or wishes. Personnel operate to ensure the mutual advantage from their common undertakings. It is similar to what the late humanistic psychologist, Abraham Maslow, referred to as "the eupsychian society"—a culture that creates an environment where people can develop their potential and satisfy their innate psychological needs. Applying this to a creative corporation, it would foster job or career fulfillment in its employees through human resources development systems, and make self-actualization possible in the work culture. It would not view the interests of the company and the individual worker as mutually exclusive, but as synergistic.

A nonsynergistic organizational culture promotes a situation in which members are fiercely competitive with one another and others, where the advantage of one individual becomes a victory over another. We all have experienced institutions where people generally psychologically aggress against and exploit one another, and climb up the corporate ladder at their fellow employees' expense. These are corporations and associations in which the majority of employees seem unhappy and under severe stress, where cooperation and mutual achievement are minimal. These we would describe as low-synergy organizational cultures.

DYNAMICS OF ORGANIZATIONAL SYNERGY

In the beginning of the Industrial Revolution, nineteenth-century entrepreneurs often exploited their employees, as well as their competitors and the society in which they operated. Indeed, the macroculture that spawned these industrial giants valued and often admired their rugged individualism, their ability to forge ahead without regard for social consequences, and their seemingly unlimited power and material success. But societies and peoples change. Today in the post-industrial scene, there is more emphasis on corporate social responsibility and environmental concerns. In the 1980s, for example, pressure exists in the United States for legislation to protect workers from the impact of sudden plant closings, or a community from the effects of nuclear plant accidents and industrial chemical wastes. Some corporate executives and firms are open and cooperative with such endeavors, while others are adamant in their opposition, taking the archaic position, "let the public be damned." Farsighted business leaders, however, realize that the trends are toward effective corporate participation in the solution of social problems, conscious of their interdependence with society. Some management consulting firms sponsor "corporate issues programs" so executives of leading world companies can discuss social, financial, and environmental concerns that impact on their businesses and which may require changes in their products and services.

In trying to predict the future, organizational administrators have too long depended upon financial plans and economic forecasts. This shortsightedness has caused many firms or agencies to be trapped by social protests, consumer activism, and changes in national moods and concerns. Lack of awareness of cultural changes or consumer needs leads to inappropriate manufacturing and marketing decisions. This explains why General Motors, with its Corvair model, missed the opportunity to anticipate the developing consumer movement for safer products, tougher liability standards, and pollution controls both in its cars and plants. Similarly, when Nestlé Company tried to promote in Third World countries its substitute for mother's milk, the artificial infant formula provoked a worldwide protest over a product that not only was too expensive for a less developed people, but also of questionable health value.

Futuristic forecasting enhances strategic planning by detecting social trends that affect not only an organization's profitability, but its survival. Synergistic planners, moreover, invite public participation in their planning, so that customer concerns can truly be met. Today even traditional corporate rivals, such as AT&T, IBM, and Sperry, are engaged in *cooperative efforts* to manage social change, and share techniques for environmental scanning, public policy research, cultural trend assessment. Some multinationals, such as Mead Corporation, have established human and environmental protection departments that involve long range plans to meet government regulatory requirements, site selection, and community sentiment regarding new plants, preventative programs for safety, and environmental standards. While these are positive signs of synergy in business, the vice-president of corporate and government relations for a *Fortune 500* company admits, "Managers with profit-and-loss responsibility only look at larger issues when they are dragged in kicking and screaming." Although some management may require motivation, such as bonus incentives, to spur them to grapple with social issues, other executives are instituting annual social audits to assess how much of a positive force the organization is in the communities where it is located.

Optimum Situations for Organizational Synergy

There are seven specific situations when synergy in organizational culture is most desirable. They are exemplified by the incidents cited in the opening of this chapter, and they include:

1. Acquisition. Whenever a corporation acquires or merges with another entity domestically or internationally, synergy skill is required. For organizational effectiveness, there must be a synthesis of two distinct microcultures, not just an imposition by the more powerful company. This is particularly true in the case of a newly acquired subsidiary. The executives from the parent company can do much to facilitate the integration process if they will take time to analyze the subsidiary's culture by the ten parameters cited on page 110. Furthermore, this merger of two organizational worlds and climates can be aided when management from the acquired firm shares its distinct culture with the other, helping them to understand policy, procedures, and processes, as well as corporate goals, attitudes, and strategies.* A week's "cultural awareness workshop" for the se-

---

* For further information on specific acquisition procedures see *Corporate Acquisitions* by Gordon Bing, Gulf Publishing, Houston, Texas, 1980.

nior management of both organizations has many "bottom-line" implications and will foster more effective colleague relationships.

2. Relocation. Anytime a company moves an existing facility and some of its personnel to another site, at home or abroad, synergistic efforts must be undertaken. People being up-rooted from a community where they are secure need assistance to integrate into the new setting, especially when there are significant geographic and cultural differences involved between the two locations. Such relocation services by the corporation must go beyond moving and new community information because employees require orientation to the realities and opportunities of the new cultural environment. "Culture shock" can be delimited within one's own country or overseas. Furthermore, the "locals" need assistance in accepting the new plant or office and its relocated employees. Popping a new enterprise into a small, unprepared community may not only offer jobs for the locals and improve their economy; it may also swamp their sewer and water facilities, and their educational and public services. Corporate management must cooperate with local officials so that the influx of people and money is planned and controlled. Further information on this issue is included in Chapter 15.

3. Structural/environmental change. When there is a major alteration within the organizational structure or environment, people should be prepared for the new shift in policy, procedure, product or service. Planned change strategies can be utilized to ready personnel for reorganization and renewal without abrupt disruption of the work climate. Sometimes the necessary changes are dictated by competition or growth. As of 1981, one hundred thirty American corporations are growing at twice the normal growth rate of the past five years. Such rapid increases shortens planning time and sharpens the potential for conflict. The quickening of the work pace on understaffed operations can lead to greater resentment, exhaustion and "burn out" on the part of employees. Pressure and stress can build up on the "fast track" even for managers. Involving personnel in cooperative efforts to regulate and control change or growth can counteract such system overload.

4. Personnel change. Whenever the composition of a workforce shifts, planned endeavors are needed to integrate the "newcomers," while reducing the psychological threat to the "old-timers" and gaining their assistance in the effort. In addition to the hiring of large number of women or minorities into work environment, there might be an influx of migrant or refugee laborers.

Sometimes, Third Country nationals or foreign executives can cause the organization to become more heterogeneous and less homogeneous. However, these individuals may also enhance synergy. The *New York Times,* for example, recently published a feature on "foreign-born executives" who are successfully moving ahead within American corporations. As mature adults from different cultures and management backgrounds, these professionals have not only integrated into, but mastered the complexities of giant U.S. companies, even to the point of receiving major appointments in the federal government. This internationalization of big business is also an example of synergy in which the "authority of competence" is considered more important than the place of one's origin, or the person's skin color and sex. It requires a reeducation of locals as to the realities of the pluralistic or multicultural workplace, and of the valuable contributions of "foreigners." European business leaders not only bring unique perspectives and talents to their American corporations, but global insights for the international markets.

5. Role change. The introduction of new technology into an organization usually means that personnel roles and relationships will change. In the traditional industrial-age corporation, work disciplines, units, and departments were fairly stable and separate. But in complex, post-industrial organizations the divisions between line and staff are fluid and often nonexistent. The superindustrial "ad-ho-cracy" requires greater collaboration between specialists and general managers. Newly created disciplines, specializations, and some work units may be relatively temporary. Thus, new interpersonal skills are required that enable personnel to form quick, intense organizational relations of a cooperative, mission-oriented nature. This is evident in today's project/product teams and matrix management forms.

6. Consortium. If an organization or a state does not have the natural, material, or human resources to undertake something on its own, it must move outside its own orbit to seek partners who will join in the endeavor for mutual benefit. Synergy is required for a combination of institutions to pool their talent and capital for a successful operation. Project management, for instance, provides opportunities for diverse departments and activities within a single organization to come together to achieve desired objectives. This approach has brought together different companies from the same or several industries, from the same or many nations. The very complexities of the superindustrial society demands such collaboration. In the decades ahead, the space colonization effort and planetary attempts to utilize the resources of the universe make international consortiums the only feasible alternative.

7. Global consulting. Whenever a group of "experts" enter the organization culture of a client ostensibly to render help, synergistic skills are necessary. Knowingly or not, the representatives from a consulting group merge their organizational culture into the client's environment. When such assistance is rendered on an international scale, the intervention may also include two national cultures. Consultants should attempt to integrate themselves into the organizational space of their customers, and not impose the mind-set or systems of the advising group. If an American accounting firm institutes a general management consulting division and expands into the world market, their accounting and financial analysis may also be culturally based and even biased. For synergy to occur in the consultation of their American representative, their consultants should examine how the financial practices and systems in the host culture work, and then what approaches of modern "American" business accounting would be appropriate.

These seven dimensions can be used, in a sense, as a paradigm, or model, for better understanding synergy in organizational culture. Perhaps some specific examples of how such synergy occurs will make the point. The following illustrations are either drawn directly from the authors' consulting experience, or from published accounts.

Synergy in the Work Culture

During the previous industrial stage of human development, there was much concern about the formation of cartels, and antitrust legislation resulted to prevent corporate collusion. But economics have so radically changed that the very survival of some business enterprises is dependent upon the sharing of information and cooperation within the same industry. Destructive competition may be a relic of the past that some national industries can no longer afford. Archaic government regulations not only need to be revised, but new laws must be formulated that will facilitate corporate synergy, especially when business entities move beyond their own national borders. The following are examples of how some corporations have addressed their synergistic needs:

Multinational acquisitions. Westinghouse Electric Corporation, Pittsburgh based, is one of the twenty largest corporations in the world. A subsidiary like Westinghouse Learning Corporation moves beyond education and acquires companies throughout the nation in school supplies, computer operations, and even bottling. Each of the firms taken over has its own particular organizational culture, sometimes reflected by the locality in which the subsidiary's headquarters are located. When Westinghouse Broadcasting moves beyond the acquisition of television and radio stations into housing and construction, the "Pittsburgh engineers" from the conglomerate's corporate headquarters are far afield and often into alien company environments. But when Westinghouse buys almost controlling interest within companies in Australia or Africa, the organizational culture is extended into "foreign cultures," which offer great challenges to the corporate executives back in the U.S.A. To promote synergy, this transnational enterprise brings managers from its subsidiaries and affiliates around the world to Pittsburgh for management development, which may range from computer seminars to cultural awareness workshops. Yet, so much more remains to be done in preparing cosmopolitan overseas representatives, especially among the legal staffs who are in the forefront of acquisitions and negotiations.

Texacana relocations. General Motors, Detroit based, established a twin plant relationship between its Mansfield, Ohio facility and a new assembly operation in Juarez, Mexico. The American management and their families were relocated to El Paso, Texas. From there the U.S. managers will commute daily across the border to the Mexican plant where they train and consult with competent Mexican executives who are to take over total operations within several years. To promote transnational synergy and link the new enterprise with other nearby GM plants in Mexico, organization development specialists from the company arranged for language and culture training at American universities for the Mexican and American managers and their families. But how much help was provided to the transplanted "Ohioians" to adjust to life in a Texas border town? A broad spectrum of "relocation services" should be offered to employees, as well as their families, if new adjustments are to be facilitated, productivity maintained, and change opportunities utilized.

Parent/subsidiary change. TRW, Cleveland based, was a traditional industrial organization. Then it got into the space business through a subsidiary established in Redondo Beach, California. But TRW Systems was unable to operate like its parent company. Its personnel were largely knowledge workers, most with advanced degrees. Its product was not primarily intended for this planet. In fact, the problems connected with "getting a man on the moon" were so complex, that entirely new management forms and organizational models had to be created. Thus, TRW Systems pioneered matrix management in which a professional might report simultaneously to several managers. To deal with the organizational problems involved, behavioral scientists within the company organized "team building sessions" so that employees would learn to work together more effectively in this different organizational culture. Eventually, the OD specialists were brought back to Cleveland to show the parent corporation how they might undergo organizational renewal in a planned way—such changes do not come easily or quickly.

Refugee influx. Coca Cola Bottling Company, Atlanta based, has plants all over Florida. In the past their employees were usually white southern males, until they began to bring in large numbers of female and black personnel. But all were still largely Americans. Then the Cuban refugees in the 1970s and '80s began to seek asylum in this southern state and went to work for the refreshment firm. Suddenly, the plant culture began to become multicultural and bilingual. Some of the new Hispanic employees were from a higher educational level than the American southerners, but not at the same financial level.

The challenge for synergy has stiffened with the influx of many exiled Haitians seeking employment with the soft drink firm. These black West Indians are of African heritage, speak Creole or French, and have come to America seeking a better way of life. They are in difficult economic straits, mainly possessing agricultural skills and limited education. With government assistance, the number of

Cuban and Haitian workers is likely to increase in the Coke plants, so many of the native white and black Americans are somewhat disgruntled about the situation. Thus, personnel changes are causing swift organizational changes, and "preventative maintenance" is in use among the work force. Management must take steps to promote a more cooperative plant climate, so that career development for all enhances its human assets.

Role challenges. N.V. Philips, Eindhoven (Netherlands) based, has a huge multinational enterprise that is linked together by sophisticated information and technical systems. From a small Dutch light bulb factory in 1891, it has expanded to a vast array of electronic productions: from cassettes and shavers to washing machines and television systems. A firm that struggled under Nazi occupation in the 1940s, it has emerged as a worldwide concern in 70 countries employing more than 380,000 people. Furthermore, it has accepted multinational responsibility in Third World countries for improving the communities in which it functions. To meet the synergistic needs of this superindustrial entity, Philips has formed a unit devoted to organizational renewal. Social researchers and internal consultants examine various aspects of work and organization in order to design more meaningful jobs, improve strategic planning, and prevent dissonance between information and control systems. In addition to such efforts to bring organizational culture in tune with contemporary work realities, industrial relations and international personnel have inaugurated sophisticated training in cultural awareness for expatriate managers. Since 1960, this Netherland conglomerate has been involved in work humanization programs. Even the roles of people on the assembly line have been changed by the establishment of autonomous work groups. As a result, Philips' internal studies indicated productivity doubled and worker job satisfaction increased.

Airbus Consortium. Airbus Industrie, Europe based, is an exceptional example of how synergistic effort can overcome corporate, cultural, and national rivalries. It successfully produces the A300 and A310 wide-body jets which by 1980 had seized a fifth of the world's commercial-aircraft market. France and Germany each own 38% of the venture, while Britain has 20%. Two German firms merged to form Deutsche Airbus and make the fuselage and vertical tail. CASA of Spain owns 4% of the project and builds the horizontal tail. France's Aérospatiale produces the cockpit, part of the center fuselage, and assembles the aircraft into final form. Despite differences in management philosophy and practice, worker organization, and even languages, this fragile balance of interests converged and achieved its goals. This technological innovation even provides the option of either the British Rolls-Royce or an American Pratt & Whitney engine.

A variety of organizational problems had to be confronted in each of the national components, but the cooperative endeavor pushed ahead with great efficiency under a flow chart that spread over the map of Europe. Decentralized production makes it easier to increase output to meet growing demand, and when extra workers are needed, they are drawn from partner companies' other projects. Technocrats have jumped traditional barriers among people on the continent, and choose personnel not "on the color of their passports" but on their ability to do the job. Even the U.S. Eastern Airlines bought the craft because it was fuel-efficient and reliable. Moving toward a European family-style operation, Airbus Industrie has resurrected the civilian aircraft business on that continent through the principle of collaboration.

International consulting. International Consultants Foundation, Washington and Stockholm based, provides a model for cooperation among professional consultants for their common benefit. Obviously, the major consulting firms have many resources to engage in a world practice. But independent consultants have limited resources, and only themselves to offer to their colleagues for professional development and support. Thus, an American and an Englishman combined their talents to formulate a network of consultants from a variety of disciplines who operate on a global basis. They have met annually in such diverse places as the Bahamas, Copenhagen, Washington, D.C., Calgary, and Dublin. From these conferences, proceedings are published on their insights, along with occasional monographs on special topics of interest to those in the consulting field. An annual registry of members provides a description of each consultant's competencies, and is used for joint marketing efforts. A periodic newsletter keeps members up-to-date on matters of concern. The executive board is multinational and multicultural, and the two key offices are rotated between Americans and Europeans.

When such international consultants collaborate on a global project, it represents the merger of national and organizational cultures. Similarly, synergy must then be sought with the client's organizational culture. Regardless of where the customer may be located in the international marketplace, the external consultant must enter into that organizational world and operate effectively within *that* space.

Occasionally, women, minorities, or handicapped personnel feel uncomfortable in a work culture that is alien or indifferent toward them. In such situations, they must take the effort to reach out and create their own synergy. The feature on page 119 is a case study in this regard.[2]

TRANSNATIONAL ORGANIZATION DEVELOPMENT

Whether an internal or external consultant, one must realize that behavioral science technology is largely a product of Western culture. Therefore, it has to be adapted or enhanced in different cultural settings. Many advanced technological innovations may or may not be appropriate in whole or part, depending on the local context. Organization development is a case in point. Richard Beckhard defined the term as follows:

How to Cope With Being Different

Jim is the only black on an engineering staff. Manuel is the single Hispanic on a college history faculty. Nora is the one female member of a commercial sales staff. Beth is the only person under 30 in an editorial group. Tom is the lone male nurse on the pediatrics floor of a hospital. Peter, confined to a wheelchair, is the only handicapped computer programmer at a bank.

As the American work force becomes increasingly diverse, more and more people share the situation of those mentioned above. No longer are religion and politics the primary social dividers among people at work. Today, lifestyle, age, sexual orientation, ethnicity and all sorts of other facets can also mark you as "different."

If you do stand out in some way from the people you work with, social discomfort can interfere with your work effectiveness.

Directly, you may be hindered by a lack of information from and give-and-take with others. Indirectly, you may be less involved in and less committed to your work if it fails to provide the meaningful interpersonal contacts that help fuse people and jobs.

Steps to Consider

Differences, however, do not have to mean barriers.

While you and the people you work with will never forget who you are, there are steps you can take to promote an easy, pleasant interaction. Consider the following:

—Take the initiative to be friendly. The initial reaching out takes some courage—from either side. The fact, probably, is that you see the need for contact with the rest of the group more than they may be aware of their stake in making closer contact with you.

One woman, distressed that her male colleagues never asked her to join them at the bar across the street for an after-work drink, finally summoned her courage and invited herself along. She was warmly welcomed and became a regular part of the group. She later realized that it had simply never occurred to the men to ask her along.

—Explain some facets of yourself, if necessary. You know a lot more about the others in your group than they probably do about you—and they may be uncomfortable asking. So it can be a good idea for you to demonstrate what they don't know about you.

A man with an artifical arm broke down the tension with his colleagues by openly referring to his disability, and explaining how remarkably the prosthesis works. A Vietnamese accountant suggested to one of his co-workers that they go out to lunch at a local Vietnamese restaurant. The co-worker was so delighted with the food and the family atmosphere of the place that he asked if they could go back the next week with some others from the work group.

—Don't attempt to obliterate the differences. In your interactions with a group of people different from you, it is vital to maintain your integrity. As a woman, you may do yourself more harm than good trying to act like "one of the boys." As a parent, you will obviously do different things after work than your childless colleagues do. The goal should be to share what you are, not to try to fit into the other's mold.

Less Isolation

—Forge bonds with similar people in other work groups.

This will serve two purposes. It will help widen your horizons on the job, which can be useful in your work. And it will make you seem less isolated among people who are different from you.

(continued on next page)

A Mexican-American hospital social worker, in a primarily Jewish department, discovered that there were several Mexican-American nurses on the staff. By becoming friends with them, and sharing coffee breaks with them and some of her colleagues together, she helped dissolve some professional and personal barriers that had existed. She also helped raise her own level of visibility on the staff.

—Ultimately, focus on the work. Your primary purpose during working hours—and that of your colleagues—is the actual job that you do. The more effectively you do that job, the more you will really have in common with your colleagues. This common ground, with time, can be a firm foundation for your relationships with others. While your differences will never disappear, they will fade from the forefront. ∎

Organization Development is an effort (1) planned, (2) organization-wide, and (3) managed from the top to (4) increase organization effectiveness and health through (5) planned interventions in the organization's processes, using behavioral science knowledge. [3]

Using that explanation as their premise, Drs. Paul Montgomery and Lois Tarkanian examined the cross-cultural implications of various OD methods in specific countries. They developed two paradigms for the selection and classification of various OD interventions, as well as the categorization of cultural traits for the target nations. In terms of trying to understand how synergy can be possible in various organizational cultures, the results of their research indicate degrees of relatedness for the selected OD interventions of Western orientation.

If care is taken to remain within the context of Japanese culture, these OD strategies might be appropriate: systems-wide interventions, individual/organizational interfaces in terms of the job and its design, personal work style analysis, and intrapersonal value analysis and relationships. They concluded that T-Groups and encounter groups should not be used.

With reference to the Mexican culture, all five of the selected interventions could be used, provided due regard is allowed for the indigenous culture patterns. That is, the researchers concluded that these approaches could be used: survey feedback and development, management by objectives, team building, laboratory training, and behavior modification.

Relative to the Neo-Confusian culture within the People's Republic of China, the findings were similar to those of the Japanese; namely, all of the above approaches could be useful except T (sensitivity training) and encounter groups whose mode of operation is in conflict with the Chinese tradition of honor and "face."

Due to the pervasiveness of the Islamic culture, the investigators thought the selected interventions were unrelated to Saudi Arabia except in two instances. That is, certain interventions could be adapted to the top Arabian managerial level where the individuals have been educated abroad in Western institutions and are involved in multinational corporations. In addition, the positive and negative reinforcement approach of behavior modification might be amenable within the parameters of Islamic religion.

The recommendations of these researchers included further studies centering upon the differences between the young and traditional management classes; upon the OD issues of leadership style and its effects, as well as power; and upon the influence of world religions on the relatedness of organizational development interventions.[4]

The implication of such investigations is that management practices and strategies around the world may be adapted outside the country of origin if we are culturally sensitive to the appropriateness or *inappropriateness* of various approaches. The adaptions may produce a synergistic synthesis that improves upon the original concept or technique. Some believe, for example that "Type Z management," the integration of American and Japanese management procedures, is superior to either approach alone.[5] Whether one is a transnational executive or consultant, creative innovators seek to use "what works or gets results" anywhere in the human family, but with due respect to local differences that might require elimination or alteration of the concept or process.

Another example of the need for culture sensitivity is international investments. Many economic forecasters envision a major trade shift from the Atlantic to the Pacific. Barry Gillman, for example, cites Japan, Australia, and Singapore-Malaysia as places that will offer best returns on stock investments. This vice-president for Citibank's International Assets Management Services is keen on the Pacific basin as an investment growth area, especially for foreign companies in electronics, finance, chemicals, and pharmaceuticals. However, for synergy to occur in such investments, the portfolio manager should have some insights into the host nation's culture and the organizational culture of the corporation recommended for investment.

Conclusions

Many scholars believe that we are now entering into the period of the "Third Industrial Revolution." Mechanization and computerization were the focus of the first and second industrial revolutions. But the current revolution, sometimes called metaindustrial, centers around the needs and aspirations of employees in the design and implementation of production and other work systems. Thus, the shift in these three work revolutions has been from products to things to people and information processing.

To humanize the workplace, Harvard professors Neal Herrick and Michael Maccoby propose the application of four principles:

1. Security—employees need to be free from fear and anxiety concerning health and safety, income and future employment.
2. Equity—employees should be compensated commensurate with their contributions to the value of the service or product.
3. Individuation—employees should have maximum autonomy in determining the rhythm of their work and in planning how it should be done.
4. Democracy—employees should, whenever possible, manage themselves, be involved in decision-making that affects their work, and accept greater responsibility in the work of the organization. [6]

Efforts to improve the organizational culture based on such premises can be found throughout the world, especially in America and western Europe. Managers, consultants, and researchers are cooperating in sharing their findings relative to quality of worklife and participation experiments.

Convergence of endeavors to "humanize the organizational environment or work culture" is happening on a universal scale and calls for more synergy on the part of corporate and government leaders.

References

1. Forbes, R. *Organizational Excellence: Using the Concept of Organizations As Open Systems of Energy.* Trumbull, Conn.: Raybestos Manhattan, 1979.
2. Uris, A. and Bensahel, J. *Los Angeles Times,* January 12, 1981.
3. Beckhard, R. and Harris, R. T. *Organizational Transitions: Managing Complex Change.* Reading, Mass.: Addison-Wesley Publishing, 1977.
4. Montgomery, P. A. and Tarkanian, L. H. *Selected Organization Development Interventions as Related to Japan, Mexico, People's Republic of China, and Saudi Arabia.* San Diego: United States International University, 1980. (Unpublished doctoral dissertation available through University Microfilms, Ann Arbor, Michigan.)
5. Ouchi, W. *Theory Z: How American Business Can Meet the Japanese Challenge.* Reading Mass.: Addison-Wesley, 1981.
6. Maccoby, M. *The Gamesman.* New York: Simon and Shuster, 1976.

7.
Synergy in
Team Management

COMPLEXITY REQUIRES TEAMWORK

In this post-industrial period of human development, traditional organizational models and managerial styles are gradually being replaced. They are inadequate and unproductive with the new knowledge workers. Therefore, a major transition is underway in social systems from "disappearing bureaucracies" to "emerging ad hocracies." In these turbulent times, leaders facilitate the transcendence from past to futuristic operations by promoting matrix or team management approaches. Whether the strategy is called a project, task force, product or business systems team, or ad hoc planning committee, work is organized around a "temporary" group that involves permanent (functional) and impermanent lines of authority. Such endeavors at organizational alteration and design are bridges from the way we have been doing work to the way we will be conducting human enterprise in the decades ahead. Today's microelectronic and semiconductor companies often result from the synergy of entrepreneurial teams.

The dictionary defines a "team" as a number of persons associated in some joint action, while "teamwork" is described as cooperative or coordinated effort on the part of persons working together. Dr. William Dyer notes that "teams are collections of people who must rely upon group collaboration if each member is to experience the optimum of success and goal achievement."[1]

The Society of Advanced Management explains "management" as a science and an art:

> Management as a science is organized knowledge—concepts, theory, principles and techniques—underlying the practice of managing; as an art, it is

application of organized knowledge to realities in a situation with a blend or compromise to obtain practical results.

The art and science of team management is emerging, especially among practitioners of project and product management. Synergy is necessary for cooperative or combined action by team members and it occurs when group participants are effective at sharing their perceptions and insights, their experience and knowledge, for common purposes. Synergy results when individuals create a new team culture—group attitudes, norms, customs, and practices—which foster the accomplishment of team objectives.

Changing technology and markets have stimulated the team approach to management, as well as awareness of the interdependence of organizational components. Furthermore, the complexity of society, and the human systems devised to meet continuing and new needs, requires a pooling of resources and talents. Inflation, resource scarcity, reduced personnel levels, budget cuts, and similar constraints have underscored the demands for better coordination and synergy in the use of "brainpower." Professors Stanley Davis and Paul Lawrence have cited three conditions for the growth of matrix organizational approaches, and have summarized the situation fostering a multiple command structure, system, and behavior:

> *First condition: outside pressure for dual focus.* The very size of some tasks, which customers, governments, or society require of the organization, forces new divisions of labor and authority.
>
> *Second condition: pressure for high information-processing.* The nature of work that is "too big" for traditional approaches also requires innovative, high-speed communication networks that keep all informed who have the "need-to-know" about work progress. An enriched information-processing capacity is essential in decentralized organizations where interdependence increases the communication load.
>
> *Third condition: pressure for shared resources.* Large scale projects demand both human economies and high performance. The pressure builds for fully utilizing scarce human resources to meet high quality standards. Matrix management permits redeployment of expensive, highly specialized talent, as well as of costly capital resources and physical facilities.[2]

In effect, the matrix or team management model causes a new organizational culture to be formulated. High technology corporations are indicative of this change, with project teams consisting of a variety of skilled specialists from mangement information systems, accounting, and new technologies. Obsolete business separations give way to synergistic, functional arrangements among those employed in manufacturing, marketing, and administration; line and staff activities overlap and often merge.

Synergy through team efforts can occur within a single enterprise, or among different organizations that were formerly in competition or that rarely mixed. The

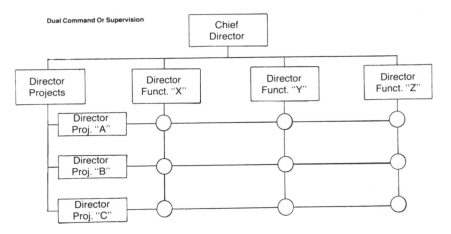

Figure 7-1. Model of matrix organizational structure.

trend is evident among companies, agencies, and associations, as well as between the private and public sectors. Davis and Lawrence maintain that matrix management is moving beyond industry to insurance, banking, accounting, law, securities, retailing, construction, education, and health and human services. This is happening, in addition to the above mentioned conditions, because of pressures created by geography, functions or services, and/or distinguishable clients. The computer has been the most powerful tool in making team management feasible, and it has fostered a revolution in organizational culture. Figure 7-1 offers a model of matrix organizational structure. The case for when and why such a management approach is recommended is summarized on page 126.

Regionalism has also promoted team management strategies. Government entities find that problems of planning, economics, ecology, conservation, and even population control are too big for local solutions. Only by the integration of overlapping jurisdictions and efforts can the public sector meet the challenges of the superindustrial age. Thus, there is a remarkable growth in the establishment of interagency task forces in planning, training, or criminal justice activities. For effective macro problem-solving in complex societies, regional commissions are sometimes formed in which local governmental power is delegated to a more comprehensive organization, which brings together a technical support staff with representatives of each local government. Then, skill in team management is necessary if synergy is to take place and improvements occur.

Regardless of the type of organization, team management calls for new skills if personnel potential is to be fully realized. Although the team is composed of knowledgeable people, they need to learn new ways of relating and working together to solve cross-functional problems and to attain synergy. To be more than a collection of persons, team building is an essential behavioral science technology that ensures group effectiveness. Experienced employees of hierarchical organiza-

---

Matrix as Transitional Bridge*

When:
- *Rapid technological advancements*
- Need for *timely decisions*
- Vast quantity of data
- Increased volume of new products and services
- Need for simultaneous dual decision making
- Strong constraints on financial and/or human resources

Why:
- Flexible, adaptive system
- Provides timely, balanced decision making
- Permits rapid management response to changing market and technology
- Trains managers for ambiguity, complexity, and executive positions
- Synergizes, motivates, and focuses human energy

---

* Courtesy of Hughes Aircraft Company.   ∎

---

tions have been conditioned to traditional organizational culture. Human factors of interpersonal relations and the dynamics of group behavior must be considered or teamwork will not occur. Teams must be concerned with task accomplishment and people maintenance. Synergy in teams must be *created*. Furthermore, the issue is not just how the team can function more synergistically, but how it integrates with the overall organization or society that it supposedly serves.

CREATING A TEAM CULTURE

For any team to be effective, members should be concerned about coordinating efforts, productive activities, and economical performance by the group. Jack Morton of Bell Laboratories once wrote of two contemporary management challenges: one is to hire and keep competent specialists who know a field of knowledge and keep current in it; the other is to get these technical specialists coupled across disciplines because today's problems are more often interdisciplinary in nature. Essentially, the same may be said for any team management endeavor.

The criterion for team selection is the *authority of competence*—the individual has some knowledge, information, or expertise that can help the group achieve its mission. The unique competence of the team participant becomes a new norm, regardless of sex, race, organizational seniority, or level in the hierarchy. Formerly, organizational group activity was arranged on the bases of commonality in product, process, function, service, geography, or even customer. Today, synergizing specialized resources requires competency in managing small- or large-scale projects, and expertise in time and conflict management. Because a technician may serve on two or more projects, while based in an existing functional area, three managers may have to share that human resource by creating integrative mechanisms that ensure the common organizational good.

Increasingly, team management is employed when the organization's activities are less repetitive and predictable. Such an approach increases the need for liaison, management by exception, and sharing of authority and information. All this is contrary to traditional organizational cultures. Management in uncertainty today challenges organizations to improve information processing, enhance integration of realistic schedules, and share decision-making, subject to continuing revision and change.

Furthermore, there is a fundamental shift in the way power is exercised. Inter-functional product teams, for example, involve a delicate balance of power among peer specialists. Because joint decisions are to be made, each member must be sensitive to the others if the contributions of all are to lead to the team's success. The product manager's task is to facilitate collaboration across functional lines. For many this will necessitate an "attitude change." In America, there is much discusssion about "reindustrialization," which demands cooperation rather than confrontation in the triple relationship between business, labor, and government. The attempts to resolve the U.S. automobile industry's crisis illustrate how essential such synergistic problem-solving is. Rather than considering each other natural enemies, these three elements must compromise and collaborate if each is to succeed. Even where a functional approach to business is still in force, labor and management can develop team relations. In Japan, to cite one illustration, quality-control circles made up of workers and supervisors meet regularly to discuss how to improve product quality.

Peter Drucker reminds us that "top management strategies are not mechanical; they are above all cultural." Thus, when an organization opts for team or matrix management, it implies a change in its ways of acting and thinking. Team management means the creation of shared values and assumptions. Thus, team members can begin to identify with one another and develop expectations of predictable behavior. But people are products of national cultures. So, while some form of team management may be characteristic of advanced technological societies, it will reflect a country's macroculture. Thus, the German *vorstand* is a board-like group with collegial decision-making and coordination among top managers. The French, on the other hand, are adverse to absolutist power and omnipotent authority, so their organizations separate authority from responsibility so as to simultaneously protect individual and collective actions. Modern matrix management typically reflects American culture, and is less popular with the British, who place more emphasis on form and ordered regularity.

Because the authors are products of Canadian and United States cultures, this book's subject matter reflects a North American approach. Therefore, the following observations on what is considered desirable in a team culture might be questioned in whole or part by readers from other national backgrounds. In any event, for purposes of discussion, here are some characteristics that we think also facilitate team success:

1. Tolerance of ambiguity, uncertainity, and seeming lack of structure.
2. Taking interest in each member's achievement, as well as the group's.
3. Ability to give and accept feedback in a non defensive manner.
4. Openness to change, innovation, and creative problem-solving.
5. Creation of a team atmosphere that is informal, relaxed, comfortable, and non judgmental.
6. Capacity to establish intense, short-term member relations, and to disconnect for the next project.
7. Seeking group participation, consensus, and decisions.
8. Concern to keep group communication on target and schedule, while permitting disagreement and valuing effective listening.
9. Urging a spirit of constructive criticism, and authentic, non-evaluative feedback.
10. Encouraging members to express feelings and to be concerned about group morale/maintenance.
11. Clarifying roles, relationships, assignments and responsibilities.
12. Sharing leadership functions within group, and utilizing total member resources.
13. Pausing periodically from task pursuits to reexamine and re-evaluate team progress and communications.
14. Fostering trust, confidence, and commitment within the group.
15. Being sensitive to the team's linking function with other work units.
16. Fostering a norm that members will be supportive and respectful of one another, and realistic in their expectations of each other.
17. Promoting an approach that is goal-directed, divides the labor fairly, and synchronizes effort.

Each team experience is different, and organizations should encourage such uniqueness, just as in departments and division. Yet at the same time, coordination and integration of team effort with other units and the whole enterprise is essential if the sum is to be greater than its parts. When team cultures contain the elements previously outlined, and are reflective of the whole organizational environment, then they become closely knitted and productive. The "deeper" into a large organization team participation is provided, and the more employees *included* in team decision-making, the healthier and more relevant will that human system become.

The teams may be part of the formal organization structure as in the case of matrix management. However, some traditional hierarchies are slow and difficult to change. Then collateral organizations of informal teams may be formulated as a secondary mode of problem-solving. This unofficial, parallel organizational arrangement is a change strategy to use with problems that are intractable in the formal system. Such an approach is especially useful to middle managers because it gives them visibility and experience in group action on high-priority, organization-wide problems that are persistent and often neglected by the traditional organization, which concentrates on structured problems of authority and production.

Team management is suitable for knowledge problems that require high-quality, creative solutions with rapid processing and high output. When complex, modern problems are *less* structured, quantifiable, definable, and past experience is unreliable, then team management is necessary.

THE CASE FOR TEAM EFFECTIVENESS

Team and matrix management seemingly came to the fore with space industry, and the NASA goal to put a man on the moon. One of the successful pioneers in such approaches is TRW Systems in Redondo Beach, California, U.S.A. We are indebted to its former vice-president and now an independent consultant, Sheldon A. Davis, for the elements of the following case constructed from his writings and interviews.

Davis defines "work culture" as the habitual patterns of communication between departments and individuals, especially with regard to the perception of each other's roles, behavior, and attitudes. He envisions "organization development" as a long-term program of systematic attention to modify and improve that work culture. Davis sees "team building" as a key OD tool to assist people whose jobs are interrelated to examine how effectively they function as a team, to identify barriers to their collaboration, and to mutually undertake means that eliminate or reduce such obstacles. The focus is upon work behavior and how it influences job performance of the individual and other team members. Consider this case for team development:*

A major aerospace firm had a number of projects underway that required the services of highly specialized employees. Such personnel were to be assigned to one or more projects on a part-time basis from their regular departmental locations. At first, line managers were reluctant to share their "manpower" with project managers because of conflicting loyalties, especially that the adhoc groups would claim too much time of this talented employee. Frankly, the line supervisors distrusted the PM's ability to consider the interests of other units in the organization equally with their own needs.

Top management insisted that this project management approach was an essential first step to a major reorganization. From occasional task force utilization, the corporation intended to move in the direction of matrix management. That meant introducing a multiple command system where one competent worker might report to two or more bosses. The company was developing a support program for this purpose, including a new computerized, management information system. The old organization chart was to give way to a "matrix" type illustration of diverse reporting relationships that included both permanent and temporary management authority.

---

*Refer to film and Leader's Guide on *Team Building*, BNA Films, 9410 Decoverly Hall Road, Rockville, Md. 20850.

To help the temporary project teams work more effectively the personnel department was introducing a new organization development program that included team building sessions. One laboratory manager resented taking his people off their jobs for such "navel gazing." But the project managers who had temporary authority over some of the same employees countered, "It's not just important to get the job done, but occasionally to examine *how* it is done and *how* we are collaborating. That's what team building is all about, plus improving the interface between the teams and the functional units."

The lab manager retorted, "We need to coordinate our activities and perform economically. If this team building will help to acccomplish that, then *maybe* it will have some 'pay-off' to replace the time my people will lose from their jobs." The PM responded, "My project is only a minimum core group for overall planning, budgeting, coordination and systems engineering. We depend on your department's expertise for the design and technical work. Eventually this matrix approach will help us all get maximum utilization of scarce, technical resources. It will help us to magnify the impact of our human assets!"

"But you and I, plus the other PM's, are all competing for the same resources and manpower," the lab manager continued. "There is going to have to be a lot of 'trade-off' on the part of all of us with managerial responsibilities, and we are not used to working like this. I can see us at cross-purposes with much conflict."

"Well," the PM remarked, "I understand that Personnel also plans some intergroup team building so that we learn new skills for this purpose. They maintain that the conflict can be managed and utilized for the common good, and that we can learn cross-functional collaboration for complex space productions. Team building is supposed to give us an opportunity to develop linking or coupling relations to avoid waste of our energies."

The lab supervisor sighed, "Those sessions better work, then, or this place is going to be in one big mess. Engineers and scientists are no-nonsense characters, not used to that human relations stuff. One value I do suspect that will come from such training is that technical types will learn some people skills that might eventually help to make them better managers when they get into supervision."

Team Development Guidelines and Evaluation

Just like the organization in general, we might have an image of the team as an "energy exchange system." When the group functions, human psychic and physical energy is utilized effectively. Team interaction is an energy exchange. As the group seeks to achieve its goals, members energize or motivate themselves and one another by their example. Team planning and changes become projections on energy use and its alteration. Every aspect of the group process can be analyzed in terms of this human energy paradigm. The key issue, then, is how the team manages its energies most productively, and avoids underutilizing or even wasting the group energies. There are ways that members can analyze their functions and performance in projects, task forces, or product teams.

Team behavior can be examined from the viewpoint of task functions, which initiate, give or seek information, clarify or elaborate on member ideas, and summarize or synthesize. It can also be seen from the angle of group maintenance or morale building, such as encouraging, expressing group feeling, harmonizing, compromising, and "gate-keeping" on communication channels.

Such data-gathering can be useful periodically to improve the group's effectiveness. Not only can the information help the person to change his or her team behavior, but when such data is combined into a visual profile, it offers a diagnosis of team health from time to time. It is recommended that teams pause on occasion for self-examination of their progress. Sometimes a third-person facilitator, such as an internal or external consultant, can be most helpful in this regard. When the group's analysis of its maturity is summarized on a newsprint tablet or overhead slide, or even in a typed summary report, the team can then view the total assessment and discuss its implications for effective energy use.

Increasing Team Effectiveness

Team participation is an intensive learning experience. When members voluntarily involve themselves and fully participate, personal and professional growth is fostered. The team is like a laboratory of the larger organizational world in which it operates. Although a temporary experience, it is an opportunity for individual and team development. Each participant shares self and insights from the basis of unique life and organizational experiences. Synergy occurs when the members listen to each other and enter into the private worlds of the others. Total team perception and wisdom then become more than the sum of the parts. To promote maximum self-actualization and energize the group's potential, the following ground rules for greater team effectiveness are recommended. Remember, these suggestions come from the authors' cultural perspectives:

1. Be *experimental*—in this learning experience test new styles of leadership and communication, different kinds of behavior and attitudes, new patterns of personal participation and relationships, joint problem-solving efforts.
2.. Be *authentic*—level in your communication; tell it like it is in your feedback; care about team members, even enough to confront them, rather than play games.
3. Be *sensitive*—express your feelings, and be conscious of the other person's feelings; empathetically respond and reflect on the sender's real meaning, not just his or her words. Be aware of the whole range of non-verbal communication and cues.
4. Be *spontaneous*—respond creatively to the here and now data produced in the group; to the person as he or she now reveals self. (Avoid being strategic

or manipulative, or engrossed in the previous there and then). Warmly receive the sharing of another and thereby be confirmed yourself.

5. Be *helpful*—accept the other's perception of self and the situation; avoid imposing your system, values, or opinions upon the other. A helping relationship means that the other must perceive your assistance as being helpful. This will occur when you help that person discover new dimensions for self; to appreciate the need to break through one's own barriers (or bag). By sharing yourself, you permit another team member to enlarge and revise one's own psychological construct (namely, the way that person reads meaning into his life experiences).

6. Be *open*—consider other viewpoints and possibilities, rather than being closed-minded or locked into your own previous conceptions. Evaluate and check feedback from others to arrive at your own determination. Be flexible, not rigid in responding to new ideas and different perceptions.

7. Be *time conscious*—the team meetings are limited in time availability for accomplishing a specific task. Avoid taking up too much "air time" or by diverting the group from its mission. Be willing to listen, but when others stray from the subject, bring the group back on target.

8. Exercise *group leadership*—team participation is an opportunity to practice the whole range of leadership skills, whether as an initiator or follower. The participative team is a leaderless group, in the sense that there is no authoritarian leader. The leadership is shared and group centered. Each is permitted to do "his or her thing," which will contribute most to group progress (from promoting the accomplishment of a task, to the maintenance of group morale).

William W. Hines, a utility training manager, describes five goals for increasing team effectiveness:

1. Look at how well team members communicate as a group.
2. Observe how they problem solve.
3. Help them better understand their own defined corporate objectives.
4. Assist the team in developing skills to manage and handle interpersonal conflict better.
5. Aid them in developing closer and more collaborative relationships.[3]

Hines proposes several types of team meetings to evaluate how the group is functioning: (a) feedback sessions with the facilitator on the results of individual interviews with members; (b) creative problem-solving or "brainstorming" meetings on obstacles to team effectiveness; and (c) weekly team building meetings to deal with identified interpersonal and work problems (usually about two hours in length).

In the process of human resource development, behavioral science consultants have created a number of methods and techniques for team development. The regular team-building session is considered an ongoing process to alter the way an intergrated unit works together, and essentially is a change strategy. William G. Dyer of Brigham Young University suggests that team-building be viewed as a cycle consisting of "problem identification, data-gathering by and among members, diagnosis and evaluation of the data, problem-solving and planning on the findings, implementation of the action plans, and then assessment of the results."

Perhaps an illustration from the experience of one of the authors (Harris) will illustrate the origin and purpose of team-building within a traditional bureaucracy:

> The top management of a very large fire and emergency department for a major California county were alarmed. The first-line managers, called "battalion chiefs," were considering turning their professional association into a union. To counteract the identification of these chiefs with rank and file employees and to strengthen their image of themselves as *managers,* the key administrators decided to initiate a management development institute for the battalion chiefs, each of whom might command upwards to a thousand employees during a major emergency.
>
> I designed a behavioral science program for this purpose, but built into the training some features of organization development. That data-gathering by means of instruments and group process produced information that was compiled into a report for upper management. The principal problem was a breakdown in communication between middle and upper level management, and it was perceived that the latter lacked synergy—they did not work well among themselves as an executive group and communicated confusion downward. Management accepted one of my recommendations and opted for team-building sessions for themselves.
>
> The two-day session was held at a fire camp away from the command headquarters. Top management first examined in depth the implication of their subordinates' feedback. Then more data-gathering was done among the chief engineers as to how they saw themselves as a team, their roles, and their relationships. I and my colleague not only provided some input on how they might become a more effective administrative group, but helped these public service executives to examine the "pay-off" functions of their own jobs. After two more off-site sessions, we compiled a report on the team-building findings and recommendations. As a result this key management group inaugurated their own plan to maintain the progress attained and confront the issues that hampered their working as a team. In other words, they committed themselves to action for internal improvement of their performance as a work unit, and strove to become behavior models for the next level of supervision.

Research in project and matrix management has demonstrated that organizations which take time for team-building usually increase their productivity. It is one of many innovative managerial technologies for organization development, which have ranged from sensitivity training and career development programs to job enrichment and videotaping of top performers in problem-solving sessions.

Because team-building strategies are still emerging, one can only review how they have been used. Dr. W. Warner Burke, editor of *Organization Dynamics*, described these five uses:

> *Start-ups*—team-building with a new group, such as plant management of a facility before it opens, or prior to the inauguration of a business systems planning group, or when several departments are relocated into a new facility.
>
> *Interpersonal relationships*—team-building sessions, usually off-site, for an intensive period together for analysis of ongoing team relations.
>
> *Content problems*—team meetings on everyday work and decision-making for effective team performance, often held on-site for short periods of time with an external facilitator. Consultation is offered on team maintenance issues, task process, norms and values.
>
> *Training*—team input sessions with an OD practitioner to provide education on group decision-making and communication, problem-solving skills, interface with other teams, etc.
>
> *Long-range planning*—team sessions on forecasting, budget planning, member replacement, impact of technological/organizational changes on the team.

Typically, an internal or external facilitator provides process consultation on how the team operates, pursues its tasks, makes its decisions, shares its leadership, sets its standards and procedures, confronts and utilizes conflict, and communicates with one another and other organizational units.

Team development should focus upon the nature of work performed, the relationships of team members who must do the work, and the way in which their work together is structured. In addition to diagnosis and data-gathering, team-building helps organizational associates to confront as a group their problems, challenges, processes, and behavior. The emphasis is upon such questions as:

- What is it like to work here?
- What kinds of things help or hinder us in working together?
- What is our job and our responsibilities?
- What are our expectations of this team and each other?
- What changes could be made to improve performance?
- What does each group member need to do differently?
- What can this unit do to work more cooperatively?
- How do other teams or work units perceive us, and vice versa?
- What commitments is each member willing to make to increase our effectiveness?

Team-building is an opportunity for participants to practice skills in data collection and analysis, human relations and feedback, negotiation and compromise, conflict management, and problem-solving. It is a chance for group introspection on "hang-ups" that affect job performance, the quality of staff meetings, the hidden agendas that undermine progress, the blocked feelings that hold back effort, the attitudes and actions that sidetrack the team. It is a synergistic system for developing organizational collaboration among knowledge workers or technical specialists. The overriding issue it confronts is "trust" and the degree to which it exists among team members and with other work units. In complex organizations in which people are so interdependent, high trust levels ensure achievement.[4]

Obviously, team-building needs to be supplemented with technical training in project or matrix management operation. In workshops on project management, the author, (Harris) provides input on the interpersonal dynamics of ad hoc groups while his colleague, Don Mabon, offers training on the technical processes for managing the project. This international engineering consultant instructs workshop participants on the project management system, organization, and objectives; and project planning, scheduling, control, appraisal, and review.

The aim of both dimensions of this management development is to promote understanding of both organizational relations and human motivation on the one hand, while teaching skills for managing temporary teams of talented people. The end purpose is to understand who is going to do what and when. Team development, as Sheldon Davis reminds us, counteracts *reverse synergy* —when people cancel each other out by not hearing, not building or working together, putting each other down, or blocking the contribution of human potential.

Conclusion

The oncoming superindustrial age will be dominated by high technology organizations. The new metaindustrial culture created in such enterprises requires people to collaborate and work in interdisciplinary, and often international, teams. Peter Drucker reminds us that any manager in a multinational business will have to learn to understand the matrix structure if that person wants to function effectively. For people conditioned by the competition and rugged individualism of the industrial age this will require training in synergy. This would include not only team-building, but education in cultural awareness and cross-cultural communication. The personnel challenge of developing global cosmopolitan leaders for transnational enterprises will extend beyond the university to corporate selection thru preretirement counseling.

During this period of organizational transition, team experience will challenge the participants to revise and expand their images of themselves and their roles. It will be a means for actualizing more of their potential, obtaining more meaning at work, and learning to develop new types of organizational relationships. Those responsible for human resource development in organizations have an opportunity through team training to increase employee awareness of the forces that influence their perceptions, attitudes, and behavior, as well as their decisions, so that they have greater control of their own work space. But the real challenge in synergistic management for both the institution and the individual is to go beyond what we are and have been, and risk becoming what we can be.

References

1. Dyer, W. G. *Team Building: Issues and Alternatives*. Reading, Mass.: Addison-Wesley Publishing Co., 1977.
2. Davis, S. M. and Lawrence, P. R. *Matrix*. Reading, Mass.: Addison-Wesley Publishing Co., 1977.
3. Hines, W. W. *Training and Development Journal*. February, 1980.
4. Martin, C. C. *Project Management: How to Make It Work*. New York: AMACOM, 1976.

8.
Synergy Among Professionals

THE KNOWLEDGE SOCIETY

The decades ahead will be years of transition. In so-called advanced nations, more and more of humankind will be transforming an industrialized society into a metaindustrial system. It is hoped, the inhabitants of preindustrial countries will use the new technology to bypass the industrial stage of human development and leap ahead into the postindustrial period. In any event, the emerging "cyberculture," or age of automation and computers, will be dominated by a marked increase in knowledge and information processing. People are becoming aware of their basic, collective *human right* to information and communication. Vocational activity will shift away from blue or white-collar designations to that of "knowledge" workers.

Adam Osborne's provocative book, *Running Wild: The Next Industrial Revolution,* predicts that of all the jobs in the industrial world today perhaps half will be eliminated during the next twenty-five years. Osborne believes the most paralyzing aspect of this ongoing microelectronic industrial revolution is the inability of lawmakers and sociologists to cope with what is occuring, because no one knows where to begin. We might start by defining what we mean by "professional." In this microelectronics/computer dominated society the new power class will be those with knowledge skills and access to relevant information.

The word "professional" is used here in the sense of one who demonstrates authority of competence in whatever he or she undertakes. Such an individual has the attitude, coupled with ability, to work for his or her own self-fulfillment and to bring to a task or occupation a thoroughness or sense of dedication in its execution. In this context this type of person professes or affirms the quality of personal

137

thinking, effort, and spirit. The word is not meant in this analysis as membership in the traditional "learned" professions. As Christoper Evans, the late innovator in microprocessors, observed:

> The erosion of the power of the established professions will be a striking feature of the second phase of the Computer Revolution. It will be marked, and perhaps more so, as the intrusion into the work of the skilled and semi-skilled. . . .The vulnerability of the professions is tied up with their special strength—the fact that they have acted as exclusive repositories and disseminators of specialist knowledge. . . .But this state of privilege can only persist as long as the special data and rules for administration remain inaccessible to the general public. Once the barriers which stand between the average person and this knowledge dissolve, the significance of the profession dwindles, the power and the status of its members shrink. Characteristically, the services which the profession originally offered become available at a very low cost.[1]

Thus, to be a professional in our discussion, one can be an athlete, technician, or programmer, as well as an attorney, physician, or social scientist. It depends on *how* one avows self in the development and use of knowledge. It requires expertise in abstract thinking without denying intuition. Increasingly, it will involve intelligent use of computers, word processors, and data banks. Tomorrow's professionals will employ and improve upon traditional research skills of data gathering, analysis, and reporting, and use them in more innovative ways. But the data collected will be interpreted and used in more meaningful ways, and on a global basis. The new knowledge professionals will be linked together around the planet and beyond by satellites, computers, and videophones. Teleconferencing and facsimile transmission will become their normal media for exchanging information. Many of them will work out of their home. The issue then arises as to whether this more rapid, enriched knowledge exchange will be used for human and not just technological development. The challenge is to utilize our immense patrimony of scientific, historical, and cultural heritage, as well as our human and natural resources, to resolve global crises and improve the human condition. This becomes possible only if there is synergy among the burgeoning mass of transnational elites.

Synergy has been described by *The Harper Dictionary of Modern Thought* in this interesting manner:

> The additional benefit accruing to a number of systems should they coalesce to form a larger system. This concept reflects the classical opinion that the "whole is greater than the sum of the parts" . . . . The word is also frequently used in a much looser way in discussions of corporate strategy to indicate general expectations of collaborative benefit. More generally still, the term is applied to the generation of unplanned social benefits among people who unconsciously cooperate in pursuit of their own interests and goals.

It is the authors' thesis in this volume that all people, especially those who might be considered "professionals," should consciously cooperate for the mutual benefit of all. The very complexity of what Alvin Toffler has characterized as "The Third Wave Culture" demands such collaboration. (In terms of human development, we can adapt Toffler's terms to explain the First Wave of Change as the Agricultural Revolution, the Second Wave as the Industrial Revolution, and the current transformation or the Third Wave as the Cybercultural Revolution.[2])

At The First Global Conference on the Future held in Toronto, Canada (1980), a panel of professional futurists sought to explain what work is. Under the leadership of Michael Wass de Czegi and Margaret Genovese, the panelists noted that "work is a way to define one's place (role) in the world; work is vision, vocation, mission, transformation, energy transfer, substantial effort toward results." Finally, one defined work as *synergy*—energy that is directed toward tasks or problems in cooperation with others, as in "team work." When one of the authors (Harris) asked this talented group to expand upon that theme, these insights were forthcoming:

1. Synergy means to produce more for less, while anti-synergy produces less for more.
2. Synergy produces dual or multiple effects by moving employees together in an ordered way.
3. Synergy at work now includes input from women whose contribution to management will create new institutional values and organizational cultures.

All of the participants in this forum agreed that there is now a need to set the stage for realization of synergistic potential—by bringing the right people or team together.

Figure 8-1 illustrates the variety and inter-relatedness of current professional development terminology. The designations on the outside of the globe refer to various "scholarly" descriptions of contemporary world society or culture. The terms inside are somewhat synonymous with the concept of synergy among professionals and describe what happens when peers work together effectively.

SYNERGISTIC COLLABORATION

Since our beginnings as a species, we humans have shared information and experience, either formally or informally. Culture itself is an attempt, consciously or unconsciously, by a people to transmit to future generations their acquired wisdom and insight relative to their knowledge, beliefs, customs, traditions, morals, law, art, communication, and habits. Peers in a particular career, trade, or profession have long banded together in pursuit of their common interest. Trade and professional associations, societies and organizations, are formed for this purpose by individuals, institutions, and industries. Through them, ideas and insights are ex-

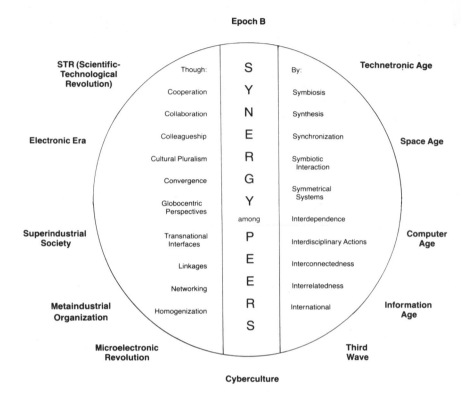

Figure 8-1. This diagram illustrates the variety and interrelatedness of current professional development terminology.

changed in meetings, seminars, forums, as well as through journals, reports, and books these entities publish. They also provide a variety of services ranging from peer evaluation, placement, and book stores, to travel assistance, lobbying, and liaison with other international and governmental agencies.

Some cultures are synergistic and their people are inclined toward cooperation. Americans, for example, have a penchant for organizing, as one glance at the annual directory of *National Trade & Professional Associations of the United States and Canada* will demonstrate (see Appendix C for more information). To promote professional and scholarly exchanges one company produces a whole series of directories for every category from consultants to research centers, as well as an *Encyclopedia of Associations* (Appendix C). In fact, in the U.S. there is even an association of associations—the American Society of Association Executives (Appendix C). Occupational and professional conferences are such big business in this nation that numerous monthly magazines and annual meeting facilities directories are produced. As a final example of this cultural peculiarity for coordination and interchange, there exists among intellectuals the American Council of Learned Societies and the Social Science Research Council.

Many of these social institutions are experiencing "organization shock" in the postindustrial age. They are not perceived as sufficiently relevant and responsive to their constituencies so they suffer declines in membership, attendance at meetings, and support for their various programs. Huge professional associations find that dissidents form splinter groups, and many practitioners do not even bother to join. Obviously, most labor, trade, and professional associations must go through planned organizational renewal if they are to survive into the twenty-first century.

Colleagues today are seeking many innovative ways for cooperating, and some of these will be described in a latter section. One development for such individuals is to move beyond the narrow confines of one's own discipline or area of activity. Thus, some professionals enter into multidisciplinary arrangements and new organizational groupings based more on mutual *interests,* rather than previous education or training. Others engage in professional activities that mix the public and private sectors, academia and industry. The point is to avoid intellectual or professional ethnocentricity in the sharing of knowledge. This synergy of professional perspectives and skills is vital in solving complex contemporary problems. Furthermore, there must be dialogue and a felt need to consult with peers, not just to inform them of one's accomplishment. True professionals confer and seek feedback before making major decisions on their research investigations, writings, and pronouncements.

For effective collaboration, certain principles must be established in the professional relationship. Reciprocity and interdependence are to be encouraged, while imposition and dependency are to be avoided. Writing on transnational social science transactions, Krishna Kumar examined scholarly transactions between industrialized (IC) and less industrialized (LIC) countries.[3] Although such professional transactions should be mutually beneficial, there is concern that in fact those from IC's may dominate their LIC counterpart, generate a system of intellectual and cultural dependency, and inhibit development of indigeneous social sciences relevant in that cultural context. Symmetry should be the goal of international professional exchanges (that is, proportionate, harmonious, equality of parts to whole; correspondence in size, form, and arrangement). Asymmetry occurs when the "inflow" and the "outflow" of knowledge and expertise are not balanced, so that one may overwhelm the other. Asymmetry must be discouraged in professional global interchanges between developed and less developed countries.

A cosmopolitan professional realizes that society in an LIC may be very developed in terms of cultural, social, and even economic aspects of its people's lives, despite the fact that it has not been fully industrialized. Just as raw materials can be drained away from the Third World populations to feed insatiable appetites in the First or Second World, so the "brain drain" may exhaust the human resources of the former. Many Third World scholars trained abroad suffer because all their professional reference groups and support services are outside their own countries.

How many institutions and professionals from the IC's are willing to invest in the Third World infrastructure for synergistic growth of all? How else will Third World scholars within their own lands be able to transform data into knowledge because they have there adequate commuication facilities and publications, computer-based data banks, and interuniversity or research centers with automated communications systems?

In his book, *Uncertain Futures: Challenges for Decision-Makers,* Robert Ayres observes:

> It is a truism that the further the world moves toward industrialization and urban living, the more interdependent it becomes. . . .This interdependence is growing inexorably, decade by decade. If every nation in the world behaved in strictly rational fashion and acted always in terms of its own best, long-term interests, the fact of growing interdependence would persuade nations to draw together and set up international agencies with power to provide some protection against possible breakdowns of international order on which all depend.[4]

Although nations may not comprehend this reality and take appropriate steps for changing international relations, individual professionals and their institutions can learn to act interdependently, especially in cross-cultural exchanges.

Issue in Collaborative Professional Relations

There are other issues to be considered in the global exchange of knowledge and information. Jacob and Jacob put the matter into focus:

> Can one recruit a "critical mass" of collaborators with the motivation, resilience, thickness of skin, sensitivity to other's feelings, humility, patience, readiness to learn, and basic know-how in conflict avoidance and resolution to hold the show together through four or five years of mounting tension and frustration?[5]

In other words, there are personality factors involved in maintaining a professional relationship. Furthermore, when the colleague has a different temperament and work style, the interpersonal relations can be a real challenge. But when the collaborator is from a different ethnic, racial, or cultural background, then skills must be practiced for confronting and transcending such differences.

Cooperation can be fostered among peers when mutual understanding is sought in advance of formal activity. When managing an international network of 80 consultants, one of the authors (Harris) developed the following guidelines:

> This resource network is intended as a community of professionals engaged in a "helping relationship" with each other, the sponsoring organization, and

the client. All members have been selected to participate on the basis of competency and responsible reputation. They have banded together to render appropriate, quality professional service that is humanistic and futuristic. As agents of planned change with individuals and institutions, our concern should be to increase organizational effectiveness and human potential. Our aim is to fulfill assignments with competence, objectivity, and integrity. Our policy is to undertake only those engagements which we feel qualified to accomplish on the basis of ability and experience, and for which there is sufficient reason to expect tangible results.

Our network will insure that there is mutual understanding on the purpose and scope of an assignment before it is undertaken, as well as the compensation involved. We will not permit ourselves to be used as a tool by clients or government to engage in unethical practice. Confidentiality will be strictly maintained relative to all data collected and privileged information obtained in the course of an assignment. Nothing will be published without the concurrence of the sponsor. All communications from or about our clients will be handled with discretion, and conflicts of interest among clients will be avoided.

In our professional practice we seek to build a climate for professional support and cooperation with each other, our colleagues, and our clients. When conflict arises, our hope is to utilize it constructively, and to be candid with each other and our clients. In searching to enhance the effectiveness of human endeavor and systems, we wish to protect individual human rights, to be authentic in communication, to foster participation, and to confront issues vital to problem solving. When outside our home cultures, we will respect the traditional values and customs of the host country, and seek to be sensitive to local accepted practice.

Creating such written consensus for a group of professionals seeking collegiality can preclude many difficulties in working relationships. It may even take the form of a code of ethics. In any event, it can facilitate specific task or project agreements.

Gordon E. Finley of Florida International University believes that when professionals undertake cooperative projects, they should be aware of potential problems in two sets of issues: personal/personnel and organizational/structural. To lessen disputes and disagreements, he proposes an interesting procedure. His system involves three conferences among participators:

Initial Conference—With all partners physically in attendance, (1) discuss the research focus; (2) review general strategy and methods to be used; (3) agree on a process for sensitive, appropriate language translations; (4) select an overall coordinator responsible for operational decisions; (5) come to specific agreements on the division of labor; (6) set up a realistic timetable and staging of activities; (7) seek funding sources in all the nations represented by investigators; (8) establish a realistic budget and acceptable appeal mechanisms; (9) set criteria for distribution of credit relative to results, and product outcome strategies; (10) ensure a "quid pro quo" exchange of benefits to participating institutions and nations; (11) devise and implement a pilot testing.

Second Conference—Again, the partners are convened to review the results of the preliminary project, and to consider (1) selection and functions of a traveling coordinator; (2) a training program for research assistants; (3) establishment of a communication network and system; (4) development of a system for processing data; (5) agreement on location and strategies for central data analysis.

Third Conference—Finally, when the findings are collected, the last principal conference should focus upon data analysis, interpretation of results, and preparation of them for publication. Consensus should be sought on division of labor for this latter purpose, equal recognition and value return to all concerned—the investigations, the sponsoring institutions, and nations. [6]

Obviously, if such careful planning does take place on a multinational, complex project, the effectiveness of the enterprise is increased to the greater satisfaction of all involved. Regardless of the size or scope of the collaboration, whether it is a formal or informal arrangement, it is essentially a trust relationship. When an individual pirates ideas, techniques, methods, materials, credits, or even clients from another colleague, or fails to perform adequately, then he or she not only jeopardizes that relationship, but possibly undermines potential associations with others. Word quickly gets around circles of professionals when a peer is unethical, undependable, or uncooperative.

Richard Brislin provides an interesting analysis of ethical issues and reviews criticisms of some cross-cultural researchers who exploit the host country and local researchers to advance their own data gathering, grantsmenship, and publications. He then summarizes the recommendations of indigenous scholars to outside professionals:

1. Learn the language of the culture being studied.
2. Communicate with a wide variety of people in the society, not just those at the top of status hierarchy.
3. Avoid generalizations about findings, and specify the exact place within the culture where data was gathered.
4. Provide evidence for conclusions based on surveys, not merely impressions.
5. Avoid journalistic-type techniques of describing specific situation, which can lead to incorrect reader inferences.
6. Be cautious in interpreting motives from behavior, and in diagnosing, seek the point of view of the locals.
7. Try to enter into the insider's world or space by reading what they read and provide independent interpretation.
8. Invite insiders to comment on outsider's thoughts about their culture. [7]

Brislin has joined with two other cross-cultural psychologists, S. Bochner and W. Lonner, in editing a volume that proposes guidelines for collaborative behavior in their field.[8] It would appear that other professionals could benefit by undertaking a similar effort to spell out the ground rules for exchanges in their disciplines.

Coping in the "Task Team" Environment

Today professional relationships are often temporary and intense. Peers may come together on a project team, a research effort, or to write a handbook or report. It is a "bridge building process" among specialists who often come from a variety of microcultures within the fields of learning, or even within the organization. The link-up effort is even more complex when the participants are internationals from diverse macrocultures. To promote synergy in such team management, four steps are evident:

1. Bring the new person "on board" quickly by various means of reaching out, briefing, and inclusion efforts.
2. Foster intense, adhoc work relationships, as well as possible outside social relations.
3. Disengage rapidly when the task is completed and re-assignment takes place, or another undertaking is begun.
4. Follow up on the aftermath of the professional activity and maintain limited communication with members of the prior consortium.

Dr. George Coelho, health science administrator for the U.S. National Institute of Mental Health, refers to this phenomenon as "coping issues in task environment."

This specialist in coping and adaptation believes that the management of self-esteem is involved when one enters a new professional environment or relationship. Dr. Coelho envisions different phases in the process. For example, in the initial phase of planning and initiation, he postulates three challenges for the newcomer:

> *Gaining entry*—that is, establishing credibility with respect to leadership, objectives, instruments of agreement, use of subjects or client relations, sources of funding, sponsorship and other institutional support systems, project clearances and blessings, and communication of results.
>
> *Observing protocol*—namely, establishing the social contact and cooperative agreements in a format that recognizes the rites, etiquette, ceremonies, proprieties customary in that local cultural setting.
>
> *Building rapport*—essentially, creating an auspicious climate for favorable social exchange and interpersonal interactions based on mutual respect and trust (for example in the use of instruments, interviews, simulations, or videotapes for data gathering).[9,10]

Dr. Coelho believes that the competence of transnational actors in such situations can be subject to assessment, and suggests the following criteria for this purpose: How well does the professional maintain his own and other's self-esteem? Manage anxiety and tension? Maintain meaningful continuity of interpersonal relationships and social supports? Mobilize a sense of autonomy and efficacy in the face of new and complex problems?

Coelho proposes four additional phases in the life cycle of temporary group relationships. After planning and initiation, there are orientation, onsite training, activities that enhance involvement and commitment and reentry assistance and evaluation. Joining others in a new vocational environment requires risk and self-management, as well as human creativity in adaptation. Participants are challenged to create a microculture that accommodates "doers and thinkers" despite the reality that this mix may produce tension and conflict. As Andre van Dam, director of planning for Corn Products Company, Latin America, asked:

> Can we learn to cooperate in a competitive world? Can cooperation (which thrives on consultation and participation) coexist with competition (which is deeply ingrained in human beings, groups, and nations?. . .
>
> Admittedly, cooperation requires trade-offs between rival ideas or interests—trade-offs imply negotiation. Cooperation hinges upon the recognition of common as well as conflicting interests.

ENSURING PROFESSIONAL SYNERGY

Social scientists are conducting significant research on what people can do in small groups to facilitate a meaningful experience and productive outcome. One exciting example of this is occurring at the East-West Center in Honolulu, Hawaii. There, at the Culture Learning Institute, Dr. Kathleen K. Wilson is spearheading an investigation with 15 other distinguished colleagues on the factors influencing the management of International Cooperative Research and Development (ICRD) projects. Their findings in this five-year project will not be fully available until 1985. However, their preliminary studies have vital implications now for any professional seeking to improve human performance and collaboration. Although the researchers are examining project team effectiveness, their insights can be extrapolated to other forms of inter- and intragroup behavior, whether it is a matrix organization, a product team, task force, or any work unit. Figure 8-2 outlines the dimensions of the ICRD analysis we will examine here.

Reporting the researchers' progress to the Australian Commonwealth's Scientific and Industrial Research Organizations in June 1980, Dr. Wilson reviewed the varied contexts in which international cooperative groups must operate. These external factors affect the environment within the project itself, and include such diverse elements as political, organizational, and cultural aspects, the size and

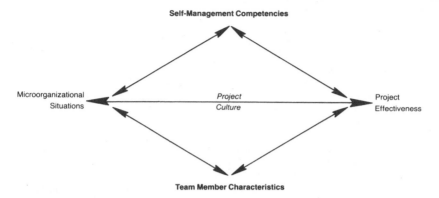

Figure 8-2. Dimensions of ICRD projects and professional synergy.

scope of the endeavor, the disciplinary background of team members, and their individual characteristics, research and development policies and problems. For our purposes, we have summarized on page 148 the ICRD observations on the human factors that can foster or hinder professional synergy. Certainly, the exhaustive listing of situations that influence a project's effectiveness points up the need for strategies managing the many "cultural" differences existing between and among professionals attempting to work together.

As part of the new team's orientation, a discussion of such "hazards" is in order. Perhaps some guidelines can be worked out for preventing some of the situations from becoming unmanageable. Such differences in perspective can be recorded on audio cassettes during project meetings, and then used to bring new team members "on board" during the life of the project. Obviously, all these human differences will not be resolved, and many will add to the richness of the team experience. At the very least, at project start-up, a review of the effects of cultural factors and conditioning on team behavior may alert the group to some of the realities and challenges involved in professional collaboration.

In terms of the individual qualities of team members, the East-West research on international cooperation projects offers some criteria that can be utilized in recruitment, selection, and assessment of professionals. *Team member characteristics* that foster group synergy are presented on page 149. Such benchmarks can be helpful in interviewing potential team members, choosing collaborators, and setting goals for self-improvement in organizational relations.

Finally, the ICRD researchers at the East-West Culture Learning Institute offer some indications for synergy assessment in professional cooperative efforts. They have established four criteria for evaluating project effectiveness and management competence:

1. Individual team member satisfaction.
2. Group satisfaction and morale.

Human Factors That Foster or Hinder Professional Synergy Within a Project:

- How project business is planned.
- Consideration of other problem-solving viewpoints.
- How the work should be organized
- Approach to R & D tasks.
- Definition of R & D problems.
- Ambiguity resolution and problem formulation.
- Methods and procedures
- Decision-making relative to recurring problems.
- Allocation of resources to team members.
- Accountability procedures relative to resource use.
- Timing and sequencing approaches
- Determining objectives for an R & D effort.
- Affiliation and liaison with external groups and degree of formality in their work relations.
- Quantity and type of project human resources.
- Qualifications, recruitment, and selection of new members.
- New member orientation and training on the project.
- Management of responsibilities
- Clarification of roles and relationships.
- Underutilization of workers relative to skill competencies.

- Motivating behavior and reward expectations.
- Coordination of long/short-term members.
- Agreement on degree of innovation required.
- Experience with cooperation especially relative to international R & D tasks.
- Official language(s) to use on project.
- Method of reporting everyone's involvement in the project.
- Coping with internal demands and visitors.
- Meeting face-to-face and having to resort to other forms of more impersonal communication.
- Involvement in making viewpoints known.
- Power differences because of institutional resources each brought to the project.
- Prestige, risk-taking, tolerance of uncertainty, and perceptions.
- Project leadership and/or organizational policies changing unexpectedly.
- Quality of work presented in evaluation methods.
- What constituted success in project work, and what to do when members fail to meet group expectations. ∎

3. Work progress relative to intended goal statements.
4. Social and cultural impact of the endeavor on people.

The East-West Center's ICRD researchers have also identified interpersonal skills that influence a professional group's situation and accomplishments. A summary of these *self-management competencies* is shown on page 149.

These insights offer a compendium of the shared leadership skills that professionals should expect to contribute in the course of group collaboration. For those organizations that provide project management training or team building for their members, these are the types of competencies to be sought in the emerging "adhocracies."

The Effective Team Member Has the Capacity for:

• Flexibility and openness to change and other's viewpoints.
• Exercising patience, perseverence, and professional security.
• Thinking in multidimensional terms and considering different sides of issues.
• Dealing with ambiguity, role shifts, and differences in personal and professional styles or social and political systems.
• Managing stress and tension well, while scheduling tasks systematically.
• Cross-cultural communication, and demonstrating sensitivity for language problems among colleagues.
• Anticipating consequences of one's own behavior.
• Dealing with unfamiliar situations and lifestyle changes.
• Dealing well with different organizational structures and policies.
• Gathering useful information related to future projects. ∎

Self-Management Competencies Permit the Project Member to:

• Recognize other member participation in ways they find rewarding.
• Avoid *unnecessary* conflicts among other team members, as well as to resolve unavoidable ones to mutual satisfaction.
• Integrate different team members skills to achieve project goals.
• Negotiate acceptable working arrangements with other team members and their organizations.
• Regard other's feelings and exercise tactfulness.
• Develop equitable benefits for other team members.
• Accept suggestions/feedback to improve his or her participation.
• Provide useful specific suggestions and appropriate feedback.
• Facilitate positive interaction among culturally different members, whether in terms of macro differences (nationally/politics), or micro differences (discipline or training).
• Accomplish required work while enjoying positive social relations with other team members.
• Build a support network for the benefit of the project team.
• Facilitate team exchanges and convert member ideas into specific tasks of accomplishment.
• Facilitate team exchanges and convert member ideas into specific tasks of accomplishment.
• Gain acceptance because of empathy expressed and sensitivity to end users.
• Encourage dissemination of project outcomes throughout its life.
• Recognize national/international differences in problem statements and procedures, so as to create appropriate project organizational responses.
• Anticipate and plan for probable difficulties in project implementation.
• Recognize discrete functions and to coordinate discrete tasks with overall project goals.
• Coordinate transitions among different kinds of activities within the project. ∎

NETWORKING PHENOMENA

Intellectuals have always formed linkages and exchanges with each other within a society or field of human endeavor. What is different in recent decades is the escalation of these phenomena on a global scale, across both cultures and disciplines of knowledge. Twentieth-century advances in communication and transportation have accelerated the process on a mass scale. The interchange of information and insight among professionals occurs on a formal and informal level. It is abetted by electronic technology, especially the computer and word processor, and contributes to the doubling, even tripling, of knowledge within fields every decade. It also contributes to professional obsolescence, and to the need for continuous professional development in order to be revelant within a vocational activity.

One's peers within a career field provide a reference group against which individual performance can be measured, recognized, and motivated. Today, such professional colleagues may be found around the world, not just within one's own country or even within one's own field of learning. As more and more study abroad, attend professional conferences overseas, or engage in career activities internationally, transnational linkages are formed.

It is interesting how people of like concerns begin to *sense* one another's compatibility of concerns. Individuals may hear a speech at a convention, spot a name and topic in a program, read an article in a journal, or hear mention of an individual from a respected professional. It may be as simple as, "This is someone you really ought to get to know." The relationship may begin with a telephone call or an exchange of letters or visits, and if there is "empathy"—a projection of self into the feelings or being of the other—then psychological involvement with one another follows. In the past, such associations might have been long and enduring, whereas in contemporary experience they may be short and intense. Even when out of contact with one another, the person is aware of the presence of his "neighbor," who may be thousands of miles away but can always be counted upon as a professional resource when necessary.

Networking is a communication concept especially appropriate for women seeking to advance in managerial and professional careers. Alina Novak, senior financial analyst at Equitable Life Assurance talks about network power for women seeking to participate in a specific organization or the business community. In San Diego, California, women in various industries and professions have formed separate networks for advancement and information purposes. Some of it is informal, like those female members of the San Diego Chamber of Commerce who formed a "downtown network." Some networks provide members with business development leads, while others gather and support women in highly visible leadership positions in business, politics, and other professions.

The collaboration may be with another person in one's career field or industry, research area or technology, or simply into a human concern that one feels deeply about—future studies, women's liberation, developing nations, ecology or environmental protection. The extent of cooperation may be only an exchange of views and data, or it may proceed to some joint venture. The latter may include contributing an article to some publication, producing a book or film, putting together a meeting or conference, undertaking research or project, or forming some organization of like-minded people. Bilateral bonds of this type can result in such endeavors as the Club of Rome, the Trilateral Commission, the UN Conference on Women, the International Monetary Fund, or The First Global Conference on the Future.

As people seek consensus with understanding colleagues, a process of examination, analysis, and diffusion of ideas takes place. The outgrowth may be a temporary or permanent grouping, some consortia of professionals into a *network*. It is a formal or informal system of people connected together for a distinct relationship or analysis. However, now there are new means available for heightening the interchange. Perhaps the preface to a work by R. Hiltz and M. Turoff best makes the point:

> This book is concerned with the recent emergence of a new alternative for conducting group communication processes among groups or networks of persons or organizations (such as meetings, study groups, teaching-learning exchanges). It uses computers and computer terminals to provide a written form of discussion or meeting. . . .Called computerized conferencing or computer mediated interaction, sometimes it is known as teleconferencing. [11]

The thrust of this movement can be appreciated in this appeal of Yoneji Masuda, president of the Institute for the Information Society of Japan, for the establishment of a "Global Voluntary Information Network":

> The GVIN has three distinguishing features: (1) it forms global supranational information space; (2) it is based on voluntary citizens as nodes with common attitudes toward global issues; (3) it uses the latest media for information lines (optical fiber cables), and personal computers. This integrated approach provides the technical basis of the network which can gather data on global concerns; analyze, present and project the consequences; study common solutions; and promote global participatory action. [12]

The potential for a new synergy among professionals through such developments is astounding. Such technology can also undermine traditional trade and professional societies, research centers, and consulting associations unless such entities renew and make use of these media possibilities. It provides a real challenge to government to sponsor public sector forums and similar opportunities for the benefit of the masses.

In these new patterns of collaboration, it is important that self-reliance is fostered in the participants and that interdependence is perceived as the basis of the network. Rudolph Rummel of the University of Hawaii reminds us that in transnational interactions, international cooperation and conflict are not necessarily irreconcilable but complementary.[13] As he sees it, the problem with the diversity of national values, goals, ideologies, lifestyles, and interests, is not to realize humanity as a single unit. Instead, synergy can be attained by developing realistic structures of mutual expectations that facilitate national interactions, while appreciating their cultural differences. Networks, in effect, represent post-industrial reference groups for professionals. They form a new microculture across the planet of people exploring for more appropriate values, attitudes, standards, beliefs, and perspectives that will be appropriate for life in the twenty-first century.

Professor Rummel reminds us that transactions occur within an existing international, regional or social order—a structure of expectations—that bridges the gap between diverse cultures and generations. He beautifully summarizes the thrust for synergy in these words:

> We are all stranded on a planet with limited resources and finite territory. We are all beginning to bump into each other. We are all establishing mutual frameworks of order within which we can cooperate, or already transacting within a preestablished structure of expectations. Underlying all these orders is a balance of national and cultural interests, of capabilities or power, of credibilities. . . .Therefore, conflict and cooperation are part of the same international social process through time.[13]

For our purposes here, Rummel's political science research provides a rare insight to professionals when he concluded:

> Cooperation thus takes place at two levels. It manifests a particular system of understanding and norms, a specific balance of interests, capabilities, and credibilities. But these balances take place in a larger order, a general cooperative framework which provides direction and guidance to all these activities.[13]

Perhaps this is illustrated in Toffler's Third Wave description of a unique global network that communicates through computer terminals in home or offices to achieve a new understanding and synergy:

> Some 660 scientists, futurists, planners, and educators today in several countries conduct lengthy discussions of energy, economics, decentralization, or space satellites with one another through what is known as Electronic Information Exchange System. Teleprinters and video screens provide a choice of instant or delayed communication. Many time zones apart, each user can choose to send or retrieve data when it is most convenient. A person can work at 3:00 a.m. if he or she feels like it. Alternatively, several can go on line at the same time if they so choose.[2]

If traditional social institutions are to survive, no less develop, then they should be assisting in the establishment of such exchange frameworks, in the indentification of interested participants, and in surveying individual resources. During 1980, for instance, three professional groups launched projects to develop data banks on members for networking purposes. The Society for Intercultural Education, Training and Research, sent out a computer form for the creation of a skill bank that will cover 442 countries and more than a 1,000 languages, including sign language. The World Future Society in cooperation with The Networking Group offered an opportunity to futurists who wish to link up with other people who share a common interest and complementary resources. The Group, after analysis of survey results, will publish a resource directory of persons, interests, and fields, an interest inventory for specific clusters of concerns, and a guide on how to make the most effective use of these tools. For those in the consulting field-seeking collaborators, the International Consultants Foundation and The Consultants Network undertake a similar service by publishing a directory and newsletter, and by establishing a referral system for its affiliates. (See Appendix C.)

Innovative Cooperation with Colleagues

Now that the concepts and means for promoting synergy in professional development have been reviewed, it may help to examine some creative approaches to the subject. Some wit has characterized those with knowledge and information as risk-takers, caretakers, and undertakers. It takes vision, courage, and risk to innovate. In 1931, Professor Neil Gordon of Johns Hopkins University had a brainchild for transmitting scientific information in a different way. Gordon wanted small groups of scientists to meet for summer seminars in a secluded and relaxed setting for informal, free give-and-take of knowledge. Today this innovative concept yields 100 Gordon conferences annually in seven New Hampshire schools and colleges for 12,000 professionals. Among the thinkers are many Nobel laureates who enjoy the relaxed exchange of data where there is no pressure, no publicity, and no need to publish.

At the other end of the creative spectrum is a financial planners network reported by Alfred E. O'Brien, C.F.P. of LaJolla, California. Both the members and their clients profit because of the weekly financial information exchange which the group shares via computer and telephone. They meet only occasionally because these astute planners are geographically spread across the United States.

When there is a coalition of people with new needs for interchange, then formal or information associations come into being. Three current examples of this are The International Organization of Women Executives (see Appendix C), whose primary aim is to help female executives excel through continuing education; the International Association Futuribles, which reports on future studies around the world through monthly journal abstracts and European meetings, as well as joint research on practical issues, such as labor conditions and lifestyles; and *Leading Edge,* a bulletin on social transformations which offers triweekly reports on innovations and emergent patterns in all aspects of society (See Appendix C for addresses of these groups.)

But what is innovation? And are there already some models of it that demonstrate synergy among professionals?

Innovation has been defined as creative idea generation, or the act of introducing something new into the established order; a change or different way of doing things from the traditional pattern. The scholars at the University of Southern California's Center for Futures Research maintain that innovation should include the invention and development of new technology, as well as entrepreneurial and managerial risk-taking to improve services and productivity. Innovation, for survival and development, should be built into the operating mechanisms or policies of all postindustrial systems. All social institutions, especially government agencies and corporations, have a desperate need to encourage creative deviations from the traditional norms and practices by professionals who will instill innovation into daily operations. As these words are written the great American industrial giant is stagnant and staggering because innovation was not advocated from the board room to the sales room. Dr. Warren Bennis reminds us that in 1930, as today, 100 companies dominated the United States economy, but 50 years later 60 of the original group have either declined or have ceased to exist. One might take the *Fortune 500* corporations in 1981 and inquire how many will be in that category by the year 2000. Those without innovative performance certainly will not be. For example, in 1960, Standard and Poors register had no category for semiconductors and related devices. By 1980, it not only provided such a classification but listed more than 180 companies.

C. Joshua Abend states there are many elements involved in organizational innovation.[14] In Figure 8-3 he proposes an institutional innovation circuit to stimulate a corporation. Does it work? The installation and application of this circuit by Abend with colleagues at Smith-Corona led to that company's development of the cartridge ribbon system for its typewriters.

The following models of innovative synergy among professionals represent a variety of approaches, from institutional to individual, from formal to informal arrangements.

It is hoped they will inspire readers to creative collaboration with colleagues that could range from individuals exchanging audio or video cassettes, which the participants create on relevant matters in their field, to trade and professional associations utilizing new media to disseminate the results of their meetings to members not in attendance.

The Twenty-Year Forecast Project—In 1980, the USC Center for Futures Research inaugurated its seventh year of collaborative futures research on the subject of "Innovation in America." Under the leadership of Dr. James O'Toole, the pro-

The Synergy of Innovation as a Total Organizational Process

Process
Methods of:
Innovation
Creativity
Problem-Solving
Idea-Generation
Conceptualization
Forecasting

Ideas
Selection
Evaluation
Training
Climate
Rewards
Acceptance Finding

**Innovation
Planning
and
Management**

People
Objectives
Company Policy
Venture Structure
Idea Transfer
R&D Organization
Criteria
Innovation Management

Organization
Screening
Product Futures
Environment
Direction Finding
Concept Assessment
Market Needs
Competition

Figure 8-3. Abend's organizational innovation circuit.

gram not only called upon the talents of its own professional staff but reaches out into the business and consulting communities for collaborative input. The purpose of this current forecast of organizational change is to integrate the results of environmental scanning, future-thinking, and long-range planning into the total organization. In addition to analysis of changes likely between now and the end of the century, the project will develop processes for implementing information about the future and the external environment into the operations of the firm. One part of the endeavor under direction of Professor Warren Bennis will deal with innovation from the perspective of the corporate board room. *Contact:* Director CFR, Graduate School of Business Administration, University of Southern California, Los Angeles, CA. 90007, USA.

The International Federation of Training and Development Organizations—In 1973, after much discussion of the idea within the U.S. Agency for International Development's Office of Labor Affairs, the IFTDO was launched. Members of the world training fraternity from 20 countries and 23 organizations took the initiative in establishing this clearinghouse of professional societies involved in human resource development. Today, IFTDO represents 37 national organizations and many thousands of professionals around the globe. In 1980 this network of training resources met in Brazil for its 9th World Congress, and its multifaceted deliberations are available in English, Spanish and Portuguese publications and audio cassettes. The American Society for Training & Development has provided a secretariat for the international group, and the special assistance of its 1,000-member International Division. *Contact:* IFTDO, Box 5307, Madison, WI. 53705 USA.

The Human Intelligence Movement—In 1979, the "intelligence revolution" took on a new dimension when the government of Venezuela appointed Luis Alberto Machado as Minister of State for the Development of Human Intelligence. This official act launched projects involving scholars from around the world in an international effort to expand human intelligence, and to close the gap between human achievement and human potential. To link together the many specialists throughout the planet doing research into the subject, a newsletter was inaugurated for the exchange of information about meetings, publications, and projects. *Contact:* Editor-Publisher, Human Intelligence International Newsletter. Box 163, Birmingham, MI 48012 USA.

International Consultants Foundation—In 1973, a group of highly qualified consultants and training specialists felt the need for greater professional integration and exchange. So they formed ICF, a relatively small and select organization with registrants from 26 countries. Committed to sharing their own innovations in developing human potential, the Foundation is concerned with the development of its own members and offering their assistance to human systems. This worldwide network of professionals publishes an annual registry, and a newsletter, monographs, and yearly proceedings. The multinational consultants meet each year in various countries for small, in-depth sessions at their own expense, and have begun to use teleconferencing. *Contact:* ICF President, 5605 Lamar Road, Wasington, D.C. 20016, USA.

Improving Performance Through High Achievers—In 1970, two colleagues collaborated to undertake a series of action research projects for clients relative to the use of high-achievement employees for problem-solving on organizational problems and to serve as behavior models to improve the productivity of average performers. The process is videotaped in performance management workshops. These videotapes then become a powerful feedback mechanism to management for organization development, as well as material for customized learning systems. With one of the originators, Dr. Philip R. Harris developed a *Performance Management Handbook* on the procedure, and both are establishing a network of colleagues from Europe to Asia to expand the research. *Contact:* President, Harris International, Box 2321, LaJolla, CA. 92038, USA.

Conclusion

On the first page of his classic work, *The Future of Man,* the late Pierre Teilhard de Chardin commented:

> It is a pleasant and dramatic spectacle, that of Mankind divided in its very depths into two irrevocably opposed camps—one looking toward the horizon and proclaiming with all its new-found faith, "We are moving," and the other, without shifting its position, obstinately maintaining, "Nothing changes. We are not moving at all."[15]

It has been the position of this chapter that true professionals are not among the latter immobilists, but develop and create *together* a better future by their human endeavors in synergy. Those areas of vocational activity that resist change, whether they are academic disciplines, unions or trade associations, professional societies, or educational institutions, will decline and be replaced by more innovative and cooperative arrangements.

Futhermore, the opportunties for professional collaboration will increase fourfold by the turn of the century. Within the next two decades colleagues located at various places on earth will visually communicate with each other, exchanging research reports, inventions, and graphic transmissions almost instantaneously. Information technology will permit a new synergy among thinking persons, and a mass interchange of creativity. Innovation will be valued in this process of consciousness-raising within our species. What Peter Drucker has said for business in this regard can be applied to all human systems:

> Innovation means, first, the systematic sloughing off of yesterday. It means, next, the systematic search for innovative opportunities in the vulnerabilities of a technology, a process, a market, in the lead time of new knowledge; in the needs and wants of a market. It means willingness to organize for entrepreneurship, to creating new businesses. . . .It means, finally, the willingness to set up innovative ventures separately, outside the existing managerial structure, to organize proper accounting concepts for the economics and control of innovation, and appropriate compensation policies for the innovators.[16]

The transformation of our traditional human society will require synergistic professionals who operate comfortably in two cultures: the industrial culture,which is disappearing, and the metaindustrial or cyberculture, which is emerging. Contemporary transnational actors must be effective bridge builders between both worlds, between the realities of the past and future.

References

1. Evans, C. *The Micro Millenium*. New York: The Viking Press, 1979.
2. Toffler, A. *The Third Wave*. New York: William Morrow and Company, 1980.
3. Kumar, K. "Some Reflections on Transnational Social Science Transactions," *International Journal of Comparative Sociology*, XIX, pp.3-4.
4. Ayres, R. U. *Uncertain Future: Challenges for Decision-Makers*. New York: John Wiley & Sons, 1979.
5. Szalai, A. and Petrelia, R. (eds.) *Cross-National Comparative Survey Research*. New York: Pergamon Press, 1977, pp. 231-278.
6. Finley, G. E. "Collaborative Issues in Cross-National Research," *International Journal of Intercultural Relations*, Spring 1979, pp. 5-13.
7. Brislin, R. W. "Ethical Issues Influencing the Acceptance and Rejection of Cross-Cultural Researchers Who Visit Various Countries," *Annals of the New York Academy of Sciences*, March 1977, pp. 185-202.
8. Brislin, R. W., Bochner, S., and Lunner, W. (eds.) *Cross-Cultural Perspectives on Learning*. New York: Wiley/Halstead, 1975.
9. Coehlo, G., Hamburg, D.A., and Adams, J. E. *Coping and Adaptation*. New York: Basic Books, 1974.
10. Coehlo, G. *Coping and Adaptation: Annotated Bibliography*. Washington, D.C.: Government Printing Office, 1980. (Contract No. PLD, NIMH 145343-76: DHEW Pub. No. 80-863.)
11. Hiltz, R. and Turoff, M. *The Network Nation: Human Communication via Computer*. Reading, Mass.: Addison-Wesley, 1978.
12. Masuda, Y. "Global Voluntary Information Network." In: *Through the '80s*, F. Feather (ed.) Washington, D.C.: World Future Society, 1980.
13. Rummel, R. In: *Bonds Without Bondage, Explorations in Transcultural Interactions*, K. Kumar (ed.), University of Hawaii, 1978.
14. Abend, C. J. "Innovation Management: The Missing Link in Productivity," *Management Review*, June 1979.
15. De Chardin, P. T. *The Future of Man*. New York: Harper & Row, 1969.
16. Drucker, P. R. *Managing in Turbulent Times*. New York: Harper & Row, Publishers, 1980.

9.
Training and Education for Cultural Synergy

LEARNING FOR THE SUPERINDUSTRIAL AGE

George Bernard Shaw once observed, "The right to know is like the right to live. It is fundamental and unconditional in its assumption that knowledge, like life, is a desirable thing." The issue in our emerging information or knowledge society is, How many can fully exercise this right completely and effectively? In what manner do the inhabitants of this planet receive knowledge and to what degree or amount? Among the major means for disseminating the wisdom of the ages, and our cultural heritage, are education and training. They are the principal mechanisms for imparting the results of present insights, inventions, and innovations, and increasingly, they are helping people plan for change and prepare the future.

In July, 1980, the First Global Conference on the Future sponsored a number of sessions on the state and opportunities of world educational systems. Among the 5,000 futurists in attendance, there seemed to be a consensus that formal institutions of education everywhere were in profound crisis. There was agreement that certainly their offerings and methods were not meeting the needs of contemporary students and trainees at all levels of learning. During an appraisal of education in the 1980s, the authors (Bowman, Kierstead, and Dede) of *Educational Futures* spoke of "the challenge for educators to shift from a reactive to a proactive reconstructionist position that takes a united professional global stand on the future of schooling"[1] Another presenter, Walter Pitman, president of Canada's Ryerson Polytechnical Institute, called for "a more complete, holistic perception of both our economy and our educational system." He challenged teachers and trainers to create an approach to learning that provides people with the skills and capacities to

159

cope and contribute in a changed economic order and a new social environment. This Toronto educator suspects that most of our current educational effort is inappropriate for this purpose, and that we presently over-train and under-educate.

Schools and colleges, institutes and universities, reflect the values and concerns of a society. But sometimes a gap develops between what is being taught and where the mainstream of humankind is moving. Currently, stunning advances in technology are forcing universities to reorganize their engineering curricula. During the hunting, agricultural, and industrial stages of human development, rugged individualism and competition were espoused, especially in Western societies. Within and without the classroom such ideals were promoted. Physical education and extracurricular programs fostered a spirit of healthy competition and individual achievement in a win/lose experience. To use the terminology of Jonas Salk, that was "Epoch A" thinking, or as Alvin Toffler might put it, "First and Second Wave" educational approaches. Even adult education, including training within industry and government, furthered such learning strategies. Management games, for instance, helped supervisors and sales personnel to be more competitive, regardless of ethics or consequences. Training films utilized athletic heros to motivate managers and workers—fierce, gridiron favorites were held up for comparable rugged, competitive, win-only play in business.

In today's postindustrial society the appropriateness of these approaches is being questioned, especially in American and European cultures, which in turn export them around the globe. In contrast to such Epoch A approaches, Epoch B education and training are likely to foster skill development in collaboration and cooperation, as well as in change-coping and change-making. The complex problems and systems of this "Third Wave" period of transition require team working and sharing by those who are from different disciplines, cultures, and countries. Synergistic education facilitates learning and working, playing and thinking, *together*. This is necessary whether we are in a classroom or on an athletic field, in a research center or on a project team.

Such synergistic education and training are already taking place, but in too limited a degree. Bilingual and multicultural education attempts to teach those from varied backgrounds to respect one another and to cooperate for mutual benefit. In the United States, for instance, legislation and programs of Equal Employment Opportunity or Affirmative Action seek to ensure that personnel of different ethnic and racial origins are judged on the basis of competence, not sex, color, culture, or religion. Today, management and executive development frequently help participants to appreciate the value of win/win for all involved, especially when joint endeavors are undertaken by labor and management, by the public and private sectors, by companies in the same industry or in similar fields, or by service agencies seeking a common goal.

"Reindustrialization" efforts within the United States clearly demonstrate the need for extending the concept of synergy in education and training. *Business Week* magazine devoted a whole issue in June 1980 to a searching analysis of what has gone wrong with the U.S. economy, and what can be learned from the highly successful German and Japanese economic models. Columnist Ernest Conine of the *Los Angeles Times* (July 7, 1980) wrote about the common thread that cuts across all the rest of this national self-examination: the need for *cooperation rather than confrontation* in the three-cornered relationship among business, labor, and government.

In successful foreign economies, there is such a cooperative relationship between the three parties. In Japan, for example, quality-control circles of workers and supervisors meet regularly to discuss product quality; representatives from business, government, and academia meet periodically to decide which industries are failing and should be phased out and which innovations should receive favorable financing and incentives. Education and training can contribute significantly in the development of such new synergistic attitudes, and in the acquisition of skills necessary for team participation and management.

In this superindustrial age, we may finally take a more integrated view of education and training, especially valuing nontraditional and informal learning. Pierre Casse, a Belgian sociologist, contends that the subject of educational endeavors, the human mind, is by nature and structure cross-cultural. That is, the mind "has the capacity to understand other people, comprehend the world in a meaningful way, and even more, cope with its own internal dialectics." Casse maintains that we have the capacity to not only understand nature and our world, but to influence both, and through this, to affect ourselves and our fate.[2] Human learning is intercultural because it involves conscious and unconscious, right and left brain qualities.

Learning's objective should be the transformation of the human being by raising his or her level of consciousness and translating this awareness into appropriate actions for the improvement of the human condition. What is exciting about our future is the new means we have at our disposal for mass global reeducation. For the first time in history, we have the mechanisms for global data gathering and sharing, world information exchange, and customized international learning. With the proper use of satellites, television, and computers, we can enrich the whole species.

To learn is to change, and the process of education and training should change the learner. Back In 1968, George Leonard wrote *Education and Ecstasy,* in which he celebrated the joy that is possible through learning. The Club of Rome maintains that human learning is the decisive factor in reversing a deteriorating situation in the human condition. These futurists take a broad approach to the meaning of "learning," in terms of knowledge and life, conscious and unconscious, experiential or simulated, formal or informal.

We have previously established the concepts of culture and synergy, so let us focus here on education and training. *The Harper's Dictionary of Modern Thought* describes three current interpretations of "education": passing on of one's cultural heritage; initiation into worthwhile ways of doing and thinking; and fostering of individual growth.[3] *The Guidebook for International Trainers in Business and Industry* defines "education" as learning or acquiring orderly, logical systems for processing new information.[4] Its author, Vincent Miller, then differentiates that term from "training," which he defines as "the process of affecting change in an individual human's behavior often applied to the acquisition of limited, job-related skills." Finally, Miller explains the word "development" as "the process by which an organization, nation, or enterprise expands or modernizes its activities." The phrase "human resource development," in a sense, encompasses all of the above distinctions.

In *Developing Human Resources*, Leonard Nadler explains HRD as meaning (1) a series of organized activities, (2) conducted within a specified time, and (3) designed to produce behavioral change.[5] Our concern in such HRD efforts is that they include an awareness of cultural differences or the cultural factors affecting behavior; and the promotion of insight and skill development in synergy, that is, cooperating or collaborating effectively with people who are different.

TRENDS IN HUMAN RESOURCE DEVELOPMENT

As we develop a new image of the human being in the decades ahead, and then act upon this vision, our whole approach to learning and the knowledge society will change. Educational efforts in cyberculture will be different, and educational systems will be vastly restructured in the twenty-first century. Contemporary trends indicate that people's education, training, and development in the next hundred years will:

1. Be more integrated with life, be a civilizing process that will take place in home, on the job, at play, as well as in classrooms.
2. Utilize home communication centers with computers, videophones, and other electronic services.
3. Reflect more individualized or customized learning, often in nonformal situations, and less mass standardized instruction.
4. Include more diverse learning through miniaturized, electronic components that store large information blocs on small chips.
5. Posses more content, information, and variety in formal instruction that will encompass global, as well as local, matters.
6. Provide more continuing education for more people at all levels, including handicapped, retired, disadvantaged, and those most discriminated against in the past.
7. Include more affective and intuitive learning synthesized with cognitive or logical learning.
8. Be more dynamic, mobile, and less institutionalized.

9. Be more tentative, exploratory, and searching and less dogmatic and rote.
10. Be more holistic, interdependent, and international, and less compartmentalized.
11. Reflect more concern for raising the consciousness of the masses, and be less elitist and ethnocentric.
12. Be more innovative and less maintenance oriented, and include educational approaches that are anticipatory, participative, and problem-solving.

Such multidisciplinary, multimedia human resource development will be futuristic, not past-oriented; concerned not only with survival, but with human emergence in dignity.

UNESCO has already launched projects and publications on "New Initiatives in Learning Research." Creative experimentations are underway throughout the world to promote educational renewal and innovative learning. A new Swiss foundation, *Forum Humanum,* is an example of this synergistic endeavor. Small work/ learning teams address problems of global importance, such as food, energy, environment, ethics, the arms race, threats to cultural identity, changing status of women, and Third World concerns. Study teams will be set up internationally, supported in their "learn-by-doing" efforts up to four years, and facilitated in their copings with world needs. The output will be joint, multimedia reports designed to influence public policy and opinion.

The Club of Rome in its analysis, *No Limits to Learning,* supports learning that is global in concern, but individual-local-societal in action. This organization urges that the transferal of educational theory and techniques from developed to less industrially developed countries harmonious with Third World cultures, so that some traditional practices of learning can be preserved and utilized. Its report cites three new research trends that offer hope that traditional learning practices can be maintained: the role of communications in learning, the development of new curricula for anticipatory learning, and "societal learning" (what, why, and how societies change or fail to change).

As humanity evolves a new culture appropriate to the technological age, we will question many of the old assumptions upon which traditional education has been based (such as, the Cartesian assumption, which distinguished between mind and the natural world, and resulted in an undue emphasis of the empirical and scientific over the experiential and intuitive aspects of learning.) A more systematic approach to education, training, and development now underway permits the learner to grasp the totality and to relate integral parts of subsystems. Joel de Rasnay proposes that the new education include concepts of interdependence, mutual causality, and dynamic equilibrium in the study of complex systems.[6] He also recommends a thematic approach to knowledge that reaches across disciplines; greater emphasis on nonrational problem-solving, and multicultural exposures to human values and world views.

Education in Competence

Our complex metaindustrial society requires that people not only work together, but that they have a degree of expertise to contribute to group effort. Thus, in modern education there is also a trend toward competency-based teaching or training. As a result of self-learning or formal instruction, people should attain something they can apply in coping with people and tasks. One dimension is technical knowledge; another is interpersonal skill. The latter includes skills in human relations, intercultural sensitivities, and synergy, or the art of collaboration for goal accomplishment. For example, one may be a very competent engineer or technician, but ineffective on a project team. In other words, the person lacks competence in working with groups, uncertainty, and dual commands. The new adhocracies require flexibility and adaptation, the ability to perform a repertoire of roles.

Another essential dimension for leadership in superindustrial organizations is to be a cosmopolitan, that is, someone who can be comfortable and operate effectively *transorganizationally*—across departments, divisions, and disciplines; *transnationally*—across cultures, countries, and national corporations; and *transideologically*—across East/West ideologies, philosophies, and religions. In the course of one year, for instance, a multinational manager may find him-or herself working in a dozen countries, with sales revenues larger than some nations' gross national products, with technology more sophisticated than that which puts us in space, and with operations that function in capitalistic and socialistic economies. Such activities demand a new type of competence.

Dr. George Coelho of the National Institute of Mental Health, U.S. Department of Health and Human Services, has defined "competence" as culturally valued performance of actors meeting task requirements by adjusting to a given environment. He believes that competence involves motivational (implicit, intrinsic human adaptation) and skill components. The latter implies that the person demonstrates abilities in performance that can be measured against a given criterion of effectiveness.

Today, as humans engage in more complex and less routine tasks, we need a greater integration of knowledge/judgment/skills, as well as more synergy—the capacity to synthesize various perspectives and input for cooperative action. Competence in a complex, transitional society or organization requires human resource development in new coping skills. Such education and training will be designed to enable the individual to interact effectively in a variety of situations and environments. Coelho, who has written extensively on his research into adaptation, believes competence is learnable, improvable, and constrained by limits. Among the constraints are personal disposition and capabilities; institutional policy, organization, or climate; cultural factors that influence role expectations, incentives and reward systems, and value orientations; and transnational situations that are new, complex, and stressful.

The emerging information society features new technologies, the automation of repetitive tasks, and the introduction of new administrative concepts on a world-wide basis. Malcolm Warren takes a systems approach to human resource development, and proposes a performance model, even when training for nonrepetitive tasks, that obtains and maintains the desired performance.[7] Warren suggests that such performance orientation can be extended to industrial, sales, administrative, technical, and professional training. He believes that training systems should focus upon *accountability* (who, what, when, where, why, how); *interface* (manner in which elements of the systems obtain information and resources); *competence* (special knowledge required in the system or program to change behavior); and *capability* (limitations of workload and budget). For Warren, the training system contains these key elements:

1. Research (related information search and application for use in the system.
2. Analysis (identification of problems, needs, performance standards, trainees, training criteria, cost and return on investment projections, and scheduling).
3. Development (actions to meet objectives of training plan).
4. Delivery (implementation of training actions).
5. Operations (administrative aspects of control and coordination).
6. Reporting (on the training).
7. Evaluation (assessment of training results).[7]

Regardless of how we develop the new knowledge worker, competence in cultural synergy must be one of the outcomes of any education and training. That means that the individual, whether dealing within macro- or microcultures or with their representatives, is capable of operating effectively through collaboration in achieving group goals and tasks. In the emerging culture dominated by technology and electronics (dubbed by Z. Brzezinski as "technotronic" society), there is an ever-increasing need for people to get out of their own space into the world of the other, so that they can achieve together through cooperation. But there are problems and risks in such endeavors, as Verner Bickley, Director of the East-West Culture Learning Institute, reminds us:

> We have seen that misunderstandings occur between individuals because of cultural and language differences. Such differences can lead to negative encounters between individuals from different cultural groups in the same country, and can also lead to negative encounters between individuals from the indigenous population and foreign residential groups, such as seasonal workers or migrants. Cultural and language differences are exacerbated by ignorance of the value orientations of individuals in other cultures, and lead to various forms of prejudice and alienation.

Counteracting such factors that can undermine intercultural cooperation is of vital importance and should be part of the cultural training for human resource development (see Chapter 5 of *Managing Cultural Differences*, Harris and Moran, Houston: Gulf Publishing Co., 1979).

Such competency in U.S. nationals is apparently decreasing if one accepts the report of The President's Commission on Foreign Language and International Studies (November 1979). The report expresses alarm at the serious deterioration in America's language and research capacity. One magazine writer put it more simply, "The U.S., a deaf and dumb giant!" The President's Commission stated:

> Americans' incompetence in foreign languages is nothing short of scandalous, and it is becoming worse. Historically, to be sure, America's continental positions between vast oceans was a basis for linguistic as well as political isolation, but rocketry as well as communication satellites render such a moat mentality obsolete. While the use of English as a major international language of business, diplomacy, and science should be welcomed as a tool for understanding across national boundries, this cannot be safely considered a substitute for direct communications in the many areas and on innumerable occasions when knowledge of English cannot be expected. The fact remains that the overwhelming majority of the world's population neither understands nor speaks English; and for most of those who learn English as a foreign language, it remains precisely that. [8]

So for those who would be competent in cultural synergy, cultural awareness and specifics, even area studies, are not enough: some foreign language skills are most necessary. The Commission makes many recommendations for improving the situation in the U.S.A., including a greater use of America's ethnic and linguistic minorities as part of the remedy. The media are urged to play a more important role in developing a more internationally informed citizen. Perhaps they can counteract the findings of a recent study of U.S. college students in which the Educational Testing Service discovered half of the sample to be remarkably uninformed about international relations.

But there is one area of the Commission's report that is important to all readers, regardless of their national affiliation. It maintained that business and labor should give more priority to foreign languages and international studies in recruitment and training of staff, while colleges and universities are asked to make such training an integral part of their programs in business and labor studies. Furthermore, they suggested that professional educational and training associations intensify their international efforts, especially ensuring that teacher and trainer education programs get such an emphasis.

Think of the cultural synergy that could be promoted if the millions of foreign students in many nations were not only given cultural and language training for the host country prior to their departure, but upon arrival in the nation they are visiting! One of the authors (Harris) testified before a Congressional inquiry for this

Presidential Commission that language education at all levels should include simultaneous cultural studies. This is especially valid in corporate foreign deployment programs. Bankers, for instance, being prepared for the world market, do not only need to know the banking laws and practices of the country to which they are being assigned, but should also receive training in its language and culture.

To further reduce misunderstanding in business and international relations, we often resort to interpreters of the foreign language. But translations are given in a cultural context, and the linguistic specialists themselves require cross-cultural training. International education and business can be facilitated by *competent* simultaneous interpretation. Linguistic Systems, Inc. of Cambridge, Massachusetts, U.S.A., reports that an international business conference can be held in 12 languages and with an audience of unlimited size. Since nine tenths of the planet's people do not speak English, communications through the oral/written word will require fast, accurate, technically precise and culturally sensitive translations. New equipment for simultaneous interpreting, graphic presentations, and later reporting have done much to foster international cooperation. The mass global use of the computer creates a universal language of another type. Also, through the wizardry of electronic technology, forthcoming inventions will translate for us, which will further breakdown the barriers between and among the inhabitants of this global village. Pocket translators, which are now available are only the beginning.

EDUCATING FOR UNCERTAINTY AND CHANGE

By nature, humans want to know what is expected of them, and what to expect in the near future. Although some cultures, such as China, are past-oriented, many cultures, such as those in the West, tend to be anticipatory or future-oriented. Today on a planet in profound transition, the only thing certain about the future is uncertainty and change (see Chapter 3, "The Manager As an Agent of Change," *Managing Cultural Differences*). Education and training at any level, but especially with adults, should focus upon preparing people to cope with accelerating change. Students and trainees can learn to be more proactive, instead of reactive to change. Workers can be trained to build change into their lifestyles, as managers can be developed to install the mechanisms for change with work systems. Citizens can be reeducated to a changing life style in which energy is conserved, waste and spending are restrained, ecology and nature are preserved, and resources and wealth are shared with the disadvantaged within the human family.

Walter Pitman writes about *appropriate* education that helps individuals cope with ambiguity, differences, and stress—facts of life in a contemporary society.[9] He proposes that appropriate and relevant education is life-long, includes the non-traditional and nonformal, and includes career development. It emphasizes balance in education for work and living. Appropriate educational systems produce specific changes in social policy, such as educational leaves for workers, expanded training by industry and service professions, or ecodevelopment values (educational activities that are sustained and environmentally responsible, restrained in costs and effective in results). This type of education and training not only provides learners with understanding of the changed economy and economic interdependence, but skill development in coping with the new economic order. How many companies, for instance, provide any consumer education to their employees trying to deal with inflation on a restricted wage, so they learn how to get the best and most with their salary?

James Botkin urges broad-based learning under institutional sponsorship, which offers coping assistance with the complexities of modern life.[10] In other words, education and training should limit the impact of "future shock" and transition from old to new ways. When editor of the report *No Limits to Learning* Botkin called for *innovative* learning as indispensable in resolving global issues and preparing people to "act in concert" in new situations. Perhaps Botkin's own words best summarize the case for anticipation and participation in education and training:

> Anticipation is the capacity to face new situations. . . . Anticipatory learning stresses preparation for future alternatives, not adaption to the present. It goes beyond foreseeing or choosing among desirable trends and averting catastrophic ones; it also enhances the ability to create new alternatives. Its opposite is adaptive, reactive learning, where one responds only to given changes in the environment, delaying search for answers until it may be too late to implement solutions.
>
> Participation is a term that powerfully and controverially evokes the aspirations of individuals and their groups to be partners in decision-making, to strive for equality, and to reject unduly limiting roles. The demand for participation has become nearly universal, and is being felt on every level, from local to global.

Synergistic education and training, then, not only teach people how to work together effectively in coping with changes in their environment, they provide experiential and cognitive learning in attitude change, planned renewal of organizations, innovation, and creativity. Their outcome should be initiative, ingenuity, and innovative actions.

Fifteen years ago one of the authors (Harris) got a telephone call from an executive of the Boeing Corporation. "Our company is going through major technological change. Our middle management is severely resisting it in a particular division. Can you help us with these 400 managers, to crack their mind-set, so that they will be more open to change?" This led to the consultant's transforming theoretical research into a training program that has since been given to more than a hundred human systems on several continents. Eventually, it was summarized into a self-learning system on (see Appendix C for more information). It is but one example of how people are being educated as to the why and how of planned change.

A change inventory used to sensitize people to the qualities necessary for survival and development in an era of transition is presented on pages 170-172. Perhaps the reader would like to use it for self-evaluation. Certainly those who would teach or train about change, should themselves be open to change.

Albert and Donna Wilson, two researchers at the Institute of the Future, have best made the case for education and training on change:

> This generation as no generation in history is consumed with change. The rapidity of technological change and its societal consequences thrust us onto a metaphorical elipsis surf-board that renders obsolete the traditional movement from one state of static stability to another by discrete steps of renewal, reform, or revolution. Unless we can discover and apply processes leading to dynamic stability, present ecological, social, and psychological imbalances will grow until they topple us.[11]

FOSTERING INNOVATION IN EDUCATION AND TRAINING

By the last quarter of the twentieth century, behavioral scientists had developed whole systems of planning change, so that synergistic educators can call upon a host of books and courses for this purpose. Simultaneously, there have been two other developments related to creativity education and future studies, which contribute significantly to the emerging art and science of change management.

In Chapter 8 we defined and provided the rationale for developing *innovation* as a norm in the professions and social systems. Here we would like to expand briefly on that theme relative to education and training if they are to produce synergy. Learning need not be by hard knocks and shocks; people can learn to anticipate and be creative. Such qualities can be found everywhere and in all institutions, but the task of leadership is to provide an environment that encourages them. One of the most creative organizations was the U.S. Navy's Public Work Center in San Diego, California. The manager not only promoted creativity workshops for employees, but rewarded innovative efforts in the repair of ships and military installations; innovation became a norm of the department.

The vice-president of Sony Corporation of America, Mike Morimoto, stated that "innovativeness epitomizes the personality" of his company. In the United States this multinational is a good example of creative synergy in the way it has integrated Japanese and American management practices. Sony likes to try new things, such as being the first to use transistors in radios.

Concept innovation, according to Magoroh Maruyama, is necessary today to cope with unprecedented problems. Maruyama maintains that potential innovators are more numerous than previously thought, and that society cannot afford to waste them. This anthropologist from the Southern Illinois University suggests

(text continued on page 172)

Change Inventory for Leaders*

Do you have a positive or negative attitude toward change? Most people fear change, but the issue is whether you let such concern paralyze you into inaction. Some persons merely react to change; other are pro-active — they plan and control change.

Part I

The following checklist includes some characteristics of effective change agents. Its purpose is to allow you to analyze yourself as an agent of change in an organization or community. Evaluate yourself on the following criteria by checking "usually," "sometimes" or "never."

	Usually	Sometimes	Never
1. *Openness*—willing to consider new ideas and people of differing opinions; tentative in communications, rather than dogmatic or closed-minded in one's approach.	_____	_____	_____
2. *Flexibility*—adaptable to new people, situations, information and developments; able to handle the unexpected and to shift position; spontaneous in responding to the "here and now" data and experiences.	_____	_____	_____
3. *Sensitiveness*—conscious of what is happening to oneself and others in the communications about the change and its effects; aware of the needs and feelings of others because of the proposed change; able to respond empathetically.	_____	_____	_____
4. *Creativeness*—respond with resourcefulness to new people and situations; avoid stereotype answers and solutions; exercise initiative, imagination and innovativeness.	_____	_____	_____
5. *Person-centered*—concerned more about people than task or mere progress; care what happens to the people involved in the change; support, encourage, inform and involve people in the decisions for change which they will be expected to implement; respect the right of dissent.	_____	_____	_____
6. *Goal-oriented planning*—develop a case for change with others which takes into account long-range objectives, while developing a plan with different stages or targets and short-term steps to accomplish the planned change; communicate these purposes and plans to all involved; state goals in terms that have positive value to those affected by the change.	_____	_____	_____

7. *Group understanding*—possess knowledge of the group process and skills in group dynamics; analyze the driving and resisting forces within the group relative

*From *Organizational Dynamics* by P.R. Harris, La Jolla, CA: Harris International, 1980.

	Usually	Sometimes	Never

to the proposed change; understand the character, structure, needs and wants of the group or organization to be affected by change; involve entire group in change process.

8. *Communicativeness*—promote open, circular interaction; able to analyze and clarify the problem and reasons for change; motivate members to desire to change and to use the available resources; develop a helping relationship with others so they can accept and live with the change.

Part II

Relative to your capacity to cope more effectively with rapid change in your own personal and organizational life, indicate your present typical response by checking the category in the right-hand columns that is most appropriate for each descriptive item in the paragraphs on the left. Be self-critical in your appraisal, for no one will receive these results but you, and it is intended as exercise in "mind-stretching."

	Usually	Sometimes	Never

9. *Changing image*—possess the capacity to reevaluate my concept of self based on new feedback, so as to expand my self-image; fluid in my self-conception, amplifying my sense of identity as a result of new encounters and experiences.

10. *Changing construct*—willing to review periodically the way I read meaning in my life; flexible in my attitudes and perceptions, so as to make "new sense" out of added inputs and insights; able to break out of "old mindsets" and to develop new rationale; able to accept, at times, inconsistencies and discontinuity in my life.

11. *Changing values*—able to sense new needs in myself and others, to develop new and changing life values, to abandon past, readymade values and ideals, to revise my expectations of self and others; and as a result, willing to re-examine the norms or standards which I have set for myself and others and to develop new ones as appropriate.

12. *Changing role*—willing to have an unclear, hazy role in life or an organization - one that is dynamic and responds to current relevant needs; able to live with a role definition which is open-ended and subject to continuous clarification; accept new role definitions for women, for parents and spouses, for colleagues, for professionals and other career people.

13. *Changing society*—able to be comfortable with impermanence or a lack of structure; capable of coping with constant alteration and perpetual transition; willing

	Usually	Sometimes	Never

to live in changing times, without the traditional stability and reference groups; able to make the most of the present moment - the "here and now" - to be "existential" or to "hang loose;" ready to combat unwarranted resistance to change in myself and the communities in which I participate.

14. *Changing goals*—concerned about actualizing my own and others' potential, as well as increasing the levels of awarness and consciousness in both; seek improvement in my capacity for feeling, and intuitiveness, for creating and risk-taking; desire more knowledge and education for personal and professional development; willing to provide cultural leadership by experimenting with new life styles of adaptation to the demands of rapid change.

15. *Changing lifestyle*—willing to be more transient and mobile within and among organizations; able to change jobs and locations when appropriate; capable of abandoning old relationships when necessary, and to search for new, more meaningful ones; willing to reject past steretypes of other people, especially various minorities or foreigners; able to participate in team efforts to solve increasingly complex problems; able to cope with stress and urban crowding, lack of privacy, noise, pollution and other modern discomforts, while seeking to improve these situations; capable of enduring discontinuities and disconnections in my life.

Note: The above-inventory items are offered with a view to stimulating your thinking about planned changes within your personal and organizational life space if "future shock" is to be avoided or minimized. There are no "right" or "wrong" answers. Research indicates that people who check "usually" are moving in the direction of developing those qualities that make for a more healthy personality in today's and tomorrow's fast-changing world. Those who check only "sometimes" or "never" are challenged by such items to set new personal goals, which would enable them to move to a state of mind or behavior whereby they would mark "usually" if they were to retake the inventory.   ∎

that we search out the invisible networks of innovators who promote the evolving harmony of natural systems. "They are not likely to be established scholars, publishing in the mainstream professional journals. But they tend to organize small symposia within large professional conferences, and to circulate their own informal newsletters or unpublished manuscripts." If effective education and training in synergy is to occur, it seems logical to begin by seeking out innovative teachers, trainers, and adult educators or HRD administrators.

Furthermore, it has been demonstrated that creativity, innovation, and futuristics can be taught. In *The Future: A Guide to Information Sources* there is a whole selection on universities, colleges, and schools that are teaching future studies, while another part of the volume describes the professionals who provide such innovative education.[12]

Leaders in industry, government, and education can be prepared for Managing in Uncertainty. Such anticipatory management may involve environmental scanning and trend impact analysis, or it may require support to creative behavior patterns within the organization. The president of American Motors—Canada, William Pickett, suggests that it may be as simple as learning to listen to the so-called "kooks" among the workforce, or what sociologists term, "the creative deviants." Perhaps such approaches explain the synergistic decision that brought about an amalgamation between American Motors and Renault of France, creating an international auto consortium.

Accepting worker feedback and insights can become an important means for maintaining innovation in an organization. U.S. business leaders and trainers began to learn from their Japanese counterparts when they introduced the Nippon "quality circle" strategy. An example of cultural synergy in training, it brings workers together weekly for the purpose of analyzing improved productivity and performance through consensus. But The Innovative Group (see Appendix C) has advanced the process by videotaping small groups of top performing personnel. High achievers are brought together in a performance management workshop not only to provide input on why and how they accomplish so much on the job, but also to problem-solve key issues that baffle management.[13] Organization development is enhanced when this information is employed in the design of training programs for average workers. In effect, the outstanding employees become behavior models and trend indicators of tomorrow's organizational norms. Creative leadership brings the right people together to cope with corporate or community needs, literally creating situations for synergy. When human systems began to seek the input of women in management, for example, synergy was fostered, and new work and institutional values were pumped into these institutions.

Synergy with the New Technology

For the foreseeable future, education and work will be dominated by the rapid development of new technology. Those with educational and training responsibilities should be developing programs to remove the fears that accompany these "smart machines," and programs to develop more synergy in "man-machine" relations. Employees, especially unions, need help in overcoming their resistance to change resulting from installation of high technology systems, and in capitalizing on new career opportunities created by retraining. As Norbert Weiner, the father of cybernetics, reminded us, ". . . messages between man and machines, between machines and man, and between machine and machine are destined to play an ever-increasing role in our lives." Psychologist Alphonse Chapanis of Johns Hopkins University put the challenge into focus with this astute observation:

> Computers guide space vehicles. They monitor complex assemblages of men and machines, warning of emergencies that are beyond human capacities to sense and comprehend. Computers keep watch over the physiological states of astronauts as well as comatose patients in intensive care units.

In the 80s, we will increasingly resort to computers to play games, pay our bills by telephone, purchase goods and services, to learn, and to enrich our lives. In 1970, E. T. Klemmer of Bell Telephone Laboratories made a careful activity analysis of how clerks, secretaries, technicians, professional people, and supervisory personnel spend their time during a working day. On the average he found that such people spend two-thirds of their time in some form of communications. With the proliferation of microprocessors into office and home, it is likely that by 1990 that percentage will rise and that new communication technology will be the principal instrument for such interchanges.

One example has been provided by Alvin Toffler as he describes the Third Wave society with its "electronic cottage," made up of "home communication centers" where families have the opportunity not only to play together, but to study and work together. Many consultants and other "knowledge" workers have already closed their "away-from-home" offices and set up business in their residences. Workforces, which are being transformed from blue to white collar or technical employment, are also being transferred to the employees' homes. Some estimates claim that up to 50% of existing manufacturing and labor can be done in home "workshops" with the installation of existing word processors, computer/telephone hook-ups, facsimile machines, teleconferencing equipment, and computer consoles. While one hears much about the revolution in office automation, companies are beginning to question if such offices are even necessary and experimenting with employee residential work programs.

In a research study on "The Practicalities of Work at Home" for a Diebold Office Automobile Program (1981), Dr. Margrethe Olson of New York University interviewed clerical workers, managers, and professionals already working out of their home. She found benefits cited for the individuals and the organizations that employed them. The personnel favored the advantages in reduced stress and costs in commuting, child and family care opportunities, and more flexibility in work schedules. But there were also problems of social isolation and the need for family cooperation. The home approach is not for every worker, but it seems to have possibilities for those who can work independently and are self-motivated, especially with software engineers, some technical managers, and data entry clerks.

If synergy is to occur in the partnership of human with computer, with office and home work, then innovative educational endeavors are necessary to prepare people for this profound transformation of our society, relationships, and careers. Such preparation goes beyond better training of computer programers and analysts, or improved communication skills with the computer, because it involves attitudinal change toward the new technology and the prospects it offers to improve the human condition. It goes beyond the expansion of computer-assisted instruction at every level of learning, or the introduction of more computer and computerized courses in the curriculum. It demands the *reeducation* of teachers and trainers toward the computer and other educational technology; similar efforts must eventually extend to the whole adult education field. True synergy occurs when First and Second World nations use this new technology to advance learning and work in Third World countries, so the less developed of the human family can "leap frog" into the emerging information society.

STRATEGIES FOR SYNERGISTIC LEARNING

There are many ways to educate personnel in cooperation and collaboration, apart from the use of electronic technology. The primary means is in the method of instruction. Experiential or affective learning, combined with cognitive and task educational activities, appears to be the most effective based on the authors' experiences. In our companion volume, *Managing Cultural Differences*, we addressed training theory and methods, especially with reference to cross-cultural human development. An observation made there is pertinent here: "To avoid a clash in cultural assumptions and training disasters, an intercultural synergy is required between trainer and trainees' needs, values, assumptions, attitudes, and information; and between human resource development needs in general and the needs of the delivery system or training sponsor." Thus, before one can teach about collaborative relations and skills, there must be a cooperative spirit and approach between the educator and the learner.

Furthermore, it is our conviction that *action learning* is a viable strategy toward any type of education and training, and that a *systems approach* is desirable. The case for this is made on pages 176-177.

Appendix C provides valuable resources for the educator or trainer seeking variety in his or her attempts to promote human synergy. Books have been suggested there that review educational methods and training techniques for this purpose, as well as sources of learning materials and aids. However, let us review here three strategies in particular that have proven effective for fostering collaborative skills and generating synergy. Most of these have been perfected by behavioral scientists in the field of human relations training:

Team Building. To facilitate cooperation within a group, such as a project team, or between organizational groups, such as between two departments, this intensive learning experience brings participants together in sessions that examine the

Orientation to Action Learning*

Those in the field of human resource development must eventually get involved in training. The design, implementation and evaluation of adult education programs for staff and clients are part of the developmental process. For these experiences to be meaningful and impactful, we suggest that the action-learning approach be utilized.

Essentially, this methodology involves the trainee in the educational process and gives the primary responsibility for learning to the student. In other words, it is based upon "learning by doing." A more formal definition of *action learning* would be—a form of training that emphasizes variety of methodology and maximum participation by the learner, usually by means of some form of group process. This approach, most appropriate in adult education, is utilized throughout this study. Learning is promoted by group data gathering, analyzing and reporting.

Rationale

In general, action learning has these characteristics:

1. *Situational:* it is inservice education or on-the-job training that has as its target *change* in the work situation or in the person who receives the training in the work or therapy situation. It is most effective when it concentrates on training a work unit or team. By providing time for practice in the learning session, the learner has an opportunity to internalize knowledge.
2. *Experiential:* it makes the prime focus of training data gathered by participants in the learning experience or provided by them from previous experience.
3. *Plural:* it emphasizes both affective and cognitive learning; its concern is for both feelings and ideas; it should be a balance of the "I feel" and the "I think."
4. *Problem-orientation:* it deals with issues for personal and organizational change and provides practice in processes for problem-solving and decision-making; it aims for action not only in the learning process, but also in the follow-up as a result of training.
5. *Systematic:* it envisions the training effort as only a sub-system of a larger system for human resource development; it is given as part of a total program for personal and professional growth; it is viewed as an essential component for broader organization development. The systems approach can also be applied to the actual training process itself.
6. *Personalized:* although group process may be utilized, due consideration is given to individualizing the learning so as to make allowance for each trainee's unique needs, perceptions and expectations. Action-learning, futhermore, provides performance standards for the trainee by setting goals. It also offers a means for self-assessment by using feedback and group evaluation.

Action-learning is based on certain assumptions about the learner and educational methodology. As stated by Dr. Malcolm Knowles, the noted adult education specialist, these assumptions are:

1. Adults enter a learning activity with an image of themselves as self-directing, responsible grown-ups, not as immature, dependent learners. Therefore they resist situations in which they are treated with disrespect. *Implication for methodology;* if adults help to plan and conduct their own learning experiences, they will learn more than if they are passive recipients.

---

*From *Organizational Dynamics* by P. R. Harris, La Jolla, CA: Harris International, 1980.

2. Adults enter a learning activity with more experience than youth. Therefore, they have more to contribute to the learning activity and have a broader basis of experience to relate to new learning. *Implication for methodology:* those methods which build on and make use of the experience of the learners will produce the greatest learning.
3. Adults enter a learning activity with a different quality of experience and different developmental tasks than youth. *Implication for methodology:* the appropriate organizing principle for adult learning experiences is developmental sequences primarily and logical subject development only secondarily.
4. Adults enter a learning activity with more immediate intentions to apply learning to life problems than youth. Therefore, adults require practical results from learning. *Implication for methodology:* adults will perceive learning experiences that are organized around subject topics.

The behavioral change sought in the learner as a result of the training should be in terms of:

1. Knowledge
2. Insight and understanding
3. Skills
4. Attitudes
5. Values
6. Interests

The conditions necessary for action-learning involve:

1. Recognition of trainee's needs
2. Integration of learner's and trainer's goals for learning
3. Encouragement of active role in the process of learning by learner
4. Provision for measurable criteria toward learning goals
5. Threat-free climate of acceptance and freedom
6. Competency and skill on part of the training facilitator ∎

impact of one's behavior on another and ways to improve interpersonal and organizational relations. In a prior chapter on "Synergy in Team Management" we described somewhat this methodology, but it can be applied to teachers on a faculty, trainers in an HRD division, top managers of an organization, or role peers from various subsidiaries. Team-building activities examine reporting procedures to supervisors; perceptions of members by members and other groups; barriers to communication and joint action; practices that enhance collaboration, role clarifications and analysis of responsiblities; improving problem diagnosis and solving; group relations and interfaces with the rest of the organization; group goal setting; and action planning. The process emphasizes "feelings" as well as "thinking," plus human factor data-gathering and analysis. It is a strategy used in organization development (OD). See Chapter 7.

Simulation. This is a form of inductive learning that creates a situation in a classroom that is similar to the real life experience. It recreates a family, social, or job environment in a controllable form. It may be a cooperation game in elementary school, or a management game in a corporation or agency, where it may involve group dynamic exercises that promote "consensus." In training sessions, organizational leaders may be asked to engage in "the in-basket exercise," which simulates the decision-making related to handling the manager's morning mail, or "the hollow square" game, which divides the group into two teams that must develop a plan for assembling cardboard pieces that form a square with a hollow or empty center. Operators within the group must then assemble the pieces according to the plan and within a time limit. Observers then evaluate the interpersonal factors during the process and report back their findings after the exercise. The real learning takes place when the total group analyzes what happened in terms of participation, cooperation, and communication during the game, and how much such behavior is found back on the job. The educator can make up such short-term group experiences, or purchase a commercial product. Simile II (P.O. Box 910, Del Mar, Ca. 92014, USA) custom designs such simulations to meet specific client needs, and then makes them available commercially. Some examples of their products useful in training for synergy are *Starpower,* a game on the use or abuse or organizational power; *Crisis,* on international conflict; *Guns or Butter,* on international relations; *Humanus,* on change and the future; *Bafa, Bafa,* on the interactions and interchanges between culture. Another useful publisher for this purpose issues an annual catalog - Didactic Systems (Box 475, Cranford, N.J. 0710, USA). They combine a cognitive with experiential learning in such simulation games as *Effective Supervision, Handling Conflict in Management, Managing in a Foreign Culture,* and *Women in Management.*

Computer simulations permit modeling of actual or potential situations, so that the learner interacts with the machine and may make mistakes in this manner, rather than in life experiences. Simulations of this type have been used to instruct pilot trainees about flying and MBA students about projected results of decision-making. Software can be obtained for marketing, production, and management games, such as the popular Harvard Andlinger Game, which IBM provides for its computers. Programmed instruction can also be combined through computers and word processors. *Simulations & Games* is an international journal of theory, design and research in this field (Sage Publications, 275 South Beverly Drive, Beverly Hills, CA. 90212, USA).

Case Studies and Critical Incidents. To avoid abuse of human energy in meaningless conflict, and to facilitate people working together effectively, the educator may create or purchase problem-solving cases of real situations or specific incidents. These may be written, video- or audio-taped, or dramatized for group analysis and learning. The Harvard case studies and methods are widely used in schools of business and in training. In our preceding text, *Managing Cultural Differences,* we have provided five different types of case studies and critical incidents for use in cross-cultural training (Chapters 15, 16, and 17). The point is to use real issues, concerns, experiences of people relative to cooperation or the lack of it in a way so that actual persons, names, events, and groups are somewhat camouflaged and cannot be identified.

When the U.S. Customs had problems of prejudice and bias within its own workforce, the authors created video cassettes of situations similar to those reported by management. The critical incidents were role played to a point of climax, and then the situation was opened to Customs' officials for problem-solving and arrival at consensus on the proper and preferred action. The same technique could be done based on feedback from expatriates on critical issues they confronted successfully on overseas assignments; then the videotapes could be used in the training of those to be deployed abroad in order to promote their acculturation.

The publications in group dynamics and human relations offer descriptions of many educational methods and techniques that can be utilized to help people work together more effectively, even when there are cross-cultural differences. These range from various forms of role play and socioguidramas, to three dimensional media in which the person responds to a film/slide creation, to brainstorming and creative problem-solving. (Obtain catalog from University Associates/Learning Resources, 8517 Production Ave., San Diego, CA 92121 USA.)

Synergy in Global HRD

Possibly the most innovative way to cultivate synergy in education and training is to go outside one's own field and or discipline, as well as one's own culture or country, to seek out new insights and approaches that work. It may require reading trade and professional journals beyond one's normal perusal, or to shift from national to international or foreign journals and publications. For example North Americans may find it worthwhile to read the Europeans *Journal of Human Resource Development or HRD International Journal* (see Appendix C). Ideally, one should be able to obtain creative ideas from "foreign" professional books and periodicals in the language in which they are originally written.

There are numerous illustrations of how transnational exchanges can promote synergy in international education. Perhaps a triad of examples will make the point here:

NIE Study of Corporation-Academic Cooperation. In April 1981, the National Institute of Education (part of the U.S. Dept. of Education) announced an invitation for proposals for a study on *The Academy and the Corporation: The Educational and Employment Effects of Cooperative Arrangements.* The project is described as follows: "Corporations have established joint ventures with educational institutions for the education of their employees. This study will analyze a sample of such ventures to determine their educational and employment outcomes and their benefits, if any, to employees, employers, and educational institutions."

Department of Defense Dependent School System. Spanning the globe and offering a unique opportunity for cross-cultural learning and synergy by teacher and student, this system enrolls 140,000 students from kindergarten through grade 12 throughout the world. Over 11,000 teachers and staff are spread out in 273 schools in 23 countries and there is a low turn-over rate. This educational system operates on an annual budget currently at $468 million.

Providing learning opportunities for children of American military dependents, it has a rare opportunity not only to produce cosmopolitan graduates, but cross-cultural education when it takes advantage of the indigeneous environment and culture. Yet one wonders how much inservice training in cultural awareness and synergy is provided to teachers, and through them to pupils?

International Professional Seminars or Conference. These gatherings increasingly offer synergistic learning that not only crosses cultures, but also ideologies. Many European professional and trade meetings bring together for an information exchange people from both sides of the Iron Curtain. The workshops and annual meeting of Diebold Europe, for instance, brings together management information specialists from democratic and socialist nations, and the intellectual transactions are extended into personal and social encounters that produce unexpected, positive results. When the Communication Association of the Pacific met in Guam in 1980, Asians and Americans shared insights with their Micronesian colleagues. Again, when The International Management Seminar of the Pacific Basin Economic Council met that same year in Taipei, participants jointly examined how the many countries in that geographic area would become the world's new investment place. PBEC provides a forum for the sharing of private sector views and understanding of transnational economic policies; and for developing a more cooperative relationship among countries bordering on the Pacific.

Therefore, whether they involves students and scholars, politicans or businessmen, international interchanges of this type frequently result in collaborative endeavors.

Another area for synergistic efforts is in the global exchange of foreign students at all levels of education. In the United States, for instance, there were more than a quarter million foreign students at the beginning of the '80s, only in colleges and universities. What incomparable opportunities for intercultural synergy in learning if American professors and educational staffs were culturally sensitive to the needs of these foreign visitors; if language and social science teachers combined their talents to further the learning and accultural of these students; and if these seekers of knowledge were encouraged and motivated to return home and make appropriate application of their new wisdom.

Synergy Through the Multinationals

Some have described the multinational corporations (MNC's) as the new educators and creators of culture. In addition to their commercial activities, such transnational enterprises are also in the business of education and training. The range extends from international conference centers where their managers and executives gather to learn to industrial training courses for natives in preindustrialized countries. Some of these companies devote whole divisions and subsidiaries to the task of human resources development. With each transfer of technology from one country to another, an accompanying instructional system must be provided. Many Third World contracts, funded by the World Bank loans, require extensive training programs. All of these educational efforts are in themselves examples of intercultural synergy. How much more impact could occur if the synergy did not occur by happenstance, but corporate HRD personnel consciously sought to teach cooperation and collaboration in representatives of both macro- and microcultures.

Professor Yoram Zeira of Tel Aviv University suggests that training directors in MNC's can be more effective as change agents in increasing organizational and personnel effectiveness. He believes an MCN's educational planning should consider these four human components: the headquarter officials, the expatriate managers, the host-country nationals, and the representatives of host-country organizations.[14] Zeira's research indicates a lack of synergy in these elements because each perceives present and desired training activities differently. By not seeking inputs from the four components for cooperative planning, effectiveness in their mutual interactions is reduced. What is hopeful is that this study of 77 MNC's throughout the world indicated a willingness of the part of the respondents to collaborate in planned change. There were enough similarities among the four groups that a training director could bring them together to limit dysfunctional impacts and promote organizational effectiveness that benefits host country operations.[15]

Opportunities for education and training through global corporations can be best appreciated in the case of one such entity, AT&T. In the U.S. Bell System, for instance, 12,000 courses are offered in 1300 training locations for 20-30,000 employees per day. In this impressive educational system in 1980, there were thousands of training support staff members involved at a cost of $1.7 billion. The HRD effort is for 1 million employees of Bell. The magnitude of corporate education can be seen in an MNC like Westinghouse, which also has its own learning corporation subsidiary and education center. It has been estimated that about 5,000 managers each year are enrolled in various seminars and work shops just in their U.S. operations with a budget of approximately $2 million.

Synergistic possibilities with such transnational enterprises occur when third parties intervene to link these corporate educational systems with each other, or with national needs. For example, many Third World contracts for MNC's require extensive training of the indigenous population by company technicians and managers. Third World governments are also issuing requests for proposals that require the contract to train their own overseas personnel in the local customs and culture. Furthermore, some developing countries sending employees to America or Europe for technical training also insist that upon arrival in the technologically advanced nation, those people receive training in English as a second language and in the host culture.[16] Another illustration of third-party involvement is the American Council on Education (One Dupont Circle, Washington, D.C. 20036, USA), which is seeking collaboration of corporations in the implementation of their Higher Education Management Institute. This is an action-oriented management and organizational development scheme using extensive needs assessment and fifty plus training modules. The American Society for Training and Development has cooperated in the endeavor to bring about institutional change in 150 colleges and universities by improvement of their own managerial practices. ACE now wishes to obtain the assistance of experienced management and organization development consultants from industry to aid in the planned renewal of these institutions of higher education, so their operations will be more effective and their offerings more relevant.

Conclusion

Those concerned about global human resource development should seek synergistic opportunities. Joint educational and training ventures between public and private sectors, between formal and informal educational efforts, and between home and host culture enterprises can be beneficial to all parties. The complicated educational problems and challenges in this superindustrial age of transition demands such collaboration.

An international approach to all education and training can become a powerful means of ensuring global human rights and dignity, and of combating prejudice and enthnocentrism. UNESCO, a powerful force for synergy in the world community, recommends that teachers be prepared to foster international understanding. In study that involved 82 countries UNESCO pointed out how educators and trainers can develop mutual appreciation of "Eastern" and "Western" cultural values, reduce intergroup tensions, and improve relationships between school and community.

References

1. Bowman, J., Kierstead, F., and Dede, C. *The Far Side of the Future: Social Problems and Social Reconstruction; Educational Futures: Sourcebook.* Washington, D.C.: World Future Society, 1979.
2. Casse, P. *Training for the Cross-Cultural Mind.* Washington, D.C.: The Society for Intercultural Education, Training and Research, 1980.
3. Bullock, A. and Stallybrass, O. (eds.) *The Harper Dictionary of Modern Thought.* New York: Harper & Row, 1977.
4. Miller, V.A. *The Guidebook for International Trainers in Business and Industry.* New York: Van Nostrand Reinhold, 1979.

5. Nadler, L. *Developing Human Resources*. San Diego, CA: University Associates/Learning Concepts, 1979. *Corporate Human Resources Development*. New York: Van Nostrand Reinhold, 1980.

6. de Rosnay, J. *Le macroscope: Vers une vision globale (The Macroscope: Towards a Global Vision)*, Paris: Editions du Seuil, 1975.

7. Warren, M.W. *Training for Results: A Systems Approach to the Development of Human Resources in Industry*. Reading, Mass.: Addison-Wesley, 1979.

8. The President's Commission of Foreign Language and International Studies. *Strength Through Wisdom*, November 1979. Available through ACTL, Room 1814, 2 Park Avenue, New York, NY 10016. USA.

9. Pitman, W. In: *Through the '80s: Thinking Globally, Acting Locally*. Washington, D.C.: World Future Society, 1980.

10. Botkin, J. In: *Through the '80s: Thinking Globally, Acting Locally*. Washington, D.C.: World Future Society, 1980.

11. Wilson, A. and Wilson, D. "Towards the Institutionalization of Change," working paper, Institute of the Future, Menlo Park, Calif., 1980.

12. World Future Society. *The Future: A Guide To Information Sources*, 1977. (World Future Society, 4916 St. Elmo Ave., Washington, D.C. 20014, USA)

13. Harris, P.R. and Malin, G.H. (eds.) *Innovation in Global Consultation*. Washington, D.C.: International Consultants Foundation, 1980.

14. Zeira, Y. "The Role of the Training Director in Multinational Corporations," *Training and Development Journal*, March 1979.

15. Freeman, O.L. "Multinational Corporations: Hope for the Poorest Nations," *The Futurist*, December 1980.

16. Kumar, K. and McLeod, M.G. *Multinationals from Developing Countries*. Lexington, MA: Lexington/D.C. Heath, 1981.

10.
Promoting
Synergistic Leadership

THE CONCEPT OF THE SYNERGISTIC SOCIETY

Leadership occurs within a context, and for our purposes, we will examine it within the framework of the world community, not as it is or has been, but as it must be. In this postindustrial period it would appear that the type of global culture, which humans need to create for survival and development, is remarkably akin to Ruth Benedict's "synergistic society"[1]—a term she developed to differentiate cultures. At first she compared cultures on the basis of geography, race, climate, size, wealth, complexity, and even "nice" or "nasty." Finally, she settled upon a taxonomy that described the function of behavior— the meaning of one's behavior in that culture. Rather than just look at overt behavior itself, she sought what the behavior purported, the character structure it expressed. "Suicide," for instance, has different meanings in various cultures. In some countries it is considered a psychological catastrophe, while in others it may be an honorable act; or the loving duty of wife/sister/mother in the extravagance of mourning and reaffirmation that in the death of the male relative, life is no longer worthwhile; or, as in some tribes, it is an accepted way of revenge by someone who feels wronged.

It was the late humanistic psychologist, Abraham Maslow, who brought these insights of Benedict to our consciousness after her death. In 1964, Maslow wrote a commentary on Benedict's lecture notes on the subject of high and low synergy, which was her way of distinguishing the general trends or characteristics of specific cultures. Maslow then added his own observations to this conceptual model for explaining why people behave as they do in specific cultural contexts.[2] The synergistic thinking of these two eminent social scientists is synthesized on page 185.

High-Synergy Society	Low-Synergy Society
• Emphasis is upon cooperation for mutual advantage.	• Uncooperative, very competitive culture; enhances rugged individualistic and "dog-eat-dog" attitudes.
• Conspicuous for a nonaggressive social order.	• Aggressive and antagonistic behavior toward one another, leading to either psychological or physical violence toward the other.
• Social institutions promote individual and group development.	
• Social idealizes win/win, virture pays, victory for all.	• Social arrangements self-centered; selfishness, not collaboration, is reinforced as desired behavior.
• Leadership fosters that wealth and advantage should be shared for the common good. Cooperatives are encouraged, and poverty is fought.	• Society adheres to win/lose approach; victory over one another.
• Society seeks to utilize community resources and talents for the commonwealth and encourages development of human potential of all citizenry.	• Leadership encourages private or individual gain and advantage, especially by the power elite; poverty is tolerated, even ignored.
	• Society permits exploitation of poor and minorities, and tolerates the siphoning of its wealth by privileged few; develops power elites and leaves undeveloped the powerless.
• Open system of secure people who tend to be benevolent, helpful, friendly, and generous; its heros are altruistic and philanthropic.	• Closed system with insecure people who tend toward suspiciousness, ruthlessness and clannishness; idealizes the "strong man" concerned with greed and acquisition.
• Belief system, religion or philosophy is comforting and life is consoling; emphasis is on the god of love; power is to be used for benefit of whole community; individuals/groups are helped to work out hurt and humiliations.	• Belief system is frightening, punishing, terrifying; members are psychologically beaten down or humiliated by the strong; power is for personal profit; emphasis is on the god of vengence; hatreds go deep and "blood feuds" abound; violence is the means for compensating for hurt and humiliation.
• Generally, the citizenry is psychologically healthy, and mutual reciprocity is evident in relationships; open to change; low rate of crime and mental illness.	• Generally, the citizenry tends to be defensive, jealous, and envious; mass paranoia and hostility; fears change and advocates status quo; high rate of crime and mental illness. ∎

Professor Benedict cited many American Indian tribes whose culture could be described as high synergy, and we all have experienced visits to cultural groups that would largely fit in the low-synergy category. Some of the latter's features seem to dominate many industrial cultures, especially in totalitarian states. Whether it be a macro- or microculture, the reader can identify groups and nations that possess high or low synergy. Our point is that leadership today in a complex, information society, must consciously work toward the creation of high synergy, whether in a government, community association, or multinational corporation.

James and Margaret Craig have written of the need for leaders to facilitate the creation of high rather than low synergy structures, interactions, and practices:

> *High-synergy* structures, interactions, and practices: any way of behaving and structuring groups that maximizes coordination, information flow, and continuity; that gives everyone easy access to information needed for conscious, informed choices. A high energy climate builds trust and good feelings, encourages truth and clear intent; fosters creativity and excellence.
>
> *Low-synergy* structures, interactions, and practices: any way of behaving and organizing—of ranking people—that concentrates power in the hands of one or a few, leaving most feeling powerless. Any thing or action that makes open communication and cooperation difficult, fosters competition, and restricts information flow so that people feel "in the dark," and cannot make conscious, informed choice. A low synergy climate diminishes trust, arouses resentments, mystifies, belittles many of the persons interacting, and stifles their creativity and contribution.[3]

IMPLICATIONS FOR LEADERSHIP

The *Random House Dictionary* defines a leader as "one who guides, directs, conducts"; while leadership is described as "the position or function or ability to lead others." We hope to build upon the groundwork on leadership layed out in Chapter 3, by providing pragmatic examples of synergistic leadership opportunities.

For the past 30 years behavioral science research has focused upon the *function* of leadership. The consensus is that leadership style should be situational; that is, appropriate to the time, place, culture, and people involved. Thus, the leader should operate within a continuum as described in Figure 10-1. However, in a postindustrial organization within an advanced, technological society, the middle to right hand range of the continuum is preferable, especially when dealing with knowledge workers. The words in the center of the continuum highlight the dominant style in each leadership posture from telling to complete delegation. The diagonal line symbolizes the delicate balance between leader authority and group freedom. This balance shifts according to whether the authority is shared or centered in the ruling person or class. For example, an authoritarian leader dictates policy and tells group members, whereas, in a group that has much freedom and authority is wholly shared, the leader abdicates total control in favor of total delegation.

In modern, more democratic societies and organizations the trend is away from leadership centered in a single person, to members of a group contributing toward

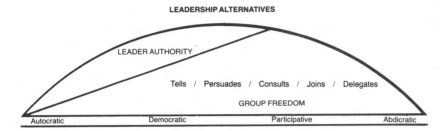

LEADERSHIP ALTERNATIVES

LEADER AUTHORITY

Tells / Persuades / Consults / Joins / Delegates

GROUP FREEDOM

| Autocratic | Democratic | Participative | Abdicratic |

Figure 10-1. Leadership is situational and operates within a continuum of alternative styles, as conceptually illustrated here.

the leadership function by sharing talents and resources. The research of social scientists confirms that participation and involvement of members in the decision-making process can result in more effective and productive behavior. In terms of participative management this principle is expressed as follows: those who will be substantially affected by decisions should be involved in those decisions. But it takes a skillful and competent leader to implement such an ideal.

Douglas McGregor distinguished between the traditional and emerging leader-ship assumptions and styles by using the terms, X and Y. A Theory X leader would be on the left side of the aforementioned continuum, while a Y leader would be at the opposite end with more consulting, joining and delegation. Likert described four human systems: Systems I/II would have X-type leaders using McGregor's terms, while Systems III/IV would be more participative. We discussed this in some depth in Chapter 8 of *Managing Cultural Differences* relative to changing organizational cultures, and in Chapter 3 of this book. What we wish to do here is to link these concepts of McGregor/Likert to Benedict/Maslow. The X leader and the I/II System are remarkably like the previously described low-synergy society or organization, while the high synergy is similar to the Y leader and III/IV Systems. McGregor's assumptions of a Y leader are that work is as natural as play; workers should be permitted to exercise self-direction and self-control in the ser-vice of committed objectives; such commitment is associated with their achieve-ment; the average human being seeks responsibility and will respond to the oppor-tunity to exercise it; many members of an organization have the capacity for crea-tivity, imagination, and problem-solving if given the chance to use it; and that the intellectual potential of the individual is being only partially utilized. The job of the leader is to provide a creative environment in which these capacities can be actualized.

For the world-be synergistic leader or manager the implications of all this is that we must first reexamine our conception of human nature and the assumptions upon which we "manage" others. Then we must literally create social or organizational cultures that reinforce the natural tendencies toward industriousness, responsi-bility, and planning for change. This requires renewal of the values that influence leadership styles, so as to emphasize creativity, collaboration, team work, mutual concern and service. Synergistic organizational or institutional forms encourage self-actualization. But throughout this process these new human systems must educate and train their members in new interpersonal and organizational skills, so that adherents can communicate and cooperate across cultures, and act together for mutual benefit. It also implies helping participants to conserve and develop human and natural resources for the common good. Finally, it means that leaders must acquire and practice a new synergistic form of power; namely, that of group initiative and cooperative action.

A Dutch business school dean has translated these concepts into the context of the modern corporation. Professor Cornelius Brevoord suggests a Theory Z form of leadership, based on goal-setting, that structures and runs the organization.[4] This is of creative benefit to its personnel and produces wealth in a socially and scientifically responsible manner. The new function of management, then, is to promote the right combination of the system's elements, that is, the interacting equal forces of people, goals, structures, and technology. Effective management enables the system to respond rapidly and adequately to a changing environment or society.

To achieve this, Thomas Horton of IBM suggests that leadership in the future will require more spirit.[5] In addition to technical mastery, mental and physical vigor, interpersonal skills, integrity and courage, he believes leaders must manifest more of their inner selves or psyche. This requires personal cultivation of one's intuition, ingenuity, sensitivity, and humanistic qualities. Then, perhaps, one may become a synergistic leader who is in tune with both intrapersonal and interpersonal needs, and who can fuse the cognitive with the affective for effective action . Only as we transcend ourselves can we transform our society. Greiff and Munter believe leadership involves the practice of the art of compromise. In their recent book, *Tradeoffs: Executives, Family, and Organizational Life* they imply that executives must create a synergy between three microcultures—personal, family, and organizational.[6]

SYNERGISTIC LEADERSHIP MODELS

Rather than being a utopian dream, there are numerous examples of synergistic leadership around us for those who can comprehend. The point of our volume is that this should become the norm in emerging cultures, not the exception. Perhaps we can illustrate our point best by citing excerpts from public or professional media that demonstrate synergy in practice.

Sharing Information. In contrast to exclusivity and secretiveness that characterized business and professional competitors in the past, trade fairs, conventions, and publications of an industry or field become mechanisms for sharing and cooperating. Two contemporary innovations elucidate the concept: The Center for International Business in Dallas and The Electronic Information Exchange System. The Center, formed by 18 major corporations in Texas, provides its members and the public with professional development opportunities and publications. It also conducts an annual trade conference and special briefings for management on crucial issues. The Electronic Information Exchange System is a pay-as-you-go information marketplace and network operated by the New Jersey Institute of Technology. It provides feedback on R and D proposals and evaluations, marketing and purchasing of services, and new computer developments and meetings.

Technology Transfer. When management and consultants from Western culture are sensitive to the needs of another culture and adapt their technology accordingly, synergy occurs. Cross-cultural use of the microcomputer is taking place for education, training, professional information exchange. For example, electric typewriters, computers, and software have been modified in Arabic, so that Middle Easterners can use the technology in both their own language and English.

The *Canadian Petroleum Daily News* reports that mobility is increasing for oil and gas company employees who are required on short notice to pick up lock, stock, barrel and family for transfer to a new job somewhere else in the world. To foster acculturation, and improved work performance and relations with the host nations, this industry publication reports on the activities of the Metzler Centre in Alberta. It offers relocation orientation seminars for personnel in the energy industry and their families. The innovative program assists the entire family to adjust and to develop realistic expectations toward working and living in their new environment.

Participative Management. Employees can become a powerful means for organizational renewal and problem-solving when management gives them an opportunity to be heard and to assist. One example of labor-management synergy is Gorivaerk AS in the Jutland peninsula. After Nils Ehrenskjold, the owner, built a $6 million factory, he was appalled 13 months later to find the ultra-modern premises a scorched ruin. As he looked upon the devastation of accidental fire, his 140 employees rallied around their employer and gave him support to rebuild the facility. The workers set up make-shift production facilities with equipment they ordered. The quick response of this tightly knit organization made sure the company lost little of its market and retained its position as Scandinavia's largest manufacturer of wood preservatives. In seven months Gori went from ruin to recovery because of cooperation between managers and workers. But the roots go back 10 years to 1970, when Nil's father introduced participatory democracy into the plant. As a result, by 1980, the firm had jumped to being a $28 million annual business, which places high priority on nonpolluting products, as well as on employee relations and motivation. A quality product is again being made in a unique and very attractive spacious building, which even provides time and facility for the managing director to play table tennis with the workers.

Retired Executives. Instead of putting their brains and experience in storage, many former executives are using their senior years to consult with managers in small businesses, or to go overseas to assist Third World managers make their companies or programs more effective. Just as older Japanese executives are used as counselors to younger managers, the U.S. government has several agencies that utilize the services of retired managers.

International Tourism. With improved global communication and transportation, there has been a mass migration of peoples across borders as travelers. The world's middle class is on the move, spending their vacations visiting each other's countries in ever increasing numbers. Airline and travel industries have been slow in providing language and cultural training to their employees. But government agencies have been experimenting with such educational endeavors. The U. S. Customs, for instance, has established a language school at various ports of entry to provide foreign language studies for their officials.

In 1980, eight million Americans visited abroad, while approximately 10 million foreigners visited the United States. Management and university consultants are beginning to provide culture specific training to business and other groups seeking to attract and serve a particular visitor group in their country. One such example is the work of Dr. Kzuo Nishiyama of the University of Hawaii who has published a book, *Japanese Tourists Abroad,* and conducts seminars on the subject to promote synergy between Japanese travelers and their American hosts.[7]

European Parliament and Economic Community. Nine nations and cultures cooperated to form the Commission of the European Economic Community and its Common Market. In 1979, the diverse populations of this area have elected 410 members to a European Parliament who will speak 6 official languages and represent 50 national political groupings. Located in Strasbourg, it brings together a variety of leaders who have rapidly become a viable, independent political force. They are beholden to voters, not governments; they review all laws and regulations for EEC and control its budget. An instructive example of the federating process, it has great implications for the relationships between the various entities. For example, when the President of France and the Prime Minister of England met in 1980, their discussions focused on European unity and Europe's role in world affairs. P.M. Margaret Thatcher commenting on these new Anglo-Franco bonds noted:

> For a thousand years, our destinies have been linked. After China and Japan, we are the two oldest nation-states in the world. For two proud nations living side by side, there are bound to be rivalries. . . . Yet it is our common interests, not our past rivalries, which need to be emphasized now. For it is my strongest conviction that in the dangerous world in which we live, cooperation among neighbors is essential to the protection of our most vital interests. Our

differences must not be allowed to obscure the longer-term benefits and external dangers.

Quite a case for synergy among nations and their leaders.

International Exchange of Students. The foreign student has always presented a unique opportunity for synergistic leadership. He or she can be a bridge builder between cultures and peoples. Throughout the world there are numerous organizations engaged in the exchange of scholars at all levels of education.

For those aware of synergy, the daily press and professional newsletters present innumerable stories of people practicing cooperation and collaboration across cultures, be they macro or micro. Our newspapers at the beginning of this decade reported these accounts:

• Sudan has an ambitious plan to expend $50 million to resettle refugees from Eritrea, Ethiopia, Uganda, Zaire, and Chad. The projects include construction of entire new self-supporting towns to house half a million exiles from neighboring states.

• The U.S. Refugee Commission has prepared a 45-page booklet, "You're on Your Way," for Indochinese refugees bound for America. The guide gives tips to new immigrants on everything from Social Security cards and seat belts, to the need for baby diapers and no haggling about prices in supermarkets. The message is for simple villagers from Vietnam, Cambodia, Laos and other Asian nations who are being catapulted into an advanced technological society.

• After many meetings and negotiations, the U.N. Conference on the Law of the Sea produced a written constitution for the oceans of the world. The treaty of 150 participating nations will cover three-quarters of the earth's surface. The Chief U.S. delegate, Elliot L. Richardson said, "Historians will look back on this year's session as the most significant single event in the history of peaceful cooperation and the development of the rule of law since the founding of the United Nations itself."

• The challenge of integrating foreign guest workers into strange cultures strains international relations. World press reports range from illegal aliens in the U.S. to racist opposition to foreign workers in West Germany to problems in the Middle East. In the United Arab Emirates, for example, the Arabs are a minority as the growth of oil industries brought a flood of foreign technicians and laborers. With oil revenues of $16,000 per head in 1979, is it any wonder that the tiny emirates are overwhelmed by 400,000 Indians, Pakistanis, Bangladeshis, and Filipinos; and 300,000 Egyptians, Syrians, Palestinians, Lebanese, Somalis, Europeans, and Americans. There are only 230,000 local Bedouins who inhabit this desert state at the southwest tip of the Persian Gulf. Even the Army is largely made up of foreigners. Mass immigration has imported a potpourri of values and cultures which erode desert traditions and produced a cacophony of sights/sounds which bewilder the natives. The world's peoples just will not sit home quietly behind their own national borders!

• Even Communist societies offer many examples of synergy in one form or another. It ranges from the solidarity teams of Kampuchia (formerly Cambodia) to the new collective leadership of China's Zhao Ziyang as premier of the National People's Congress with Hua Guofeng, the Chief of the PRC's Communist Party. The latter will serve as co-captains of a team of technocrats, administrators, and economists. . . .Ancient Bulgaria has developed an interesting partnership with the modern Soviet Union. Long survivors of many invasions, the Bulgarians have acquired great skill going with the tide, maneuvering, getting by and managing. They adopt or copy Russian styles and practices in everything from uniforms, mausoleums and alphabet to media, party or political structure, and foreign policies. After all, the Russians did twice invade Bulgaria in its 1,300 year history, literally liberating the inhabitants from their oppressors—first in 1875, and again in 1944. . . .Soviet refugees also find it hard to grapple with life in an open society, but most eventually integrate into their new cultures. Some who come to America are baffled by a lack of an authoritarian system to direct their lives, by having to cope with democratic practices and opportunities.

• An intriguing demonstration of synergy is present in the Japanese American. The Nisei, so harassed in World War II, have produced the Sansei (third generation) who are providing synergistic leadership in the arts, rock music, filmmaking, and law enforcement throughout the United States. An increasing number of these acculturated citizens are faced with greater freedom and myriad career choices. One UCLA sociologist, Gene Levene, heads a massive Japanese-American Research Project indicating that one-third of the 2,000 surveyed were in professional occupations. USC anthropologist, Akemi Kikumura, notes that Sansei inherit the legacy of their parents' success and their Japanese grandparents' cultural heritage, so that they now go forth themselves into diverse fields and cultural diffusion. The UCLA psycholgist predicts the Sansei interracial marriage rate will jump from 55% today to 75% in the near future.

• In a knowledge revolution with its demands for instant technology transfer, strange bedfellows and synergies can be produced. Now the Portuguese who first settled in Angola centuries ago (1575) are returning to their former colony five years after they fled the revolution there. The same thing is happening in Marxist Mozambique. The reason is simple. The Portuguese have know-how, language skills, and need jobs. The newly freed African countries have crippled economies, shortages of trained people, and a need for foreign technicians and professionals. Despite the faults of their previous colonialism, the Portuguese did two things right in Africa—they built beautiful cities and intermarried to produce a multicultural society, of all colors in its citizenry. . . .Farther south in the native "kingdom" of Lesotho, the Outward Bound program brings together black and white South Africans for leadership development. In contrast to apartheid practiced by Afrikaan neighbors, the races here are mixed to promote racial harmony. Blacks and whites are linked together in mounteering exercises and team problem-solving. One of many Outward Bound camps in 17 countries, this effort gets its support from multinational corporations operating in South Africa.

• A recently elected prime minister of Japan, Zenko Suzuki, was chosen for his peacemaking abilities among the factions of his country's politics. A mild-mannered, soft-spoken man of infinite patience, Suzuki built his reputation within the Liberal Democratic Party as a "coordinator"—a person able to dispose of thorny issues while minimizing conflicts an soothing emotions of opposing interest groups. Coordination for him has been a technical exercise in resolving conflicts. In a former post, he stressed the need for socialization of capital and equipment in the fishing industry, and was responsible for transforming that industry by cooperatives. It was something encouraged by the then U. S. occupiers and which transformed the lives of poor fisherman.

Thus, evidence of synergistic leadership can be found in all countries, systems, and cultures. Obviously, from our earlier statements, some cultures lend themselves to cooperation and collaboration. Our thesis is that today's global interdependence makes it essential that leadership within a world in transition promote synergy. Modern leaders literally must be bridge builders across culture differences. This is true whether the challenge be national or organizational cultures. The whole trend in Europe toward codeterminism or industrial democracy is illustrative of this concept in action.

WOMEN SYNERGIZERS IN GLOBAL MANAGEMENT

In the literature of education and training today there is increasing emphasis on use of left/right brain learning activities. It appears that certain capacities are associated with either side of the cortex. Similarly, it is known that every person has qualities that are associated with either the female or male psyche. Holistic learning of males would include cultivation of those aspects commonly associated with the feminine character, and vice versa for the female. Furthermore, it has also been observed that one of the major problems with world leadership, whether political or corporate, is it male domination. Key decision-makers tend to be chauvinistic and skewed toward the male perception of "reality" and the male approach to problem-solving. If we are to have synergistic leadership, male and female thinking and powers must be intergrated. Perhaps the planet's persistent, unsolved problems—mass unemployment and hunger, violence and aggression, underutilization of human resources, etc.—exist partly because our attempts to manage them have been so lopsided. That is, over one half of the human race, women, are too frequently excluded from the decision-making process and the halls of power.

Human development will never achieve its potential as long as women are denied their right to share fully in the management of our social institutions. Some will argue that such a situation was only in the past, and characteristic of the hunting and agricultural stages of the human condition. But even in this so-called age of enlightenment, there are industrial societies that consistently deny women an opportunity to fully particpate in worklife, especially at the managerial levels. There are many factors throughout the world that constrain female leadership, but there are three that must be overcome if true synergy is to be achieved: (a) obsolete rural mindsets that restrict the role of women within a culture to that of wife and mother; (b) women's own inadequate self-images, which psychologically handicap them from greater self-fulfillment; and (c) male chauvinism, which underutilizes female talents or misuses women's competencies. Each of these constraints requires massive reeducation and attitude change, which is the objective of the universal women's liberation movement. Synergy is thwarted as long as beliefs, attitudes, and traditions in which distinctions are made of people's intrinsic worth on the basis of sex prevail. Whether aware of it or not, the sexist believes women are inferior and behaves accordingly. As with racism, it causes humankind to restrict development of its potential.

The following excerpts from "Women's Roles: A Cross-Cultural Perspective" illustrate the importance and ramifications of this issue:

The International Women's Year in 1975 marked the beginning of the United Nations Decade for Women. These activities were the catalysts for a global reexamination of the roles of women in present-day society. Development of active strategies to achieve equal participation in all aspects of economic, social and political life, and to increase the status of women were set as goals for the '80s.[8]

The near-universal recognition of women's political rights and the strength of their voting number in many countries are nowhere reflected in their direct role in government. . . .Though 99.5% of the women in the world are legally entitled to participate in politics, the number of women in public office remains in most countries appallingly low. In very few countries do women fill even 10% of such positions.[9]

The international manager needs access to a full range of behavioral and attitudinal skills. . . .Whereas women have been excluded and excluded themselves from most international assignments, a small group of women is beginning to demonstrate that the female international manager can be effective overseas. . . .Further research needs to be conducted on the decision-making criteria of women candidates themselves and of personnel responsible for overseas assignment decisions. . . .Through such investigations, management's ability to increase the effectiveness of their international personnel, regardless of gender, will be greatly increased.[10]

Relative to female workers in Japan, a White Paper issued from the Prime Minister's Office in January of 1978, stated that women's labor is valued at about one-half that of men. . . . .Culturally, the distinction between private self and public self, between inner feelings and expressed opinions, between one's actual talents and outward humility and modesty, are behavior patterns of long standing. Historically, education in both school and home has prepared women to become one who can be depended upon for nurturance, support, and service to others. Finding a personal sense of worth and strength through being depended upon is a strongly sanctioned social pattern. . . . .The necessity to cloak inner strength in outward passivity, however, can be a cultivated and often frustrating technique. There are those Japanese women who are confused by switching the self they present on the job. As one young unmarried women working in a radio station remarked, "I am often very puzzled sometimes when my boss wants me to come up with creative, original ideas, and then I have to walk behind him down the hall. Other times I offer a suggestion and he looks at me as if to say, "stay in your place." [11]

Readers concerned about women leadership should consult Appendix C for further information.

TOP MANAGEMENT AND SYNERGY

International Management, (1980), reports that chief executive officers (CEO) today may be spending 40% of their time in external activities as compared to 10% ten years ago. This is but one of the measures of the changing role of the CEO, particularly as a public figure demonstrating corporate social responsibility:

> Interdependence between the company and outside political, social, and economic forces, coupled with a climate of participation within the company, have profoundly affected the nature and scope of the job. The CEO has far less freedom of action than in the past. The notion of the leader working by consensus through a team has largely replaced that of a traditional power figure. Which is why the CEO has become a diplomat as well as a manager, a communicator as well as a decision maker.

Key executives are faced with increasing outside pressures, changing corporate boards, increased business operational complexities, greater uncertainities amid faster telecommunications, and altered value systems. Collaborative projects and joint ventures are the norm for top management as dynamic shifts of power occur among individuals, organizations, national and international institutions.

A study was conducted in 1981 of the perceptions of chief executive officers regarding the impact of contemporary socio-economic changes upon managerial and leadership activity. The researcher, Dr. Gerald Goll concluded:

1. That socio-economic change had substantial impact upon such activity, especially in terms of prioritization of the executive's time and energy

for such concerns. The CEO's perceived themselves as agents of change charged by those to whom they were accountable for increasing operational efficiency and responding to community needs.

2. That these executives perceived their leadership roles to be transformational; finding better ways to motivate subordinates toward achievement of organizational goals.

3. That these chief executives described themselves as interacting with two societies—the internal or organization, and the external or community. They then expressed frustration over the lack of control over these environments. [12]

The new role requires top leadership to be power brokers who promote synergy between and among the board, management teams, staff, and support services in a high-speed management information situation. The art is learning to grapple with uncertainties, intangibles, and unpredictables in a very dynamic and fluid global business environment. The *International Management* Eurosurvey confirmed again that top management must not only provide a model of motivation, but be skillful in communication, especially listening, and human relations. Furthermore, such a person must be a generalist, able to deal with the interrelated factors of the single management task, as well as be knowledgeable in group dynamics. Above all, the organizational leader must trust his or her own intuitions about people and situations, and utilize this talent often.

It is interesting to note here relative to some of the previous observations that most employees from various cultural backgrounds in several subsidiaries of a single multinational corporation preferred participative management. According to the cross-cultural study of Dietrich Schaupp, these same workers perceived that their leadership gave them less opportunity to participate. [13]. Although the sample is limited, the authors suspect that while much lip service is given to the necessity for leaders to promote participation and team work, there are still too many transnational enterprises where human resources are underutilized on that score.

The whole lifestyle of the corporate executive is undergoing profound change. Although willing to jet around the international marketplace, more are becoming unwilling to relocate families often. Spouses now frequently have careers of their own, and the "professional couple" needs skill in meshing their vocational lives in a satisfactory manner. The quality of executives' lives is taking on more significance. Thus, synergy is also called for in relation to professional and personal lives, office and home obligations.

Another dimension of executive leadership, which was discussed in a previous chapter, is the need for innovation and creative risk-taking. One critic of the American automotive industry, for example, wrote about the lack of executive invention and flair being responsible for too little significant technological innovation. Our research on the subject of high-achieving employees indicates that innovative, top-performing personnel at all levels need organizational support, especially from top management who themselves become success models of such behavior.

The whole thrust of both this book and its predecessor, *Managing Cultural Differences,* is that leadership should be culturally sensitive and skillful. Now two UK lawyers have written a book on *Troubleshooting International Business Problems,* which substantiates our position. Duckworth and Blackshaw maintain from experience that the multinational corporate troubleshooters must not only be sincere and trustworthy in international negotiations, but demonstrate respect for cultural differences. Perhaps their position is worthy of summary here:

> It is often said that the main obstacle to an increase in world trade is the lack of understanding of cultural differences. . . .To that extent, courtesy is more important than hard selling or bargaining. A knowledge of what is "appropriate" for the conduct of business or negotiation in any particular country pays dividends.[14]

Recently, a management consulting firm conducted a survey of 256 U.S. international executives, of whom 75% were born in America and spent an average of 88 days on business annually outside of North America. Almost 60% of the respondents spend 2-4 months abroad each year, while 25% spend more than 4 months overseas annually. Sixty percent of these international executives have lived outside their country in the course of their business careers for a median of 3.3 years abroad. Yet, only 44% expressed fluency in another language than English.[15] Since the question was not asked, one can only speculate on the degree of cross-cultural training that they had received in either their university education or from their companies. Such data not only underscores the need for human resource development, but points up the value of the recommendation of the President's Commission on Foreign Languages and International Studies. This government report (1979) specifically urged American business and labor to give more priority to foreign language and international studies training in their staff recruitment, as well as encouraging colleges and universities to include such studies in their business and labor offerings. Certainly anyone hoping to exert leadership in international business should have developed such competencies.

In 1980, Systran Corporation of Chicago surveyed a hundred American companies operating overseas. They found an average employee early-return rate of 30% and typical cost of $70,000. Further replacement costs relative to these same workers can rise to an additional 53% excess over that originally budgeted for the assignment. Finally, the study found that the average cost of transferring an international executive for foreign deployment to be $130,000 per family. Such figures should be incentive enough to top management to have a system for recruitment, selection, and orientation of expatriate managers and technicans, as well as to include cross-cultural training in any such leadership development. It is inconceivable that without this, the international executive would be in a position to promote synergy in the world marketplace.

Rensselaer Polytechnic Institute has developed a system for spotlighting leadership capabilities in MBA students. It is centered on three dimensions: daily management activities, targets or the people who are on the receiving end of the manager's actions, and relational factors. The relational factors include three different roles; director, motivator, and evaluator. Based on data from 400 managers in six companies, the findings emphasize the ability to motivate a technical or professional team as crucial.[16]

Executive recruiters also offer their experience on what is required for successful leadership in the executive suite. The use of such "headhunters" has spread rapidly in both Europe and the United States. They seek top management candidates who have a track record of accomplishment, and are flexible and mobile. Yet, a 1980 study by the National Association of Corporate and Professional Recruiters showed that only 60% were successful in their research for the right leader when relocation was involved.

Further, a synergistic leader must be able to manage stress in his or her own professional and personal life, and not overly induce such tension in subordinates. Frequently, the type who climbed to the top of the corporate ladder in the past was a Type A personality. Research confirms this to be achievement-oriented, competitive behavior, which also happens to be a significant factor in heart disease. Such leaders have been described as those who must do several things or tasks at once, schedule more activities into less time, fail to notice beauty in their surrounding environment, have difficulty sitting down and doing nothing, and become unduly irritated when forced to wait or to move slowly. They measure success in numbers or quantity, and play every game to win even when playing with children. They put excessive stress upon themselves, their fellow workers, and their families, and in effect, become anti-synergistic. This Type A profile seems prevalent within cultures, such as American, where children are conditioned to such behavior.

One cannot be a successful synergistic leader at the expense of self-deterioration or the deterioration of others. Yet, *Fortune* magazine succinctly described some CEO's of large corporations who were seemingly successful at the cost of exploiting their subordinates and competitors. Some admired them for their toughness and brutalization of their colleagues, whose time and service they absorbed at an unrelenting pace. For a time this industrial-age dinosaur may linger in the executive suite, but will eventually will become extinct. Contemporary transnational enterprises require a new leader capable of self-actualization through cooperation and collaboration with others.

Changing leadership patterns can be best illustrated in the emerging high technology field. Japan currently challenges America for domination of this new industry, and its major electronic manufacturers lead in sponsoring such innovation. In the United States, on the other hand, the *Fortune 500* corporations, such as General Electric, Westinghouse, and Western Electric, are bound by the traditional bureaucratic structure of the industrial age and have forfeited the high-tech leadership to small, maverick manufacturers. These new manufacturers' executives do not follow the old leadership patterns of the aging industrial giants. A collegial tone typifies the new superindustrial organization, characterized by young technicians who ignore corporate formalities and "perks" of the past. As James Flanigan observed:

> There is no executive dining room in the Dallas headquarters of Texas Instruments Inc, world's largest manufacturer of semiconductors with $3.2 billion in annual sales. . . .At the Palo Alto-based Hewlett-Packard Co., world leader in electronic instruments, the office of Chief Executive John A. Young is an 8-by-10 foot area with linoleum covered floor, set apart by two glass partitions. At Intel Corporation in Santa Clara, the $660 million sales, 12-year-old pioneer in microcomputing, the chief executive wears an open-neck shirt and a gold chain. Many of the employees are less formally attired—in jeans.[17]

The knowledge workers create a new style of management in which informality, egalitarianism, and creative risk-taking are very much in evidence among these forward-looking business innovators. Bright university graduates avoid the tired bureaucracies with their layers of management procrastinators, and seek competitive challenge in smaller entities marked by rapid information flow and decision-making, *collegiality,* and more shared responsibility. This new type of worker is involved in his or her own job design, goal-setting, and self-assessment. These new adhocracies tap employee creativity and entrepreneurial aggressiveness, and respond quickly to changing opportunities. The values of such organizational cultures feature simplicity over status, alternative career paths and rewards over titles, and management meetings in which people are expected to present and defend unusual ideas. Executives are expected to motivate by example, and set the pace for a confident and exciting business environment filled with creative tension and security for top performers.

OPPORTUNITIES FOR SYNERGISTIC LEADERSHIP

The world today needs individuals of all sexes, races, and nationalities who will exercise planetary leadership in promoting cooperation among opposing or complementary forces. There are numerous human endeavors that may get nowhere in their solitary independence, but may flourish if their participants realized their interdependence on the "others" and practiced collaboration. Perhaps the best way to illustrate these occasions for synergy is through the following series of quotations:

> • A new way of thinking, according to Buckminster Fuller, is *synergy,* which helps to free one from outdated patterns and can break the shell of permitted ignorance. To this futurist the word means "the behavior of whole systems that cannot be predicted by the behavior of any parts taken separately." It is a somewhat reverse explanation of the usual definition of the term. For exam-

ple, from ancient to contemporary times scientists have made observations about the mathematical coordination between the planets and the sun. Yet there is nothing in one of the bodies that tells us whether it is going to attract or be attracted by another. Only by observing the macro/microbehavior of the universe, we get clues. The very integrity of the universe, Fuller maintains, is implicit in synergy, and there is a hierarchy of synergies. There is nothing in atoms that predicts the behavior of molecules; nor do the latter predict behavior of protoplasm; nor in that latter that predicts ecological energy-exchanging, and regenerative coordination of all living species. . . .The universe is a synergy of synergies. Fuller says the corollary of synergy is that known behavior of a few of the parts enables discovery of other parts. But in order to really understand what is going on, we have to abandon starting with parts, and we must *work instead from whole to particulars!* To be successful in cyberculture, we need to overcome obsolete conditioning or inadequate systems.[18]

• Joint ventures and mergers, according to Charles Tavel, can produce international cooperation through the concept of "coupling." The author of *The Third Industrial Age* explains that as the formation of a holding company for diverse partners from different countries and cultures. It permits the transfer of technology and information among relatively independent partners, and leads to complementarity. For example, a company from Western Europe may have developed a product that is effective and captured the market on that continent. Similarly, another corporation in North America has a complementary product which has done something similar with the market on its continent. The two firms then couple and exchange products and markets. They cooperate in R & D, product diversification, capital investment, and global policy. These independent partners may even establish a world-wide polycentric organization as a result of their synergistic experience.

• Third World transnational enterprises, according to Krishna Kumar, are increasing rapidly among the developing countries themselves. The East-West Center scholar's several books on the subject point up the compatability of Third World nations who have foreign subsidiaries and joint ventures in other nations at similar stages of economic development. Firms from countries such as Argentina, Brazil, Hong Kong, India, Singapore, South Korea, Taiwan, and the Philippines have taken the lead in this regard. These multinationals work in every sector of the world economy, and their representatives are more mutually sensitive to one another. Dr. Kumar believes they tend to introduce into each other's lands more appropriate technology and supervision.

• Civil and human rights is an arena for global synergistic leadership. The opportunities are limitless and the range of need extraordinary as the following listing will demonstrate: (a) freeing political prisoners worldwide who differ with the local ideology, a la the efforts of Amnesty International in London; (b) promoting the understaffed and underfunded efforts of a multitude of UNESCO and World Health Organization projects; (c) counteracting cultural stereotypes of foreigners and minorites in mass media, such as the false image of Arabs presented in the Western press, radio, and television;

(d) overcoming bigotry and prejudice against some group which becomes a scapegoat, whether it be the Gypsies in Spain, the Jews in France, or the French in Canada; (e) combatting the exploitation of children whether it be by kidnapping or malnutrition or sexual abuse, as the Geneva Anti-Slavery Society for Protection of Human Rights has done relative to child slavery among the 200 million "forgotten people" under 15 years of age who are forced to work in unsafe conditions; (f) helping exiled refugees not only to obtain safe haven, but to acculturate in strange lands, as in Los Angeles County where organizations banded together to aid in the resettlement of approximately 1,500 Indo-Chinese who were arriving there monthly in 1979-80.

• Synergism for achieving export goals in troubled economies was the subject of a presentation by Harvey Trilli, President of the Pullman Swindell Company. Quoted in *The International Essays for Business Decision Makers* (1979), this address for the Center for International Business deals with economic difficulties being experienced by industrialized nations. Trili calls for more synergisim between government and business and other institutional sectors. He cites as examples of this concept the successful models of the Export-Import Bank, the World Bank, Overseas Private Investment Corporation, the International Monetary Fund, and the Domestic International Sales Corporation. His points are underscored by another contributor to that same volume, Adlai E. Stevenson on "Facing the Realities of Interdependence," who calls for government stimulation, not restriction, of international business for new economic cooperation to enhance the security and welfare of all.

High-Synergy Strategies

There are numerous techniques and methods that leaders can employ to facilitate synergistic teamwork. In our prior volume, *Managing Cultural Differences,* Chapter 20 outlined some ways to be more effective in the multinational environment. Ross Goble in *Management for the Future* provided a summary of qualities for nontraditional leaders.[19] We have refocused and presented these on page 202.

Assuming Goble's leadership strategies are already employed by the cosmopolitan manager or administrator, what are some other approaches that will promote synergy in the organization? The following are offered as indicators of what could be done to change institutional culture.

Positive use of power. Power, like conflict, is energy that can be used or abused, depending on whether the leader employs it for positive or negative purposes. Barry Oshry, who has developed a conceptual approach to power and systems, believes the term "power" need not mean trouble and that too many people in organizations feel "powerless." Skill training can empower leaders to recognize the capacities for constructive use of power within themselves and others, as well to employ that competence to make positive things happen in a corporation or government agency. The collective or synergistic use of power can become a driv-

---

Synergistic Leadership Style

- Emphasizes quality of life, rather than just quantity of good /services.
- Promotes concepts of interdependence and cooperation, rather than just competition.
- Encourages work and technology in harmony with nature, rather than conquering it and avoiding ecological considerations.
- Is conscious of corporate social responsibility and goals, rather then just technical efficiency and production.
- Creates an organizational culture that encourages self-achievement and fulfillment through participation, rather than dogmatism and dependency.
- Restates relevant traditional values such as personal integrity, work ethic, respect for other's property, individual responsibility, and social order.
- Encourages in self and other the capacity for intuition, creativity, flexibility, openness, group sensitivity, and goal-oriented planning.   ■

---

ing force for organizational change. The following extract from Oshry's book on *Power and Position* makes the strategy clearer:

> Organic Power, A Self-and System Perspective—In whatever position we are in, we shape human systems and they shape us. . . .Organic power is self-and-system-centered influence; the ability to influence our own condition within a social system and to influence the condition of the system itself. Organic power differs from purely self-centered power orientations. . . .[20]

Relative to power and powerlessness, Dr. Oshry envisions three possible roles for us. The *directors* focus and channel system energy, while managing the tension between change and stabilization. The *members* enrich the system's visions and structures when cooperating with or rebelling against the system as it is. The *middle position* influences the director/member communications and interaction patterns, and is responsive to both while maintaining a degree of independence. This conceptualization of the director is comparable to the authors' view of the leader as an organizational energizer. Oshry believes that power is the ability to do what we need to do and to do what the system needs having done. He prefers an approach that develops a integrated *and* differentiated system:

> The system has the capacity to differentiate— a process in which members experience and develop their differences: and to de-differentiate—a process in which members experience and develop their commonalities and oneness. . . .
>
> The system has the capacity to integrate—a condition in which all differentiations, pull together in a common effort; and to dis-integrate—a condition in which all systems differentiations are able to go their own ways. The system can harness the energies of differentiated forces in the service of the system

survival or protection, and it can allow for dis-integration in the service of freedom, liberty, and self-development.

The system has the capacity to be system-conscious, and to be aware of itself—what it is, what is going on, what its problem and potential are. It can then choose whether to continue as is or to change form and direction. . . . And the organically powerful system has the capacity to submerge system-consciousness, to suspend the process of self-examination, in order that members can get about the business of doing whatever has to be done.

Organic power is the management of system energy. . . . The goal is to develop an organism of which we are a part, that can be aware of itself, that can respond complexly and effectively to its environment, that can maintain itself as it is, that can transform itself as the situation requires. The goal is to develop a system in which we as members are alive and alert—recognizing and realizing our unique potentials.[20]

Thus, a synergistic leader does not create a system that crushes, underutilizes, or abuses its human resources, but rather a system in which power is used to foster cooperation and collaborations for both system and self-improvement.

Trend scanning and interpretation. In a sense, a synergistic leader is a futurist, always seeking the big picture by peering over the horizon. Through technological forecasting or other means of future studies, this leader gets a sense of new directions, so that he or she may not only prepare subordinates for tomorrow, but help to create the future. This leader reads futuristic periodicals and newsletters (World Future Society's *The Futurist, Futures Survey,* or *Education Tomorrow)* and perhaps, "plugs into" some futures research center and obtains their reports, or utilizes their techniques.

The University of Southern California's Center for Futures Research, for instance, proposes that top executives use QUEST, Quick Environmental Scanning Technique, which permits managers and planners to share their views about trends and events in future external environments. It is a systematic way to develop shared understandings about priority issues that affect corporate policies and planning. It involves about a dozen executives reviewing a notebook on major environmental trends and events in their industry. Through structured series of dicussions, they spectulate on divergent views about performance indicators and probabilities relative to critical issues. A report is eventually prepared on this input, which also contains three to five scenarios incorporating the major discussion themes. Another session then review the implications and identifies feasible strategic options for coping. These are ranked in order of probability and given to a planning team for further development of leadership strategies.

Another approach, entitled "Innovating with High Achievers in HRD," describes a method for videotaping top performing employees in a problem-solving workshop.[21] These outstanding performers are used as trend indicators, because they circumvent obsolete rules, regulations, policies, and procedures in order to achieve, thereby creating tomorrow's organizational norms and standards. If a leader wishes to reduce organization shock and get a fix on future personnel practices, then bring together the top producers in a performance management workshop. The videotapes that result not only provide feedback to management, but can be used in training average performers through behavior models. The word "power" comes from a Latin derivative meaning "to be able." Certainly, the achiever has power that should be harnessed for organizational renewal.

Reversing viewpoints. For the leader who wishes to bring opposing perspectives together in some form of synergy, it helps to try and understand the other viewpoint. That is, to get out of our own private world and into the life space of the other. Thus, we may be in a position to empathize and to perceive somewhat as that other person who differs with us. Then, if a sharing of two distinct perceptual fields takes, there can be an enlarging or overlapping of life spaces and the conditions for synergy.

Each of us operates in a unique space, which has been conditioned by culture, beliefs, life experiences, socio-economic status, environment, education, etc. To communicate effectively, especially in cross-cultural situations, requires that we enter into the receiver's field of experience and patterns of ideas. Because each of us can equate meaning with various communication symbols, we must put verbal and nonverbal inter action into a specific context. Therefore, we should try and enter into the other's mindset, or psychological construct, which is the way one reads meaning into his or her life. It is from one's perceptual field that each person exchanging messages proceeds to decode, interpret, and respond to such interaction. The challenge is to enter the other's perceptual field.

Such endeavors are essential if leaders are to promote cooperation and collaboration, to resolve conflict and cope with differences. The principle applies to superior and subordinate, team leader and team member, labor and management negotiations, domestic and international business. It is valid when members of two different professions or diciplines attempt to work together, or when two different departments or divisions within an organization are interdependent. The process is like reverse role playing, and it is as applicable to two diverse persons in a marital relationship seeking to collaborate, as it is to two antagonists forced by circumstances to tolerate each other and overcome barriers between them. Even when we speak the same language, we may not have shared cultural assumptions, so we may misread each other. Many assumptions upon which the receiver operates may be hidden or unknown to the sender. But when we try to "feel" as the other, then we have taken the first step in bridge-building over human communication gaps. This happens when free-enterprise North Americans try to understand the socialist society and spirit of the Soviets; or when United States citizens examine the past twenty-five years of their country's foreign policy and impact on Iran from the perspective of the average Iranian. Only then can Westerners understand the significance of the Russian and Islamic revolutions in this century. Only then do we take the first giant step toward accommodations and peaceful coexistence, culminating in trade and cultural exchanges and, finally, cooperation.

Collaborative behavior is based upon interpersonal trust, which can occur while we tolerate differences in people by learning to understand *their* space or world. An effective leader is one who is capable of facilitating high interpersonal trust in others, something confirmed by behavioral science research.

To exercise any leadership in complex systems in transition today is a challenge. The neat, orderly world of the past is gone, and traditional leadership approaches are inadequate. It is an illusion that the single leader or decision-maker can make the difference, and this explains why so many people internationally are disillusioned with contemporary political "leaders." Now, only the combined brainpower of multiple executives or teams is most appropriate, so that many become involved with their unique resources and mobilized toward complex solutions. People are culturally influenced and do not always act rationally, so we do not yet collectively manage the planet. Therefore, leaders should think globally, but act locally with the clear understanding of the interdependence of human and natural systems. Hazel Henderson said it best in work on *The Politics of Reconceptualization;* in which she counteracted the past entrapment of leaders:

> . . . .At the same time, we must internalize the view of the indivisible human family, biologically and genetically one species with no scientific bases for the superstitious, parochial divisiveness based on minor differentiations, whether of skin color, ethnic stock, sex or social and reproductive functions.
>
> This next evolutionary leap in our expanding consciousness, imagination and empathy is the only potential we possess that can hope to counter the increasing entropy we are creating on a planetary scale. . . .
>
> To put our planetary house in order will require concerted human effort involving examination of our value systems as clinically as we can. . . .
>
> To devise workable ethics for the Solar Age will require that we begin the co-operative, global task of inventorying the world's value systems, religious beliefs, and cultures, past and present, assessing those behavioral outputs and hardware configurations which they produce. . . .
>
> The confusion of hierarchical thinking as it collides with real-world cybernetics is evident. . . .In any case, in a thermostat's functioning, the feedback from the rest of the system are governors - actually the reversal of our hierarchical concept of governance from center or top down. . . .
>
> These realities, when accepted, deal a death blow to our either/or, hierarchical, dichotomizing, objectivied, location-specific Westernized logic, and clear the way for more subtle, soft-focus, intuitive, simultaneous cognition, typified by the Oriental worldview, folk wisdom, and mystic tradition.[22]

Henderson's observations provide a fitting conclusion, and remind the new leaders who will be creating *cyberculture* of the necessity for synergy in our conceptualization and use of global human mental powers and insights.

References

1. Benedict, R. *Patterns of Culture*. Boston: Houghton Mifflin, 1934. (Quoted in F. Goble, *The Third Force*, published in 1970 by the Thomas Jefferson Research Center, 1143 North Lanke Avenue, Pasadena, CA. 91104, USA.)
2. Maslow, A. *Journal of Individual Psychology*, vol. 20, 1964, pp. 153-164.
3. Craig, J.H. and Craig, M. *Synergic Power*. Berkley, Calif (Box 296): ProActive Press, 1979.
4. Brevoord, C. In: *Management for the Future*, L. Benton (ed) New York: McGraw-Hill, 1978.
5. Horton, T. In: *Management for the Future*, L. Benton (ed.) New York: McGraw-Hill, 1978.
6. Greiff, B.S. and Munter, P.E. *Tradeoffs: Executives, Family and Organizational Life*. New York: New American Library, 1980.
7. Nishiyama, K. *Japanese Tourists Abroad*. University of Hawaii, 1973.
8. Newmark, E. In: "Women's Roles: A Cross-Cultural Perspective," *International Journal of Intercultural Relations*, vol. 3, no. 4, 1979.
9. Newland, K. In: "Women's Roles: A Cross-Cultural Perspective," *International Journal of Intercultural Relations*, vol. 3, no. 4, 1979.
10. Adler, N.J. In: "Women's Roles: A Cross-Cultural Perspective," *International Journal of Intercultural Relations*, vol. 3, no. 4, 1979.
11. Brannon, A.P. and Ramsey, S.J. In: "Women's Roles: A Cross-Cultural Perspective," *International Journal of Intercultural Relations*, vol. 3, no. 4, 1979.
12. Goll, G.E. "Perceptions of Chief Executive Officers Regarding the Impact of Contemporary Socio-Economic Change Upon Managerial and Leadership Activity." Unpublished doctorial dissertation, United States International University, 1981. Available from University Microfilms, Ann Arbor Michigan.
13. Schaupp, D. *A Cross-Cultural Study of a Multinational Company: Attitudinal Responses to Participative Management*. Praeger Publishers, 1978.
14. Duckworth, D. and Blackshaw, I. *Troubleshooting—International Business Problems*. London: Oyez Publishing Ltd., 1980.
15. Egon Zehnder International, Inc. Survey appearing in *Personnel Journal*, June 1980.
16. Rensselear Polytechnic Institute, *"Early Identification of Management Talent Project,"* 1980.
17. Flanigan, J. *Los Angeles Times*, October 14, 1980.
18. Fuller, R.B. *Critical Path*. Washington, D.C.: St. Martins Press/World Future Society, 1981.

19. Goble, R. In: *Management for the Future,* L. Benton (ed.) New York: McGraw-Hill, 1978.
20. Oshry, B. *Power and Position.* Boston: Power and Systems Training Inc., 1977.
21. Harris, P.R. "Innovating with High Achievers in HRD," *Training and Development Journal,* October, 1980.
22. Henderson, H. *The Politics of Reconceptualization.* New York: Anchor/Doubleday, 1980.

Unit 3

Cultural Specifics
and Synergy

11.
Synergy with Asian Management

THE TWAIN MUST MEET

The human brain has two sides which have separate functions, yet work effectively together for the benefit of the whole body. So too in the geopolitical body, there are two unique dimensions of the human experience — East and West. Traditional mythology has espoused this questionable comment on global behavior: "East is East, and West is West, and never the twain shall meet." The human family in its diverse groupings is so interdependent today, that the "twain must meet" and synergy promoted despite Oriental/Occidental cultural differences.

Although the concentration of First and Second World economic development seems to be in the West, there is the economic miracle of Japan, which is certainly in the First World category. Furthermore, though we think of multinational corporations as largely centered in the West and the First World, there are many emerging Third World multinational companies, and a preponderance of these are in Malaysia, Singapore, Hong Kong and Taiwan. Despite the historical reality that many of the great trade routes of the past were in the Far and Middle East, modern Western business leaders often focus their attention on the North Atlantic community, missing the action in the emerging Pacific Basin market because they are culturally and commercially myopic. To be a cosmopolitan manager, one must be open to the contributions of Eastern and Western cultures, because only in the interchange between these respective hemispheres can full human potential be achieved.

Asia has a diversity of peoples and cultures in various stages of economic and technological development. A fourth of mankind lives in the rapidly developing People's Republic of China. The potential of Indonesia is mind-boggling. As one views Asia and its management, can we afford to overlook Australia? But the East is so large in terms of geography, human and natural resources, and disparate business practices that total coverage is beyond the scope of this unit.* So, in this chapter we examine several Asian peoples and apologize to other ancient cultures in the area which space limitations force us to exclude. But the insights shared in this representative sample of the East will help global managers to be more sensitive and appreciative of their Asian counterparts, so that greater collaboration and cooperation may be fostered through international commerce.

Nearly two billion people in Asia, about half the human race, are experiencing dramatic changes in their lives. The Chinese are attempting to modernize their country, while Japan is learning to live with the successes of modernization. The U.S. involvement in Vietnam is over and the era of major war in Asia is over. An era of accelerated trade, diplomacy, and cooperation centered around the Pacific basin is beginning. The U.S. Department of Commerce advised "in the first five months of 1980, U.S. exports to the Far East and South Asia increased by 25% over the same period in 1979, significantly faster than our imports from the region."[1]

The five nations of the Association of Southeast Asian Nations (ASEAN) — Indonesia, Malaysia, Philippines, Thailand, and Australia — are becoming a powerful regional economic force. All of these countries ended the decade of the 1970s with strong growth rates and these are predicted to continue despite a worldwide recession. Yet, these nations of the Far East also have a variety of problems that undermine international business synergy. For example, writing in the *Asian Wall Street Journal* (March 2, 1981) Syed Hussein Alatas reminds us that rising corruption saps Asia's strength. He believes that only Singapore has seriously fought and overcome entrenched corruption, which in other countries seems to have increased in scope and depth.

In this chapter, we provide practical background information on several countries in Asia, so that important cultural differences are understood and synergy can be promoted by international business leaders.

WORKING IN MALAYSIA

The Federation of Malaysia, consisting of 13 states, was formed in 1963 at the end of the British rule. Eleven of the states are part of peninsular Malaysia and the two states of Sabah and Sarawak are separated by 400 miles of the South China Sea. The land is approximately 90% forested and both the peninsula and the states of Sabah and Sarawak are characterized by flat coastal plains rising to steep mountain ranges. Malaysia's major exports are rubber, tin, palm oil, timber, and petro-

---

*Chapters 17 and 18 of *Managing Cultural Differences* address many aspects of Japanese and Chinese culture.

leum; the major imports are machinery, transportation equipment, and consumer goods.

Kuala Lumpur is the capital of Malaysia and is the location of the federal parliament and the prime minister. In addition, each of the 13 state governments have parliaments and prime ministers and 9 have sultans. The present government policy promotes Malay participation in business and the dispersal of industry to less developed areas. The government is a parliamentary democracy under a constitutional monarchy. Its economic policies are laid out in its Third Malaysian Plan.

Cultural Concepts

The population of Malaysia is approximately 12.3 million, with 10.4 million residing in the peninsula. The multicultural population is reportedly 53% Malay and other indigenous people, 35% Chinese, 10% Indian, and 2% from various minority groups. Courtesy, etiquette, gentleness, and good manners are hallmarks of the Malay culture.

A fundamental concept surrounding the ethical system of the Malay people revolves around the concept of *Budi*. *Budi* illustrates the ideal behavior expected of a Malay. Its basic rules are respect and courtesy, especially towards elders, and affection and love for one's parents, as well as a pleasant disposition and harmony in the family, the neighborhood, and in the society as a whole. There are two forms of *Budi: Adab,* which means that the individual has a responsibility to show courtesy at all times; and *Rukun,* which means that the individual must act to obtain harmony either in a family or in society.

Malays do not seem to value the pursuit of wealth for its own sake. They do, however, believe in hard work and self-reliance. Life is viewed as a passing thing, and family and friends take precedence over self-centered interests, such as the accumulation of profit and materialism. The Malays' love for children is reflected in the gentle and tender manner in which they raise them.

Gestures and Greetings

There are several forms of nonverbal communication that one might use while in Malaysia that could easily be misconstrued or insulting to the Malay people. Therefore, familiarity with greetings and certain gestures to avoid could lead to a more successful business trip. The following are a few examples. In meeting a Malay, the elder person should be mentioned before the younger, the more important before the less important, and the woman before the man. In rural areas, it is customary for men and women to shake-hands with each other. When meeting a man, a Malay woman may *salaam,* which is bowing very low while placing the right palm on the forehead, and then covering their hands with cloth. However, men and women in the cities generally shake hands if they believe that a person is unaware of the social etiquette pertaining to handshaking. The traditional Malay greeting resembles a handshake with both hands but without the grasp. The man offers both hands to his friend, lightly touches his friend's outstretched hands, and then brings his hands to his breast. This simply means that "I greet you from my heart."

In Malaysia, instead of pointing to a place, object, or person with the right index finger, which is considered impolite, it is more common to point with the thumb of the right hand with the fingers folded under. In calling for a taxi, one uses the fingers of the right hand, moving them together with the palm facing down in a waving or "come here" gesture, which is opposite to the typical American beckoning of a taxi. A gesture to avoid is patting a child on the head. The head is considered to be the center of the intellectual and sacred power, and is therefore holy and should not be touched.

Values and Attitudes of Malayans

The following contrasts are intended to be especially helpful to the business person working in Malaysia. It will cover a number of basic considerations and cultural contrasts in attitudes towards work, motivation, leadership, planning, as well as a number of basic differences between American and Malay society and way of life. Many of these ideas were derived from a cultural analysis prepared by George W. Renwick of Intercultural Press, Inc.[2]

Religion. Islam is the predominant religion in Malaysia and exerts a great influence not only on the method of worship but the Malays whole way of life. Therefore, any foreign business representative hoping to function effectively in this environment should have an understanding of Islam, as it is very important in order to obtain a total picture of Malay culture. Whereas Americans' religious practices are generally confined to Sundays, Malays' religious concerns seem to be on a more profound daily basis. The Malays stress the importance of their belief about God and the hereafter in their language.

A person is guided by the prescriptions of the Koran, which spells out and details rules of behavior that include all social and business activities. As Muslims, they are expected ro recite the creed, "There is no God but Allah, and Muhammad is his Prophet," and they must pray five times a day and worship Allah as the only true God. Providing charity, helping the needy, fasting during the month of Ramadan, and if possible, making a trip to Mecca are additional practices that the Muslim Malays are expected to follow. They should also refrain from eating pork or drinking alcoholic beverages. In the main portion of the Mosque, the Muslim place of worship, Malay women sit apart from the men and are not allowed at any time to mix casually or to eat with them.

Tradition. The Malays deeply respect traditional customs but, in some cases, these customs do not complement their religion. In these instances, the practices of Islam have been adapted to fit more effectively with the traditional customs. These traditional practices and beliefs are called *Adat*, the Malay word for custom. The importance of these *Adat* are illustrated by their proverb, "Let the child perish but not the *Adat*."

Nature and Human Nature. Man is considered basically good by the Malays, which is somewhat different from the Protestant ethic and the concept of Original Sin in western Christianity. Throughout the history of the United States, an underlying belief has been that man can overcome nature. Mastery and control over nature is even becoming more evident in view of how America is attempting to deal with the shortages of fuel, water, and food. In the Islamic faith, the Malay position concerning man's relationship to nature is one of being subject to or living in harmony with nature. At times, a Malay feels subject to the elements because of his fatalistic attitude and belief of the supremacy of God's will. A Malay also believes that he is part of the natural world, which reflects his belief in animism — the notion that plants and animals have a spiritual dimension.

A Malay pays little attention to what has happened in the past and regards the future as both vague and unpredictable. Planning for the future or hoping that the future will be better than either the present or the past is simply not their way of life. Americans, who are seldom completely satisfied with the present and have little respect for the past, place a high value on change and feel most comfortable in looking towards the future.

Individualism and ambition also offer significant contrasts between the two cultures. Whereas individualistic talents and characteristics are held in high regard in America, the Malay places the utmost importance on relationships with relatives, friends, and colleagues.

In the United States, ambition generally means to strive for worldly success, financial and social. There is generally a lack of such ambition in Malaysia, which could be attributed to a variety of causes. In the past, the chances of a Malay succeeding in worldly terms were very small and did not depend on the efforts of the individual Malay. Furthermore, if in fact he did succeed, there were laws that prohibited the accumulation of wealth by Malay peasants. A third reason for this lack of ambition is that from the perspective of the Islamic faith, there is a strong sense of fatalism as indicated by the common expressions such as "God willing" or "If God wants me to be something I will, if not, God's will be done." These factors favor a lack of motivation for worldly success, which is replaced by a motivation to develop deep and lasting relationships with friends and relatives. Therefore, Malays have traditionally felt that in receiving material success, they might lose the highly valued respect of their family and friends.

In contrast to the American tendency to change the environment and concentrate most energy in working to get ahead, a Malay's energies are directed in many areas. Furthermore, the hot and humid climate in Malaysia is a drain on energy; thus, little attempt is made to alter the environment.

Trust, respect, and leadership. Trust for a Malay is fundamental to a successful interpersonal relationship regardless of the nationality of the person with whom he is interacting. A person's capability for loyalty, commitment, and companionship are the key characteristics upon which the Malay generally bases his trust. On the other hand, an American bases his or her trust on a person's capacity for performance, level of expertise, and position in the social structure. For Malays, the process for developing trust is more internal and personal whereas for Americans, the emphasis is on external and professional aspects. For an American respect must be earned, but for Malays, it comes with a person's status.

There also exists a subtle difference between Americans and Malayans concerning the interaction of formality and respect. Malays show respect initially through formalities, however, as a relationship progresses, formalities are slowly dropped until an informal atmosphere is reached. Americans also start out formally, but the progression to a less formal situation occurs much more rapidly. The slower transformation from formality to informality often confuses Americans who are unaware of the differing progression. Although an American generally respects a very aggressive person who demonstrates that he can get what he wants, the Malay respects a compromising person who shows that he is willing "to give and take." In Malay negotiations the person who compromises is the most respected person and will often receive more than he anticipated.

When a Malay meets a stranger, he not only evaluates the person but also his background, family, and social position. An American generally evaluates a person in terms of his accomplishments. Therefore, the American might not pay the Malayan the respect that the Malay feels that he deserves, due to this difference in orientation. These attitudes reflect the fact that America is a very "doing" oriented society, whereas the Malay is oriented toward "being" or "existing."

In U.S. organizations and institutions status is usually attributed to someone demonstrating leadership capabilities. In Malaysia, the process is somewhat reversed. Malays are born into a certain social position or status, and if the status is very high or important, then they are expected to demonstrate leadership capabilities. Americans and Malays base good leadership on different personal qualifications. To be aggressive and confident are basic to the American concept of leadership. For a Malay, the most important quality of a leader is confidence and the ability to understand people. A leader in Malaysia is also expected to be religiously devout, humble, sincere, and tactful. One's position in Malay society is also important. Even if a person is not worthy of respect, his position might demand that he receive it. A Malay feels most comfortable in a hierarchal structure with a clearly defined role, and emphasis is on room for growth in interpersonal relationships.

Work Ethic. Since the Industrial Revolution, the Protestant work ethic has been a mainstay of American achievement in business, as well as other areas. Idleness has been looked upon as the work of the devil. The distinction between action and idleness is not as clearly delineated in Malay culture and language. Work is viewed as one of many activities by the Malays. A large percentage of the time in a Malay's life is spent developing deeper relationships with family and friends in ways that would appear as idle time to many Americans. This contrast is clearly illustrated by the differing perspectives of how the elderly are viewed in Malaysia and in America. When a person reaches old age in the United States, the fact that he can no longer work generates the feeling that he is no longer useful, whereas in Malaysia, an elderly person is regarded as a wise counselor who plays an important role in society.

The concept of promotion is another aspect of the working environment that differs between the Malay and American culture. A Malay would never take the initiative to request a promotion for himself. When a Malay receives a promotion, it is when his superior respects and thinks very highly of him, and this is of utmost importance to the Malay.

Malaysia is composed mainly of fishing and farming villages with only a few large cities. This factor has important ramifications concerning the educational and technical abilities of the Malay people in contrast with Americans, who are for the most part, raised and socialized in an urban environment. In the past the Malay found it unnecessary to learn about business or to specialize in one field. In general, the Malays do not go up to college and those who do often major in liberal arts as opposed to business or engineering. American business people in working with Malayans often complain about this lack of specialization and technical sophistication.

Politics and Power. Of fundamental importance to anyone working in Malaysia is an understanding of the pluralism among the Malays and Chinese. In order to succeed in Malaysia, one must understand some of the differences and difficulties between the two cultures. Traditionally, the Malay has not been involved in the economic sector of the economy. As mentioned earlier, he has farmed, fished, and earned only enough to support his family. In Malay society there was an occupational void which was largely filled by the Chinese, who eventually, gained virtual control the economic sector of Malaysia. The political situation was reasonably stable until 1969 when there was serious rioting. A high-tension level between the Malays and the Chinese was touched off by election results that favored the Malays. Since then, the government has taken a very pro-Malay stand.

A twenty-year development plan, which favored the Malays, was initiated in 1970. The plan contained two principal economic objectives. First was to check the dominance of Chinese economic control by requiring a definite percent of the labor force to be Malay at all levels of business. Second, the plan stated that the foreign share of the Malay market would be reduced from 60% to 30% by 1990. Due to the general lack of interest in business by the Malays, it has been difficult to reach the designated percentages and, in spite of the efforts towards modernization and education, the results have not been completely satisfactory. Another barrier is the strength of the Malay traditional values: the government cannot force people to change these values. Concerning the second point, even though there will be a decrease in the Malay market allocated to foreign investors, there is still room for expansion of the present foreign-controlled market.

The fact that a near balance of power exists between Malays and Chinese requires close cooperation between the two cultures. However, due to the differences in customs, culture, and values, there has been a great deal of tension between the two groups. As a result, the climate in Malaysia is unstable. An atmosphere of mistrust and feeling of exploitation has led to a defensive stance and negative perceptions and expectations of each group. The unpleasant balance of power between the Malays and the Chinese seems to be more permanent than in other multicultural societies, due to the strong cultural differences; for example, the Chinese Buddhist background versus the Islamic practices of the Malays.

An additional cultural obstacle that hinders the American understanding of the Malay-Chinese relations stems from the fact that the American comes from a low-context culture. When communicating, the American uses and expects explicit messages. For the American, it is the words that convey meaning and information. Malays and Chinese, however, have grown up in a high-context culture, where they depend more on non-verbal means of communication than on verbal messages. Unlike many Americans, persons from high-context cultures usually depend on a traditional structure that resists change or modification, and such persons tend to be group-oriented, rather than individual-oriented.

Foreign business persons coming to Malaysia are challenged to apply synergistic skills to their relationships. This will foster not only cooperation between themselves and the Malays, but will contribute to collaboration among the country's diverse inhabitants.

UPDATE ON THE PEOPLE'S REPUBLIC OF CHINA

Since 1979, when our initial volume, *Managing Cultural Differences,* explored doing business in the PRC, a great deal of water has flowed along the Yantze River and the number of U.S. business people and others visiting mainland China has steadily increased. Visitors now report luxury goods, such as color televisions, are being marketed on the streets of the major cities, and the message is clear to all Chinese: "Work hard and these things can belong to everyone." China is attempting to respond to problems of low productivity, obsolete technology, and other issues affecting their desires to increase the average monthly wage from $40.00 to over $1,000 per year by the year 2000. Previous economic systems that did not work because of ineffective decision-making, and the inadequate training of managers, technicians, and laborers are being changed to incorporate aspects of a free market economy. Mainland Chinese are now appealing to overseas Chinese to assist in revitalizing the "mother land."

The following observations are taken from many sources and present diverse viewpoints and interpretations of the changing situation in China. They range from the simple to the profound, and provide a synthesis of insight about an immense country and an ancient culture in the midst of rapid change.

From an interview with Professor Yao Nien-ching of the Beijing Institute of Foreign Trade:

> The Foreign Trade Department started to enroll post-graduates since 1978. The purpose of our taking post-graduate students is to train people with a higher standard. For those in the English Department, our aim is to train a more competent teacher in that particular department and since we are a school of foreign trade, not an ordinary language institute, we don't go about trying to train them too much in linguistics or literature — though they must have some of these. The main purpose is they must be able to speak English with foreign trade and economic content.

> . . . I am a professor in the English Department, and also the vice-chairman of the academic committee, which is a group newly formed to assist the school leadership on academic affairs, an advisory organization.

> . . . Before that I worked for 10 years as a research economist in the Institute of Economic Research of the Ministry for Foreign Trade.

> *What are the backgrounds of the professors? How many women are there at BIFT, in the faculty?*

> Few of them have been abroad. There's several, quite a few, who studied in this country. One, a statistician, studied at the University of Chicago. One, in New York University. Females, about half of the faculty in our department, in all departments. But, they are mostly junior faculty, but with professor's rank, including associate professors, there are less women than men.

> *How were you placed, did you have to take a test?*

> No, we started work and then there was a meeting among all the members to ascertain our ranks . . . essentially.

> My official title was associate research fellow, but I was made a full professor last year. An associate research fellow is really equivalent to an associate professor in rank . . . At the beginning of 1966, that is when the cultural revolution was unleashed, there was no possibility of any academic teaching, any schooling . . . anyway we were classified as people who helped to push the revisionist line so we were criticized. The president of our institution was called a capitalist rogue, and ah . . . well it . . . was rather unpleasant. And, then after a few years, in 1969, we went down to the countryside to what was called May Seventh, Cadre School, c-a-d-r-e, means anybody who is not a shopworker or . . . who works in the hills. It's very difficult for you to understand . . . anyway, it's called May Seventh Cadre.

> I worked in the paddle fields at first, planting rice, weeding in the fields, you know, water fields. Later, I was a laborer on a construction site, carrying cement, water. Later, my job was to manufacture indigenous bacteria fertilizer. Ha! A great interesting life. And mind you, I don't mind so much this life. I think to be with the people, farm laborers, and to go through what they have come through or what ordinary workers come through is a great experience for

me, naturally. What made us suffer was really the doubtfulness in its various manifestations of ultra left. It was part of the agony. But, however, we don't take that personally. They are in jail, the gang of four, and will be shortly on trial. And we are free. And, then I was called back in 1972 first to write the teaching materials for basic English.[3]

From *Forbes:*

China's great need for modernization becomes readily apparent to the visitor. In wintry Peking, one finds bureaucrats wearing heavy clothing inside because many government office buildings lack sufficient heat. Go to a store: The abacus is used instead of a cash register. Go to a construction site: There are few trucks. Dirt is removed in carts pulled by people in harness. One sees cement blocks weighing perhaps 1,500 pounds being hauled on flatbeds, each pulled by one man. Horsepower in China is literally just that. Outside Peking, work animals, thin and calloused, are everywhere.

The Chinese make no secret of all of this. Wherever one goes — factory, school, commune — the officials invariably end their speeches with something like, "We are backward and we are looking for assistance from the industrial countries."

China recently shocked Japanese businessmen by delaying or cancelling large orders for industrial equipment. The Chinese have been dragging their heels with a number of European and American businessmen as well.

This, of course, is a significant change from only a few months ago when China seemed to be on an international spending spree. But now, bureaucrats have been adding up the cost of their original modernization plans and they're starting to realize that they can't do everything at once. As one official put it to this writer. "The goals have not changed, but the stress has. Before you build a copper smelter, for example, you must first develop the copper mines."

In addition to the lack of money, another serious problem is China's shortage of skilled workers. Some of our group ran into several European engineers working at a supposedly secret Chinese factory utilizing advanced foreign technology. The engineers' tale of woe was long. The Chinese didn't know how to operate the sophisticated machine tools; inventory control and quality control were alien ideas. Said one engineer, "It takes 16 weeks for them to do one or two weeks' work."

The lack of skills was exacerbated by the Cultural Revolution. The visitor quickly learns how devastating this movement was to China's development. Universities were closed down. Studying was condemned as "bourgeois" and "selfish." Research and development ground to a halt. A generation of youngsters lost a critical decade of education.

It would be a mistake to underestimate this country's ability to modernize, however. The desire to learn is palpable. More important, the Chinese seem now to recognize the potency of incentive. Everywhere officials will tell you, "Politics should not interefere with economic laws."

Take China's communes. Farm laborers earn "work points." The more you do, the more work points you are awarded. When cash is received for the crops, the amount of money the peasant receives is determined by the number of work points he has earned.

The Chinese government is no longer embarrassed by the private plots. At one commune we were told that while private plots made up only 7% of the tillable land, they produced 25% of the value of the brigade's output. Under new government rules, the more a commune produces, the higher the price per increased unit of output the commune receives.

The Chinese are experimenting with incentives for the factories as well. When one of our group asked trade union leaders what their chief function was, they replied, "To increase worker productivity." The Chinese are not only interested in merely enlarging output. One official asked this writer, "Do your engineers study economics and finance? How are they taught to be economically efficient in their work?"

All this, of course, should not be taken to mean that China has become a hotbed of laissez-faire capitalism. Far from it. But ideology is taking a backseat to economic development.[4]

From the *New York Times:*

Sipping tea at the Chinese Mission to the United Nations, Rong Jiren appeared confident and at ease in a pale blue Western-style suit, receiving with grace the small deferences of several other Chinese officials — nearly all of whom were attired in an austere dark gray Mao style.

For their part, Mr. Rong said, "foreign companies too often fail to understand China's requirements. Some of them think the projects they propose would be the ones we need," he said. "They are not quite satisfied when our reply is that their project is not needed by China."[5]

From the *Christian Science Monitor:*

Can China make it? Can one billion Chinese move from the bicycle age to their own version of the automobile age by the end of this century? Can they achieve what Chairman Hua Guofeng and Vice-Chairman Deng Xiaping call the "four modernizations" — of agriculture, industry, science and technology, and defense — and turn China into a "relatively advanced" industrialized country; in other words, become a country with a gross national product of about $1,000 per person, modest enough in per capita terms but totaling somewhat more than Japan's GNP today?

The task China's leaders have set themselves and their people is arduous and the road ahead is long. Nevertheless, by the end of this year, answers may begin to emerge regarding three key questions essential to success:

1. Can the leaders energize the masses?

2. Can they get their own Communist Party cadre moving?
3. Can they find a framework firm enough for the Communist Party to remain in control, yet flexible enough to promote the innovation, initiative, and creativity required to transform the Chinese economy?[6]

Also from the *Christian Science Monitor:*

Since the downfall of the "gang of four," the People's Republic of China has steadily shifted its emphasis from ideological purity to economic development.

This trend has been accompanied by China's willingness to increase its contact with the West, at least in terms of obtaining financial and technological assistance, to hasten its drive towards modernization. As a result of these new policies, the People's Congress promulgated the Statute on Joint Ventures last July 1. The statute allows foreign participation not only in the management but also in the ownership of an enterprise. It is a radical departure from past practice.

As it promulgated the statute, China set up the Commission for Foreign Investment and the China International Trust & Investment Corporation to facilitate forming joint ventures and transferring capital and technology from abroad.

Because the statute contains general principles rather than specific guidelines, the Chinese are drafting other statutes and regulations necessary to apply the statute. Among those under active consideration are detailed rules to enforce the statute, tax laws for joint ventures and foreign personnel, corporation law, laws relating to the protection of industrial property, customs and tariff laws, foreign-exchange regulations, and accounting laws. Until these laws are enacted, Chinese authorities will negotiate specific details and incorporate any understandings into each joint-venture agreement.

Chinese officials have indicated that they particularly welcome proposals for transferring technology and for ventures that will enable China to earn hard currency within a relatively short period. For political as well as economic reasons, those involved in promoting joint ventures with foreigners would like to see quick successes so that they might quiet opposition from those who have doubts about recent developments. Although the statute provides that a joint venture's products may be sold domestically at this juncture, products intended primarily for Chinese markets are not encouraged.

Up to the time of this report (February, 1980), although no joint ventures have actually materialized, negotiations are reportedly under way for 40 to 50 joint ventures, and two "agreements" on construction of a hotel in Peking and a woolen-goods factory in Xinjiang (Sinkiang) have been signed.[7]

From the *New York Times:*

The ice cream soda, an American cultural import, has reappeared in Peking after an absence of 14 years.

"The Dung Fang Department Store in central Peking tried offering sodas June 8. Response was overwhelming, and the store now is hurriedly building a permanent soda fountain," said the shop manager, Wu Silu.

Served in glasses resembling root bear mugs, the sodas cost the equivalent of 27 cents. Chinese shoppers queued up to buy them. The shop was open for only four hours each afternoon because of a shortage of syrup and ice cream, but it sold 1,500 sodas a day in its first three days.

Ice cream sodas in Peking date back to the era of foreign domination before the Communist Revolution in 1949. They were mostly a luxury for foreigners. They survived until the start of the Cultural Revolution in 1966, when foreign luxuries were regarded as decadent."[8]

Because for hundreds of years traders exploited the Chinese people and resources, today's multinational representatives must practice synergy to overcome fears of foreigners and encourage cooperation for mutual benefit. China has much to contribute to the West and it needs Western science, technology, and capital investments. Synergistic principles and practices can bridge East and West, and foster respectful interchange.

Now to another Asian country which represents a challenge for synergy.

INDONESIA: UNITY THROUGH DIVERSITY

Geography and Government

"Bkinneka tunggal Ika" translated "unity through diversity" is the national motto of Indonesia. This nation of islands represents a rich variety of local customs and traditions found among its diverse people.

Indonesia is an archipelago situated across the equator between the continents of Asia and Australia. It is the largest archipelago in the world, with 13,677 islands of which 6,044 are inhabited. It stretches 3,330 miles from east to west, and 1,300 miles from north to south. There are four main island groups in Indonesia. The Greater Sunda Islands are composed of Java, which has population of 80 million, Sumatra which is the sixth largest island in the world, and two other large islands. The other three groups of islands include the Lesser Sunda Islands, the Malukus, and West Irian.

With the present population estimated at approximately 150 million, Indonesia is the fifth most populous country in the world, exceeded only by mainland China, India, the U.S.S.R., and the U.S.A. Its labor force is approximately 45 million people and growing at approximately 1½ million people per year. However, it is estimated that 18 million people are unemployed or underemployed. The average per capita income is approximately $150 per year, with many millions of families earning less than 50 cents per day. There is a deepening discontent among many groups of people about differences in living conditions between the very wealthy and the very poor.

Although Indonesia is primarily an agricultural land, it is not self-sufficient in food. Approximately 8% of the land in Indonesia is cultivated and most of this area is on Java, where the population is extremely concentrated. There are many small farms on Java, but the farming methods are old and very time consuming. Thus, farm life is generally hard and not profitable.

Over 60% of the national income of Indonesia is derived from oil. Recent significant oil finds have prompted estimates that the country has about 90% of the known and proven oil reserves in Southeast Asia. These reserves are of very high quality and are extremely low in sulphur.

The second five-year plan, 1974-1979, called for an expenditure of $12.4 billion (U.S.) for consumer goods such as food, clothing, and housing. Foreign investments are significant in Indonesia and tourism is increasing rapidly.

Formerly known as the Dutch East Indies, Indonesia remained the territory of the Netherlands until 1942 when it was occupied by the Japanese. Although Indonesia gained its independence in 1945, it continued to struggle with intermittent guerrilla warfare until 1949 in order to gain total independence from the Dutch. In 1949, the Dutch transferred sovereignty of nearly all of the land of the Dutch East Indies except West Irian, which is now known as the Netherlands New Guinea. The new country became known as the Republic of Indonesia in 1950, and in 1963 West Irian also became part of the nation. General Suharto, a leader of the counter-coup, was formally made President of Indonesia in 1966 and was reelected for two more five-year terms in 1973 and 1978.

Suharto's "new order" remains a strongly centralized government based on the Constitution of 1945, which was amended in 1950. As President, he is subordinate, as well as responsible, to the People's Assembly, although this assembly, consisting of 1920 members, is basically a ceremonial body that elects the President, approves his programs, and meets every five years to organize the election. The House of Representatives is made up of 460 representatives who meet annually. Three hundred sixty of these 460 seats are elected on a proportional system, and the other 100 persons are appointed by a coalition of different parties and functional groups. In Indonesia, there are a total of 27 provinces. Voting in Indonesia is the right of anyone over 17 years of age or who is married regardless of the age of the person.

In 1920, an Indonesian Communist Party was formed and in 1927, Suharto and his followers formed the Indonesia National Party. For many years, these groups have struggled for life and growth.

In Indonesia, there has been and continues to be a long tradition of government corruption, which has been labeled "speed money" and means basically that which gets things done. Since 1970, the government has spent enormous time and energy in attempting to reduce corruption in high places, although how much has been is questionable. In addition, there has been considerable unrest in Indonesia, but the hopes have been that these energies could be channeled into constructive directions.

Indonesia is the largest Islamic land in the world. Indonesians mix Hindu and Moslem prayers and allow various kinds of religious beliefs to meld with the ideas of the prophet Mohammed. Generally, people do not strictly adhere to the rules of the Koran, rather the village law or *Adat* prevails in Indonesian rural and urban areas. Even though Indonesia is a Moslem country, women have never been veiled, nor have they been secluded like other Moslem women in the Middle East. On many of the islands, women vote and hold leadership positions. However, in spite of the fact that women have been guaranteed full and complete rights, Indonesia is a male-dominated country. Education of women is a problem with women comprising only 30% of the students at the university or college level. Thus, with this disparity in education, the Indonesian woman's position is behind that of her male counterpart.

Cultural Concepts

In Indonesia, the family is the basic unit of Indonesian life. It is a highly complex system with many interlocking relationships in the vast network of an extended family system. For most Indonesians, the family is the first priority. There are many young people in Indonesia, with nearly 70% of the total population under 30 years of age. The customary law or *Adat* permits polygamy, but it is not practiced by many persons. In December, 1973, a bill was passed requiring free consent for girls with the minimum age of 16 and for boys with the minimum age of 19 in the sharing of property acquired in marriage. In the case of divorce, the children are often assigned to the custody of both parents, and in court, men desiring to practice polygamy must still prove that all of their wives will receive equal treatment.

A basic concept in Indonesian daily life both in a social and a business context is the importance of avoiding making someone feel *malu*. The word literally means ashamed or embarrassed. Criticizing or contradicting a person in front of others will cause you to lose face with the group and the person will feel *malu* as a result of your action.

Also important to Indonesians are the concepts of unity and conformity. They do not strive, as many Americans do, to become individualistic.

Behavior Modes

A common courtesy that should be respected is not raising one's voice or demonstrating externally intense emotions. Head-on confrontations are embarrassing to most Indonesians. Thus, they prefer to talk indirectly and ambiguously about areas of difference until common ground can be found. *Semdah* is the art of paying respect to one's superiors who are generally persons of higher rank or position either by birth, by economic status, or by age. One form of demonstrating *semdah* is by not questioning one's superiors.

In Indonesia, there is a subtle but very hierarchical approach to interpersonal relationships that is related not only to family and to the village, but also to the larger community and to the government. Leadership is very paternalistic and consensus is the mode followed by all persons. Young persons defer to old people, though in the cities this is changing somewhat. Indonesians are known for their friendly hospitality.

It is suggested that foreigners working in Indonesia never refuse an offer for food or drink, but at the same time, it is customary not to finish it completely.

Gestures and Greetings

There are certain gestures that should be avoided while in Indonesia. For example, never touch the head of an Indonesian as it is thought to be the place where the spirit resides. Kissing and embracing in public should also be avoided because it is considered rude and coarse. In addition, personal questions should not be asked as this may be interpreted by Indonesians as probing into territory that is none of one's business. The use of the left hand for eating or for passing of gifts should be avoided because it is considered the unclean hand. Pointing is also considered rude in Indonesia, and therefore should be avoided. Handshaking has become customary in Jakarta among Westernized Indonesians. However, in general, there is no physical contact. The traditional greeting is a bow with the hands together, a nodding of the head and a gracious smile.

Business Interactions

Indonesians are extremely indirect in business contexts. Therefore, it is very important to circumvent a subject before the critical issues are mentioned. Everything is negotiated in Indonesia, and the people love to bargain. With the exception of the major department stores, there are few fixed prices. Once a person is respected as a bargainer, a merchant will offer far more reasonable prices.

Indonesians do not like to be pressured or hurried. Time in the United States can be wasted, spent, utilized, and saved. In contrast, time in Indonesia is viewed as a limitless pool. There is a phrase in Indonesia describing this concept that translates as "rubber time," so that time stretches or shrinks and is therefore very flexible.

It is difficult to find acceptable housing in Jakarta, a city with over 6 million people. Most business people rent a bungalow with a garden, which usually costs over $2500 per month. Alternatively, there are several suburban areas about thirty minutes by car from the Jakarta business section and many foreigners live in these areas. Before signing a lease, it is important to investigate the water supply in the area, because this is often a problem. Electricity in Jakarta is 110/130-volt alternating current, which is convenient for American appliances. However, the city has recently converted to 50 cycle/220/380-volt alternating current, and the international hotels use 220-volt alternating current. Thus, it is important to be careful with small appliances. Electrical power facilities also present problems and very often there are "brown-outs."

The national language of Indonesia, Bahasa Indonesia, was officially adopted in 1928. At the time of this decision, Bahasa Indonesia was a regional language spoken by only 5% of the total population of Indonesia. In order to achieve a higher ideal of the unity of the Indonesian people, the major sub-races such as Javanese (47%), Sudanese (14%), and others pushed aside their regional feelings and adopted the idea of a common language.

With such diverse cultural groups Indonesia is in need of massive "synergizing." One of the principal contributions that external transnational enterprises could make to this emerging nation is to help it attain its goals. The only hope the multicultural Indonesian people have for success as a group is by practicing collaboration in their society and with foreigners.

WORKING IN THE PHILIPPINES

Geography, Government, and People

In this multicultural society, Tagalog is the principal language, but English is widely spoken because of Western influences, primarily U.S.

Hospitality, friendliness, and sincerity are prominent aspects of the Filipino culture. Am ambience filled with gaiety is the result of over 400 years of the Spanish influence. Filipinos are predominantly of Malay stock, with Chinese and American cultural influences. The Philippines' 700 islands cover approximately 115,000 square miles in the South China Sea. The eleven largest islands comprise over 95% of the total land area and population, with Luzon being the largest island, and Mindanao being the second largest. Although Manila, located on Luzon, is the most well-known area, Quezon City was declared the capital of the Philippines in 1948. However, most government activity still remains in Manila.

Great contrasts in terrain and climate exist throughout the Philippines. Northern Luzon is mountainous, the southern islands are comparatively dry, while other parts are dense jungle areas. In addition, throughout the islands there are a number of volcanoes. The Philippines are located within the tropic zone with the low areas having a warm, humid climate and only slight variations from the average temperature of 80 degrees Fahrenheit. The monsoon season lasts from June to November, and periodic typhoons pass over the island causing immense floods and damage to crops and homes.

The military government of President Ferdinand E. Marcos remains in power under martial law declared in 1972. In 1981, restrictive provisions are being lifted and elections were held. Under the current Constitution, the government was established as parliamentary with executive power vested in the prime minister. The president is the head of state and he, as well as the prime minister, are elected from the membership of the National Assembly. The prime minister appoints his cabinet and initiates most legislation. The traditional parties in the Philippines are the Liberal, and the Nacionalista, and also a small Communist group which has essentially operated independently.

The foreign policy of the Philippines is based on a close alliance with the United States and in cooperation with many other Asian countries. The United States, the Philippines, and six other countries signed the Manila Pact in 1954, which established the Southeast Asia Treaty Organization, or SEATO.

Western business people have generally reported that the Filipino government is inefficient and that having contacts in high places of government is essential in cutting through the bureaucratic red tape. The people basically work on the "mañana" system, since they seldom complete things on time despite deadlines. However, in their own fashion, things do get done. "Almost, but not quite" is the foreigner's conclusion.

International businesses are worried that the current favorable business climate might end if Marcos should be replaced. These concerns seem less significant when one considers the largest portion of his cabinet is constructed of technocrats rather than politicans, who would continue the "new society." Thus, the current political setup in the Philippines seems to assure investors that business and contractual agreements can be carried out in a normal manner and enforced. The Philippines' commitment to free enterprise and friendly relations with Western nations still exists even with the recent establishment of relations with many Communist nations in the past years.

The Philippines' economy is based on agriculture, forestry, and fishing, which employ more than half of the total labor force and account for more than 50% of all exports. The agricultural sector consists of the production of food crops essentially for domestic consumption (rice and corn), and cash crops for export. The country's major exports are sugar, copra, copra meal, coconut oil, pineapple, tobacco, and abaca. The Philippines is also one of the world's leading producers of wood and wood products. Although fishing contributes to the Philippines' economy, the fertile fishing area has not been developed to its full potential. The Philippines are rich in mineral resources with nickel, copper, and other mineral deposits among the largest in the world. However, only a small portion of these have been surveyed and exploited. Government programs have recently been initiated to strengthen the industrial development and have included protective import duties and taxes. Until 1970, the U.S. was the leading trading partner of the Philippines. However, trade with Japan has now surpassed that of the U.S. because of considerable tourist and business investments.

The Philippines' population has doubled since it received independence from the United States in 1946. With a population numbering approximately 46 million, the Philippines has one of the highest birth rates in the world. Manila, the largest city on the islands, has a population of around 2 million persons, and Quezon City, the capital, has nearly a million inhabitants. People have come to the Philippines from many South East Asian countries, such as Indonesia, Malaysia, and China. The blend of these cultures has formed the Filipino race. The most significant alien ethnic group residing in the Philippines are the Chinese who have played an important role in commerce since the nineteenth century, when they first came to the Philippines to trade. With a million and a half Moslem Filipinos on the island, Moslem practices are also prevalent.

The present culture strongly reflects Hispanic influence. The education system was influenced by the presence and the relationship of the Philippines to the United States from 1898 to 1946. Education is highly valued and a family will make great sacrifices in order to educate the children. The literacy rate is approximately 85% and nearly one-fourth of the nation's budget is spent on education. However, the goal of compulsory education has not yet been realized completely because of the lack of facilities and qualified teachers.

The standard of living in the Philippines varies, with only a few families owning a large percentage of the rural and urban real estate. These wealthy few control profitable businesses and the universities, and they live in luxury. Reform, especially in land ownership progresses slowly.

The Filipinos are a conforming people who rarely create disturbances. Thus, they are willing to go along with conditions rather than trying to change them. Their belief in *pakiksama*, which literally means the ability to get along with people, emphasizes the Filipino attitude of submission as opposed to disturbing those around them with whom they might disagree. Confrontation is avoided. Consequently, the true feelings of the Filipinos are often hidden behind an agreeing facade, and the foreign business person in the Philippines should attempt to read these hidden signals that are given him.

Cultural Concepts

Filipinos generate warmth and friendliness. The everyday greeting for acquaintances and friends is a handshake greeting for men and women, and occasionally a light pat on the back for men. Older people should be shown respect and should always be allowed to take the lead. Filipinos place great importance on the family. The well-being of the family supersedes every other desire, therefore questions concerning the family are very important. The Filipino does not strive to accumulate money and power for his own sake, but rather in order to better his family position. Large extended families, including cousins and friends, reflect the great interdependence of the family in the Philippines.

Hiya or shame is an important social force for Filipinos, and the idea is instilled in their children at an early age. To accuse a person of not having this *hiya* trait is a gross insult because it indicates that a person is unable to feel shame as well as all other emotions. Therefore, it is very important never to criticize another person in public or in front of his friends because it shames him, and is thus the greatest of insults.

The negative ramifications of *hiya* are that the Filipinos avoid change, innovation, or competition simply because if the result is failure, it would cause him to shame his family. Consequently, the Filipino family and the Filipino businessperson will "save face" at any cost.

The Filipinos are a very fatalistic people. An everyday saying in Tagalog is "bahala na," which translates either as "accept what comes and bear it with hope and patience," or "God wills it." Success in the mind of the Filipino is often a function of fate rather than individual merit, and therefore, most people are content in their social position only because they feel fate has placed them there. Expressions such as "never mind," "it doesn't matter," or "it was my fate" are common reactions to problems such as typhoons, epidemics, and crop failures. Another demonstration of their belief in fate is that the Filipinos frequently gamble and play games of chance.

The Filipinos also have some ancient beliefs with regard to spirits and ghosts. At times, the Filipino will use the excuse of these phantoms when he fails to keep an appointment or a promise, which is difficult for Western people to understand.

Due to the Spanish influence, the Filipinos are a somewhat emotional people, and very sensitive. They are loyal friends and demand the same kind of loyalty in return. This aspect is reflected in social situations, as well as business interactions. They are reluctant to share or to do business with a person unless there is a mutual sincerity. This has been a great obstacle in the past, as Filipinos have described American businessmen as being overly aggressive and insensitive to feelings.

The Filipinos are hospitable and enjoy entertaining. When accepting invitations, one should inquire if the starting time is "American time" or "Filipino time." In the case of American time, one should arrive at the hour requested. However, if the arrival time is on Filipino time, it is not necessary to arrive until an hour or two later than requested.

The concept of individualism is valued by the Filipinos. If a foreign businessman fails to treat a Filipino as an individual, the foreigner will be refused help. It is important to take time to talk with adults and children and not to be judgmental. The Filipinos will make every effort to maintain their reputation as being a hospitable people. In return, foreign business people should be polite and respectable towards the Filipinos.

Another influence brought to the Philippines by the Spanish is the machismo attitude. Many married Filipino men may keep a *casa chica,* or concubine, which is generally accepted by their wives. However, this attitude has been changing with the development of human rights and the women's liberation movement. The Philippines prides itself on being one of the few Asian countries with a large percentage of women in government and politics.

Nonverbal Communication

There are several nonverbal communication techniques utilized in the Philippines, and the following are some examples that can be helpful in a business context. The raising of the eyebrows indicates an affirmative reply, namely a "yes." A jerk of the head downward means no, while a jerk upward means "yes." Like the

Japanese, the Filipinos rarely say "no" as we do. They resist confrontation and may say "yes" verbally while putting their head downward, namely a nonverbal signal for "no." To indicate "come here" one would extend the hand out with the palm down moving the fingers in and out as in a scratching motion. When calling a waiter or a waitress in the Philippines, it is customary to hiss in order to get service. Filipino women use fans in this tropical climate and have developed a nonverbal gesture system using various fan movements to signal messages.

Religion

The Philippines is the only predominantly Christian country in the Far East primarily due to the Spanish influence. Over 90% of all Filipinos are Roman Catholic, which affects their culture and daily activities. There are several phrases in Tagalog that incorporate Catholic traditions that are used every day. For example, if someone indicates that he or she is frightened, one would say to that person in Tagalog, "May the Blessed Virgin Mary protect you." At the turn of the century, there was a significant Filipino resentment against the foreign domination of the Catholic Church, which led to a group of native Filipino priests splitting off and forming the Philippine Independent Church, now the second largest church in the islands.

A significant minority striving for human and religious rights is the one and a half million Filipinos who are Moslems. In southern areas of the islands, Islamic practices and militants dominate.

The Idea of Right and Wrong

Although the concepts of morality and ethics are much the same in the Philippines as in the United States, there are certain contrasts. According to American tradition, also present in these islands, right and wrong behavior reflects the relationship between an individual and the Almighty God. Theoretically, punishment or rewards are according to divine judgment. The individual may see certain behavior as sinful, and thus feel guilty if he has sinned. To most Filipinos, however, religion is less specifically related to daily behavior. What is "correct" behavior is more likely to be defined by tradition and related to the family and other reciprocal obligations. Failure to measure up in terms of family expectations and traditions produce feelings of shame.

As in most developing nations, including the Philippines, corruption is prevalent in the public services, government, and business. It is not uncommon for many complications in business and government bureaucracy to be speedily resolved by the payment of a favor. Such practices are the result of long historical and cultural development, rooted in the Spanish tradition in the Philippines.

The Filipinos have produced an extraordinary synergy among their diverse cultural groups. They are a people open to cooperation and collaboration with outsiders.

SOUTH KOREA

Asia, or the Far East, is puzzling and generally difficult for most Western businesspeople to understand. Until recently, Japan was the market and the country most well known. With the normalization of diplomatic relations between the United States and the People's Republic of China, much work and study have been conducted in that area. But Korea was virtually unknown to the rest of the world until the great struggle and war in the 1950s. At that time, it became a focus of world attention in a clash between the East and the West. Korea became a battleground of communist and democratic ideologies. Thus, today it is a divided country, with the U.N. maintaining a buffer zone of peace between the socialistic system of the North under control of the Communist party, and a somewhat democratic, but totalitarian military regime in the South. The two Koreas are clients of the U.S.S.R. in the North and the U.S.A. in the South.

The Economy

South Korea, whose economy is strong, proudly compares its unprecedented economic progress since 1955 with the quick economic recovery of Japan and the Federal Republic of Germany after World War II. Compared with the United States, however, Korean economic standards are still relatively low, but the standard of living is rapidly improving and a strong middle class has begun to emerge. The Korean economy relies heavily on exports. However, with recent industrial development, the emphasis in South Korea has been on the manufacture of consumer goods for shipment overseas. A large percentage of South Koreans are employed in agriculture, and significant effort has recently been made to raise agricultural productivity and marketing systems and to renovate antique farming techniques.

Religion

The underlying ethic of Korea is Shamanism, but the people have also been strongly influenced by Buddhism and Confucianism. Shamanism is the religion of ancient Koreans for whom the elements of earth, mountains, rivers, etc. were sacred. Shamanism was introduced in Korea in the fourth century and has the longest history among the organized religions in Korea. Confucianism also has been a strong force, and the most influential of the newer native Korean religions is Ch-ondo-gyo, which was founded in the mid-nineteenth century on the belief that every person represents heaven. Christianity was introduced in Korea in 1783 by Korean diplomatic delegates who came into contact with the Bible in China.

Cultural Concepts

"What makes a Korean tick?" is a question that has intrigued Western businessmen since their first contact with Koreans many years ago. What do Koreans really think? How can you get to know what they are really thinking? Someone observed that Orientals were called inscrutable because Westerners were too lazy to find out what they think and why. The following comments are intended to help one understand Koreans.

A vital concept to understand in Korea is *kibun,* which is one of the most important factors influencing the conduct and the relationship with others. The word literally means inner feelings. If one's *kibun* is good, then one functions smoothly and with ease and feels like a million dollars. If one's *kibun* is upset or bad, then things may come to a complete halt, and one feels like eating worms. The word has no true English equivalent, but "mood" is close. In interpersonal relationships, keeping the *kibun* in good order often takes precedence over all other considerations.

In business functions, businessmen try to operate in a manner that will enhance the *kibun* of both persons. To damage the *kibun* may effectively cut off relationships and create an enemy. One does not tend to do business with a person who has damaged one's *kibun.* Much of the disturbance of *kibun* in interpersonal relationships has to do with lower class persons disturbing higher class persons. Thus, for example, a teacher can scold a student in the class and no individual feels hurt or no one's *kibun* is especially disturbed.

Proper interpersonal relationships are all important among Koreans, and there is little concept of equality in relationships among Koreans. Relationships tend to be almost entirely vertical rather than horizontal, and each person is in a relatively higher or lower position. It is essential for one to know the levels of society and to know one's place in the scheme of things. In relationships, it is often necessary to appear to lower oneself in selfless humility and give honor to other people. A well-respected Korean often assumes an attitude of self-negation and self-effacement in social and business contacts. To put oneself forward is considered proud arrogance and worthy of scorn.

Protocol is extremely important to Koreans. When meeting others, if you do not appreciate one's actual position and give it due recognition, then one might as well withdraw on some pretext and try to avoid future contacts with those who have misjudged one's true status. A representative of another person or group at a meeting is treated with even more care than that person or group because the substitute may be sensitive to slights either real or imagined and report it back to his colleagues. This is very difficult for Westerners to understand, but a Korean who fails to observe the basic rules of social exchange is considered by other Koreans to not even be a person — he is an "unperson." Foreigners to a certain extent and in a certain sense are considered by Koreans as unpersons. Koreans show very little concern for an unperson's feelings, his comfort, or whether he lives or dies. In short, such an unperson is not worthy of much consideration. When relationships are broken among Koreans, some people tend to resort to violence, but every effort must be made to remain within the framework of polite relationships.

Deference or Respect to Elders

Elders in Korean society are always honored, respected, pampered, appeased. To engender the anger of an elder means serious damage, because his age allows him to influence the opinions of others, regardless of the right or wrong of the situation. In the presence of an elder, one remains at attention and one does not even smoke or drink. Like children, elders must be given special delicacies at meals, and their every wish and desire is catered to whenever possible. The custom and manner in which elderly people are sometimes sent to old persons homes in the United States is extremely barbarous and shocking to the Koreans. Every home in Korea, no matter how poor, allocates the best room in the house to the honored grandfather or grandmother.

Etiquette

Koreans are considered by others to be among the most naturally polite people in the world when the proper rules of etiquette are followed. In personal relationships with strangers or associates, Koreans tend to be very strict in observing the rules of etiquette. To touch another person physically is considered an affront to his person, unless there is a well established bond of close friendship or childhood ties.

In modern Korean society many businessmen now shake hands as a sign that they are modernized. However, they will very often bow at the same time that they shake a person's hand. To slap someone on the back or to put one's arms around a casual acquaintance or to be too familiar with someone in public is a serious breach that may effectively cool future relations.

To embarrass someone by making a joke at his expense is highly resented even if done by a foreigner who does not understand the customs.

After a few drinks, businessmen often become very affectionate, but at the same time apologize for being a bit drunk. The next day they will tell their colleagues that they are sorry for imposing one's good nature while being a little tipsy.

When appearing in public to speak, perform, or whatever, one bows first towards the audience and then towards the chairman of the meeting. Businesspeople should learn the proper bowing procedures and etiquette of Koreans. Korean businessmen do not seem to worry about keeping time, being on time, beginning on time, or leaving on time to the same extent that Western businessmen do. However, this is changing now and there is more of a tendency to follow the same time schedule as in the West.

Introductions. It is not the custom among the Koreans to introduce one person to another. Instead, one would say to another, "I have never seen you before" or "I am seeing you for the first time." The other person repeats the same thing, and then usually the elder of the two persons in age or rank says, "Let us introduce ourselves." Each person then steps back a little, bows from the waist, states his own name. They are then formally introduced. Names are stated in a low, humble voice that cannot be heard accurately, and then calling cards are exchanged. One may learn the new person's name and position at leisure. Do not say, "Sorry, I did not get your name. Would you tell me again?" Calling cards are very necessary in Korea and should be utilized by foreign or Western businesspeople at all times.

The use of names in Korea has an entirely different connotation than in most Western countries. To the Confucian, using a name is presumptuous and impolite, as a name is something to be honored and respected and it should not be used casually. In Shamanism, to write a name calls up the spirit world and is considered bad luck. One's name, whether it is written or spoken, has its own mystique, and is that person's personal property. To call someone directly by his name is an affront in most social circumstances.

In Korea there are relatively few surnames, thus there appears to most Westerners to be an inordinate number of Kim's and Park's. When a Western businessperson uses a Korean's name to his face, one can usually observe a slight wince around the eyes of a Korean. It is almost always there. A Korean is addressed by his title, position, trade, profession, or some other honorific title such as teacher. As opposed to our U.S. training of saying, "Good morning, Mr. Kim," a polite good morning is better or "Good morning, teacher" is acceptable. Many Koreans work and live next to each other for years without even knowing their full names. The president of Korea is referred to by high officials as "excellency," even in his absence, because it is considered too familiar to use such a high person's name in conversation. A Korean's name is usually made up of three characters — the family's surname is placed first, and then the given name, which is made up of two characters. It is used by all members of the same generation. By knowing this name, a person's generation in the family tree can be recognized.

Privacy and Propriety. Privacy is a luxury that few can afford in Korea, and Koreans have learned to make imaginary walls about themselves. A visitor calling on a person on a hot day may find this person in his undershirt with his feet on his desk, fanning himself. The visitor coughs to announce his arrival, but he does not knock. This person does not "see" the person he has come to visit, nor does this person "see" the visitor until he has risen, put on his shirt, coat, tie and adjusted himself. Then they "see" each other and begin the formality of greeting. To have privacy, a Korean withdraws behind an imaginary curtain and undresses, or does what he has to do, not seeing or being seen by those who, by the literal Western eye, are in plain view. It is considered discourteous to violate this screen of privacy once it is drawn about a person. A discrete cough is intended to notify the person behind the screen that an interruption is impending.

Table manners are based on making the guest feel comfortable. The attitude of a servant is proper for a host with his guest. At meals, the hostess is at the lowest place, the farthest from the place of honor, and often will not even eat in the presence of a guest. Before beginning to eat, the host will often make a formal welcome speech stating the purpose of the gathering and paying his respects to his guest. Often food is served on small individual tables, each with many side dishes of food, a bowl of soup, and a bowl of rice. One removes the top off the dish of the hot rice and places it on the floor under his place at the table. Korean food tends to be highly seasoned with red pepper, thus a careful sip of the soup is advisable before taking a large mouthful. To lay the chopsticks or spoon on the table is to indicate that you have finished eating. To put them on the top of a dish or bowl means that you are merely resting. A guest may show his appreciation for the meal by slurping his soup or smacking his lips. Guests are not expected to clean their plates, and to leave nothing indicates that you are still hungry and embarrasses the host by implying that he has not prepared enough food. The host will continue to urge his guest to eat more, but a firm refusal is respected. A good healthy belch after a meal is a sign that one has eaten well and enjoyed it.

Gift Giving. Koreans give gifts on many occasions, and the appropriate etiquette surrounding the giving of gifts is often a problem to Western businesspeople. In this context, every gift expects something in return, and one rarely gives an expensive gift without a purpose. The purpose may be to establish an obligation, to gain a certain advantage, or merely to create an atmosphere in which the recipient will be more pliable to the request of the donor. To return a gift is considered an affront, but in some instances it may be better to return the gift than to accept it with no intention of doing a favor in return. Some Koreans have a special ability to work their way into the affection of foreigners and form personal relationships that may later prove embarrassing and/or difficult to handle when some impossible or very often illegal and unlawful request is made. In Korean, "yes" may merely mean "I heard you," and not agreement or intention of complying. To say "no" is an affront and could hurt the feelings, and thus is poor etiquette. Many Koreans often say "yes" to each other and to foreigners and then go on their own way doing quite the opposite with little sense of breaking a promise or agreement.

Business Attitudes

In business, flattery is a way of life, and without subtle flattery, business would come to a halt. One must begin on the periphery in business relationships and gradually zero in on the main business in narrowing circles. To begin directly a discussion of some delicate business matter or new business venture is considered by Koreans to be the height of stupidity and dooms the project to almost certain failure. Impatience to a Korean is a major fault. A highly skilled businessman moves with deliberation, dignity, and studied motions, and senses the impressions and nuances being sent to him by the other businessman.

To Korean businessmen, Western business persons often appear to make contracts on the assumption that all the factors will remain indefinitely the same. They take a gamble that society will allow them to complete the agreed conditions of the contract. In Korea a written contract is sometimes of little value, though this is currently changing. It may be only a paper contract, and there may be no understanding that it will be kept if the conditions at the time it was made should change. A change in the economy, the political situation, or personal reasons of one of the contractors may invalidate the completion of the contract without any sense of misdeed.

Since there are many similarities between Korean and other Oriental cultures, cross-cultural skills that are effective in this society have application elsewhere. For example, there is a large minority population of Koreans in Los Angeles and their native language is the third largest spoken in that California city. In many ways Korean is also a synergistic culture, except for the political division of the peninsula.

Conclusions

Cultures are complex and multi-dimensional. Researchers, cultural anthropologists, intercultural communication specialists, and business people tell us that more problems exist between nations or groups of people where there are large numbers of cultural factors subject to variation. When working in Asia, physical appearance, language, religion, social attitudes, and basic assumptions about oneself are factors that differ significantly. Differences and difficulties are realities.

Many cultures and business systems in Asia were not discussed in this chapter. However, in the resource appendix at the back of this book are several books that will assist the business person to understand the "realities of differences" and through reflection move towards cooperative interactions or synergy. John Feig in his work *Thais and Americans: Two Distinct Yet Complementary Cultures* ended his excellent analysis with this statement of synergy:

> Each has a gap that could be at least partially filled by drawing on the strengths of the other society. Thus the cultures complement one another, and Americans and Thais, working together as partners, can help one another pick and choose the ingredients which will improve the quality of life of both countries. Thais can try to approach the high American standard of living, and Americans can try to reach the high Thai standard of contentment.[10]

References

1. U.S. Department of Commerce. "World Trade Outlook," *Business America* July 28, 1981.
2. Renwick, G. "Malays and Americans: Definite Differences and Unique Opportunities." Intercultural Press, Inc.
3. Yao, N.C. *The Thunderbird,* Glendale, Arizona, Winter 1980.
4. Forbes, M.S., Jr. "A Poor Country Learns About Modernization," *Forbes,* April 1979.
5. Smith, P.L. "Western Involvement Sought in China's Modernization Effort," *New York Times,* June 21, 1980.
6. Oka, T. "The New 'Long March' to Modernize," *Christian Science Monitor,* March 11, 1980.

7. Huang, T.W. "China Pens Rules for Ventures," *Christian Science Monitor,* March 13, 1980.

8. UPI. "Ice Cream Sodas in China After 14 Years," *New York Times,* June 15, 1980.

9. Feig, J. *Thais and Americans: Two Distinct Yet Complementary Cultures,* Chicago, Illinois: Intercultural Network, Inc., 1978.

12.
Synergy with
Middle Eastern Management

> In the space of a few short centuries, man has moved from a world in which
> life was a simple, straightforward matter of earning one's bread, raising children
> and obeying the commands of God and king, to a world where everything is
> complex, nothing is permanent, and man, himself, is often seen as a vicious
> animal.[1]

Most cultures in the Middle East are traditional and Moslem, and caught in the midst of conflict and change. Synergy is needed to help them build a bridge between traditional and modern cultures, between pre- and post-industrial ways of life. There are numerous examples of why the Middle East could make an excellent laboratory in fostering more collaborative human relations.

Israel, although largely Jewish, must cooperate with its Christian and Arab minorities, as well as its fellow Semites in neighboring lands. Lebanon may not make it into the 21st century as a national entity unless it can produce synergy between its Christian and Islamic factions. Iran must overcome unsynergistic tendencies in its culture to not only bring together its own diverse populations, but to live in peace with its neighbors. It is a prime example of what happens when national leaders do not plan change, and try to bring a people along too fast from the agricultural to industrial stage of development. The repercussion is revolution, which not only plunges its Persian adherents into turmoil, but affects the world. The returned American hostages understand that reality now. Their ordeal might have been avoided if First World America had been more culturally sensitive to Third World Iran and its religious past.

Perhaps no country is more fearful of such "progress" than Saudi Arabia. The anomaly is that while this country has invested billions of oil revenue dollars to create an infrastructure and industry in a tribal nomadic society, which is faithful to Islam and opposed to change, there is considerable opposition to such modernization as was expressed by armed religious followers who, in 1980, took over the Great Mosque in Mecca. Although fears were expressed that Saudi Arabia is vulnerable to the same kinds of forces that operated in Iran, the policy in Saudi Arabia of rapid economic growth and continued development is pursued.

As Stan Windass observed:

> Intermediate technology was originally thought of as technology appropriate to underdeveloped countries, a step toward development. It began when people realized what destruction large industrial enterprises could cause in developing countries. A big plastic-sandal factory might be introduced, say, into an Arab country where sandal-making was already a traditional craft, but one diffused throughout the countryside and involving many supporting crafts besides the sandal-making itself . . . New machinery makes vast quantities of plastic sandals, which flood the market, dislocate the social structure, employ little labor, and draw out wealth for investors in foreign countries. When the machinery breaks down there is neither the local skill, nor the materials with which to repair it. The havoc is completed by closure of the plant.[2]

Another example of unexpected technological impact was presented by Donald Heynemann, when he showed how the construction of the giant hydroelectric irrigation dams in Africa brought unintended and unforeseen consequences, such as parasitic worms:

> As each project begins, its planners speak glibly of the need for information from many disciplines, but once the dams are authorized, they are viewed largely as problems in engineering. Construction is justified on the basis of economics, and considerations of public health or social and cultural change are often sacrificed in the course of dealing with other problems.
>
> One deleterious outcome of this emphasis on engineering has been the creation of conditions that allow parasitic organisms that have afflicted human beings since antiquity to increase their levels of infection beyond their normal intensity or range. The result is disease of unprecedented severity or extent . . .
>
> The high dams of Africa are paradoxical examples of the widespread changes wrought by technology and of the environmental interaction that frequently results in outbreaks of parasitic disease. The three principal African rivers — the Volta in Ghana; the Zambesi between Zambia and Rhodesia, and the Nile of East Africa, Sudan, and Egypt — have been controlled and domesticated though the greatest building efforts since the construction of the pyramids . . .
>
> Eliminating the annual flood has created its own problems. Nitrates and phosphates that fertilized the land every year when the Nile deposited its silt need to be replaced. Phosphates are abundant and can be mined from desert

with energy generated by the dam, but nitrates must be imported. The silt also contained trace elements and other soil nutrients. As reserves of these minerals are used up, people will pay more for artificial fertilizers . . .

One infection peculiarly tied to the increasing number of irrigation canals is schistosomiasis, a snail-borne parasitic disease that afflicts some 175 million persons in Africa and the Middle East, in parts of the Caribbean, and in much of South America and the Far East, particularly the Philippines and China. Outbreaks of schistosomiasis and other water-related diseases were predicted prior to construction of the Aswan High Dam, but economic necessity, the need to resettle thousands, to build towns for them, and to work out the complex logistics involved relegated disease control to a low priority. The human results of this and other projects in Africa appear in World Health Organization reports on tropical diseases spread by water; thousands of children with livers swollen by schistosomiasis; Nigerians and Ghanians blinded by onchocerciasis, a parasitic-worm disease carried by blackflies, which breed in fast-flowing water; Sudanese with visceral leishmaniasis, a frequently fatal disease carried by sand flies, and outbreaks of tsetse fly-borne sleeping sickness among people and domestic animals . . .

The community's children play a primary role in maintaining the cycle. Youngsters carry most of the viable eggs and they deposit them freely in the canals. Children cannot be kept from the water because the habits of defecation and urination in running water are considered clean and appropriate . . .

Formerly, the land of Upper Egypt was cultivated only after the annual flood. The land dried out between the floods killing most of the snails. Rarely did more than 5 percent of the population show evidence of schistosomiasis. As permanent irrigation canals were built and people were continuously exposed to infected snails, infection rates in some areas soared to about 85 percent in less than a year after people moved into the new villages . . .[3]

The effect and impact of technology changes that result in significant environment changes is difficult to judge over a short period of time. But we must be aware of the needs of other cultural groups and retain cultural values and pride in the ancient culture while, at the same time, introducing appropriate technology. The following "culture specific" examples from several countries in the Middle East suggest what some of these cultural synergistic challenges are.

THE ARAB WORLD

Approximately 40% of the world's oil is being produced in the Middle East and Arab Africa, and about 70% of all proven oil reserves are located there. These figures clearly illustrate the necessity of cooperation and synergy between the Western world and the Arab world.

When Jack Grey asked foreign managers what bothered them about working with Americans, their answers indicated why U.S. business people have difficulty working in an intercultural situation. The answers, which clustered around six responses, serve as a warning to any representative of an advanced technological culture seeking to be effective in a more traditional culture:

1. *Americans display feelings of superiority; they know the answers to everything.*

   It is not enough to give; it is how you give that is important. Giving, and leaving the impression that you can easily afford it, is not making a favorable impression on the receivers of your help. Feelings of inferiority and superiority occur. And nobody likes to feel inferior.

2. *Americans want to take credit for what is accomplished in joint efforts.*

   If one thinks he is superior, it will be difficult for him to recognize the input of the others, whom he perceives as being inferior. Since Americans are extremely geared to competition, performance and fast-track careers, it is not surprising to see some of them using this universal tactic. But already having the "American image" it is not forgiven, where it might be for the local man.

3. *Americans are frequently unable or unwilling to respect and adjust to local customs and cultures.*

   The American way of cutting meat is considered by the Europeans as primitive and is the subject of a lot of jokes. Eating with only a fork is considered as being impolite. The way most Americans treat wine and flowers make the French talk about "massacre and barbarianism."

4. *Americans fail to innovate in terms of the needs of the local culture.*

   The U.S. is, in comparison with most countries, more advanced in technology. The danger exists that the American manager (or consultant) will look for innovations based on the American situation, whereas the overseas employee is looking more for a less sophisticated solution . . . A lot of innovations are inspired by American situations and are therefore welcomed with reservation if not with hostility.

5. *Americans refuse to work through the normal administrative channels of the country.*

   Local management sometimes has a tough job in making the U.S. manager understand that he has to respect the legal and contractual stipulations as well as the local existing administrative procedures.

6. *Americans tend to lose their democratic ways of working and acting when on a foreign assignment.*

   The most surprising tendency is that some foreign (American) managers want to instill fear in their local subordinates. They think it is a successful management style. Even if it would be in terms of results (getting the sales or production targets), the image they leave after their departure is a serious handicap for their (foreign) colleagues taking over.[4]

The Arabs possess a common culture that has united them by religious and historical factors. Their life is interdependent and many of its elements are inseparable as each aspect of life depends on another. The Western world has been cognizant of the Arab world for centuries, but the Arabs have often been approached with suspicion. Equality, trust, mutual respect, and admiration have not been characteristics of the relationship.

The presence of Aramco in Saudi Arabia is an example of cooperation and the fruitful interaction of diverse groups of people. The first agreement was signed between the Saudi Arabian Government and Standard Oil Company of California in 1933. Since that time the original terms of the agreement have been successfully renegotiated several times to the benefit of Americans and Arabs.

Chapter 3 presented aspects of Arab culture regarding the resolution of conflict.* Now we focus on some synergistic opportunities and obstacles for foreigners in this diverse part of the world.

In turning to Iran, we would like to refer to the ABC News three-hour presentation "America Held Hostage: The Secret Negotiations," originally shown on January 22, 1981, shortly after the hostages were released. The program was a behind-the-scenes examination of the efforts to find a way to release the hostages. The program's reporter, Pierre Salinger, concluded that the United States spent more than a year trying to negotiate the hostages' release with Iranian officials who were powerless to end the crisis. Salinger stated there were large "cultural gaps" and errors and misunderstandings on both sides. The executive producer of the program, Robert Fry, said:

> . . . We (U.S. negotiators) approached the crisis with a Western mind-set. We dealt with government officials. What better people to deal with? But in Iran, it's the religious leaders who are the political power. It's impossible to realize the turmoil that surrounded the circumstances, the nibbling away, and the erosion of the political climate in Iran.

Had the U.S. negotiators more fully understood the cultural aspects of the crisis, communication might have been facilitated and the crisis cooled. A manager on international assignment should at least be able to answer the following questions concerning the country or culture in which he or she is working:

1. Do you know the names and responsibilities of the persons you will be meeting?
2. Will these persons be able to make the decisions related to your assignment?
3. What do you know of their background?
4. How would you describe the political process?
5. What are the interest groups and how do they express their concerns?
6. Is there a state religion? How many religions are there?
7. How does religion influence the people?

---

*See Chapter 19, "Working in the Middle East," of *Managing Cultural Differences* for further detail on Arab culture.

8. What are some differences between your religious beliefs and the beliefs of this religion?
9. What is the relationship between this country and the U.S.? Presently, in the past ten years, and before that time? What is the projection of their future attitude?
10. Are Americans liked, disliked, and for what reasons?
11. What is your attitude toward the people? Do you feel superior? Inferior?
12. Do you know any effective ways to persuade?
13. What else do you think you should know about this culture in which you will be a "foreigner"?

A synergistic solution was achieved to the hostage impasse when the U.S. enlisted Moroccans as intermediaries in the negotiations.

U.S. exports and technology transfer to the Middle East and North Africa are expected to dramatically increase in the decades ahead. Since the United Arab Emirates are a microcosm of Islamic culture, we asked Leslie K. Healy to prepare the following overview based upon her experience in Abu Dhabi, working for a Middle Eastern multinational organization. Her observations should assist readers who hope to do business there in a culturally sensitive and synergistic manner.

The United Arab Emirates

The United Arab Emirates is located in the Eastern Arabian Peninsula, bounded on the north by the Persian Gulf. The United Arab Emirates include Abu Dhabi (where the federal capital is located), Dubai, Sharjah, Ajman, Umm al-Qawain, Ras al-Khaimah, and Fujaira.

Abu Dhabi is the largest and wealthiest of the emirates, and the site of the federal capital. Other emirates lie along the shore of the Arabian Gulf, with only one emirate lying on the eastern coast.

Dubai, for centuries an ancient hub of trade, is the major commercial center and the most populated of the emirates. Major drydock complexes and large industrial projects are underway in Dubai. The emirate is quite cosmopolitan, with a distinctive international atmosphere.

In Sharjah, an emirate about eight miles north of Dubai, light industry, ore development, and tourism are developing. Sharjah hopes to be the service center for the U.A.E. and is establishing itself in this regard.

Ajman and Umm al-Qawain lie further north, near the Strait of Hormuz. Agriculture is a major source of income. Some oil discoveries have been made, with fishing and quarrying other major activities.

Fujairah lies entirely along the east coast, along the Gulf of Oman. It has a high rainfall, with beautiful mountains and coastal scenery. Fujairah has touristic ambitions along with fishing and agriculture being major sources of income for this emirate.

The U.A.E. has been formerly known under various names, such as the Trucial Sheikdoms, the Trucial States, the Trucial Coast, and Trucial Oman. European and Arab pirates roamed the Trucial Coast area from the seventeenth century well into the nineteenth century; hence the former name, the "Pirate Coast."

The U.A.E. has had a long relationship with the United Kingdom. The U.K. and the Trucial States established close bonds in many treaties throughout the nineteenth and twentieth centuries.

In an 1892 treaty, the Trucial States agreed not to enter into relationships with any foreign government other than the United Kingdom without its consent. In return, the British promised to protect the Trucial Coast from all aggression. This relationship continued well into the twentieth century, and British culture impacts the Emirates. However, in 1971, the U.S. ended the treaty relationships with the Gulf sheikdoms. Bahrain and Quatar became independent in September, 1971, and the United Arab Emirates followed suit on December 2, 1971.

The United Arab Emirates is actually a federation of seven states. In the U.A.E. the Supreme Council of Rulers is the ultimate authority, supported by a council of ministers, and a federal national assembly. The legislative branch consists of a 40-member National Consultative Council. Secular legal codes are being introduced; however, Islamic law is highly influential. Each of the seven emirates is largely self-governing. There are no political parties and no voting.

The U.A.E. has an estimated area of over 80,000 square kilometers (about the size of Maine). The shore of the island-dotted Gulf Coast is low-lying with many *sabkha* (salt flats). The Oman mountains run north-south, close to the east coast. On the western edge of the mountains there is a plain with many fertile patches. The coastal plains gradually give way to the rolling sand dunes, which cover most of the territory.

The population of the United Arab Emirates was estimated at 900,000 in 1979. The population of Abu Dhabi, the capital, is approximately 300,000. Immigrants were attracted by the development of the country, and they form the largest part of the population. The indigenous population is estimated at less than 25% of the total. The population in each emirate is concentrated largely in its capital.

The main ethnic groups are Arab, Indian, Pakistani, and Iranian. The official language is Arabic; however, English is widely spoken, as is French. Other common languages include Farsi, Hindu, and Urdu.

The United Arab Emirates has shown many achievements in development and in the spread of federal activity. The federal government is responsible for education, medical care, low-rent housing, communications and transportation. In many economic matters, the individual emirates develop their own interests, and do not publish budgets.

To be sure, the economy of the U.A.E. is founded on oil and natural gas, accounting for almost all of the country's export earnings, and providing great opportunities for productive investment. Gross domestic production (GDP) was about

$16 billion in 1979, because of significant increases in world oil prices. Per capita income was estimated at $16,000, one of the world's highest.

It must be mentioned that the boom of the 1974-1977 period has ended in the U.A.E. Two bank failures triggered a recession from which the U.A.E. is only now slowly emerging. Local construction has slowed considerably. Major new products are rather unlikely, although projects such as roads, schools, and hospitals are still planned in the emirates. The central government budget was $2.8 billion in 1978, with defense spending comprising nearly 30% of the budget.

The U.A.E. continues to increase its import levels; its major imports being machinery, consumer goods and foods. Imports reached about $5.3 billion in 1978. The major trading partners of the U.A.E. are Japan, the U.K., and the United States. As mentioned earlier, petroleum dominates the emirates' export earnings.

The United States has enjoyed rather friendly, informal relations with the U.A.E. for many years, based on private U.S. contacts in the Gulf area. Upon federation of the U.A.E. in 1971, the U.S. immediately recognized the United Arab Emirates and established formal diplomatic relations.

Cultural Concepts

Greetings, Business Customs, and Courtesies

The Arabs use elaborate and ritualized forms of greetings and leave-takings. Knowledge of these formalities and protocol are essential for the foreign business person visiting in the U.A.E.

The visiting business person may have a long wait before seeing his host, as the Arab sense of time is much more leisurely than the Western. Once having met the host, interruptions may be frequent, constant visitors are usually arriving, messengers being sent and received, etc.

It is very rude to show impatience or to fail to respond to social preliminaries. The visitor will always be offered a refreshment as a sign of hospitality, and this offer should always be accepted.

Business cards are essential, and are usually presented upon the first meeting. This gesture usually results in an exchange of cards. Business cards should be presented in English on one side, with Arabic on the other. The Arabic side of the business card should face up in every presentation to an Arab.

A meeting usually begins and concludes with an offer of coffee or tea. Such an activity is a normal sign indicating that the meeting has ended, and that future meetings should then be arranged.

Titles are not in general use on the Arabian Peninsula, except for royal families, ministers, and high-level military officers.

At the conclusion of the first or second visit, one might present a modest gift. A novelty or souvenir item from the visitor's home country would be quite suitable.

In short, the first business visit and initial business dealings should be approached as a leisurely "getting to know each other" process. Conversation may not get to business for several days, and it is considered rude for the visiting businessman to press the issue.

The people of the United Arab Emirates are generally friendly and courteous. One word is paramount in viewing social customs throughout the U.A.E; in fact, throughout the Arab World. That is, *religion*. Religion is part of a Muslim's daily life, not just on the Sabbath. A visitor who shows respect for the Islamic religion will gain favorable receptions almost everywhere.

The people of the U.A.E., as with all Arabs, place great importance on manners, generosity, and hospitality. The guest or visitor should accept all friendly, gracious gestures.

In regards to Arab generosity, a visiting business executive must take care not to praise or admire anything that his host owns, because the host will feel obliged to give it to the admirer. This is a tradition, and one may diplomatically decline the gesture. However, it is wiser to initially take care not to express too much admiration of any object one's host owns.

Also very important to recognize is that the system of hospitality is based on mutuality. An invitation must be returned; an equal gift must be offered in return. The offer of hospitality to visit an Arab's home must be accepted. Refusing this gesture of friendship is taboo and almost unforgiveable.

Today you may be the guest, but tomorrow you must play the host, according to social customs and courtesies. Be aware of this.

Arabs are generally very status and rank conscious. Take care to acknowledge and pay deference to the senior man first.

Another important thing to remember for any visitor to the U.A.E. is never berate or criticize a person publicly. You will make him lose "face" and you will also be looked down upon for doing this. Don't show signs of condescension towards others; mutual respect and worthiness is expected at all times. This is just not typical of the U.A.E., but is present in all Arab and Middle Eastern customs.

For social contact and entertainment, Arab person-to-person contact is quite ritualistic and private. Any use of first names should be initiated by the Arab host. Any and all opening social moves should also come from the Arab host.

Consumption of alcohol at social events should generally be avoided. When the Arab businessman has visited your country, he certainly may have drunk liquor, but once again in his home country, he returns to customs. A general rule: take your cue from your hosts.

It is expected for one to argue to pay the check at a restaurant. One should make many efforts to pay the bill, though whoever proposed the outing is usually the host. As earlier mentioned, social gestures of hospitality should be returned, with you being the "host."

Most social customs are based on the Arab male-dominated society. Women are usually not part of the entertainment scene for traditional Muslim Arabs. Gulf Arabs, in particular, carry on separate social lives.

Conversational topics of a general nature can be discussed readily, but it is wise to follow your host's lead in this respect and to show agreement and harmony in conversation. Arabic is a high-context language; language and conversation are important. However, the following conversational guide should be followed:

1. *Avoid* bringing up subjects of business before getting "to know" your host. This is considered rude.
2. *Avoid* any questions or comments about a man's wife or any female children over the age of twelve. This is a major taboo.
3. *Avoid* any colloquial questions that could be misunderstood and taken wrongly by the Arab host.
4. *Avoid* any swear words; this is highly distasteful. Off-color jokes are also not appreciated.
5. *Avoid* pursuing the subjects of politics, religion, or financial matters.
6. *Avoid* any discussion of Israel. This is not a pleasant topic for most Arabs.

Often a foreigner seeing two Arabs speaking together may believe they are engaged in an argument of some sort because of the wise gestures, raised voices, and animated facial expressions. This is probably not the case. They are most likely engaged in some lively discussion concerning business, politics, or the like. Contrary to Oriental reservedness, emotional displays are commonplace among Arabs.

Arabs stand much closer together when talking than do Westerners. The conversational distance is often only about ten inches, and to express a point, the Arabs tend to use bodily contact; i.e. tapping a person gently, resting a hand on the other's shoulder or knee, etc. However, Western "backslapping" is considered rude and rather vulgar by most Arabs.

Eye contact is also much more intense than Westerners are usually comfortable with. However, when an Arab businessman meets you for the first time, he may restrict his eye contact because he does not yet know you.

The Arab handshake may appear limp when compared to a hearty Western handshake, but the Arabs do not generally like the hard-pumping Western handshake.

Kissing on the cheeks is also common when men greet each other or when women greet each other. Also, handholding among men friends walking along is a common sight. As previously indicated, much more bodily contact is made between Arab men than between Western men.

Some Arab gestures and expressions may be quite confusing to a Westerner. There is much nonverbal communication in the Arab culture. This includes much talking with the hands, and a profusion of facial expressions. A raising of the eyebrows, or a clicking of one's tongue (or a combined response of the above) signifies a negative response. A positive response is usually given nonverbally by a side nod of the head.

As mentioned before, the Arabs use their hands often. The right hand is for public matters, the left hand for private. Be careful of your hand gestures. Do not accept or give anything with the left hand, the "toilet" hand. Particularly, do not eat with the left hand.

Also, placing hands on the hips may appear to be a challenging gesture to an Arab. Consider your gestures before making them.

Bodily functions, such as sneezing, nose-blowing, etc., are all down-played. The ritual burping after a big meal is no longer considered acceptable in polite circles. Also considered very impolite is exposing the soles of your feet to those present.

The Arabs conduct business in a leisurely way. There is no "one-stop" business dealings in the United Arab Emirates. This is often one of the most frustrating things when a Western businessman is visiting the U.A.E. Negotiations may take months to reach fruition.

The general approach to business does not relate to time. One frequently hears "insh'allah" or "God willing" as an answer to a question. Patience is a virtue, and the visiting businessman may have to return to the U.A.E. again and again, before business is completed.

To get started in business in the U.A.E., one must find a local sponsor. A foreign concern must be represented by a local agent or sponsor in the U.A.E., as in many of the Arab countries.

Extensive preparation should be made before visiting the U.A.E. Contact should be made with several local sponsors, and, even then, surprises should be expected upon arrival in the U.A.E.

Requests for appointments should include a statement identifying the purpose of the visit. It is wise to remember patience; the businessman wishing to establish initial contacts will find it necessary to spend at least a week in the U.A.E. to obtain initial appointments.

Connections are essential in conducting business in the U.A.E. "Well-connected" people progress faster, and more easily gain access to public and private decision-makers.

Bargaining is a Middle Eastern art, and the visiting businessman must be prepared for some old-fashioned "haggling." Establishing a personal rapport, mutual trust, and respect are essentially the most important factors leading to a successful business relationship. The Arab businessman does business with the man, not with the company, or the contract.

Culture Tips

There are some wise points for a traveler to remember when visiting the Middle East:[5]

1. Knowledge of a few sentences of Arabic, even a few words, can do wonders to enhance one's image.

2. Knowledge of some aspects of Islamic culture and religion will be highly appreciated.
3. No casual religious references should be made. Respect your host's religion.
4. The Persian Gulf is the *Arabian Gulf* to an Arab, particularly someone from the United Arab Emirates or any other Gulf states.
5. Political, religious, and personal discussions are best kept to a minimum.
6. All Middle Easterners are not Arabs or Muslims (Iranians are not Arabs).

Synergistic Opportunities

The new relationship being established between Israel and Egypt is an example of what can happen when persons develop and apply problem-solving skills in resolving long-time conflicts. Simply sitting down, talking, and trying to understand each other better was not what brought Israel and Egypt as far as they have come. A mediator of stature was necessary. Analyzing the conflict, exploring each side's perspectives, and developing new solutions (synergy) are important. Mediators to international conflicts attempt to create the conditions to accomplish this analysis and problem-solving. Nations cannot be treated as individuals, but individuals with a common heritage share much in common, and these common perceptions can be explored and understood.

The Middle East is but a short jet hop to Europe, and the interchange of people from both continents has vastly increased, for business and pleasure. Arabs fly regularly to Europe to study, invest, engage in commerce, seek medical assistance, or vacation. Many reside permanently or temporarily on that continent, especially in the U.K. On the other hand, Europeans go to the Middle East for new markets and as tourists. The potential for synergy is there if the Europeans and Arabs learn to understand each other's cultural differences and historical developments, respect one another, and consciously search for cooperative endeavors for mutual benefit.

The reader is referred to Appendix C for more detailed readings on the Middle East.

References

1. Anon. "The Battered Human Ego," *The Futurist,* June 1978.
2. Windass, S. "An Alternative Society," *Yale Review,* Summer 1976.
3. Heynemann, D. "Dams and Disease," *Human Nature,* February 1979.
4. Grey, J. "The Most Common Criticisms of American Technological Assistance by Foreign Co-workers," paper presented at Texas A&M University, College Station Tex., 1975.
5. Assi, R. "Saudi Arabia: The Kingdom and the Power," *National Geographic,* September 1980.

13.
Synergy with European Management

These comments by Dr. Carl Zimmerer express a controversial viewpoint, but also provide food for thought for the North American hoping to be effective in European trade.

For many years, European businessmen looked up to American managers with admiration, but those days are long gone. Gone is the belief that losses can be turned into profits simply by selling ailing European companies to American corporations.

In France, the Netherlands, and Belgium, American-managed firms had endless disputes with the authorities because managers did not stick closely enough to the employment agreements they signed with the respective governments in return for relocation subsidies.

The British media wrote scathing reports about American companies that wanted to shut down their British subsidiaries because of lagging labor productivity. In Germany, several U.S. parent corporations suffered losses in the millions because they closed down their affiliates in haste rather than slowly selling them at low cost, thus avoiding employees' severance pay.

Moreover, the American policy of "hire and fire" has resulted in many European managers leaving companies acquired by U.S. corporations. This forced U.S. parent companies to search for new managers on the open market. Those they brought in either had been fired from other jobs because they did not meet standards, or they were pirated away from other companies at salaries sometimes twice as high as their market value.

Nobody likes to work for the Americans. Executives don't feel like heads of companies but like messenger boys.

Then, there are language problems; American managers who have been stationed abroad with a subsidiary of a U.S. corporation fail to speak the host country's language even after living in the country for many years. When a major American bank acquired majority interest in a European bank, the manager sent there by the U.S. bank demanded that his colleagues and employees conduct all business in English.

American executives are accused of hiding their lack of decision-making power behind their refusal to speak with the workers' councils in their native language.

American corporations are no longer backed by a government that has to be everybody's guiding light. Indeed satellite nations have become stars in their own right. They know they can do more on the American market with their irrational operating methods, their lack of long-range planning, their outmoded accounting systems, and their outdated products than American companies can achieve on the European market with glamour products and Harvard MBA's.[1]

Still another perspective was provided by a panel of American executives in a seminar sponsored by the World Trade Association of San Diego and the U.S. Department of Commerce. They advised those hoping to be successful in doing business in Europe to:

- Locate a U.K. plant on the continent and use a European label on products; it provides better market penetration.
- Emphasize customer service in the selling because that is where European competitors are weak, especially in repair of home appliances.
- Publish a price list in terms of local currency, not U.S. dollars, and lease all office equipment in Europe.
- Hire only those North Americans willing to make at least a two-year commitment to working in Europe, and insist that sales representatives tell the truth about products and service as a manifestation of their knowledge and competence. Sales personnel are key people in Europe.
- Provide continuity in Europe, avoid an economic seesaw, and hang on in bad economic times as a demonstration of commitment to the area. Representatives should demonstrate long-term effective performance, because Europeans are very resistive to change, even in personnel.
- Strategic planning is needed to penetrate the European secondary market of Spain, Greece, Yugoslavia, and Eastern Europe because of censored communications and government restrictions.
- Be prepared to do business indirectly, such as using an Austrian trading company to do business with the Eastern bloc of nations.
- Be ready for technical difficulties and know local business customs. For example, beside language difficulties, forms may be of different lengths and not

copied on standard machines, or ink may not reproduce well. Using titles properly, even when honorific, is important. Equipment nomenclatures may have different words or meaning than in America.

- Europeans like personal contact, personal mementos. To the European, what is being sold may not be as important as who you are. A favorable impression (cemented by a token gift) often can mean a sale even when the competitor's price is lower. The American firm's business representative must be carefully chosen and checked (orally, because if the person is a European, others will not commit opinion about the individual on paper). Europeans take business a lot more personally than Americans, and that refers also to business relations.[2]

In this chapter, we will consider some aspects of European management, as well as the realities of the cultural differences. Only then is one prepared to promote cultural synergy. In *Managing Cultural Differences,* a case study was provided on doing business in England and Ireland, while Chapter 13 offered some insights on commerce and its cultural dimensions in France and Eastern Europe. Here, we will provide some further culture specifics on the French, and include some new material on the prosperous West Germans whose country is a miracle of economic recovery from WWII. Doing business in Europe with cultural sensitivity requires acceptance of the continent as two economic and ideological blocs of nations — the West, as part of the First World of free enterprise and more democratic governments; and the East, sometimes designated as the Second World because it is part of the worldwide communist bloc. Trade, technological and scientific, and cultural, exchanges have been the instruments of synergy in a divided Europe. The East Europeans also have their multinational corporations and attend international professional meetings. Regional economic groupings, whether they are the West's Common Market or the East's COMCOM, are steps toward synergy for the whole continent.

WORKING AND DOING BUSINESS IN GERMANY

Proverbs influence subsequent generations because they embody human reality and experience in symbol, and thus are unique to a culture. A Scottish saying "As the people, so the proverb." We begin our material on Germany with examples of some German proverbs, which are intended to give further insight into areas of differences and the potential for synergy.

German Proverb	Meaning
"Work makes life sweet."	Work is a reward.
"Create, create, build houses."	Be constructive.
"An ax in the house spares calling the carpenter."	Do things for yourself if you can.

"Without diligence, perseverance, and effort, there is no reward."	Work hard.
"No oak falls with one blow."	Be patient.
"All beginnings are hard."	Patience, especially at the start.
"From the word to the deed, there is a long time."	Talking is easy; doing is difficult.
"Punctuality is the the courtesy of kings."	Be on time.
"Do not put off until tomorrow what can be done today."	Dependable people do not procrastinate.
"Morning hour has gold in its mouth."	Those who rise early will reap rewards.
"Order is heaven's first law."	Orderliness.
"Hoping and waiting makes a fool of many."	Work hard.
"A friend to all is a friend to none."	Be selective.
"A good conscience is a soft pillow."	Be good and you will be treated fairly.
"Less is often more."	Value small things.
"The Donau and the Rhine do not flow together."	Two large (powerful) things don't belong together.
"He who doesn't stoop for a penny is not worth a pound."	Appreciate the small yet important aspects of life.
"The rich man can eat with only one mouth."	More is not necessarily better.

German Management

These proverbs are in some instances similar to proverbs in the United States and in other cases different. They indicate ideals that people strive for and provide areas of cooperation.

Top German executives and senior officers have traditionally come from the aristocratic families in Germany. This has resulted in a great deal of prestige for the business elite and it also has been instrumental in introducing the values of the aristocratic society into business. After World War II this changed somewhat when many of the aristocratic families lost their past importance and, as a result, top management positions became available to young businessmen trained in management, regardless of birthright.

Research has indicated that in many ways German management has been influenced by American strategies and models of management. For example, German management texts contain chapters on Management by Objectives and the Delphi Technique, as well as a variety of other U.S. management strategies and philosophies.

The organization of German firms influences many management functions, because German firms have traditionally had a distinct hierarchy of managers and personnel, and a sometimes rigid approach to change. At the management level, there are several groups in the organizational structure that include top managers, senior executives, middle managers, and lower managers. The autocratic and rigid structure of many German firms is accentuated by a centralized authority, which results in an "ultimate authority," whereby a manager expects obedience of his subordinates. The manager, then, becomes a kind of benevolent dictator.

A typical German manager is extremely authoritarian when compared to the typical American manager and participation in the decision-making process by subordinate German managers does not play as great a role as in an American organization. German managers show a reluctance to delegate authority and are less open with information, believing that it is not necessary for subordinates to know everything. U.S. managers working in German organizations or with German firms often complain that more information is necessary for successful job performance.

Loyalty and hard work are important factors determining the success of a manager in a German firm. The road to senior management can be viewed as a pyramid with each level being defined by a precise title, salary scale, and specific fringe benefits. This system works well because of the sense of order it instills in its members. Being status and title conscious, a German manager will accept promotion readily and will be aware of the responsibilities of his new position and his chances for promotion. Respect for one's superiors is demonstrated by a strong sense of formality, both on the job and off the job. Even managers who have worked together for many years but are of different status levels use the formal address form *Sie* (you) rather than the informal *du*. It is also not appropriate to use first names when speaking to one's colleagues.

Codetermination Act

This act which became law on May 4, 1976, required that companies with over 2,000 employees give the workers parity with the shareholders on the firm's supervisory board or the board of directors. In the event of a deadlock between the union members and the shareholders, the decision of the shareholders will prevail. The board's chairman is chosen by the board members, but, if the necessary two-thirds majority cannot be achieved in selecting this person, the shareholders have the ability or option to chose whomever they want.

Work councils and codetermination, as well as representation on the board of directors in large German corporations is a way of life in German organizations. These procedures and structures have resulted from old German codetermination laws that date back to 1920, when the first law providing for work councils was enacted. Presently, work councils are necessary in all organizations that employ more than twenty people.

In addition to work councils, German workers also have representation on the board of directors in organizations that employ more than 2,000 people. Prior to 1976, workers in industries other than iron, coal, or steel had only one-third representation. However, with the enactment of the Codetermination Act of 1976, the principle of parity representation in all organizations was extended.

The purpose of the work council is to serve as a kind of barometer, which measures the overall labor relations climate in an organization. It also allows management and workers to respond to problems very quickly. In the United States, the labor-management relationship is usually strained, if not adversary. H. C. Jain states:

> Work councils provide a legitimizing context for joint cooperative programs (such as improving the quality of work life at the work place), which might otherwise be perceived by the unions as unilateral and manipulative management schemes. Furthermore, European experience tells us that, despite differences in size, composition, and the competence of work councils or work committees among different European countries, they have demonstrated a capacity to find solutions to major problems in the enterprise before they evolve into hardened issues.[3]

In the United States, management and labor are expected to fight for their members and to receive the largest possible slice of the pie. German unions on the other hand, are characterized as wanting to help in the "baking" of the pie. Besides the policies resulting from codetermination laws, there are a number of other differences between German and U.S. management. Peter F. Drucker, states:

> Foreign managers increasingly demand responsibility from their employees, all the way down to the lowest blue collar worker on the factory floor. They are putting to work the tremendous improvement in the education and skill of the labor force which has been accomplished in this century. The Japanese are famous for their "quality circle" and "continuous learning." In Germany, a highly skilled senior worker known as the "Meister" acts as a teacher, assistant, and standard-setter, rather than as a "supervisor" and "boss."[4]

The "Meister" system in German management and organizations is not new, and it has been used in a variety of contexts over the years. However, as it is presently employed, it dates to post-World War II, and basically restructures the role and responsibilities of a first-line supervisor. This system breaks the barrier between lower and higher levels of management, and develops or attempts to develop a cooperative relationship between supervisors and subordinates.

It is important for American managers who are considering investment in Germany to realize that it is expected and required that there be substantial employee representation on the policy-making board. This representation is involved in major plant openings and closings, hiring and lay-offs, and day-to-day plant operation. The effect of the worker representation on the decision-making advisory board has other implications in long-range management planning.

Attitudes and Values

Perhaps the German worker is the key to the amazing reconstruction of Germany that has occurred since the end of World War II. The German worker is deeply ingrained with a sense of order and discipline in contrast with many American worker concepts of individualism and a laissez-faire attitude toward work.

There are also differences between German and American workers regarding their orientation towards time. Most Germans are more inclined to work from the past to the present, and the American is inclined to move from the present to the future. The future-orientation of American workers leads them to respect values such as vitality, mobility, organization, abundance, and informality. Whereas, the Germans' attachment to the past leads to his respect for stability, wisdom, quantity, diversity, and convention.

German managers have a strong sense of order, and traditional German values have been influenced by the Christian ethic. The good German manager is honest, hard-working, intelligent, thorough, and strong in body and character. German people perceive themselves as being trustworthy, industrious, efficient and creative. German managers strive for perfection and meticulously seek out details.

German people place a great deal of importance on a close-knit family. From the secure base of the family, Germans feel better able to face an unsure world. The male in a traditional German family maintains an unchallenged dominant position in the home. His wife is expected to obey him and his children are expected to respect and submit to his authority.

Friendships are highly valued and are as strong as family ties. Friendships are based on strong emotional connections, which lead to a common identity, as opposed to many American friendships that are based on mutual interests.

German people are very status conscious and often have relationships that are based on social status rather than on personal or emotional ties. Formality and aloofness are characteristically German. Only if the relationship is close is it considered socially correct to use first names, and then only by mutual consent. It is deemed presumptuous to inquire about another's personal affairs or to neglect to use one's title where applicable.

The two most important characteristics and values of the German people might be those of order and discipline. An orderly life is of critical importance for the German person and this is accomplished by striving for discipline. German people might submit themselves to the authority of the society or the controlling group in order to accomplish this discipline, even though it may contradict their own values.

Most German managers or executives will not see visitors unless the time has been arranged in advance. This requirement from the German's perspective is based on a keen sense of order and an aversion to surprises. In making contact with German organizations, American managers should seek appointments with persons at the highest possible level of the organization. In very large organizations, it may be impossible to contact the chief executive officer and very often the lower level managers will participate in initial contacts.

The typical German manager is not professionally mobile and most have had only one or two employers in their lifetime, as compared with the American executive at the same level who has had seven or eight employers. This results in a strong degree of company loyalty. Power in German organizations flows from the top down and very carefully from one organizational level to the next. In general, German management theory has been dominated by highly technical concerns. Many German managers have engineering backgrounds.

German technicians and consultants are promoting synergistic ventures around the world. Their automakers, for example, have opened plants in the U.S., which develop a German-American manufacturing approach. According to Dr. Georg Dittmar, international franchise consultant, they have adopted American fast-food and food marketing strategies, such as the convenience store chain, but then give such operations in "Deutschland" a special German dimension. German service organizations have promoted synergistic projects in many less developed countries.

WORKING AND DOING BUSINESS IN FRANCE

Chapter 3 discussed aspects of the decision-making process as learned in the United States. For purposes of comparison, we illustrated aspects of the Japanese decision-making process — the ringi seido — of which many international managers are well familiar. As an illustration of the complexity of conducting international business in Europe, we will focus upon one aspect of French organizational culture — decision-making.

A Historical/Cultural Perspective

During the last century and a half, France has experienced many profound economic changes that have directly contributed to its newfound status as one of the wealthiest and most technologically advanced societies.* The nation has managed to sustain a faster rate of growth than any other European country, and, according to economic forecasts, promises to be, by 1985, the biggest economic power in Eu-

---

*This material on France is from a paper by Christine Reddy.

rope. While many ascribe this tremendous economic revival to the planned nature of the economy under "Le Plan" and the close association between government and industry, more directly, it is attributable to a post-war resurgence of new planners and pioneers who pushed aside the old industrialists and filled many of the key positions in industry in defiance of the pre-war penchant for gerontocracy. In speaking of the cause for change in French industry, Landes refers to

> . . new ideas and attitudes . . . largely imported into the business world from outside by three groups: economists and bureaucrats who had been exposed to Keynesian and post-Keynesian economics, often in the course of wartime exile; a small number of young men trained in business or engineering schools abroad; and the postwar graduates of French commercial and technical schools, who found much greater opportunities than their predecessors simply because the advance of technology and corporate business organization made formal training increasingly valuable if not indispensable. The influence of the new outlook depended, however, on the readiness of the great mass of old-line businessmen and officials to accept these carriers, listen to their expansive message, grant them positions of power.[5]

The majority of economists agree on this view of the French revival, but find it baffling that it cannot be explained by pure economic factors. Professor Charles Kindleberger writes, "to conclude that basic change in the French economy is one of people and attitudes is frustrating to the economist but, after examining and discounting a number of economic explanations of the French recovery, it does seem to be due to the restaffing of the economy with new men and new French attitudes.[6]

Prior to the war, the structure of French industry was characterized exclusively by the family-owned enterprise, which had developed from historical feudalistic lineages of medieval France. Single proprietors, artisan workers, and family businesses constituted the mainstream of French production and commerce. A special study of the 1936 census showed that with the exception of the iron and steel industry, relatively few establishments employed more than a handful of workers. In most branches of industry, production units had rosters ranging from an average of thirty-eight employees to five and even fewer.

In comparison to the neighboring European countries whose production units tended to be much larger and infinitely more specialized, France suffered from an archaic manufacturing capacity. French workers avoided the new developing technical structures in favor of the small-scale, unstructured and commercially isolated enterprises managed by the interests and business strategy of the family unit. The firm was perceived by its owners as a financial extension of the bourgeois household, and more important than free enterprise, they believed that the firm's self-sufficiency and independence were of paramount significance.

Borrowing was kept at a minimum in order to avoid any obligations to the banks and also to avoid any monetary risk that might result in failure and thus, disgrace the family name. In order to remain independent, stable and secure, profits were the goal rather than growth.[7] According to Crozier's study, the firm's interests were subordinate to family imperatives:

> The essential unit of social strategy is the family and not the individual. Business life is deeply influenced by the battle which bourgeois families sustain against each other in order to maintain and improve their respective positions. This game is extremely tight. It does not call for taking risks and moving boldly ahead; its natural economic consequence is the model of safe management. Traditional bourgeois businessmen would indulge simultaneously in petty economics and in conspicuous consumption, but would have difficulty embarking on an aggressive investment policy.[8]

Consequently, the complexities of a large firm were deemed to be beyond the managerial capacities of the family members. Therefore, in lieu of expansion, they concentrated on securing a steady source of income in order to preserve the family's status. Patrimonial and conservative business strategies guided the family entrepreneurs. Management authority resided in a single individual, the head of the family, whose responsibility it was to oversee all aspects of the business. His prime function was to safeguard the company for the family succession. Management, as a rule, was not shared with family members, and, most certainly, not with outsiders. Authority was thus highly-centralized and direction was autocratic.

Following World War II, the French economic and social structure witnessed a decline in the small family unit for three reasons: first, suitable heirs could not always be found to carry on the business; second, the government began imposing heavy death duties; and third, and perhaps most significant, to keep abreast of the competition from the United States, Japan and the neighboring European countries, it became evident that investments would be required, which necessitated much larger amounts of capital than could be extracted from a handful of individuals.[9]

Today, French industry is a peculiar mix of the old and the new. "Behind the glittering technological triumph of the Concorde and the insolent innovation of Citroen motorcars, the backward and fragmented structure of many parts of industry still survives unharmed."[10] Large monolithic corporations, which have for the most part been nationalized, preside next to a growing number of private enterprises and the traditional family groups of artisan workers, who are for the most part, still engaged in business on their own account. Thus, in spite of its drive towards modernity, and decades of upheaval and restructuring, France is still a market of family empires and paternalistic traditions. In any study of French management, one must realize that the remnants of this country's feudalistic heritage are so deeply rooted within the French spirit that it often accounts for the conservative and autocratic nature of their business methodology.

While the recovery of the French economy was directly attributable to a new and dynamic breed of civil servants and elites, they have not done much to change the French management philosophy. Because the former members of the Grand

Corps, the civil servants, restaffed French industry after the war instead of return-ing to government, very little has been done to expand the field of management. Their transfer from the government to commerce has merely reinforced an already class-conscious and distinct elite whose management philosophy is based on the traditional family unit. As Ehrmann points out,

> . . . The Grand Corps, those civil servants occupying posts that govern or in-fluence economic matters and interests, move quite readily from the administra-tion to high positions in industry and commerce, while only a grave national emergency would induce a businessman to accept a post in government. The number of former functionnaires employed in business is steadily increasing. For the most part they are simply returning to the milieu from whence they came after enjoying, partly at the expense of the state, the still highly regarded training afforded by public service.[11]

Citroen, Michelin, Peugeot, and Panhard are just several examples of many of the large industrial structures that, until recently, operated strictly within the framework of the traditional bourgeois entrepreneurial system. But, one by one, because of competition, growth, and the high cost of maintaining technical progress, they are undergoing radical transformations, in order to attain the re-sources and expertise that the family unit can no longer supply. Today, only Peugeot can claim to be a real "family" company. Five members of the Peugeot family preside over the eleven-man board and the effective managing director of the group, Francois Gautier, joined the clan by marriage. It is interesting to note that in spite of its paternalistic traditions, Peugeot, over the past several years, has consistently been ranked as the most successful of the French car companies.[12]

Renault and The Compagnie Electro-Mecanique, on the other hand, are two ex-amples of companies that espouse the new liberal management philosophy. How-ever, while they both disengaged themselves from family ties and claim to have adopted a decentralized management structure, they nonetheless, are governed autocratically.[13]

The basic creed of European managers is Fayolism, introduced by Henri Fayol in 1916. Fayol was largely responsible for the idea that business management is a unique activity that could be studied and improved upon. In his major work, *General and Industrial Administration,* he analyzed the functions of a business enter-prise and expanded on how the head of a firm should conduct his administrative duties — planning, organizing, coordinating, commanding, and inspecting. His management philosophy was authoritarian in nature and highly centralized and it reinforced the family industrial mentality that the businessman is supreme in his domain. Fayol believed that "in all human associations, in industry, commerce, army, home, state, dual command is a perpetual source of conflict. A body with two heads is, in the social as in the animal sphere, a monster and has difficulty in surviving."[14] Instead he proposed his principles of Unity of Command and Unity of Direction under which an employee should receive orders from one supervisor

only; "one head and one plan for a group of activities having the same objective."
Fayol believed that as soon as "two superiors wield their authority over the same
person or department, uneasiness makes itself felt and should the cause persist, the
disorder increases and the malady takes on the appearance of an animal organism
troubled by a foreign body."[15] (Obviously, this belief conflicts with modern matrix
management.)

Fayol's doctrine of management was the core for many industrialists and his principles still constitute much of the current managerial philosophy in France. His
autocratic stance and his conviction that people must be centrally governed reinforced the managerial pattern of the Grand Corps and the French family barons.
Consequently, centralized management characterizes the greater part of French
industry.

Up until fairly recently, schools of business administration, and indeed, formal
preparation for business were virtually nonexistent within France. However, as the
heads of European enterprises began to realize that management is a distinct occupation for which particular professional skills are required, and for which specific
intellectual training can be undertaken, more and more young European managers
possessing business degrees have emerged and are trickling into the French corporations. More recently, Europe has witnessed a mass import of American managerial methods and a mass migration of their youngest managers to American
business schools. Consequently, French managerial thought is gradually becoming
a blend of the traditional Fayolist philosophy combined with the American influence of systematic management education.

In the United States and France, the hallmark of the manager is his decision-
making authority. An individual can only rightly be classified as a manager when he
acquires or receives the authority for making decisions. This managerial "right" is
as important in the doctrine of Fayol as it is in American corporative thought.

French Management

The preceding information makes it clear that the French centralization of control means that decision-making powers are vested in the *homme seul*, or lone
leader. Most of the strategic decisions are concentrated at the top of the managerial
hierarchy and there is also a pronounced tendency not to communicate the reasoning behind these decisions to those at lower management levels. As a result, the
initiative of subordinates is often severely stifled, the talents of middle managers
are wasted, and more often than not, a big gap in communication exists between
the top and lower rungs of industrial enterprises.

The technique of "brainstorming" which is a form of collective thinking widely
used in American management circles, has not been very well accepted within
French industry, even in corporations that have sought greater decentralization of
authoriity and participative management. Consequently, committees are far less
important in the French managerial process than they are in the United States.

Preference has always been given to high-quality individual thinking and decision-making, rather than to group thinking.

In a survey conducted by Bass and Burger in which they assessed international managers on the basis of similarities and differences in attitudes, values, and beliefs, France ranked among the nations that least favored group decision-making. They ranked higher than average in indicators of risk tolerance and reported themselves as being quick decision-makers, but not impulsive ones. [16] It would seem from these results that French managers are not adverse to making decisions under conditions of uncertainty; however, they seem to devote more time and rationality than their American counterparts in arriving at important decisions.

Farmer and Richman in *Comparative Management and Economic Progress,* observe that French industrialists tend to be rather conservative risk-takers and they believe the lower achievement drive is an important factor, in addition to other sociological and cultural factors. [17] The French are preoccupied with a great urge for security and this attitude manifests itself in the decision-making practices of French management. But, according to Farmer and Richman, it is possible that the conservatism is changing, mainly as a result of the French Economic Plan and "the provision of more relevant information for micromanagerial decision-making in business (which) is leading to a somewhat less conservative view toward risk-taking and to a somewhat more expansionist business attitude." [18]

French management is also being introduced to the scientific method and its use in the decision-making function. As compared to practices in the United States, less use tends to be made of scientific methodology and a far greater reliance is placed upon intuition. Presently, this is largely because organized management theory and processes are only just beginning to make their debut in European industry. As previously mentioned, the French are adverse to decisions made on a collective basis, as they feel that the man at the top has exclusive rights to this management function. As a result, considerably less use is made of staff specialists, consulting firms, and various other aids, including data analysis, which would assist French management in solving their business problems. [19]

Theoretically, authority in industry must be shared with the workers through *comités d'enterprise,* which were prescribed by French labor laws in 1945. The comités d' enterprise were designed to bring the employers and the workers together for regular meetings to discuss specific subjects. They were the first move towards labor-management cooperation which later developed into participative management. Like its successor, the comités have not been very successful as the employer sees in them a possible threat to his authority.

Labor unions, which have been a feature of French industrial life for many years, are also viewed by the French manager as a potential threat. Since the unions' inception, the French worker has demanded the right to control and even participate in management decision-making. The autocratic stance of the industrialists has placed labor and management in a historical and deep-seated conflict which is reinforced by the wide social and economic gap that separates them. And, it is this very gap that has persuaded management to withhold from labor any sharing of responsibility for running the business. Consequently, even when companies, such as Renault have claimed to operate according to the principles of participative management and purport to having a large number of workers' councils, the top hierarchy have not allowed them to place any great restraint on their decision-making activity. In reality, these councils have merely helped to give the workers the feeling that they are more involved in the business society than in the past.[20]

Because the concept of an organized and systematic management method is basically new to French management circles, there is very little that has been written on how the great industrialists actually go about determining company goals and defining plans. Other than the fact that decision-making in France tends to be much more autocratic and centralized than decision-making in America, the French have elaborated very little on the way they consider alternatives and choose a position. According to Grosset, who has studied executive teams in France and Europe,

> The trend to create a corporate executive within the large corporations reflects the awareness of the senior executives of a need to expand the basis of their decision-making. However, as in the United States, it is very difficult to assess the scope of management decision-making as very few corporations have declared how their executive decisions are made.[21]

As the top of the French managerial hierarchy becomes charged with a new and young breed of European middle managers who have acquired skills and knowledge in a systematic management method, then such functions as problem-solving and decision-making will, no doubt, take on a more structured approach. However, because the idea of the *homme seul* or the *père de famille* is deeply imbedded within the French character, it is doubtful that French decision-making will be very quick to change from its centralized position to a more participative one in the very near future.

In doing business with the French in the last decades of the twentieth century, four realities should be considered:

1. The drive for E.C.C. leadership seen in the development of new technologies in France and attempts to serve as headquarters of the European parliament.
2. The political attempts by France to steer a neutral course in competition between Europe's Western and Eastern bloc. The French have not only maintained an independent position with the communists in the Soviet bloc, but with Islamic countries as well. The 1981 election of a socialist adminstration portends other challenges for change in that country's position in the international market.
3. The 1981 election outcome will significantly change French business and industry. President Mitterand and the socialists are moving the country toward decentralization of power and nationalization of many industries.
4. Finally, the French are rugged individuals and somewhat culturally unsynergistic.

PROMOTING SYNERGY IN EUROPEAN BUSINESS ENDEAVORS

One's success in doing business in Europe depends on many factors, but a necessary prerequisite is a knowledge of the local business environment of the country in which one intends to work. An important element of this prerequisite is to remember that Europeans are not all alike. Although the European business microculture has many similarities, national cultural differences are an important consideration in Europe. For example, Switzerland and France are neighboring countries, yet business techniques and modes are quite different.

Switzerland is a multicultural and multilingual society. Swiss executives are precise, prompt, and meticulous. This precision is often reflected in their characteristics, dark suits and ties, and formal greetings. Business meetings are for specific purposes, and pleasantries should be kept to a minimum. The Swiss are well known for their financial acumen, honesty and integrity, as well as for their emphasis on time. To foster collaboration one must do business on their terms.

The ways of the French are quite different from the Swiss. Whereas the Swiss executive will be in the office at 8 a.m. or earlier, the French executive rarely arrives before 10 a.m. The Swiss may wish to immediately get down to business, but the Frenchman enjoys exchanging pleasantries and light conversation. He considers it rude to launch into business right away. The French are actually quite conservative in regards to business, despite their sometimes avant-garde reputation. They are formal, and there still exist many social and class distinctions. Exhibiting good taste and making a good impression is vital.

Another important aspect to doing business in Europe is to remember that most of the business representatives you will meet in Europe (outside the United Kingdom) will have learned English as a second language. They may need more time to understand what is being said. One should speak slowly, clearly, and avoid slang and colloquialisms. Then seek feedback to determine if your message was understood. Above all, a Canadian or American businessperson should show patience and understanding for someone having difficulty expressing himself in English.

In addition, those who speak English will probably speak British English, which has different spellings and meanings from American or Canadian English. For example, the British equivalents to the American cigarette, restroom, drug store, and subway are fag, lou, chemist, and underground or tube, respectively.

Besides language and local customs, there are perception problems between North Americans and Europeans, as illustrated by a Russian observer:

> . . . Phoenix, the capital of the State of Arizona, where Soviet journalists, with rare exceptions, are for some unknown reason not allowed to go . . . Twice I ran into a sandstorm, and once, walking a few blocks in the city at noon, I almost suffered a heat stroke. But worst of all was the constant thirst . . . Although water here is worth its weight in gold and contains salts that tend rapidly to cause kidney stones, this did not discourage those who dreamed of becoming owners of plots of land in their declining years.[22]

There is great room for expansion in the international operations of many corporations. Some U.S. companies, have been reluctant to deal in foreign countries, and American business people have become discouraged because they do not understand the mentality and culture of the people they are dealing with. While there is much to learn about the complexities of doing business in Europe, taking certain steps in advance, such as consulting government, commercial and trade departments, and doing one's cultural "homework," will greatly enhance the prospect of synergy with Europeans "on the continent," as well as with Europeans in North America.

Finally, North and South America are experiencing an unprecedented influx of European capital, business representatives, and tourists. Many European companies are establishing operations throughout the Americas, so the prospects for mutual synergy are considerable. In fact, the continent of Europe is a laboratory of synergy as the multiple countries and cultures struggle toward a more cooperative and unifying approach. The European economic community and the new European parliament are illustrative of this trend. Furthermore, European business interests and both sides of the Iron Curtain have many joint efforts, economic and professional interchanges, that move that continent's peoples beyond political and ideological barriers toward greater European collaboration. The growth of economic regionalism "guest" worker exchanges, and increased trans-European trade are indicators of synergistic trends.

References

1. Zimmerer, C. "Nobody Likes to Work for Americans," *Christian Science Monitor,* December 12, 1978.
2. Reported in *San Diego Business Journal,* April 27, 1981.
3. Jain, H. C. "Worker Participation: Lessons from the European Experience," *Management Review,* May 1980.
4. Drucker, P. F. "Learning from Foreign Management," *Wall Street Journal,* June 4, 1980.
5. Savage, D. *Founders, Heirs, and Managers.* London: Sage Publications, Inc., 1979, p. 31.
6. Andagh, J. *The New French Revolution.* New York: Harper & Row Publishers, Inc., 1969, p. 14.
7. Harbison, F. and Myers, C. *Management in the Industrial World.* New York: McGraw-Hill Book Co., 1959, p. 127.
8. Cozier, M. *The Bureaucratic Phenomenon.* The University of Chicago Press, 1963, p. 275.
9. Rowley, A. (ed.) *The Barons of European Industry.* New York: Holmes and Meier Publishers, 1974, p. 6.
10. *Ibid,* p. 18.
11. Harbison and Myers, loc. cit. p. 218.

12. Rowley, loc. cit. p. 7.

13. *Ibid,* p. 8.

14. Merrill, F. *Classics in Management.* American Management Association, Inc., 1970, p. 195.

15. *Ibid.* p. 195.

16. Bass, B. M. and Burger, P.C. *Assessment of International Managers.* New York: The Free Press, 1979, p. 132.

17. Farmer R.N. and Richman, B.M. *Comparative Management and Economic Progress.* Bloomington: Cedarwood Publishing Co., 1970, p. 209.

18. *Ibid,* p. 209.

19. *Ibid,* p. 189.

20. Harbison and Myers, loc. cit. p. 213.

21. Grosset, S. *Management: European and American Styles.* Belmont: Wadsworth Publishing Co., 1970, p. 115.

22. Andronov, I. *The New York Times Soviet Weekly of World Affairs,* September 1976.

14.
Synergy with
Pan American Management

A CONGLOMERATION OF CULTURES

An Ancient Stone Anchor Found Off the California Coast Indicates the Chinese Were in the Americas, 2200 B.C.

So ran the headline of a recent feature article on the latest archeological findings that implied that Asians, not Europeans, may have been the first to discover the New World. Scholars have found evidence that Phoenician merchants, Viking warriors, Irish monks, and Polynesian seafarers reached this Western Hemisphere centuries before an Italian navigator got the credit for this great feat. Of course, the Eskimos, or Inuit as the Eskimos prefer to call themselves, of Mongolian descent, may have already crossed the Bering Sea and settled in North America long before the Phoenicians, Vikings, Irish, and Polynesians arrived.

This great land body, which extends almost from the Arctic to Cape Horn, was named "America" after another sixteenth century Italian explorer, *Amerigo* Vespucci, who was also a merchant. Trade was to be a dominant force in the discovery and development of these unknown territories between the Atlantic and Pacific Oceans. Although all the inhabitants today of the Americas have right to the title, "American" — and many think of themselves as such — it was the people in that portion called the United States, who popularly appropriated the designation.

The Americas — north, central, and south — have a diversity of cultural heritages, and a synergy of sorts is being forged. It is like a huge laboratory of human relations in which a mixture of cultures from Europe, Africa, and Asia are merging. Geographically, one tends to think of North America as primarily "Anglo-Saxon" types who largely speak English. The only trouble is that Canada is bilingual with its second language of French, while the United States is moving in that direction with Spanish. For convenience, we refer to that area south of the Rio Grande River as *Latin America,* because the language there is mainly of Latin origin. Apart from numerous Indian languages, Spanish is dominant in Mexico, Central, and South America, while Portuguese is the major language of Brazil (plus Italian and Japanese to a lesser degree).

For our purpose, *Pan America* will designate those peoples who inhabit that land mass of some 15 million square miles from the Arctic Ocean south to the convergence of the Atlantic/Pacific Oceans at Drakes Passage. The Americas involve approximately 30 *national* cultures, plus Eskimo and Indian cultures.

For international managers seeking to function effectively in the Pan American market, it is important that they have the "big picture" about the peoples and cultures on these two vast continents linked by that land bridge called Central America. Furthermore, for managers and other leaders from the north who do business in the southern part of the Americas, and those from Latin America who seek trade and commerce in the northern part, geoeconomic and cultural insights will facilitate the processes of business and acculturation.

There are four major indicators that provide a quick insight into the Americas, and help to explain why North America is referred to as First World, while most of Latin America is considered Third World. (This information comes from the special issue of "Economic Development" from the September 1980 *Scientific American.*) The first criterion is *food.* The United Nations Food and Agricultural Organization (FAO) divides the world into developed and developing countries. From this perspective, only four are seen as exporters of cereals — U.S., Canada, Argentina, and Australia — and three are within the Americas, two in the north and one in the south.

The second indicator is *energy.* The International Institute for Applied Systems Analysis divides the world into seven major energy-related regions. Region 1 is North America with a highly developed market economy, rich in energy resources. Region IV is Latin America, a developing region potentially rich in energy resources.

The third factor is *human resources.* Relative to the rate of natural population increase, North America is less than 1% and has a population of approximately 238 million persons. Whereas, Latin America has a range of 1-3% of natural population increase, and about 340 million inhabitants. The most populous countries of 3% or more are Mexico, Venezuela, Guatemala, Peru, and Paraguay.

The final factor to consider is *economic wealth.* Garret FitzGerald developed seven economic categories based on world data collected by economists Kravis, Heston, and Summers of the University of Pennsylvania. North America falls within the rich category because its gross domestic (G.D.P) product per capita is more than $5,000. In the area of Latin America, only one country falls in that category, Netherland Antilles.

Between $3,500-$5,000 G.D.P., which the researchers designate "near-rich," are Argentina, Venezuela, Trinidad, Puerto Rico, and the Virgin Islands. Between $2,500-$3,500 G.D.P., the "upper-middle rich," are Brazil, Surinam, Uruguay, Mexico, and Martinique. Between $1,425-$2,500 G.D.P., the "lower-middle," are Cuba, Guatemala, Nicaragua, Colombia, Ecuador, Peru, Dominican Republic, Monserrat, Antigua, Dominica, St. Lucia, Barbados, and Granada. Between $875-$1,425, known as the "poor one" category are El Salvador, Bolivia, Paraguay, St. Kitts/Nevis, St. Vincent, and Guayana. No Pan American country is classified in the "poor two/three" categories, which reflect G.D.P.'s below $875.

Perhaps this issue can be brought into sharper focus when one considers that Latin American poverty is deepening, and that it affects 36 million children under the age of six years. Despite brisk economic progress in this region, a 1981 CEPAL report (U.N. Economic Commission for Latin America) estimated that approximately 10% of the continent's total population now live in poverty. The trend, according to these U.N. experts, is that 16% of this Latin population will be poor by the end of the century. There is a shift from rural to urban emigration and poverty, so that by the year 2000, it is expected that there will be about 160 million urban poor and 85 million rural poor. This means growth in the shantytowns or misery villages (called "favelas" in Brazil) surrounding urban areas. The situation continues to fuel political and social unrest, often triggering terrorism and violent revolution.

Table 14-1 provides some other contrasting indicators between "Anglo" and Latin American countries. Naturally, the information contains some generalizations because many specific differences exist within the cultures. For example, while North America is generally influenced by the Protestant religious cultural tradition, the United States and Canada do have a large and growing minority of Roman Catholics, the dominant religion in Latin America. While one may say the Christian religious tradition prevails in Pan America, there are numerous other religious minorities ranging from Jewish to Moslem. Also, the ancient animist religions linger on, and are most evident in Haiti and Brazil with Christian overlays. Thus, in seeking themes and patterns in the diverse cultures of the Americas, there are minority cultural differences aplenty. Social class also brings a life-style and perspective that cuts across national cultures. There is much in common among the cosmopolitan upper class throughout the Americas, despite national cultural differences.

SYNERGISTIC POTENTIAL

To achieve synergy between the northern and southern parts of this hemisphere, its inhabitants must overcome a cultural and an economic/technological gap. Despite ancestoral similarities between the North and Latin Americans, there is a lack

(text continued on p. 272)

Table 14-1
Pan American Culture Contrasts

North America		Latin America
Population (approx.)		
Canada	24 million	
USA	214 million	
Total	238 million	340+ million people
Land Mass (approx. sq. mi.)		
Canada	3.5 million	
USA	3.6 million	
Total	7.1 million	8 million
National Cultures		
2 countries		24 countries
2 indigenous peoples		1 commonwealth (PR)
(Eskimo/Indian)		(12 island countries
		of West Indies ?)
		Variety of Indian cultures

Major Cultural Inputs	*Major Cultural Inputs (Latin America)*
• Native North American Eskimos and Indians (nomadic aboriginals).	• Native Indians (descended from ancient, highly developed civilizations of Incas/ Aztecs).
• European—originally Spanish/French/ English and later diverse immigration from the continent.	• Europeans—in most countries largely Spanish with lesser influences of Germans and Italians, except in Brazil where dominant input was Portugese; some English input.
USA	
• African, including lately Haitian.	• African.
• Asian—originally Chinese, some Japanese, Polynesian, and recently Indo-Chinese.	• Asian—ancient Polynesian influence, and some Japanese input in Mexico and Brazil.
• Mexicans and Cubans, and lately variety of other Latins.	
Canada	
• Ukranians and variety of Commonwealth peoples (e.g., Indians and Pakistanis, West Indies).	

Socio-political Developments	*Socio-political Developments (Latin America)*
• English common law system.	• Napoleonic Code of laws.
• In Canada the struggle of the English/ French colonial powers still affects national sense of identity and relations, and government struggles for its own constitution in British Commonwealth.	• Feudalistic societies of Spain/Portugal imposed by conquerors on developed Indian civilizations.
• After a revolutionary war, USA declared independence from colonial power in 1798, and expanded from East to West; eventually into the Pacific, Alaska and Puerto Rico.	• French/Austrian royality/empire imposed on Mexico; the latter was center of revolutions in 1821, 1824, 1838 which impacted on South America.
• Egalitarian, democratic, individualistic, materialistic with emphasis on organization and self-development.	• Family oriented with authority centered in the father and often extended to the "father of the nation" a strong dictator.
	• Universities and republics from the 19th century with great dependence on military institutions/control.

Table 14-1 (continued)

North America	Latin America
• Problems of race/minority relations—in Canada, it is principally the human/ political rights of the French-speaking group in the dominate English society; in USA, it is principally the total rights and integration of black citizens, of slave ancestory from Africa, into the society; and Hispanics. Protests have been largely peaceful and through political/legal action for equal opportunity.	• Problems of social class integration— although there was much intermarriage of the races, the powerful elites from an economic/social/political standpoint control and dominate the poor, often peasants of Indian heritage. The disenfranchised have moved beyond political/ military protest for social justice to terrorism as a means for changing the status quo.
• Economically and technically advanced in post-industrial stage of development; into space exploration and development, as well as global leadership.	• Economically and technically developing, and in the process of moving from the agricultural and through the industrial stage of development; energy discoveries and development in Mexico can dramatically forge a new relationship with its neighbors.
• Religiously pluralistic with wide variations from severe fundamentalism to major shifts to Eastern religious traditions or moving beyond religious attachments. Majority consider themselves Christian with large Jewish minority.	• Although significant growth in spiritualism and Protestantism, the Roman Catholic tradition is still dominant, but undergoing profound role change—instead of traditional support for the oligarchy, many clergy providing leadership in a revolution for social justice.

Education

• In the English tradition; public and privately supported institutions of higher education, with unique system of community colleges and technical institutes. In Canada, public support is provided to schools administered by religious organizations, largely Catholic. In USA there is strict separation of church and state, so there are many public elementary/secondary schools and no public support to the parochial and independent school systems. Universal education required by law usually to 12th grade, and many go on to college studies.	• In the European tradition, especially Spain/Portugal/France. Ancient and traditional university education with emphasis on the humanities, especially studies in law, medicine, and engineering. Colegios are more numerous than American secondary schools and offer the equivalent of junior college. Upper classes tend to send their offspring to private schools and universities, often conducted by the orders of the Catholic Church. Although literacy is increasing many in the population overall do not receive more than a very few years of primary education; notable exceptions in the larger countries which provide more education. Rigorous examination competition for university entrance. Technical education also on the increase and use of mass media.

of shared cultural assumptions. Thus, even if the North American speaks Spanish or Portuguese while trying to do business in Latin America, that person will find communication, at times, a strain on both sender and receiver of messages. The communicators are not sufficiently socialized in each other's major cultural differences.

Sociologist Raymond Gordon notes even after extended periods of residence in Colombian homes, American guests still did not know appropriate cultural routines, and misunderstandings were often provoked. How much more might this be true in the arena of international business or economic development within the Americas? In his book, *Living in Latin America,* Gordon quotes the experience of the late Senator Robert Kennedy whose attempts at rousing goodwill in South America lead to some hostility. A speech in Santiago began with a neutral crowd reaction and ended with chants of "Yankee go home!" The offending words that triggered the inhospitable response was "Let us learn together" by which the Senator sought to convey an attitude of friendly equality. Unfortunately, that exact phrase had been used previously by North American politicians on Latin American territory, so according to a Chilean official, it had this special meaning:

> The phrase, "Let us learn together," would have gotten by in Italian, Swedish, or Russian. This audience assumed when an American says it, he is being a hypocrite because he is representing a government which has repeatedly taken advantage of Latin American countries through the use of both military, political, and economic might. Often when the United States is about to put the pressure on us to do something, they make it clear that we are working together.[1]

That is a significant Latin perception of North Americans whom they tend to think of as the Yankees or "gringos." The typical Latin seems to be neutral about Canadians because they are so far north. Canadian contact with their southern neighbors beyond the U.S.A. has been limited. Many Latin Americans have a love-hate relationship about the States. They admire its equality and economic progress, and at the personal level may like many Americans; many seek to live in the U.S. because of its opportunities. But many Latins also distrust, envy, and fear "Big Brother." This is especially true for Latin countries that border or are near the U.S., such as Cuba or Mexico (that is why there is an expression, "Poor Mexico, so far from God and so near the United States"). Too many North Americans, on the other hand, ignore the needs and possibilities in Latin America, and do not pursue collaboration with these neighboring states and peoples; Europe or Asia gets all their attention. Even government officials tend to ignore and treat the Latin countries with benign neglect until a crisis erupts. The United States and Canada lack clear-cut Latin American policies and programs, especially of a long-term nature, that would promote mutual cooperation between north and south, as well as improved cultural understanding. It is as if Latin Americans have yet to truly enter into the North American consciousness, while the latter seems to be in the Latin consciousness in too many negative ways.

The U.S.A. has made many efforts to build better relations with its Pan American neighbors. Though such endeavors may have been premature, unsuccessful, or underutilized, they contain seeds for future synergism.

However, before examining these efforts, let us review some insights from Professor Gordon's case study of Latin American cross-cultural communication. He came to some generalizations that may help us to promote better interactions in the Americas:

1. *Syllogistic nature of meaning* — be alert to covert assumptions which may act as the context for interpreting the meaning of an overt message from another of a different cultural background. The message is only the raw material for interpretation, and one should attempt to consider the silent assumptions.

2. *Situation-associated assumptions* — link particular assumptions for interpretation with a situation, not just with words, gestures, or voice tone used in the message sending. The concept of situation, whether speaking Spanish or Portuguese, or operating through an interpreter, is to seek out the objectives of the situation; the time and space patterns of the activities involved; the roles of actors in the situation; the rules governing the interaction in that local Latin situation. The word "familia," for example, connotes much more to a Latin American than the American sense of family.

3. *Dissonant cross-cultural assumptions* — occurs in communications if the sender tries to impose his or her cultural assumptions upon the foreign assumptions behind the interaction. The problem in U.S.-Canadian interfaces is that both too often assume they are quite similar, whereas the subtle cultural differences may escape each other. North American bankers or Catholics can make many misassumptions about their Latin American counterparts.

4. *Values, conflict and communication* — the real difficulties in cross-cultural communications may be occurring because value systems are in conflict. While northern and southern Americans at a Pan American conference, for instance, may be in agreement on general goals, the conflict might be anticipated in the means to achieve such goals. That is, the time, place, division of labor, sequence of actions and other factors. When one is not open to consideration of the other's values, then emotions may rise and disagreements increase.

5. *Trivial actions and profound effects* — in cross-cultural negotiations, the seemingly trivial aspects may lead to an accumulation of misunderstandings that have profound impact upon the relationship. North Americans, for example, when guests in a Latin home or office may overlook mundane details to their own detriment and a fruitful intercultural encounter. If one does not have sensitivity in "small matters," it can lead to misinterpretation of intent or motives.

6. *Making allowances for foreigners* — although members of a host culture may make normal allowances for guests' alien behavior, some of the foreigner's behavior may not be forgiven for the native does not comprehend the other's context and reason for such unacceptable actions. More often the North American gets into difficulty by not making allowances with self because of foreign status, as well as not attempting to conform to behavior norms of a given situation.

7. *Vicious circle effect* — minor communication breakdowns can escalate and be exacerbated so that the natives make judgments about the visitor's desires and motivations which may indeed be false, and create negative images in the mind of the host. This may lead to social isolation of the foreigner, making it more difficult for the visitor to understand the host culture and people. To move beyond a superficial level of communication, this vicious circle must somehow be broken by the foreigner or he/she becomes a prisoner of isolation.

8. *Blind leading the blind* — amateur observers of a foreign culture may provide ethnocentric distortions of reality produced by systematic misinterpretation of the cross-cultural experience. Thus, a business person from North America about to be assigned in Latin America may seek out a colleague for input about the culture because that other person had already done business there. A manager should check out the feedback of a single colleague with objective data (e.g., books and reports) and then only make tentative judgments before living in the host culture for some time.[1]

For successful Pan American exchanges and collaboration, Professor Gordon's research indicates that each party in the cross-cultural encounter *must learn:* (a) to recognize symptoms of miscommunication in oneself and the other; (b) to separate fact, interpretation, and conclusion; (c) to derive silent assumptions about major premises in the interpretive process from the foreigner's minor premises and conclusions; and (d) to request information from the host country citizen in such a way as not to bias or inhibit the response.

POSSIBILITIES FOR PAN AMERICAN COOPERATION

The prospects for Pan American synergy in the twenty-first century are bright. The last half of the twentieth century has seen some remarkable progress in the Americas. First, there has been relative peace between the nations of this Western Hemisphere, despite internal upheavals within various Latin states. World War II brought military cooperation among many countries of these two continents against a common external threat.

There have also been some noble efforts toward economic cooperation that lay the groundwork for real collaboration in the future. It takes time for such diverse cultures to learn the value and skills of joint endeavors. But the ground for synergy has been broken in such undertakings as the Organization of American States, the

North Atlantic Treaty Organization, the Central American Common Market, the Andean Pact, the Alliance for Progress, and the Latin American Free Trade Association. One hopeful sign relative to United States involvement in such activities is the shift away from unilateral foreign aid to sharing of resources through multilateral institutions, such as the World Bank and the Inter-American Development Bank. Lately, the concerns of the various American nations have shifted more to the social arena with the establishment of such entities as the Inter-American Commission on Human Rights.

To resolve some of the serious inequities and exploitations within Pan America during this complex period of social transition demands collaboration among the people of this hemisphere. Numerous organizations in the private sector have made substantial contributions, but the natural and human resources in Pan America are enormous and the potential for improvement of the human condition in this area of the planet is staggering. It requires cosmopolitan leaders with vision who can set goals that capture the imagination of all Americans, north and south, and then energize them to actions toward mutual social and economic development. John F. Kennedy was such a leader when he joined with other Latin statesmen in signing an agreement at Punta del Este in 1961, which launched the Alliance for Progress. Some will claim the U.S. was naive and only self-interested in promoting this scheme; others will claim it was a failure. Perhaps these words of Galo Plaza, a Secretary General for the Organization of American States, will put the matter into a larger perspective when he said in 1971:

> As I see it, the Alliance for Progress is very much alive. As a slogan, it may have lost some of its early appeal, but the concept of multilateral cooperation to achieve more rapid economic growth and greater social justice is as valid as ever, and it has been incorporated as a treaty obligation in the amended charter of the Organization of American States.
>
> The contribution of the United States and other external sources has played an important pump-priming role, but the greater share of the effort has been Latin America's, even more so than anticipated ten years ago . . . In some areas, such as tax reform, literacy, school enrollment, life expectancy, and urban water supply, the Latin American countries took significant strides toward the Alliance for Progress *goals.*
>
> The experience of the sixties has also served to underscore the need for maintaining Latin American unity toward the rest of the world on development issues, without trying to prescribe a uniform strategy for individual Latin American countries . . . But this has not impeded the trend toward greater Latin American cohesiveness and solidarity, which has been evident in the OAS Special Committee for Latin American Coordination.

In 1970, The Peterson Report offered unique guidance relative to inter-American affairs; namely, not to impose one's cultural values or institutions upon another state, but to have as development objectives "the building of self-reliant and healthy societies . . . an expanding world economy from which all will benefit, and improved prospects for global peace." Señor Plaza reminded North Americans of Latin America's importance to the United States and Canada as a multi billion-dollar market for goods and services, a source of raw materials for North American industry, an arena for private investment which yields high returns, and as a strategic cite for defense and the advancement of human welfare and security. Such pragmatic reasons should stir investments in their southern neighbors by Canadian and Yankee traders, as well as their governments. But it will take more than altruistic assistance by such groups as the Canadian International Development Agency or the U.S. Peace Corps. The challenge in Latin America is to provide management development and self-help undertakings.

Those with vision will set goals to close the Pan American poverty gap within the next fifty years. Those who look beyond the horizon appreciate the wisdom of a Raul Prebish when he reminded North America of the interest and commitment we should have in Latin America, "the inevitable corollary is a systematic long-term effort in which the scale of the means is in reasonable proportion to the magnitude of the end pursued."

In a 1980 *Los Angeles Times* interview the new chief of OAS, an Argentine diplomat named Alejandro Orfila, noted that the principal issues facing the Americas is a fairer distribution of wealth to break up patterns of the past:

> Concentration of wealth must be mobilized, in a democratic way, to serve the majority of people. Neighbors need to help neighbors in resolving conflict, as when the OAS provided observers to reduce the crisis of near warfare between El Salvador and Honduras in 1976. That was a typical example of helpful presence without interference . . .
>
> With reference to the gap between rightist landowners and leftist politicians and peasants, Nicaragua's recent experience has had an impact in Latin America. The violence of the revolution there was something nobody wants to repeat. People in their right minds are not going to come up with a solution that destroys everything. Like the Nicaraguans, they will try to create a balance of interests.

The new secretary general reminded us that underlying all of Latin America's difficulties is the need for integral development in the areas of education, health care, and opportunities for self-development. Orfila emphasized the interdependence of North and Latin America, and the need of one part of the hemisphere for the other. He is encouraged that economic development is now horizontal in the Americas, and not just vertical. He commended the industrialized nations of the south, such as Brazil and Argentina, or oil producers like Venezuela and Mexico, for contributing to the welfare of their neighbors. In addition to the economic power of that big four, he pointed to the organizing progress of the Andean Group of five — Bolivia, Colombia, Ecuador, Peru, and Venezuela — in forming a common market. Orfila believes that one of the big recent changes in the hemisphere has been the recognition by all member states — democracies and nondemocracies — that they must deal with each other and strive for understanding.

This opinion was confirmed on December 18, 1980 when eight Latin countries issued the "Declaration of Santa María" marking the 150th anniversary of the death of Simón Bolívar. Along with the Spanish government and the representatives of the Andean group nations, other signatories included Costa Rica and El Salvador. The 1,200-word document pointed out that "a new and vigorous effort to cooperate is indispensable" to create the conditions for a more just social and economic order. The chief executives agreed that there would be no intervention in other nations' internal affairs, in the unity of peoples, or the sovereign will of citizens.

One reason for optimism about the future of relationships in the Americas is the accomplishments and prospects of the Pan American Development Foundation. It is a nonprofit, private voluntary agency established in 1962 through leading citizens of the Americas and the General Secretariat of the OAS. Its objective is to help the lowest-income people in Latin America and the Carribeans to participate productively in the socioeconomic and cultural development of their societies. PADF activates the involvement of the local private sector, especially the business community, through the formation of national develpment foundations in the various countries.

Through these foundations, PADF becomes the catalyst for local civic and business leaders to promote programs in health services; tools/equipment for training in vocational schools; communication services to assist public service broadcasting devoted to economic, social, and cultural development; and "Operation Niños" to focus attention on needs and resources for the care and development of children.

"Synergizing" the Pan American potential presents a macromanagement challenge:

1. To better manage the national resources of all states in the hemisphere by more effective collaboration of public and private sectors in each country, and between north/south regional relations.
2. To manage the transfer of technology and information for mutual development of North and Latin American peoples.
3. To contribute to economic and social development of Latin America through the exercise of corporate social responsibility by multinational enterprises on both continents.

We are not only suggesting a more effective trilateral partnership between business, labor, and government in the Americas, but we are proposing that transnational corporations throughout Pan America apply their management skills in developing human and natural resources in the hemisphere. Here are some possible scenarios for synergy:

1. Multinational companies within the "big four" countries of Latin America form joint ventures with their smaller and less fortunate neighbors to develop those countries' resources.

2. Canadian and U.S. multinational corporations operating in Latin America set up major training and health centers in the vicinity of their facilities, not just for their own employees, but for the benefit of the community nearby.
3. Establishment of a Pan American job or peace corps movement for youth to become involved in hemispheric development projects, as a means of promoting a skill exchange and combatting youth unemployment.
4. Promotion of Pan American human resource development and population control goals and plans for the 1980s and '90s — a joint endeavor of foundations, corporation, and government agencies with specific targets for the turn of the century.
5. Feasibility studies for regional development projects on a macroengineering or economic scale that would direct the energies of people in the Americas outward toward economic and social improvement, especially for involvement of the military in such endeavors in place of warfare (e.g., Army Corps of Engineers type programs).

Let us focus our attention now on some of the cultural changes underway in the three major geographic areas of the Americas which deserve leadership priorities.

NORTHERN AMERICAS' CULTURAL DEVELOPMENT

Eskimos and Indians

In the far north of the Americas are two native peoples caught in a culture gap — the Eskimos and the Indians. Essentially nomadic hunters by tradition, they have both been harmed and helped by the rapid advancement of "white civilization" into their lives. With the introduction of U.S. and Canadian government health and education programs, their life expectancy and levels of consciousness have risen. But so has their frustration, despair, and social deterioration. Some of these indigenous peoples have acculturated to the modern way of life of their North American counterparts, have graduated from universities, and hold important posts in government or business. Others have succumbed to alcoholism, drugs, or even suicide, especially the young. Their problems and potentials are similar on or off reservations; whether in the U.S. state of Alaska or the Canadian Northwest Territories; whether above or below the U.S./Canadian border.

In reality, tribal or aboriginal peoples everywhere face the same dilemma brought on by accelerating social and technological change. Whether an Inuit in Hudson Bay or a Navajo in northern Arizona, the confrontation with too rapid cultural change leaves the natives bewildered, confused, and almost overwhelmed. The rate of innovation in traditional societies is slow, while it rises astronomically in modern societies in the midst of transition. The traditional culture is past oriented, while the modern society is future-oriented, interpreting history as progressive movement. Unfortunately, Western ethnocentrism — even among anthropologists — labeled these peoples in the hunting stage of development as primitive and backward. A racist mentality would view such people as "underdeveloped" because of some biological inferiority. In fact, such peoples may be quite developed within their own context, and more in harmony with nature than modern persons. They seem to possess a better sense of ecology, energy conservation, food distribution, and overall happiness than many of their so-called civilized counterparts of today.

In the process of trying to enhance the native peoples of the Americas, corporate tycoons, political leaders, and welfare administrators might do well to try to understand and appreciate the values and assets in such "primitive" cultures. Then we may be in a position to create a synergy with them relative to their contribution in modern society, and how our modern systems might better meet their needs. Thus, when transnational enterprises, like giant energy corporations, move into the territories of Eskimo, Aleuts and Indian peoples, a cooperative approach that demonstrates concern for the natives is more productive for all in contrast to a destructive/exploitive strategy.

Within the ecological zone of North America, anthropologists classify the varied cultures by geographic area that share similar traits. The primary substance activities of native peoples usually center around hunting, fishing, gathering, and some planting. The individuals are organized into families or tribal bands, some of which may be large and well organized. The village becomes the basic political unit, and some have been known to create rather sophisticated hierarchal societies. Such groups demonstrate wide degrees of skills in art, architecture, crafts and clothesmaking; most seem superbly adapted to their environment when left without intrusion from modern man.

Such societies are called "primitive" in the sense that their way of life is relatively simple and basic in terms of adapting to meet fundamental human needs. The culture is tied into the local environment, and roles/relationships are clearly differentiated on the basis of sex, ability, and age. For centuries they have survived by adapting, so that today we find Eskimos functioning effectively in San Francisco and Indians doing steel work in Los Angeles. To try and preserve this vanishing way of life, the nations of North America have provided reservations and cultural centers, but many Eskimos and Indians abandon the traditional way of living for the "benefits" of modern civilization. Since much needed natural resources, especially energy, are found on the lands still possessed by these primitive people, the issue is whether technological man will seek a synergy with these natives, or simply exploit them and destroy their cultures entirely.

Culturally sensitive management of petrochemical companies is beginning to work with tribal leaders so that the Indians can develop their own energy companies with technical training and assistance. Similarly, Eskimos, are being assisted in establishing cooperatives so that they may develop their own economic units in the fishing industry. The U.S. Government and courts have been ruling favorably about honoring old treaties and making financial restitution for lands stolen from the Indians. Under new government policies the native peoples are being urged and trained to provide management leadership in agencies that affect their lives, such as the Bureau of Indian Affairs and Public Health Service. They are even provided assistance through the Small Business Administration to start up their own minority enterprises.

The Eskimos and Indians of North America have paid a high price for acculturation. Many of their peoples suffer mental and physical, as well as economic, handicaps that range from alcoholism to suicide. But with cooperation and collaboration by their fellow citizens, these proud and resourceful peoples can be developed to help themselves and create a new place in the superindustrial age.

As we try to provide a cultural overview of the other inhabitants of this hemisphere, we would like to recommend a resource of culture specific information on the Americas, as well as other geographic areas in the world: the Language & Intercultural Research Center, Brigham Young University, Provo, Utah 84602.

Canada

Canada is a bilingual and bicultural country, whose 24 million people live in 10 provinces, 2 federal districts, and the Northwest Territories (which comprise a third of Canada), and the Yukon Territory in the Far North.

Canada is a nation in the midst of an identity crisis between its two major cultural heritages — English and French; and with a powerful southern neighbor, the USA. When the matter is resolved and the process of national maturation is completed, Canada may either become a world superpower, or split into a new geographical realignment. Futurists speculate that if Quebec were ever to become independent, then in time the western Canadian provinces might align themselves with the western USA states to create a separate political entity or some new regionalism, while the north east provinces might do the same with the northeast States. Meanwhile, the country is legally governed under the British North America Act of 1867 and only the House of Commons in the United Kingdom can amend it. At this writing, the Canadian Prime Minister is struggling with provincial premiers to "patriate" and bring home the consitution in time for Canada's 114th anniversary of birth-July 1, 1981.

Foreign multinational managers seeking to do business in Canada or form joint ventures with Canadians should better understand this country's vast resources and potential, and complex ethnic groups.

Throughout Canada, the family is the center of society, and homes are often passed along from one generation to another. Nowhere is this more true than in the central province of Quebec, the heart of French Canada. If you have some insights into Latin Europe, you may better comprehend the French-Canadian.* It is a culture that is somewhat unsynergistic and very individualistic. People tend to be

---

*In Chapter 13 of *Managing Cultural Differences* some culture specifics on the French were presented which might help in understanding French-Canadians.

more reserved until you get to know them well. As a minority in Canada, the citizens of French heritage feel they have been discriminated against and a separatist movement has been launched. This human rights struggle has raised the consciousness of both groups in the country, and has increased the legal privileges of the French-speaking in employment and other social arenas. Remember, French sovereignty existed in this part of Canada since Cartier landed in 1534 until 1763 when "New France" was ceded to Britain. The Roman Catholic tradition dominates, though some schools are operated by Protestants. The major industries are mining, forestry, hydroelectricity and agriculture.

As the task of a nation building toward unity proceeds, Canadians are more aware of their rich cultural diversity and natural resources. The country's economic wealth is centered in forests, petroleum, natural gas, and iron ore. In sprawling Canada, the native Indian population of 250,000 form 500 tribes, of which three fourths live on reservations. Democratic Canada has one of the world's highest standards of living and its people are very industrious. From a management standpoint, workers are very punctual, but the fun-loving French Canadians are more easy-going and less time-conscious. Operating a bilingual business is a challenge, but then French-speaking citizens can be an advantage in international commerce. The English spoken in Canada is slightly different from the American version (e.g., British pronunciations, Scottish diphthong sounds like "about"). Proud of their country, sensitive about their relations with the U.S. and comparisons to it, fiercely independent while self-deprecating as a people, Canadians resent being lumped together with the other "Americans" below the 49th parallel — many of whom they consider pushy, showy, and arrogant. Despite that and the U.S. media/economic dominance, the relations between North Americans is generally good and friendly. There is tremendous potential for synergy between the northern neighboring countries who in many ways are more alike than different.

United States of America

That is the official title, and the citizens refer to themselves as "Americans," while many others call them "Yanks" or "Yankees," a nickname that originally referred to the inhabitants of the New England or northeastern States. The nation consists of the mainland — the central portion of the North American continent, or 48 States; the State of Alaska in the northwestern tip of the hemisphere; the State of Hawaii which is located west of the mainland in the Pacific Ocean; the District of Columbia with its federal capital of Washington. The Commonwealth of Puerto Rico will be discussed, along with the Virgin Island Territory in the next section on the Central Americas. Since the end of WW II, the USA has administered 11 trust territories in the South Pacific over which it has gradually been relinquishing control. Between 1975 and 1980, accords were negotiated with the native islanders to establish the Commonwealths of the northern Marianas, the Marshall Islands, and the Federated States of Micronesia; and the Republic of Palau. The 1980 census indicates a population of 226.5 million people, with a 17% increase of black Americans to 26.5 million. There are 1 million American Indians and 3.5 million Asian and Pacific Islanders. This federal republic will probably have 250 million people by the year 2000.

The U.S. is a multicultural society on the way to becoming bilingual. Although the American version of English is spoken with a variety of dialects (18 or more), Spanish is emerging as a second language. American speech is as varied as the country's geography and climate, which is temperate on the coasts, subtropical in the south with extensive deserts and widely different seasons/rainfalls. The part that western Europeans find most difficult to comprehend is the immense size and difference of the mainland. The fourth largest nation in the world, the USA has been thought of popularly as a "melting pot" of diverse cultures. It is true that it is a land of immigrants — from the time of colonists (English/French/Spanish), plus the African slave and nineteenth century European influx, to the present waves of refugees from IndoChina, Cuba, and Haiti. The population is largely white, Anglo-Saxon, but the significant, growing minorities of Hispanics, blacks, and Asians as well as the native American Indians, are rapidly changing that configuration.

A free enterprise economic system prevails, and the nation's industrial/agricultural/technological leadership in the world market is awesome but under challenge. A quick overview of the culture might reveal these generalizations, subject to many differences among people and in specific places:

1. Goal and achievement oriented — Americans think they can accomplish just about anything, given enough time, money, and technology.
2. Highly organized and institutionalistic — Americans prefer a society that is strong institutionally, secure and tidy or well kept.
3. Freedom-loving and self-reliant — Americans fought a revolution and subsequent wars to preserve their concept of democracy, so they resent too much control or interference, especially by government or external forces. They believe an ideal that all persons are created equal; though they sometimes fail to live that ideal fully, they strive through law to promote equal opportunity and to confront their own racism or prejudice. They also idealize the self-made person who rises from poverty and adversity, and think they can influence and create their future. Control of one's destiny is popularly expressed as "doing your own thing." Americans think, for the most part, that with determination and initiative, one can achieve whatever he or she sets out to do and thus fulfill that individual's human potential.
4. Work oriented and efficient — Americans possess a strong work ethic, though they are learning in the present generation to enjoy leisure time constructively. They are very time conscious and efficient in doing things. They tinker with gadgets and technological systems, always searching for easier, better, more efficient ways of accomplishment.
5. Friendly and informal — Americans rejected the traditional privileges of royalty and class, but do defer to those with affluence and power. Although infor-

mal in greeting and dress, they are a noncontact culture (e.g. avoid embracing in public usually) and maintain certain physical/psychological distance with others (e.g., about two feet).

6. Competitive and aggressive — Americans in play or business generally are so oriented because of their drives to achieve and succeed. This is partially traced to their heritage of having to overcome a wilderness and hostile elements in their environment.

7. Values in transition — Traditional American values of family loyalty, respect and care of the aged, marriage and the nuclear family, patriotism, material acquistion, forthrightness, and the like are undergoing profound reevaluation and the people search for new meanings.

8. Generosity — Although Americans seemingly emphasize material values, they are sharing, as has been demonstrated in the Marshall Fund, foreign aid programs, refugee assistance, and their willingness at home and abroad to espouse a good cause and to help neighbors in need. They tend to be altruistic and some would say naive as a people.

In terms of U.S. social institutions, three are worth noting here. Education is viewed as a means of self-development, so participation in the process and within the classroom is encouraged — it is mandatory until age 16 and 97% finish at least elementary school, so the literacy rate is fairly high. There is a public (largely free of cost) and private school system up through the university level of education; the latter are either independent or religious affiliated schools. The average family is nuclear, consisting of only parents and children, if there are any. More than half of American women work outside the home, and females have considerable and improving opportunity for personal and professional growth, guaranteed by law. The home has been matriarchal and child-oriented, though today there are many single-parent families and childless couples by choice. The society is youth oriented, and usually cares for the elderly outside the home in institutions. It is experimenting with new family arrangements from couples living together without the legal sanction to group communes. Politically, the government operates on the Constitution of 1787 and the Bill of Rights, which provides a three-branch approach of checks and balances. Currently, there are increasing problems of disillusionment in political leaders, corruption in public offices, and a push toward decentralization or the confederation of states concept (e.g., emphasis on states rights and less government regulation over individual lives).*

The Americans too are in the midst of profound social change, and even an identity crisis. Among the factors contributing to this maturation challenge are:

1. The lessening of world leadership and influence forces a reassessment of the national self-image. After much success in its war abroad, Korea and Viet-

---

*For more detailed information about U.S. macro- and microcultures and doing business in the U.S., see chapters 14 and 15 of *Managing Cultural Differences*.

nam proved to be costly and questionable conflicts that mass media brought into American homes. In addition to inflation and economic setbacks, American confidence was also undermined by the hostage crisis in Iran. All of this coupled with assasinations of the country's leaders in the 1960s led to an undermining of the national will, organized public protests, and the need now to reexpress national goals.

2. Latinization of the U.S. is affecting the character of the country and its communication. (This will be discussed later.)

3. Transition into a post-industrial society is happening first and faster in the U.S. than in most other countries because of scientific and technological advances. The values and life-styles brought on by the industrial stage of development are being reexamined and new replacements sought for more effective coping in cyberculture. (A later section on the future of America will explore this further.)

The impact of such contemporary trends depends on where you are in America, for there are considerable regional differences and subcultures. For example, the clear-cut distinctions since the Civil War between Northerners and Southerners are eroding, as many northern Yankees move south to the "sun belt" for jobs, retirement, or improved quality of life. Above all, Americans are a very mobile people — geographically and organizationally. There is also a big difference between eastern and western life-styles and attitudes: the eastern U.S. is thought to be more establishment, conservative in thinking, over-organized and deteriorating; the western U.S. is seen as more casual, innovative, and flexible.

One aspect for foreign readers to note is that Americans are becoming less isolationist and provincial in their thinking and actions. Mass travel abroad, international communications and business, more foreign students and visitors have affected American perceptions. Furthermore, the impact of foreigners is currently considerable — more outsiders are being transferred to the U.S. for business or professional purposes, and more foreign capital is being heavily invested here. (Corporate acquisitions and property purchases by Canadians, Japanese, Europeans, Middle Easterners and South Africans are considerable, and have even caused some fear and backlash.) Foreign tourism in the U.S. has increased dramatically. The influx of refugees and legal and illegal immigrants has strained existing social systems. But Americans are generally of a cooperative spirit, so they are open to international influences in their society, and usually support endeavors that will promote regional or world synergy. The presence of the United Nations headquarters in New York City is symbolic of this.

Hispanic America

From the viewpoint of cultural differences and synergy, one of the more fascinating developments in the U.S. during this century has been the rapid and rising Latin growth and influence in the country. After wars and treaties, the Spanish seemingly gave up their claims, principally along the southern borders of the U.S. from east to west. Culturally, however, the Spanish influence in Florida, Nevada, Arizona, California and Texas has always been most significant, principally by way of Cuba, Puerto Rico, and Mexico. Now the very face of America and many of its major cities are being vastly changed by the Hispanic peoples in their midst. The 1980 U.S. census revealed that of the minority population of 16.8%, 61% were of "Spanish" origin.

It has been predicted that Hispanic Americans will become the largest minority in the U.S. before the turn of the century. Raul Yzaguirre, director of the National Council of La Raza (The Race), an umbrella organization for Hispanic-Americans, maintains the 1980s will be their decade. Just on numbers alone a valid argument can be made to support his thesis. And it should be noted that the "numbers" do not necessarily reflect an accurate count of the number of Hispanics in the U.S. because many such people are either overlooked in the census taking, or avoid being included for fear of legal actions. Also, the 1980 census did not include Cuban refugees. The Hispanic population is largely Roman Catholic, and therefore generally do not believe in birth control, so it is evident what the outcome will be in the future relative to changes in numbers relative to the "Anglo" citizenry and the traditional Protestant American culture.

The Hispanics are a people who are only beginning to organize to gain political power and representation. One of their goals will be bilingualism in the American society, and they already have achieved some success with bilingual public education.

The Hispanics were on this mainland for centuries before the U.S.A. became a nation. Today they bring distinctive flavor and diversity to the American cultural mainstream. Strong regard for family and kinship in a patriarchal society is the first contrast. Other contributions to note are: gentleness and considerateness, especially with regard to women; lively, colorful music, art, and food; industrious entrepreneurs and hard-working laborers; large Spanish-language media capabilities and influence; and many other such Latin qualities to be described in the rest of this chapter on Latin America. Latinos offer the United States an amalgam of buoyancy, sensuousness, and flair that will either enrich the nation, or cause a schizophrenia with those of "Anglo-Saxon" heritage.

This Hispanic expansion is not just in the southwest or southeast, but throughout the U.S. with major concentrations in urban areas such as Miami, New York, Chicago, and Los Angeles. The exploding ethnic population of that largest California city, which was settled by Spanish colonists 200 years ago, is radically changing that area. Latinos, combined with Koreans, Chinese, Filipinos and other foreign minority groups, have now become the majority in that city and downtown Los Angeles on a weekend is a babel of foreign languages and skin complexions. Considering that 20% of the voters in Los Angeles, and 30% of the city's school enrollment is Hispanic, the future of the "City of the Angels" is evident. At the other end of the country in the East, Florida struggles to absorb its latest influx of refugees from Cuba and Haiti. Miami is fast emerging as Latin America's "capital." Not only have the Latin American divisions of multinational corporations chosen it for its headquarters, but Venezuelans, Chileans, Peruvians, and Argentinians have discovered it as a shopping haven. Despite the social unrest caused by more than 700,000 Cuban refugees descending on Dade County, Latin American trade and tourists have ignited a commercial boom. Miami is already more than 50% Hispanic and the bilingual signs everywhere are symbolic of a changing community, a harbinger for the whole country. *World Press Review* (November 1980) quotes a West German newspaper on this phenomenon as follows:

> Eighty years after Theodore Roosevelt's America liquidated the remains of the Spanish empire, the language of the former adversary returns. But the struggle does not involve simply two European influences. Mexican-Americans so clearly bear an Indian heritage that their advance seems less a return of the Spanish empire that than the revenge of Montezuma!

One small indicator of how the internal character of America is being altered was seen when the U.S. Equal Employment Opportunity Commission proposed that employers not require bilingual workers to speak only English on the job unless business necessity dictated otherwise. Such guidelines will assist the more than 10.6 million people in the U.S. who speak Spanish as their primary language.

These Hispanic developments in North America have enormous implications for managers who do business in or with the U.S., and offer tremendous opportunities to promote new synergies. In fact, the whole blending of the American and Latin cultures on the U.S. mainland is an unconscious model of synergy. Two other such paradigms of cooperation can be cited in San Diego, California. Increasing trade with its adjoining urban metropolis of Tijuana has prompted San Diego business leaders to join with their Mexican counterparts in developing a Mexican-American trade center, and participating in their World Trade Association. Why? Because 79% of San Diego imports are from Mexico, and 90% of its exports go to Mexico. Perhaps trade along the international borders can become a major force for more synergistic efforts by these two great national neighbors.

The other synergistic model is the "Program in United States-Mexican Studies" at the University of California-San Diego. Dr. A. Wayne Cornelius has brought together leaders from both countries in the creation of a center for research, training, and public service activities between Mexico and the U.S. The scholarly effort will address problems and interactions between the two peoples, develop a library and data bank, and promote interdisciplinary, international seminars on public issues of mutual concern. It is a long-term program in international collaboration that will bring about an exchange of information and practitioners.

Before closing this section on North America by forecasting its future, it might be advisable to look beyond the horizon for U.S. Latinos. Robert Anson reminds us that Hispanics comprise a varied tapestry reflecting Spanish, Indian, mulatto, and Afro-American heritages, and today comprise a substantial proportion of the

U.S. population. A federal government policy analyst, his trend forecasts are worth noting here:

> The future safety and security of the U.S. is linked with developments in Mexico and Latin America, creating a greater sense of interdependence than in the past. Economically, for instance, the U.S. imports $17 billion worth of Latin America's products, while Latin America is the U.S.'s third largest export market. In the next three years Mexico, for instance, is planning to double its energy productions and represents a major potential source of gas and petroleum for the U.S.

> The U.S. is already the fourth largest Spanish-speaking nation in this hemisphere and will be the third-largest by 1990. Los Angeles, California, contains the second-largest single group of Hispanics in the world. By 1990, one half of California, one third of Texas, may be Spanish-speaking; by 2000, Hispanics may be the majority population in four states. The Hispanic market in the U.S. is the fastest growing, having increased by 25% since 1970. Forty-two percent of the U.S. Hispanic population is under 20 years, and by 1990 that increased number will impact the political-economic landscape. Within the next two decades, Hispanic minorities will comprise 27% of the total U.S. population, and California may become its first Third World state.

> The social and cultural fabric of both Anglo and Latin American influences will affect both groups and produce a new synergy. The mariage of economic and political realities, according to UNESCO ambassador, Esteban Torres, will promote and solidify the socio-economic and political efforts of the Hispanic community. Hispanics are learning to use information and the multiple channels of communication in this society to influence change as a result of their growing economic and political strength.[2]

Literally, the Hispanic Americans can become the synergistic bridge to the whole of Latin America, whose present population of 300 million estimated may double by the end of the century.

The Future of North America

Some futurists, like Victor Ferkiss, forecast that the twenty-first century may see the emergence of quasi-nations or regional groups in the northern hemisphere. These regions, which would extend beyond national and state boundaries, would be defined by the socio-political-economic needs of the people in them. For example, "MexAmerica" would encompass Mexico, Texas, Arizona, New Mexico, and southern California. "The Breadbasket" would include the mid-western U.S. and central Canada; "The Foundry" would contain the industrial northeast; "Dixie," the southeastern U.S.; and "Ecotopia," northern California, Oregon, Washington, and western Canada.

Such continental integration and technocratic movements, according to Ferkiss, could become a North American common market in fact, if not in political agreements. Energy and agriculture are the major ingredients propelling such economic integration. Though precise boundaries of these new regional alignments are difficult to forecast, Professor Ferkiss believes there are significant other cultural and demi-political forces moving the three countries in such directions. It has long been evident that the immigration and customs policies of the three nations are obsolete, and that the massive exchange of information, goods and inhabitants, requires a new approach that goes beyond traditional borders and cultures. Ferkiss concludes that in the near future, the status quo will be maintained while extensive population migrations go on among the three neighboring nations. As the new geopolitical regroupings occur and other patterns emerge, expect to see vast changes in these countries' immigration policies toward one another, starting with a more effective guest worker program.

Currently, most Americans are confused and uncertain about their future, but open to technological changes. Yankelovich and Leftkowitz[3] conclude that at all levels of society a search is underway for a new collective consensus about painful social choices that must be made. Their research indicates that the American public:

1. Wants to retain some of the gains made in affluent years, and will make only those sacrifices necessary to maintain economic stability and the necessities of life.
2. Seeks to strike a balance between hard work and leisure, and is willing to slow down the pursuit of pleasure for the exploration of self-fulfillment.
3. Desires to curb expansion of certain government services, while reducing taxes and invasion of privacy.
4. Is willing to make modest cutbacks to conserve energy, and a new antiwaste morality is gaining momentum.
5. Searches for a more balanced life style in which the needs of the spirit will be integrated with material aspirations.

Some of these same trends have been confirmed by the 1980 election results in the U.S., and by Stahrl Edmunds, the Dean of the Graduate School of Administration at the University of California, Riverside. Edmunds observes the public in the next two decades will react strongly to its disillusionment with political leaders over inflation, lower economic growth rates, growing unemployment, and mounting tax squeeze, unless policy-makers alter the direction of social change.[4] But Americans tend to be future-oriented and optimistic as a people, so Edmunds concludes, "In other words, the future is in our own hands, if we so wish."

Latin Americas' Indians

The Mesoamerican culture area encompasses the chiefdoms and states in the highlands of Central Mexico and Guatemala, and the lowlands of the Yucatan and adjacent regions. The best known of these "empires" are those of the Aztecs in the

Valley of Mexico, and the Maya states of Guatemala and Yucatan. In pre-Columbian times these people had a very advanced civilization — they measured time precisely by movements of the heavenly bodies, built pyramids and immense cities, developed a sophisticated calendar, domesticated corn and gave numerous fruits/ vegetables to the world, developed mining skills, and were magnificent jewelers. Only a visit to the great anthropology museum in Mexico City, or to an exhibit of ancient Indian art and artifacts can help one comprehend the high state of advancement in these civilizations.

Thus, the Indians in the past and present can be classified mainly by the geographic or ecological zone in which they lived, developing a culture suitable to that place. In ancient times, highland Incas linked together an empire that extended from modern-day Ecuador to Chile with a network of roads, suspension bridges, and relay runners. Where the original natives were not exterminated by the colonists, their societies simplified and deculturated. The Andean Indian highland culture utilized sophisticated irrigation for intensive agriculture and this led to large communities. Art, architecture, crafts and political leadership was of high quality. The Tropical Forest peoples in river lowlands and dense forests are typified today in Amazon river tribes that the Brazilian government alternately aids and hinders in their struggle for survival against modern settlers in that country's interior. The Marginal area people are in the largest contiguous location from northern Uruguay to the Strait of Magellan, including the Chilean archipelago.

CENTRAL AMERICA'S CULTURAL DEVELOPMENT

Going south of the Rio Grande River from the United States one enters the Third World and Latin America. This is also true moving southeast of Florida, but there one encounters in the Caribbean Sea area a series of small nations that represent a curious mix of British-French cultures. Considering that some of these West Indies occasionally changed hands between Britain and France, an unusual cultural synergy has occurred which goes beyond a language interchange between French and English. Among eight major nations in the mid-continent and fourteen adjoining island states to the west, we will begin with the largest and most powerful.

Mexico

Situated on the Pacific Rim and extending eastward to the Gulf, Mexico is a land of contrast and promise. Over 761,000 square miles in land mass, this country has an expanding population of more than 70 million people. Its diverse peoples have increased a hundredfold in the past forty years. Half of that burgeoning population lives in the central highlands, which constitutes half of the country's total cropland. With an annual population increase of more than 3%, this nation is expected to have 100 million people by the year 2000. This has enormous social and business implications not only for Mexico, but especially for the "Norte Americanos." With 31 states in the United States of Mexico, 14 million people are concentrated in the Federal District capital of Mexico City. Like many developing countries, the young greatly outnumber the old, and the life expectancy is 65 years, contrasted to 73 years in the U.S. Other interesting population trends are:

1. Thirteen percent are of Indian pure blood ancestry, 10% of European heritage, 75% mixed.
2. Increasing urbanization - 65%.
3. Decreasing infant mortality, but still a death rate of 70 per 1000 (in contrast to 13 per 1000 in the U.S.).
4. Rising literacy rate — now 84% of the population, plus a rising educational level (in 1980, 15 million in elementary school, 4 million in secondary level, and 800,000 in higher education).
5. Rising income per capita ($2,100 annually in 1980 per person average), but still 18 million underprivileged people, largely in rural areas.
6. Inadequate diet, medical care, housing and social security still plague the nation.

One fourth the size of the U.S., Mexico has a topography that features desert, tropical, mountainous and temperate regions with equal parts divided by the Tropic of Cancer. The lofty central plains are the main agricultural region, but only 24 million hectares of the agricultural land is cultivated. In the next five years, it is anticipated that another 3.3 million additional hectares will be developed. Although predominately an agricultural nation, Mexico is rapidly industrializing and is a leading exporter of metals, especially silver. In addition to spectacular growth in manufacturing and tourism, Mexico's hope for a better economic future lies in its recent discoveries and developments in oil and gas. Its energy supplies may rival those of Saudi Arabia with a proven oil reserve of 40 billion barrels, and a potential of 220 billion barrels.

This is altering Mexico's whole relationship with the U.S., which has been somewhat stormy since the Americans invaded the country in 1846. After the war Mexico ceded almost half of its original territory to the U.S. by the Treaty of Guadalupe (this included Texas California, Arizona, New Mexico, and part of Utah/Colorado). No border on earth separates two more widely divergent standards of living between two nations. Despite conflicts over illegal immigration, trade and drug smuggling, the American and Mexican peoples are generally friendly, and the prospects for Mexican and American synergy are promising.

From a business perspective, multinational managers need to understand that:

• The nineteenth century in Mexico was marked by political unrest, the twentieth century by economic progress, and the country may really come into its own promise and potential in the twenty-first century.
• Discovered by Hernan Cortez in 1519, Mexico revolted against Spanish rule and achieved independence in 1821. It defeated French influence and interfer-

ence by 1876, and survived a series of revolutions, achieving political and economic stability by 1940. One political party has dominated since 1930. The federal government consists of an executive, legislative, and judicial branch, and the military does not play a significant role in governance. Government seized and nationalized all Roman Catholic Church properties and reduced the power of that religious organization by anti-clerical laws (culturally, the people are still influenced by Roman Catholic morality and spirituality).

• The structure of capital and labor is somewhat different here from other countries in Latin America. The old, landed oligarchy has lost a major share of its property and power. A large rural bourgeoisie has grown among a large group of small landowners who today provide the capital for industrial and financial development. There is a growing salaried middle class, some of whom also cultivate their own land. An agrarian revolution has created a new type of peasant class, benefiting by government land distribution policies, or becoming a major source of U.S. agricultural manpower, as well as the Mexican industrialized workforce. Relative to returns for capital and labor, two thirds go to the corporation and only one third to the employees.

• The large public sector and public corporations contribute 44% of total investment, and is part of the state's power. State-owned companies implement public policy to generate jobs, goods and services, and an ability to negotiate with other nations or their corporations. The power of the state is limited by its single market orientation toward the U.S., which accounts for two-thirds of its imports and exports. Mexico is America's fourth largest trading partner, and its attempts to sell more in the north are blocked to a degree by obsolete, protectionist U.S. trade policies, regulations, and unions. Its new energy strength could force a change in that economic relationship.

• In the '70s, multinational corporations in Mexico (95% American controlled) provided 93% of the payments for imports of technology; and in the '80s, 80% of the technology employed is still foreign. Multinational corporations occasionally obtain slightly lower but safer profits on their investments in Mexico than they do in other Latin American countries. By 1980, the growth rates of public and private investment increased by 18%. Trade balances, employment, family planning, consumer price index, worker wages, and other indicators of economics well-being all continue to improve in Mexico.

Some of the above insights come from Pablo Gonzalez Casanova.[5] He reminds us that Mexico is a country in major transition, seeking to broaden its social and democratic basis, to control tensions between the evolving middle class and the disadvantaged masses, and to contain radical and revolutionary forces within the society.

The Mexicans are a relaxed, hospitable, and warm people who may relate more to their Indian than Spanish heritage. They are proud, patriotic and family oriented, and very hard working. Emotional, with a leisurely sense of time, they are generally comfortable with themselves and others, and are very person oriented. External business people should take time to talk and socialize, and above all be culturally sensitive and respectful.

Central Caribbean Complex

On the western side of the Caribbean Sea is a land bridge between the northern and southern continents of the Americas, which also fronts on the Pacific Ocean. The seven nations located between Mexico and Colombia are usually referred to as Central America — all but Belize are primarily Latin in culture.

If ever there was a need and case for synergy, it is in these Central American states. The nineteenth century federation called the United Provinces of Central America may have been premature, but it provided a cooperative model for the future — if not politically, at least economically. Only by collaboration, such as in Europe's Common Market, can this bloc of countries overcome their chronic poverty, illiteracy, violence. Perhaps where political and military power-types have failed, local business leaders and multinational managers may succeed in raising the standards and quality of living for the populace. Sandwiched between North and South America, this area cries out for synergistic solutions and contributions from both the Anglo-Latin cultures.

Central America has been described as "the land of the smoking gun," where terrorism and turmoil imperil hopes for moderate reform. Unfortunately, too often in the past these "banana republics" became comic-opera fiefdoms of U.S. commerce, especially United Fruit Company. Despite bustling capitals, the 20 + million people in this strife-torn and suffering region are, for the main part, gentle peasants who have been exploited too long. This strategic land mass is a glaring challenge to the more affluent in the Americas to right the unequal distribution of wealth and land, a festering source of political instability. As General Wallace Nutting reminds us, "All of Central America could easily radicalize, and a very substantial wedge would be driven between north and south." But consider another scenario under the aegis of the industrialized Pan American countries in which: educational technology is used to provide mass education and literacy; cooperatives are formed on a massive scale to include the peasants into a better way of life; scientific and technological know-how is shared to improve the economies, the health services, and development of the region; and social justice is brought to all levels of society.

Panama, conceivably, which has never considered itself part of Central America and has been spared the regional strife, might become a laboratory, along with Costa Rica, to create demonstration models that would influence the other states to join in a regional entity for self-improvement. Efforts by such new governments, as in Nicaragua, to liquidate $1.5 billion in war debts by ambitious reforms from agrarian redistribution to a literacy campaign should be encouraged. Application of new techniques to promote social peace and reduce internal political violence, as in El Salvador and Guatemala, should become the concern of Pan American social scientists. Simplistic, anti-communist and military approaches will not solve the region's problems and tap its vast undeveloped human and natural resources. In contrast to North American bribery and support of corrupt officials, Mexico and Venezuela have provided an example of synergistic magnanimity by concerned neighbors: these major oil producers agreed to provide regional importers with a 30% credit. Perhaps Latin American commercial leaders are in the best position to assist Central America?

The West Indies

On the eastern side of the Caribbean Sea, facing outward toward the Atlantic Ocean, is a group of island nations generally referred to as The West Indies. Thirteen of these independent states are part of the United Nations, while two are affiliated with the U.S. — the Commonwealth of Puerto Rico and the Territory of the Virgin Islands. Puerto Rico, along with Cuba and the Dominican Republic, are thought of as part of Latin America because of their Spanish cultural heritage. The remaining represent a mix of African, French, English and even Irish cultures. (The Irish influence resulted from descendants of political dissidents brought there by the British.)

All of these former colonies have full U.N. voting rights as sovereign states, but are not likely to make social/political/economic progress on their own. Attempts by the British government to form confederations out of some of them failed. In a special on "Turmoil in the Caribbean," *World Press Review* (September 1980) described the Central American and Caribbean region as a "microcosm of global conflict" and a hotbed of imperialism in the struggle between Western capitalism and Cuban communism. Because the major powers lack a cohesive and consistent Pan American policy, moderates in these microstates are hard pressed between radical elements on the right and left of the political spectrum. While a few countries, such as Canada and Venezuela attempt to offer positive mediation in the Caribbean Basin, violent change is spearheaded by the radicalized and disenfranchised. Distress signals continue to come out of the central portion of the Western Hemisphere calling for synergistic solutions and peaceful progress.

As the tiny states swing left and right on an ideological seesaw, Barbados manages to provide a model of hope in a sea of chaos. In contrast to the intense rivalries and economic despair around it, Barbados runs well with a balanced budget, healthy growth rate, efficient democratic elections, neat and orderly public service. The 6.5% annual economic growth is due to stability, record tourist arrivals, manufactured exports, sugar production, construction boom, and a happy, industrious population. With intelligent and sober governance, its defense forces have been called upon to police their tiny neighbors. After three centuries as a British colony, its parliamentary system works independently. Even the lovely, nearby Netherlands Antilles with its Dutch cultural overlay is not immune from social unrest as riots and fires at the Shell Refineries proved. The future of these peoples lies in cooperation and collaboration, but who will show them how to accomplish this?

SOUTH AMERICAS' CULTURAL DEVELOPMENT

As the multinational manager flies over the twelve countries that compose the southern continent of the Americas, one is struck by the immensity of this land mass and the potential resources down below, especially in Brazil and Argentina. Nine of these Latin peoples have, in addition to their ancient Indian heritages, a Spanish cultural base, and one nation each has Portuguese, French, or Dutch cultural inputs. All but Surinam share the Roman Catholic cultural tradition. Most have been enriched by African cultural influxes. Centered between the Atlantic and Pacific Oceans, South America has been a multicultural cauldron for mixing Asian, East Indian, as well as European and African, cultures in a curious synergy.

South America is a place where we can simultaneously be amazed at the beauty of the pre-Columbian art and civilization, or the very modern and colorful art works and high-rise architecture; and be appalled by the poverty of the masses and the great wealth of the few, by the violence and terrorism and by the dominance of a powerful military or dictator. We can be encouraged by the progress in education and literacy, improvements in health services and population control, changing images and aspirations of South Americans. (See Appendix C for sources of available information on these national cultures.)

Despite the great diversity in Latin America, there are common themes and patterns. After the development of fairly sophisticated Indian civilizations, there was a period of European colonization and exploitation from the fifteenth through eighteenth centuries, followed by wars of independence and attempts at federation during the nineteenth century. Since the early twentieth century, Latin American nations have been engaged in internal and external conflicts. Yet, the last half of this century has seen relative peace between the nations of Central and South Americas, and significant economic progress.

These countries also share another factor — a Roman Catholic cultural tradition that not only pervades their history, but ways of life and thinking. The Spanish and Portuguese explorers and conquerors brought the missionaries with them to convert and "civilize" the pagan inhabitants. Accompanying the military from South America up through North America were Franciscans, Dominicans, and Jesuits. At first, the clergy protected the Indians and helped through their missions to educate the indigenous populations. Their agricultural and trading centers became the great cities of South and North America. With the passage of time and increase in wealth, the Church became part of the establishment, despite the notable successes of priest revolutionaries, like Father Miguel Hidalgo, who espoused the causes of nationalism or the peasants. As a major land owner itself, the Church has not only supported the oligarchy, but opposed population control, divorce, and social change. But recently, in opposition to the continuation of feudal conditions and serfdom for peasants, a group of socially-minded clergy have provided Latin leadership.

With the encouragement of Pope John XXIII's Second Vatican Council in the 1960s, the promotion of social justice became a Roman Catholic priority in Latin America. A series of episcopal conferences confirmed the efforts, while Latin bishops such as Leonidas Proaño of Ecuador, the martyred Oscar Romero of El Salvador, and Dom Helder Camarra of Brazil, became forces for change in their dioceses and nations. Some priests and religious became militant and even joined the guerrillas or Marxists. Others suffered harassment, beatings, torture, and death in their defense of the poor and human rights. Bishop Proaño stated their case in these dramatic words:

> Exploitation, oppression, and repression of one group by another is socially sinful. God created the world for all, not just a few landowners or large corporations. It is therefore our duty in the Church to protest such conditions and develop a conscious awareness of the causes of oppression among the poor, encouraging them to unite and develop their own political solutions and leaders.

The growth of the militant theology and activities in the Latin American Church caused Pope John-Paul in his visits to the Western Hemisphere in 1980 to protest social inequities, and yet warn the clergy of the need to concentrate on their spiritual mission. In any event, no modern manager operating in Latin America can afford to ignore the Church as a cultural force. One author (Harris) has personally witnessed in Venezuela a decade of positive effects of a movement called "Faith and Happiness" which brought about a synergy on behalf of community development by religious organizations and executives. Cooperation and collaboration for social improvement in Latin America can be significantly advanced when business cooperates with institutions for human development.

The great Latin American liberator, Simón Bolívar, envisioned hemisphere solidarity 150 years ago. Consider this plea for Latin synergistic contributions:

> We are a small race of men; we possess a world apart, surrounded by wide seas, which is new in almost all the arts and sciences, although to some extent old in the uses of civil society.
> . . . Racing ahead to coming ages, my imagination looks at future centuries and observes there, with admiration and wonder, the prosperity, splendor, and way of life this vast region has received. I feel carried away, and I seem to see this region in the heart of the universe, extending out over its long coasts, among those oceans that nature had separated, and that our country joins together with extended and wide channels. I see it serving as a link, a center, an emporium of the human family. I see it sending to all corners of the globe the treasures harbored in its mountains of silver and gold. I see it distributing health and life to suffering men of the old universe through its divine plants. I see it communicating its precious secrets to the wise men who do not know how superior the sum of its culture and the riches that nature has lavished upon it are. I see it seated on the throne of Liberty grasping the scepter of Justice, crowned by Glory, showing the old world the majesty of the modern world.[6]

MANAGEMENT SYNERGY IN THE AMERICAS

In this chapter, we have sought to provide Pan American managers a kaleido-scopic view of the Western Hemisphere in terms of its diverse national cultures and their development, as well as their problems and opportunities for synergy. Our realistic appraisal has analyzed human and natural resources from the Alaskan state in the far north to the Patagonia state in the far south, covering unique peoples from Eskimo hunters to Argentinian sheepherders. To improve the quality of life for all the hemisphere's inhabitants, effective and ecologically controlled utilization of resources on these twin continents is a *major management challenge.* Trained and experienced managers in transnational enterprises throughtout the Americas may be able to accomplish in the decades ahead what politicians, dictators, revolutionaries, and soldiers have failed to accomplish in the past centuries — Pan American cooperation and collaboration.

In some ways, the old Spanish administrators provided us some potential models for the economic integration and regional cooperation that will be the highlight of the Americas in the twenty-first century. Thomas Mooney reminds us that the Spanish captain-general who lived in Guatemala City over three centuries ago administered a region extending from the southern Mexican border to what is now the northern Panamanian frontier.[7] From other great Latin American centers like Lima and Mexico City, the Spanish promoted regional and international trade. In conjunction with the nineteenth century independence movements, visionaries such as Simón Bolívar, promoted cooperative entities, such as Gran Colombia, which may be harbingers of tomorrow's collaborative schemes, if not politically, at least socially and economically. The signs of the future are already evident in undertakings, such as the Organization of American States, the Central American Common Market (CACM), Caribbean Common Market (CARICOM), the Latin American Free Trade Association (LAFTA), the Andean Pact (ANCOM), and other emerging attempts at synergy in this hemisphere. Many such efforts under the stimulus of the U.S. government were perceived as "imperialistic." Perhaps the time has come to take the north-south issue of cooperation in the Americas out of the political arena. Perhaps transnational managers operating in the international marketplaces of North/Central/South America may offer the innovative leadership necessary to develop the potential of our two continents?

The German political scientist Gottfried Dietze offered international executives a rare insight into the differences between North and South American organizations and management styles when he wrote:

> In Hispanic America the hierarchical order of the state was complemented by
> that of the army and the Catholic Church, whereas in English-speaking America
> a more liberal political order, the absence of a strong army, and the prevalence
> of civilians with their families were complemented by more democratically or-
> ganized churches.

> The strong executive in Latin America is as much a result of the heritage of the Latin American nations as popular government is the outcome of Anglo-Saxon traditions.[8]

Aware of Latin America's heavy European cultural dependence, as well as continuing immigration from that continent, Canadian and U.S. Americans should realize that if they do not take the initiative in promoting synergy in the Americas, others abroad may do it for them. Bernard Lietaer, head of organizational planning and computer department for the National Bank of Belgium sounded the alert when he said that Western Europe and Latin America are following economic policies that will lead to disaster unless they start playing "the positive sum game," where both sides win. Lietaer believes that this requires a basic change in the relationships between developed and developing countries. He argues that both continents can avoid severe economic depression in the next two decades by cooperating to solve each other's problems. This Belgian economist, who proposes a Western Europe type "Marshall Plan" to foster Latin American industrial development and markets, asserts that with increasing U.S. withdrawal from its domination of Latin American trade, South America becomes a very attractive potential partner for Western Europe. He envisions the multinational corporations as the bridge for accomplishing this collaboration.[9] Those North Americans seeking greater synergy with their counterparts in the southern part of the hemisphere take note.

The culture capsules previous presented illustrate the great contrast, complementariness, and the synergistic potential among the peoples in the Americas. We will conclude our analysis with a last look at some paradigms and issues worth considering.

Trans-American Synergistic Models

From the middle of the twentieth century Argentinian companies have been promoting successful programs of multinationalization. Over $8 million investments by these corporations in other Latin American countries have worked to the economic benefit of Brazil, Paraguay, and Uruguay, especially in manufacturing.

Brazil's Petrobras has undertaken foreign venture projects for oil exploration and refining in nine other Latin American nations. After $60 million investments in their neighbors, Brazilian multinationals are now penetrating the African markets.

Ecuador, graced with virgin jungles, fertile mountains, and miles of ocean shores, keeps uncovering its natural treasures. In the last century, it was pearls, cacao, coffee, and bananas. Now it is oil and sea harvesting. It has opened its doors to vast reserves of oil, to industrial potential, and to 70 million consumers in the five member countries of the Andean Pact. Furthermore, with the help of American entrepreneurs, it is going into shrimp farming in a big way. The Andean Pact, plus the International Monetary Fund, have opened new development horizons for its own citizens and neighbors.

Mexico has been encouraging the establishment of twin plant operations with U.S. firms. The facilities not only provide jobs in Mexico, but improve their economic and technological skills. As a result, the illegal alien drain on the USA is reduced, and American cars and computers have parts in them made in Mexico through cooperation between neighbors.

Canada has made a major commitment to Carribbean development. The nation will increase cooperation in trade to CARICOM and raise Canadian economic and technical assistance to the regions. Canadian high commissioner to Ghana John Graham recently observed:

> We are aware that if Canada cannot come to an understanding on the contentious and difficult North-South issues with the Caribbean, we will have great difficulty building bridges with other parts of the Third World.

For such synergistic undertakings to succeed, cultural sensitivity and skill is necessary for international business transactions. For our readers interested in fostering similar synergistic relations, we recommend a remarkable document entitled, *Reference Manual on Doing Business in Latin America.* [10]

Table 14-2 provides insightful comparisons between North American and Latin cultures in terms of business practice.*

Increasingly, Inter-American business negotiations are conducted by attorneys through teams. Writing in the above cited ABA reference manual, Robert Radway discussed "New Dimensions of Negotiating in Latin America." The transnational corporation's negotiating team is usually interdisciplinary. Thus, if synergy is to be achieved, cross-cultural sensitivity and skills must be applied within the team because the professionals come from different microcultures (see chapter 7); and with the clients who represent different macrocultures. Then potential context and conflict difficulties can be managed more effectively, and mutual cooperation fostered.

Another strategy to consider in facilitating Pan American management synergy is to try and enter into the foreign manager's life space and perceive situations as that person might do. It is a kind of reverse role play which can be done singly or in groups, literally or figuratively. One author (Harris) has done this when consulting on twin plant projects that involve managers from two different cultures in the Americas. For example, in a management development session composed of executives from both sides of the U.S.-Mexico border, each group was asked to take a turn sitting in the center of a circle with their fellow nationals and listing what they liked and did not like about the management style and practices of their counterpart in the other culture. Imagine the Americans' surprise, for instance, when they heard themselves described by the Mexicans as "cheap." Later their colleagues from Tijuana explained to the Californians, "When you are visiting our plant on a Friday afternoon at the end of a work week, we appreciate an invitation later by you to go out and socialize. But when we arrive at the *taberna,* you say 'It's Dutch - we all pay for our own drinks.' Now you may do that in your country, but in Mex-

---

*For more information on Latin cultures see Chapter 15 in *Managing Cultural Differences*.

Table 14-2
Inter-American Cultural Contrasts in Business

Aspects* of U.S. Culture	Alternative Aspects of Latin American Culture	Examples of Business Functions Affected
The individual can influence the future "where there is a will there is a way."	Life follows a preordained course and human action is determined by the will of God.	Planning, scheduling.
The individual can change and improve the environment.	People are intended to adjust to the physical environment rather than to alter it.	Work and motivation planning.
An individual should be realistic in his aspirations.	Ideals are to be pursued regardless of what is reasonable.	Goal setting.
We must work hard to accomplish our objectives (Puritan ethic).	Hard work is not the only prerequisite for success; wisdom, luck, and time are also required.	Motivation and reward system.
Commitments should be honored (people will do what they say they will do).	A commitment may be superseded by a conflicting request, or an agreement may only signify intention and have little or no relationship to the capacity of performance.	Negotiating and bargaining.
One should effectively use his time (time is money which can be saved or wasted).	Schedules are important but only in relation to other priorities.	Long- and short-range planning.
A primary obligation of an employee is to the organization.	The individual employee has a primary obligation to his family and friends.	Loyalty, commitment, and motivation.
The employer or employee can terminate their relationship.	Employment is for a lifetime.	Motivation and commitment to the company.
The best qualified persons should be given the position available.	Family considerations, friendship, and other considerations partially determine employment practices.	Employment Promotions Recruiting Selection Reward
A person can be removed if he does not perform well.	The removal of a person from a position involves a great loss of prestige and may only rarely be done.	Promotion
All levels of management are open to qualified individuals (an office boy can rise to become company president).	Education or family ties are the primary vehicles for mobility.	Employment practices and promotions

(Table 14-2 continued on page 300)

* *Aspect* here refers to a belief, value, attitude, or assumption that is a part of culture. It is shared by persons in any culture.

Table 14-2 — Continued

Aspects* of U.S. Culture	Alternative Aspects of Latin American Culture	Examples of Business Functions Affected
Intuitive aspects of decision-making should be reduced and efforts should be devoted to gathering relevant information.	Decisions are expressions of wisdom by the person in authority and any questioning would imply lack of confidence in his judgment.	Decision-making processes.
Data should be accurate.	Accurate data is not as highly valued.	Record-keeping.
Company information should be available to anyone who needs it within the organization.	Withholding information to gain or maintain power is acceptable.	Communications.
Each person is expected to have an opinion and to express it freely, even if his views do not agree with his colleagues.	Deference is to be given to persons in power or authority, and to offer judgments not in support of the ideas of one's superiors is unthinkable.	Communications.
A decision-maker is expected to consult persons who can contribute useful information on the area being considered.	Decisions may be made by those in authority and others need not be consulted.	Decision-making.
Competition stimulates high performance.	Competition leads to unbalances and to disharmony.	Promotion.
A person is expected to do whatever is necessary to get the job done (one must be willing to get his hands dirty).	Various kinds of work are accorded low or high status and some work may be below one's "dignity" or place in the organization.	Assignment of tasks Performance Organization
Change is considered an improvement.	Tradition is revered and the power of the ruling group is founded on the continuation of a stable structure.	Planning.
What works is important.	Symbols and the process are more important than the end point.	Communication Organization Planning.
Persons and systems are to be evaluated.	Persons are evaluated but in such a way that individuals not highly evaluated will not be embarrassed or caused to "lose face."	Rewards Promotion

* *Aspect* here refers to a belief, value, attitude, or assumption that is a part of culture. It is shared by persons in any culture.

ico, you pay if you invite us out to join you." The reader may say that it is only a small matter. But Latins are generally very warm, sociable people; sensitivity to such seemingly small cultural differences builds the kind of personalized business relationships that lead to Inter-American collaborations.

Conclusion

John Condon in *Inter-Act Mexico,* reminds us of the Latin vision of a cosmic race. It is expressed in the words *la raza,* the often mystical idealization of the Latin culture. In this collective image, the spirit speaks through the race. As one contemporary Mexican philosopher eloquently commented:

> The American will become, with centuries, the sum and synthesis of humanity, spiritually as well as physically.

That gets to the heart of the message in these pages. Cosmopolitan managers in transnational enterprises are in a unique position to cultivate Pan American integration and synergy. They can create cooperative models that will be emulated in other regions of the globe.

References

1. Gordon, R. *Living in Latin America.* National Textbook, 1974.
2. Anson, R. "Hispanics in the United States: Yesterday, Today and Tomorrow," *The Futurist,* August 1980.
3. Yankelovich and Leftkowitz (polling organization). "The New American Dream," *The Futurist,* August 1980.
4. Edmunds, S. "Which Way America?" *The Futurist,* February 1979.
5. Casanova, P.G. "The Economic Development of Mexico," *Scientific American,* September 1980.
6. Quoted from *Americas,* by R. Caldera, April 1981.
7. Mooney T. In: *Doing Business in Latin America.* T. A. Gannon (ed.) New York: AMACOM, 1968.
8. Dietze G. "Government of the People: A European Looks at the Americas," *Americas* Vol. 33, no. 5, May 1981. (Published by OAS, General Secretariat Building, Washington D.C.)
9. Lietaer, B. *Europe + Latin America + the Multinationals.* Farnborough, U.K. Saxon House, 1979.
10. Shea, D. R., Swacker, F. W., Radway, R. J., and Stairs, S. T. (eds,) *Reference Manual for Doing Business in Latin America.* American Bar Association's National Institute on Current Legal Aspects. (Available through Professor D. R. Shea, Director, Center for Latin America, University of Wisconsin, Milwaukee, Wisconsin 53201 USA.)

15.
Transnational Managers As Cosmopolitan Synergizers

INTERNATIONAL PRODUCTIVITY STRATEGY

At the turn of this decade two best-selling novels appeared on the subject of Japanese culture. James Clavell's *Shogun* was eventually televised and viewed by millions of Americans and Japanese. The $20 million film production was in itself a classic example of both cultural differences and synergy. The production crew was made up of Japanese and American nationals who not only came from different cultural backgrounds, but also from two distinct approaches to film making. Naturally, there was some conflict as each cultural group started with somewhat inflexible stances on film techniques and procedures. The Japanese also experienced culture shock at the important managerial role of females among the American film crew members. But eventually, both groups made professional compromises, learned from each other, combined their talents, and produced a significant cinematic work. Not only did vast audiences enjoy the fruit of their mutual artistic efforts, but this multitude of viewers gained greater insight into both Eastern and Western cultural mind-sets.

The other work of fiction was *Ninja* by Eric Van Lustbader, and it is cited here primarily for two quotations of the hero in that novel. Speaking of the essence of Japanese culture, he observes:

> There is firstly respect. Then there is knowledge — sought and assimilated. There is acceptance of what is and what was — the understanding of one's role within the matrix. Then there is curiosity to know the unknown. And lastly there is love.

Somehow these words sum up the challenge of intercultural encounters. The book's principal character finally adds this astute statement:

But in business one must learn to be cosmopolitan in one's thinking, especially when it comes to the matter of your client's personal tastes. I do not believe it is a good policy to be closeminded — traditional. This world supports a myriad of cultures. Who is to say which is more valid?

Wisdom can be discovered anywhere, even in works of fiction. The above quotes get at the heart of the message which we authors have been trying to convey. As we come to the closing chapter of the second volume, perhaps it is appropriate to review here what it is we have attempted to communicate to our readers.

Managing Cultural Differences encourages multinational managers to revise their image of their role in the world marketplace, and suggests that such leaders should be more cosmopolitan in perspective, and less ethnocentric. It proposes the acquisition of new skills in intercultural communication and planned change. The book reminds them that they not only transmit their own culture in the course of international business, but their own culturally-conditioned view of management. It offers a paradigm to better understand both macro- and microcultures, and then applies that conceptual model to facilitate comprehension of organizational culture and its impact on human behavior. Furthermore, it shares ways for delimiting culture shock and facilitating acculturation through improved cross-cultural training and foreign deployment services. To this culture general input, the first book in the International Management Productivity Series adds some culture specifics, especially in the form of case studies on doing business abroad in various cultural contexts. The principal theme is the need to be more aware of how cultural differences affect behavior in international business and development, as well as how one can improve coping skills in cross-cultural situations that may occur within or without one's native land.

Managing Cultural Synergy supplements this thesis and complements its message by highlighting that the very differences in the world's people can lead to mutual growth and accomplishment. Then, there is opportunity for more than the single contribution of each party to the intercultural transaction; we can go beyond awareness and our own cultural heritage to produce something greater by cooperation and collaboration. Cultural synergy builds upon similarities, and fuses differences resulting in more effective human activities and systems. The very diversity of people can be utilized to enhance problem solving by combined action. Those in international management have unique opportunities to foster synergy on a global basis. But they must first appreciate the many facets of the comparative management process, especially the cross-cultural factors in motivation and decision-making, power and conflict, and business communications. Thus, we examine some of the issues involved in international organization development. This exploration indicates how synergy could be enhanced through organizational culture, with team management, and among professional colleagues by transnational training and education, and through participative leadership. The final unit of this volume

(Chapters 11-15) focuses upon culture specifics in synergistic management. By considering global concerns that can be influenced by managerial activities and approaches, we hope to demonstrate the potential contributions of collaborative managers. In this closing chapter we will review eight particular opportunities that cosmopolitan managers have to promote greater synergy in the world marketplace:

1. Global leadership
2. New images and paradigms
3. Changes in organizational cultures
4. World trade and development
5. Multinational cooperatives
6. Relocation services
7. Educational innovation
8. Cultural interdependence

SYNERGY THROUGH EFFECTIVE GLOBAL LEADERSHIP

First, in his or her exercise of leadership, the international manager must continually update and broaden his or her understanding of culture and its impact on our lives. Although there may be no valid management theories that can be universally applied across all cultures, there are many principles and practices of leadership that can be adapted to various countries despite cultural differences. Professor Andre Laurent has been collecting data at INSEAD on a variety of European managers. Laurent discovered that despite the fact that French managers strongly disbelieve in matrix organization because it seemingly violates unity of command, one French MNC subsidiary had a long history of successful team management. Thus, despite the cultural differences in managerial approaches, it is possible to produce cultural synergy in the pragmatic operations of management.

Another example of how cross-cultural research within international management may help improve cosmopolitan leadership has been provided by Professor Teruyki Kume. His investigations at the Department of Foreign Studies, Nanzan University in Nagoya, Japan have centered on one aspect of the management process — that is, decision-making. Since more than 200 Japanese plants have been established in the United States, Kume's research examined the ways Japanese managers in these factories introduced their approaches to decision-making, and under what conditions American managers would favorably adopt Japanese styles of choice-making. It is an excellent illustration of synergistic research at a time when much of the management literature in America emphasizes the value of group decision-making. Kume found, however, that American cultural factors, such as individualism and self-reliance, tend to inhibit the transfer of the Japanese style:

Namely, Americans tend to control, dominate, and compete in various group situations, causing a conflict with the Japanese approaches. Their tendency to specialize in certain areas and their sense of urgency are also likely to inhibit them from using the Japanese style of intense horizontal and vertical coordination. The Japanese, whose major motives are security and safety, tend to be more cautious and thorough in their analysis of problems that require solutions. In contrast, the Americans, whose major motives are achievement and accomplishment, are more likely to be quick and impulsive in making decisions. Not being apprehensive about making the wrong decisions, they are willing to live with the outcome. Contrary to "common sense" expectations, it was found that the Japanese are more egalitarian than Americans who are more hierarchal at least in the process of decision-making.

The authors believe that such findings from intercultural management research, while insightful, also offer managers a mirror image of their national approaches to leadership for comparative analysis. Foreign managers are forced to rethink their positions when they realize that the success of Japanese decision-making is based on a management philosophy that fully recognizes every member of the organization as an important person who can help the company achieve its goals most effectively. Such leadership practice is culturally conditioned.

For effective global leadership, the transnational manager must also be able to think big and think ahead. Therefore, one must have the capacity to envision the increasing interdependence of all facets of human life. The late statesman, Adlai Stevenson demonstrated this sense of leadership in his activities with such words as these:

> We travel together, passengers on a little spaceship, dependent on its vulnerable reserves of air and soil; all committed for our safety to its security and peace; preserved from annihilation only by the care, the work and the love we give our fragile craft. We cannot maintain it half fortunate, half miserable; half confident, half despairing; half slave of the ancient enemies of man, half free in a liberation of resources undreamed of until this day. No craft, no crew can safely travel with such vast contradictions.

D. L. Hawk, vice-president of the Center for Creative Leadership (Greensboro, North Carolina 27402, USA) underscored the same theme more recently. Writing in the Center's newsletter about "Leadership 2000," Hawk reminded us that participation in an interdependent world system is required even though goals are diverse, power is dispersed and conflict is inevitable. He cited these examples of synergistic possibilities:

> When a common purpose can be found, then diverse interests of individual parties can be subsumed . . . and smaller goals can be accomplished within the framework of that larger purpose. Chrysler Corporation's bailout by a coalition

of government and banks is an example of how a superordinate goal overcame the parochial interests of individual bankers . . . When superordinate goals are found, they minimize the disruptions of the ripples of change. Basic agreement on purpose and direction reduce conflict, and produce a center of gravity to hold a group together. Such a center of gravity allows groups to act quasi-independently within their interdependent relationships.

In addition, leaders of the future will need to be able to show people how to work with and for others without sacrificing their individuality, betraying their values, or silencing their consciences. To provide clear leadership, leaders will need to act independently . . . yet collectively . . . So, effective leaders of the future will build coalitions, influence others skillfully; and solve problems with consensual, not compromised, solutions.

Perhaps the founder of the American organization, *Common Cause* put our point on this matter best. John Gardiner stated:

> Leaders have a significant role in creating a state of mind that is society . . .
> They can conceive and articulate goals that lift people out of their petty preoc-
> cupations, carry them above the conflicts that tear society apart, and unite them
> in the pursuit of objectives worthy of their best efforts.

The cosmopolitan manager in global enterprises is now in a position of influence not only to provide such vision for his or her own organization, but for the world community. Such sensitive executives have a rare opportunity to contribute to the creation of cyberculture, the new post-industrial way of life, as well as to design the new meta-industrial organization culture.

In any event, it is culture that has a powerful influence in giving a people identity. Culture is the collective meaning a people put into their unique life-space. It is the pattern of attitudes, beliefs, customs, traditions that generally express the way the average person in that place think and behave. When a people isolate themselves and communicate only with one another, they delimit their capacity to cope with diversity and the challenges of an increasingly "global village." Such an approach is contrary to the mainstream trend wherein the human family worldwide is seemingly creating a new planetary culture based on the refinement of its diverse cultures. The growth and rapid defusion of communication and technology has been the catalyst in this process.

Leaders must become more transnational and transcultural in their thinking, planning, and involvement. Medieval or industrial-age mindsets on the part of executives and top administrators are inappropiate. As the old cultural structures disintegrate and we struggle to create contemporary substitutes, true "leaders" keep their minds-eye on the post-technological culture yet to come into being. Such a person is R. Buckminster Fuller, who understands that the greatest revolutions in human history are now underway, and he envisions it as a "geosocial revolution." For Fuller the twentieth century has been a turning point in which unplanned, human inadvertencies in weaponry development have lead to technological spinoffs that could vastly improve the human condition. Fuller points out that the standard of living for average workers in advanced societies has risen from less than 1% for all humanity to 44% within the first two thirds of this century. Because of advances in scientific industrialization, world leaders now can extend that success model to all of humanity.

What then holds us back? The International Federation of Institutes for Advanced Study published a report by A. Peccei that indicates one answer. Its fascinating and well-argued conclusion is that only by a cultural revolution that changes the human quality can we control and orient the material revolution. A further insight is provided would-be cosmopolitan synergizers by still another IFIAS report by A. King on *The State of the Planet*. The conclusions reached are that while interdependence of all societies and all ecosytems make it imperative to think globally, in practice each social group and its leaders must solve problems locally. Appendix A "Towards Human Emergence," further elaborates on this theme and focuses on the significance of the cultural transition underway. It offers a rationale for leaders working for more synergy.

Public opinion polls indicate that citizens have more confidence today in business leaders to resolve community problems than they have in political or educational leaders. Executives in multinational and world corporations are in a unique position to promote synergy within their own sphere of operations, and between their own organization and its multiple interfaces. A recent study by Management Centre Europe (1979) of 500 top managers confirms that management thinking and practice do transcend national frontiers toward a unified European business scene. This European survey covered nine Western countries on that continent, and emphasizes that the pressures on management have greatly increased in the past decade, and that managers are not responding as effectively as they should to social pressures. Further, these key managers envisioned a dearth of really effective business leaders in the near term. These findings are significant for our theme here: overall, 51% of the respondents called for closer cooperation between business and education, while 66% felt the need for more effective management training.

In another study of 20 chief executive officers, Dr. Gordon Lippitt reported these major concerns for the 1980s:

> 1) increased multinational markets; 2) selecting new organizational structures; 3) managing increasing organizational complexity and uncertainty; 4) coordinating mission and goal in view of diversifications and decentralizations; 5) clarifying roles and accountabilities; 6) responding to changing worker values; 7) managing change and conflict; 8) encouraging performance improvement and appraisal; 9) reducing inter-unit competition and encouraging collaboration; 10) maintaining proper financial perspectives; 11) promoting effective utilization of human resources; 12) motivating new workers with multiple loyalties; 13) coping with ambiguity through innovation; 14) increasing interface between systems; and 15) improving management's role as human resource educators and developers.[1]

To conclude this section on global leadership, we turn to Dr. Charles Tavel, Chairman of the Committee on Industrial Innovation in the Organization for Economic Cooperation and Development, who maintains that this "third industrial age" calls for a *strategist*. In complex, interrelated, and interdependent activities, such a person is the brain, the synthesizer who assigns everything to its proper place. Tavel feels that this is one organizational function that cannot be assigned to a group of people, but that the executive strategist must make decisions and take responsibility for them. That strategist not only formulates but implements strategy relative to organizational structures and processes, task assignment, performance and motivation/reward. Furthermore, the corporate or government strategist is a generalist who can promote teamwork among specialists. Tavel believes the character of the strategist implies determination, originality, and commitment to personal and professional accomplishment. To these observations, we add Peter Drucker's comment that one needs strategies for tomorrow that anticipate the areas in which the greatest changes are likely to occur. In his *Managing in Turbulent Times,* he speaks of developing strategies that enable a business or public service institution to take advantage of the unforseen and unforseeable:

> Planning tries to optimize tomorrow the trends of today. Strategy aims to exploit the new and different opportunities of tomorrow.[2]

This is one reason why cosmopolitan synergizers must also be futurists and familiar with such literature as *Future Survey Annual* and *Future-Abstracts* (see Appendix C for addresses).

SYNERGY THROUGH NEW IMAGES AND PARADIGMS

Another opportunity through which transnational managers could promote synergy is in their conceptualizations. In the previous section we implied that leaders have a responsibility to contribute toward society's state of mind by articulating goals that move the populace to action and lift them above mundane preoccupations. Mental images influence human behavior in all spheres.

One aspect for the exercise of international leadership is helping people to cope more effectively with varied life identity crises by the creation of new images. Such crises, which contribute to future and organizational shock, may be seen as a series of concentric circles, which begins with the individual as the inner circle and expands to roles, organizations, nations, and, finally, species.

Starting in the center with the *individual,* it is apparent that our various self-images are threatened by accelerating changes within various global cultures. Traditional human conceptions are breaking down under the impact of contemporary events. We are forced to conjure up new perceptions of ourselves, both individually and institutionally. The increasing gap between where technology is and where culture lags, contributes to identity crises for many persons on this planet. We thought we knew who we are, but the old absolutes give way, and we are uncertain. We are people in transition, caught between disappearing and emerging cultures.

Not only is the self-concept for many in doubt or inadequate, but traditional *role* images in society are being undermined. What is a woman, a black, a teacher, a manager, a parent? We thought we knew, but again rapid change makes us unsure, causing us to redefine our roles. Nowhere, for instance, is such crisis more pronounced than with the Arab women today. Contrast the upper-class, educated Arab female in chic clothes who may jet around the world, with her Islamic sister in the peasant class — uninformed to a large extent and with a life wholly centered around her family and village. Both represent strikingly different roles in a Moslem world turned upside down.

Similar representations may be made of *organizations,* because human systems — collections of people — also suffer identity crises. Caught between a disappearing bureaucracy and an emerging "ad-hocracy," the institution may experience down-turns in sales, poor morale, membership reductions, bankruptcy threats, obsolescence of product lines and services, and increasing frustration with unresponsive management. Organizations, then, are challenged to go through planned renewal and to reproject their public images.

So too with *nations.* When the social fabric unravels or wavers, there are national identities in crisis. Three such examples are: the U.S. which lost "face" in Vietnam and had its diplomats seized as hostages in Iran; Great Britain, which lost its empire and nearly went bankrupt as a nation; and Japan whose very economic and technological progress threatens its traditional culture. Whether one goes to Canada, Pakistan, or China, the peoples of various countries seek to rediscover their collective selves in the post-national period.

Finally, Homo sapiens struggles with an identity crisis for the *species.* We thought we were earthbound, but now we have launched out into the universe. What are the limits of human potential? Is our real home out there? Cosmopolitan leaders can help in promoting synergy between past and future conceptions of our selves, which so powerfully influence our behavior and accomplishments.

William Christopher in *Management for the 80's* suggests that business itself has an identity problem in the emerging superindustrial age:

> If we have no concept of what we are as a business enterprise, our journey into the future will be haphazard . . . If our actions, adjustments, and reactions derive from a philosophy in tune with the world around us, we will find some kind of identity . . . that is consciously articulated and made central to every action taken everywhere in the organization . . . .

Christopher suggests that this search for a more relevant identity seek answers to such questions as, What business are we in? What are we as an organization? What should we become? The authors would add two more: Who are our customers? and where are our markets? Many corporations are afraid to enter into the world marketplace, cope with diverse customs and import/export regulations, or to go beyond their own borders. The "wise man" of Sony Corporation, Akio Morita points out how European firms have successfully penetrated the Japanese market, while many U.S. companies are fearful of this unfamiliar business environment. Sony's chairman cited this example:

> If you look at the electronics industry, there are no American companies which are international. RCA doesn't have any business outside the United States and Canada. And the same goes for Zenith and General Electric. The only non-Japanese company in consumer electronics which is international is Philips of The Netherlands. The failure of American firms in most fields to commit themselves to long-term investment is one of the reasons why the United States sells so few manufactured products to Japan.

Some may argue that the reason American electronic firms do not enter Japan is the restrictive laws there upon foreign investment and companies. Others may point to the firms in Taiwan. But Morita's statement should force American managers to rethink their own approach to the world marketplace. There may also be historical and cultural perceptual blinders that cause some nation's leaders to be too isolationist and hesitant for global trade.

In *Managing Cultural Differences,* Chapter 1 made two related points. First, a paradigm is a conceptual model that influences our basic way of perceiving, valuing, thinking, acting — a particular vision of reality. Second, we confirmed Willis Harman's observation that the industrial-era paradigm is no longer viable for modern ideology or a way to view the world. Too many corporate and government leaders are operating upon "old pictures" of the cosmos and human nature, including the nature of work, the worker, and the management process itself. Executives in transnational enterprises should join the common struggle for a world cultural rebirth, and assist in conjuring up the new visions that will energize or motivate the human family.

Psychiatrist Robert Jay Lifton put the matter succinctly:

> In times of severe historical dislocation, social institutions and symbols — whether having to do with worship, work, learning, punishment, or pleasure — lose their power and psychological legitimacy. We still live by them, but they no longer live in us. Or rather, we live a half-life with one another.[3]

Dr. Lifton reminds us that the essence of human growth occurs when old routines break down, and larger spheres of change are created as replacements. Communal resymbolization then takes places in all aspects of human existence. The leaders contribute to the formulation of more relevant life-enhancing imagery for the culture, and even the counter-culture forces effect the reconceptualizations by which humankind lives. Just as the individual goes through passages in the life process, and is challenged to renewal by transitional experiences, so too our collective selves. It is a continuing open search for meaning that causes the phenomenon of passing over and coming back to one's own culture with new insights and life-styles. Whereas in the past such transformation was caused by great innovators, today large numbers of people participate in the resymbolization task. It is the authors' thesis that transnational managers, because of their knowledge and experience, are in an unusual position to join in the process of renewal. Their role in global enterprises offers an opportunity for recreation of cultural assumptions, norms, and practices on a planetary scale.

Too many industrial age traditionalists are culture-bound in their perceptions of profitable enterprises. Thus, big manufacturers failed to anticipate the boom of "high tech" (micro electronics) "gen tech" (genetic engineering) and "space tech" (space technology and spinoffs).

Recently (1980), John Naisbitt, senior vice-president of the polling organization Yakelovich, Skelly, and White, addressed the Foresight Group of Sweden on the restructuring of society. He spoke of the shift to the information society, power decentralization, trend toward a global economy, high technology and break up of mass instrumentalities. He also reviewed the dinosaur effect — the attempt to grow by merger in order to survive before going under — used by some major professional associations and unions, and he analyzed the restructuring of the work environment from top down to bottom up. Naisbitt then urged the establishment of monitoring or tracking systems to monitor the rapid changes, and warned against conjuring holocaust, and gradual adaptation of international industry to cyclical movements of the environment. He urged an open mind and flexibility in action for survival in the '80s. What this eminent forecaster did not do is provide a frame of reference or paradigm for his listeners to better understand the transitions underway and to have hope. (The authors trust that Appendix A might provide their conceptualization in this regard, so we will limit this section to consideration of two additional analyses.)

Rifkin and Howard have noted that our current human paradigms took shape 400 years ago with Newton and are already obsolete.[4] They maintain that the entropy law from the field of thermodynamics will be the ruling paradigm over the next period of history in human development. The principle is expressed in two metaphysical laws, which Albert Einstein called supreme for the whole universe:

> First is that all matter and energy in the universe is constant, and cannot be created or destroyed. Only its form, never its essence can be changed . . . The second related entropy law is that matter and energy can be changed in only one direction — from usable to unusable, or available to unavailable, from ordered to disordered. Entropy then is a measure of the extent to which available energy in any subsystem is transformed into an unavailable form. Accordingly, whenever a semblance of order is created anywhere on the earth or in the universe, it is done at the expense of creating greater disorder in the surrounding environment.

Jeremy Rifkin claims such a notion destroys the concept of history as progress, or of science and technology creating a more ordered world. Our generation, he believes, will be very uncomfortable with such a paradigm, but our descendants will act easily upon it. It is a conservation law, every time energy is transformed, a penalty is exacted — a loss in the amount of available energy to perform some kind of work in the future. Work, in this view, occurs when energy moves from a higher level of concentration to a lower level, so that less energy is available to perform work the next time around. In our companion volume, the authors have suggested that the organization be viewed as an energy exchange system. If that paradigm were synthesized with the entropy one, then we all should work smarter, conserving human energy by our personnel practices and occupational tasks and not wasting it or abusing this psychic and physical energy. For waste, in any form, is dissipated energy.

Rifkin believes that many economists and political scientists will be unhappy with this paradigm for it undermines some of their present theories. Many anthropologists, he counters, may be more comfortable with it because they have long recognized that the energy basis of a given environment is the primary determinant for shaping culture, and divides the history of change in society in how people organize their environment. This exposition, then, would hold that technology does the world no favor if it speeds up energy flow, nor do affluent societies which burn up energy at such an exhorbitant rate compared to less developed ones. In this line of thought, the earth is a closed system in which humankind must make peace with nature and live cooperatively with the rest of the ecosystem.

Regardless of whether we agree with this conceptualization or not, it does force macrosystem managers and innovative technicians to rethink their impact on both internal and external environments. It challenges us to redefine "progress", for the paradigm looks upon technology as a transformer. Each major breakthrough in the modes of human tools or technology transforms a specific type of energy in our environment. Thus, the Industrial Revolution came about in order to transform coal energy from beneath the earth, but then reaches a level when it can no longer sustain the level of energy transformation on which society can then depend. Eventually the technology "bottoms out" when it reaches its entropic watershed. Even institutional development can be viewed as the way work in a society is allocated for the transformation of energy. Rifkin, like others, questions whether the multinational corporation is only a temporary phenomenon:

> Anyone who has looked at the escalating costs associated with giant multinational corporations and huge government bureaucracies cannot help but notice that more and more energy (or work) is expended operating them, while less and less work is gotten out of them. The institutional complex which was supposed to facilitate the flow of energy through the culture becomes a parasite, sucking up the remaining energy source. All along the energy line, the flow slows up, and the society begins to atrophy.[4]

Rifkin describes the latter stage as the "colonizing stage" which emphasizes energy flow-through. He offers hope in that intelligent humans will mobilize to move to the "climactic framework." This he envisions as a slowing down of increasing complexity and centralization by minimizing the energy flow-through. A climactic existence, then, favors small, decentralized institutions with a steady low-flow use of energy. An entropic world view is based on conservation of finite, and envisions the end of the age of nonrenewable resources, or Industrial Age. It would urge Third World peoples to avoid high-energy, centralized technologies as in Western industrialized cultures, and seek intermediate technologies. It sees the transition to a Solar Age with a complete reformulation of economic activity and a shifting of energy base. It advocates innovative solar use of energy to slow the use of the planet's fixed terrestrial resources. It implies also a revolution in values, for a low-entropic society deemphasizes material consumption and self-indulgence. In a low-entropy culture, private property is retained for goods and services, but not for land and other renewable/nonrenewable resources, replacing the latter with public guardianship. The move toward a low-entropy approach would not only impact upon the economy, but requires controlling the population explosions. (From the beginning of human existence to the Industrial Revolution that growth was only 1 billion people; from 1800 to the year 2000, another 7 billion is anticipated.)

In such formulations, reformation of all social institutions from education to law are implied. Whether the human race will accept all or part of this paradigm, it is in harmony with many of the concepts of ancient Greek philosophers, and Judeo-Christian teachings. It calls for accommodation to the natural order, and self-sacrifice, the highest form of love, before we transcend beyond our physical existences to another state of being or consciousness.

The final conceptual model comes from Mahbub ul Hag, director of policy planning for the World Bank, in the form of six economic goals for the next decade. These goals, presented at the First Global Conference on the Future (1980), are intended to turn the world from its present path toward destruction:

1. New institutions of world interdependence that permit a majority of mankind to influence international institutions.
2. A system of global management instituted between producing and consuming nations, for a just distribution of the world's resources.
3. An international commitment to put a definite floor under absolute poverty before the end of the century, so that the basic human needs of the deprived majority will be met.
4. Acceptance of responsibility by developing countries to restrain their own ungoverned population growth, so that resources will be used wisely and equality of opportunity can be achieved by their own peoples.
5. Creation of a world of relatively open borders for the better movement of goods, capital, and people.
6. Reallocation of massive defense spending to remedy economic inequalities in the world and political injustices, thus creating a new global security in contrast to nuclear insecurity.

Mr. Hag's image of the future is a noble statement that could promote more synergy internationally. Some might reject it as too idealistic, but considering it comes from a prominent international banker, it offers food for thought. *What if* macro-system managers were to adopt such a vision in their everyday operations, and devoted their energies to such goals?

The issue we raise here for would-be cosmopolitan synergizers is that the paradigms of our era are eroding. The industrial model favored individualism and unrestricted free enterprise, material progress with social responsibility the concern of government. It offered such goals as capital accumulation, efficiency, continued growth of production and consumption; and espoused division of labor and specialization, planned obsolescence and waste, exploitation of common resources. It results in economic elites and mass poverty, alienation of persons from community and nature and counteracts humane purposes. That analysis is the outcome of research by Dr. Willis Harman who called for new conceptual models that will transform our culture toward a transindustrial society. Dr. Harman predicted a painful transition for humankind in the near term, including economic and social disruptions.[5] But this distinguished futurist advocated a radical vision with adaptive incremental strategies based on the understanding of the interrelatedness of separate actions.

It was present in the U.S. Declaration of Independence with its emphasis on individual human rights and dignity, and the national goal for government to guard such rights, while ensuring the growth and development of the human person. Perhaps the time has come for world leaders to declare a new "Declaration of Interdependence." Dr. Warren Schmidt sketched a beginning for such a document in his award-winning film, "Is It Right to be Always Right":

> All persons are created equal, but each should be
>   permitted to develop in a unique way;
> All persons are endowed with certain inalienable rights
>   but each must assume inevitable responsibilities for
> the happiness of all depends upon the commitment of
>   each to support both quality and difference . . .

When such a declaration is completed and acted upon, then adversaries may discover their common beliefs and realize also that "you may be right and I may be wrong." Awareness of our interdependence and need for one another may become the principle by which we can shape our future together.

In this search for new paradigms, Harman suggests these high-priority tasks:

1. Encourage business institutions to move toward synergism with societal needs through changed corporate goals.
2. Promote measures to foster a strong, broadly responsible volunteer, nonprofit sector.

3. Foster private/public/voluntary sectors joint action to develop new work roles; promote social innovation; encourage *frugal* technology and society; inaugurate future-oriented, global planning.
4. Devise incentive structures and organizations to make multi-national corporations more effective agents of Third World development.

Harman also suggests that the conceptual revolution underway will emerge with a social model that incorporates:

1. Complementarity of physical and spiritual experience.
2. Teleological sense of life and evolution with ultimate reality perceived as unitary with transcendent order.
3. Value postulates that include levels of consciousness or awareness, and probe the potential of both supraconsciousness and subconsciousness.
4. Goal orientations that create social institutions for the purpose of developing human potential.
5. Seeks complementary views of the world from science, supernatural teachings, world philosophies, and other sources to create a new synergy of meaning.

SYNERGY THROUGH CHANGES IN ORGANIZATIONAL CULTURES

When such conceptual models begin to be translated to the environment of social institutions, then the microcultures of human systems will be altered. Perhaps then workers or members will find new meaning in their work and organizational affiliations. We have applied the insights of cultural anthropology to organizations in Chapter 8 of *Managing Cultural Differences,* and Chapter 6 of *Managing Cultural Synergy.* There, we have made their case for change and synergy in organizational culture. Max Ways, who directs the Future of Business Program at Georgetown University, summarized some of the changes that have occurred and will continue in the last half of this century:

> The distribution of formerly concentrated power put strain upon the organization. Coordination within and among organizations could be maintained only by an expanded and improved "nervous system" devoted to communication. The general trend throughout business was for the replacing of commands from the apex by explanation and persuasion at all levels. An amazing humanization and democratization in the workplace is taking place.[6]

Such humanization and democratization of organizational culture seemed to get its start in Europe. Gary L. Cooper, an American who holds a chair in management at the University of Leeds, reported such developments in six countries of that continent. He described a variety of change efforts including introduction of autonomous work groups, greater worker participation, and improvements in the quality of working life. In the long term he contended such innovations will improve industrial relations, solve some of the problems caused by technological change, and meet the deeper needs of workers.[7]

The culture of a work system must be adapted to the macro-culture in which it operates. Yet organizational leaders everywhere can learn from each other, regardless of where in the world the entity functions. As Edwin Reingold reported after touring Japanese auto factories:

> Calisthenics before plunging spiritedly into their day's work. Japanese workers are imbued with a sense of mission — doing a good job is important to them, to their union, to their families, and to their nation. Worker alienation is almost unheard of, and sabotage is unknown . . . Instead, workers and management share the same objectives. Each plant has its quality control circles to analyze standards of work and ways to improve the product. The rewards for usable ideas are mostly psychological . . . The goal of labor-management relations was enunciated as . . . "harmony over opposition." . . . Japanese companies guarantee lifetime jobs, listen to workers' suggestions or complaints, and share their good times and bad.[8]

Is it any wonder that Peter Drucker suggested that it is no longer a case of "what can we learn from American management, but what can American managers learn from foreign management?" Here are a few of the trends abroad he suggested worth emulating:

- Management demanding responsibility from workers down to the lowest level of the organization.
- Customized employee fringe benefits based on individual need, which may include housing allowances, insurance options, etc.
- A sense of marketing that means knowing what is of value to the customer, thinking in terms of market structures and specific markets, and aiming at global markets.
- Marketing and management strategies based on innovation, replacing the old, outworked, or obsolete — many foreign business planning starts with the question, "What are the new things we are going to do?"
- Separation of short from long-term expected results, permitting a second budget in corporations for expenditures over a long period of time.
- Managers who perceive themselves as national assets and leaders responsible for development of proper policies in the national interests.[9]

Drucker points out that many such overseas management trends may have originated in the United States, but were not put into practice here. Perhaps this explains why in the week that the U.S.'s three largest automakers announced the largest losses in their history, the chairman of the board for Sony said that the problem in America is not so much the workers who are "fantastic," but the managers.[12]

Akio Morita, the wise man of Japanese management, has established and managed plants in the United States, so his comments on our work culture are not to be taken lightly when he observes:

> American management hires other people at their own risk, and when they (American executives) create a problem, they fire these people. But the fault is not with the worker. The fault is with management!
> . . . Another problem is too much emphasis on immediate results. The annual bonus of some American executives depends on annual profit, but the executive who knows his firm's production facilities should be modernized is not likely to make a decision to invest in new equipment if his own income and managerial ability are judged only on annual profit . . . .
>
> Good labor-management relations are the ultimate strength of our industrial system. Americans often write off smooth labor-management relations here as a product of a culture and a homogeneous society (Japan). . . . Japanese firms worked to attain harmony in labor-management relations since major strikes paralyzed their auto industry in 1953. Japanese executives are aware that American post-war occupation policies turned their country into one of the most egalitarian societies in the world.[10]

In this critique of American management's need for change, Morita noted that U.S. executives are paid too much and have a life-style too far apart from the ordinary worker. Japanese measure management success, not on the size of your salary, but how well you made the work pleasant and promoted the joy of participation and teamwork.

At the same time Morita's comments were being reported, American executives at Coca-Cola in Atlanta, Georgia were spouting with pride, "Coca-Cola is a power for good in the world. Not only because of the economies it helps in towns and countries, but because of the understanding we foster abroad, too."[11] While these management myths were being swallowed, the business world knew that it had been a confusing year for that soft-drink giant, when six high-powered executives vied competitively for a job that only one would win; and after the individual was chosen, the other five and their factions were supposed to close ranks and work for the common good. *Business Week* in a somewhat superficial and naive article provided the reader with some useful insights on American corporate culture:

> Culture implies values, such as aggressiveness, defensiveness, or nimbleness, that set a pattern for company activities, opinions, and actions. That pattern is instilled in employees by managers' example and passed down to succeeding generations of workers . . . But a culture that prevents a company from meeting competitive threats, or from adapting to changing economic or social environments, can lead to the company's stagnation and ultimate demise unless it makes a conscious effort to change.
>
> Just as tribal cultures have totems and taboos that dictate how each member will act toward fellow members and outsiders, so does a corporation's culture

influence employee actions toward customers, competitors, suppliers, and one another. Some times the rules are written out. More often they are tacit. Most often they are laid down by a strong founder and hardened by success into custom. Culture gives people a sense of how to behave and what they ought to be doing.[12]

The article then cited examples of these concepts within U.S. corporate cultures, such as:

- IBM, whose service philosophy drives the whole company.
- Digital Equipment Corporation, where emphasis on innovation creates freedom with responsibility.
- Delta Air Lines, where a focus on customer service produces a high degree of teamwork.
- Atlantic Richfield Company, where entrepreneurship encourages action and operating managers have great autonomy.
- Pepsi-Cola, whose employees are conditioned that success exists in beating the competition.
- J. C. Penney Company, which seeks long-term loyalty, fairness to customers, security for its employees.
- American Telephone and Telegraph, which is altering its service-oriented culture to give equal weight to marketing, including flexibility in responding to customer needs.
- 3M Company, where the unwritten rule is "never be responsible for killing a good idea."[12]

Organization culture is subtle, but identifiable. It can be changed, but it happens slowly and the leadership must come from top management. Rather than propping up industrial cripples, chief executives should seek to renew their corporate environments, which may lead to abandoning archaic lines of business and adopting new ones.

The directions of the new organization culture have been plotted. For instance, Raymond A. Katzell's *Work in America: The Decade Ahead* points out these trends:

1. Traditional economic significance of work will give way to rising concern for its psychological qualities and social meaningfulness.
2. A shift away from hierarchical control to participation and involvement of workers in decisions.
3. More knowledge work and less proportionately that is routine and unchallenging.
4. Nonwork (family, community, voluntary service, and retirement) will rival work for income in importance.
5. The workforce will exhibit wider attitude diversity on the subject of work itself.

The emerging corporate cultures of space, genetic, medical and other high technologies are quite different from the industrial environments of the past. They are the pacesetters for tomorrow's organizational climates.

Obviously, the microculture of the organization is influenced by the macroculture of a particular society, and vice versa. Changes in national culture impinge upon corporate cultures, as collective changes in organizational cultures can affect a country's culture. When the changes in both are synergistic, then the whole people move forward to a new state of being. But this will require a reeducation of management and workers, a national attitude change. Economics professor Robert LeKachman of City University of New York highlighted this lack of synergy in the American work culture:

> Cultures resist sudden change. Ours notoriously is a society animated more often by the ideal of competition than of cooperation. Confrontation is more popular than tedious progress toward consensus.
>
> Unions prefer to bargain at arm's length with employers rather than collaborate with them. Union leaders who become too chummy with the bosses are immediately suspected by the rank and file of plotting to sell them out.
>
> The adversary model is equally popular in managerial circles. It is the rare chief executive officer who perceives much benefit in cooperating with either unions or public officials.

There is much that can and should be done in management and labor leadership development to help personnel appreciate the value of striving for synergy with others.

Global management is in itself a subculture in worldwide human activity. Synergy can occur when managers in various countries begin to learn from one another, and influence each other's managerial styles and organizational models. Unit three in this book is devoted to input about comparative management — not just the differences, but the innovations worth adapting.

SYNERGY THROUGH WORLD TRADE AND DEVELOPMENT

Down through the ages there have always been people characterized as having a "trading culture." Perhaps if we developed an international trading culture, the world economy and the human condition would be the better for it, and there would be less poverty and war. Cooperative international development would rule out rich nations exploiting poor ones, or technologically advanced peoples draining the resources of less developed members of the human family to support their own wastefulness. Furthermore, it has always been understood that business flourishes when there is political and economic stability. As we move into the twenty-first century, prosperity can only be achieved by a trilateral synergy between business in the form of the transnational corporation, and the home/host governments. Orville

Freeman, president of Business International Corporation, addressed that theme in another way relative to "Global Opportunities for Business." He proposed a new synergy between the industrialized countries mostly in the Northern hemisphere with their management and technological skills, the OPEC nations with their financial power from oil, and the Third World peoples (mostly in the Southern hemisphere) with their natural and human resources, as well as consumer needs. To bridge this "North/South" gap, Freeman called for a global "Marshall" type plan on a planetary scale for which the multinational corporations would provide the initiative and infrastructure. Tens of thousand of people in Third World countries are already being developed in business, technology, and management under MNC auspices. The very cost of sending American managers abroad, for instance, has stimulated the training of Third World indigenous managers.

There is a growing awareness and action relative to the expansion of corporate social responsibility. Lloyd B. Dennis, chairman of the social policy committee at United California Bank put it this way:

> There is something happening in the relationship between business and society. I believe that the most influential segment of the business community — certainly a large number of the Fortune 500 companies, the multinational corporations — has accepted the notion that business should, nay, must be more socially responsible. They are recognizing that it is important to combine maximizing profits with upgrading the quality of life. A key reason for this is that many corporate heads are finding . . . their peers who are attempting to solve social problems that in one way or another threaten profits are ahead — in many ways other than profits — than if those problems are ignored.

If synergies such as have been previously suggested could be fostered, then we might begin to grapple more effectively with the earth's poverty/population problems. Addressing the 141-nation International Monetary Fund at the turn of the decade, Robert S. McNamara reminded his audience that one-quarter of the world's population lives in countries where the per capita income does not exceed $200 a year. Stepping down as chairman of the World Bank, he spoke of a sustained attack on poverty as a continuing social responsibility and an economic imperative. During his term of office, McNamara focused on world cooperation to improve the human condition. In the distribution of $12 billion in international loans, he proved that cooperation can be effective.

A recent issue of *Scientific American* was devoted to world economic development. It came at a time when the United Nations launched a special session to launch global negotiations regarding an agenda for better management of the world's economy. At issue is the asymmetry that now prevails between the relations of the 30 industrially developed nations, and the 130 nonindustrial developing nations. In the opening article, K.K.S. Dadzie confronted the significance of this disproportion:

The momentous questions underlying this agenda touch the interests of everyone, but particularly the poor who constitute more than half of mankind. To increasing numbers of the poor around the world, economic development means not only betterment of their material condition, but also greater human dignity, security, justice and equality. It is a transformation of their lives, a liberation from drudgery. Development therefore implies profound change in the economic arrangements within, as well as among, societies.[13]

The antisynergistic connection between poverty and population is illustrated in Figure 15-1.

Other articles in this momentous *Scientific American* edition made these points, pregnant with meaning:

- The goal of economic development is to improve the well-being of the human family. Health is not just the by-product of development, but a primary lever for initiating the process.
- The task of feeding everyone on the planet adequately calls for an agricultural investment of more than $100 billion. Without a fairer distribution of income, many will still go hungry and the number of needless deaths will escalate.
- An adequate supply of water for agriculture, industry, and people depends on human intervention in the water cycle and development of water resources on and under the ground surface.
- The future growth in the global demand for energy will come mainly from the less developed countries. If the demand is to be satisfied, then technology transfer from developed countries is not only essential, it must also be appropriate.
- The first input-output model of the world economy suggests how a system of international economic relations that features partial disarmament could narrow the gap between rich and poor nations, so that technological innovation for development purposes would be emphasized over its use in weaponry.

To achieve such noble objectives requires the type of cosmopolitan synergistic leadership that has been proposed throughout this volume.

The transactions between developed and less developed industrialized countries (LIC) should be advantageous to both parties. In his many writings on the subject, Dr. Krishna Kumar describes a position that generates a system of intellectual, economic, and political dependence in the LIC recipient as "localite." An approach of dignity and respect that seeks to help the Third World help itself would be designated "cosmopolite." The latter sees any dependence as temporary, and does not perpetuate it. Industrialized countries, institutions, and their representatives who are cosmopolites would avoid exploiting the LIC's material and human resources in order to increase their own GNP. Rather they should undertake collaborative, joint ventures for mutual advancement. Transnational enterprises become the means for

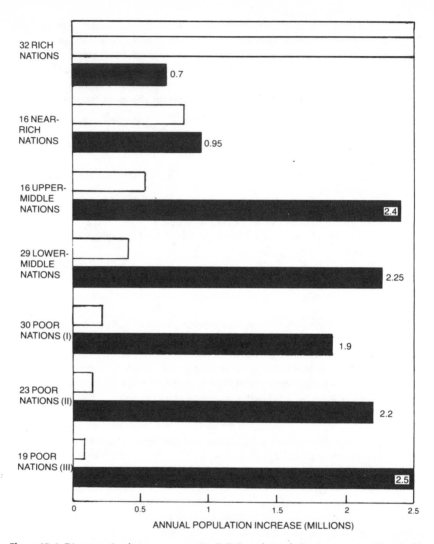

Figure 15-1. Disproportion between per capita G.D.P. and population increase is evident in this comparison of the data for world economic categories. For the rich and near rich (per capita G.D.P. of $3,500-$15,000) the percent of annual population increase is less than 1. For the other five categories (with G.D.P. between $275-$3,500) minimum percent of increase is 1.9, with an average of 2.25. Reprinted with permission *Scientific American,* Sept. 1980, K.K.S. Dadzie.

contributing to effecting synergy between East and West, North and South. Synergy results from an egalitarian and participatory policy toward world trade and development. It is a sharing of planetary resources through the medium of MNC's and governments with the facilitation of World Bank, International Labor Office, UNICEF, World Health Organization, and like international entities. Synergistic attitudes encourage a self-help process in which people in need of assistance are no longer passive recipients of foreign handouts, but collective participants.

There are numerous organizations and publications fostering such synergistic trends already, and some are listed in Appendix C.

Perhaps one of the most dramatic examples of improvement in international relations and bridge building between the First and Third World is going on relative to the People's Republic of China and the United States of America. Almost daily one reads of this new East-West synergy:

> The largest trade show the United States has ever mounted opened in Peking . . . Two hundred fifty-one American companies exhibited their wares to increase Chinese awareness of their technology and industrial products. At the same time, the occasion permitted the Americans to do market research on China's needs in modern industrialization. More than 200,000 Chinese officials, economic planners, engineers and industrial managers attended the 11-day session. Sixty percent of the U.S. representatives came from industrial giants who were projecting a trade relationship for the next decade. Preparations were made by the cooperation of the China Council for the Promotion of International Trade. Never have so many Chinese leaders come into contact with American business delegates.

> New Sino-American venture gets underway in Beijing. Ground was broken for a 528-room luxury hotel that was designed by a Chinese-American architect from San Francisco and is to be built by PRC labor. It is one of a handful of projects approved under China's year-old joint venture law. The pattern calls for the Chinese to have the controlling interest and to appoint the chief director. The latter's deputy will be Clement Chen, the San Francisco architect who will own 49% of the hotel. Under contract approved by China's Foreign Investment Commission, the American side will operate and manage the hotel for the first five years and gradually turn over responsibility to the Chinese staff. A rationale has been devised to split profits until 1991 when the PRC takes over full ownership.

From all over the world China is now inviting human resource, management, manufacturing, and technical experts to visit their country, study its needs, and share their insights. Through China Enterprise Management Association, the Association of Teachers of Management was asked to send a party of 15 representatives from Italy, U.K., and the U.S. The academics discovered enormous resourcefulness in using obsolete technology and machinery, and a management renaissance underway. The PRC looks not only for Western materials, but its knowledge, especially relative to management skills. What an opportunity for a cosmopolitan manager to promote synergy.

There are numerous demonstration models around the world where trade and development projects can break down barriers and misunderstandings among peoples who are different and lead to peaceful collaboration. For example:

- Powerful Japanese business interests are moving to open the trade doors with North Korea. An East Asian Trade Research Board has been formed to assist the Communist nation in its efforts to seek more assistance and trade with the outside world.
- Israel moved closer to a bold engineering plan that would link the Mediterranean and the Dead Sea by a canal. The hydro-electric power project would require the cooperation of Egypt and Jordan to succeed ultimately. It is projected as being operational in 10 years, and could deliver over $1 billion worth of megawatts of power in the following 50 years.
- The new International Law of the Sea Treaty was decided upon by consensus of 156 participating countries and 24 nongovernmental organizations. This most significant achievement in international relations since the U.N. charter provides a sea constitution affecting boundaries, ocean transit, seabed mining, fishing, marine environment, and jurisdictional agencies. Synergy became possible despite a kaleidoscope of seemingly conflicting interests.
- Macroengineering projects are being planned that would put a tunnel under the English channel, a bridge across the Strait of Gibraltar, a highway connecting Poland to Greece, a North-South motorway for Eastern Europe, etc. By the turn of the century these and other macroengineering feats may bring together peoples who are culturally different in an ever closer fashion. The European Community Transport Committee is an example of one of many agencies working on such transnational planning.
- The Dutch aerospace company, Forker B.U. has asked Japanese firms to join a project they have underway with the American aircraft manufacturer, McDonnel-Douglas Corporation. The joint venture is to study the building of a new-generation, 150-seat, medium-range jet plane.
- Major urban centers throughout the world are becoming increasingly cosmopolitan and multicultural because of the impact of international business. For example, there are 3,000 foreign companies in New York City, 42% of which were established since 1975. They directly employ 140,000 people in that metropolitan area, and indirectly another 25,000 work for them.

Unless international development and trade on a cooperative basis is increased on a massive scale, such as in these examples, the human family can expect a very troubled twenty-first century of transition. Many studies into the future, such as *The Global 2000 Report to the President* (U.S. President's Council on Environmental Quality), provide us with dire warnings for managing in an uncertain world. The horrendous problems to be faced in population control, food production, environmental regulation, energy resources, and other such global concerns make it evident that they are so complex and interdependent that only synergistic international solutions will provide lasting results. The message to our readers is that we have no choice but to cooperate with those whose views differ from our own, and to develop collaborative coping strategies.

SYNERGY THROUGH MULTINATIONAL COOPERATIVES

Cooperatives are voluntary associations created for mutual economic assistance. They are usually owned by their members or patrons, annually redistribute the earnings; and are run by directors who usually come from among the members. A nineteenth century movement formulated in Britain and France, they are most suited to the superindustrial age where there is much emphasis on participatory democracy and involvement. Their ideology is articulated by the International Cooperative Alliances as follows:

1. Voluntary membership without artificial restrictions or social, political, or religious discriminations, and based upon need for its services and acceptance of membership responsibilities.
2. Cooperative societies are to be administered democratically by persons elected or appointed in an agreed manner by the members, all of whom have equal voting rights and participation.
3. Share capital should only receive a strictly limited rate of interest, if any, while saving surpluses are to be equitably distributed to avoid one member gaining at the expense of others.
4. Cooperative societies should make provision for the education of members, officers, employees, and the public in the principles and techniques of cooperation.
5. All cooperative organizations should actively collaborate in every practical way with every other such coop organization at the local, national, and international levels.

The cooperative movement has grown steadily in the twentieth century, so that small entrepreneurs and consumer groups have banded for effective action in such diverse fields as agriculture and fishing, construction and energy distribution, merchandising and financing. The credit union is an example of a type of banking cooperative that has swept across the world. The synergistic approach has been applied to the needs for rural electric power to urban development. Many of society's problems — inadequate housing, high cost of food, health and child care services — can be realistically solved by formal establishment of a cooperative. Apparently, Canadians think so, for nine million of them belong to some form of cooperative. They even have formed a Co-operative Future Directions Project (Scott Library, York University, 4700 Keele Street, Downsview, Ont. M3J 2R2, Canada). Based on the theory that cooperatives form a unique sector of the economy, distinct from the public/private divisions, the effort concentrates on managing in turbulent times; the need for new cooperative vision, the elaboration of the co-op system; and information and research. To accomplish this, the cooperators use such methods as scanning, analysis, vision discussion groups, and coordinated research studies. Networking, working papers and annual reports, and visual aids become their means for disseminating their findings and forecasts.

Just as corporations had to move beyond national borders and cultures to solve complex, interdependent problems and meet the challenge of the world market, so too cooperatives have had to go multinational. The leading researcher on this is Dr. Jack Craig, a sociologist in Canada's York University. He defines a multinational cooperative as a combination or federation of cooperatives which have joined together to provide international goods and services. Contrary to the profit oriented corporation, cooperative earnings are returned to members, or put in reserve to generate other benefits for members, or to help other groups in society set up autonomous cooperative ventures.

Dr. Craig's thesis is that cooperatives provide a technique for organizing economic activity on a global basis, and can provide developing countries with a means for multinational exchange of technology, information, and resources. In *Multinational Cooperatives: An Alternative for World Development* Craig examines such transnational cooperatives operating in the areas of insurance, credit, manufacturing, and consumer services.[14] The following extracts from that significant volume are offered to our readers to indicate how the cooperative movement can be a powerful tool for synergy, and to encourage further study of this technique. If cooperatives were to benefit from modern developments in the management and information sciences, they could become a international force in synergistic improvements such as these:

- The *International Cooperative Insurance Federation* consists of 71 insurance cooperatives in 26 countries. Founded in Europe, its Insurance Development Bureau assists Third World Countries in establishing insurance co-ops through Allnations Inc., Columbus, Ohio, which makes loan guarantees. Premium income of member ICIF organizations is well over $2 billion, and now includes affiliates in North and South America. At triennial congresses of the International Cooperative Alliance, members share experiences and present papers on their financial activities. ICIF acts as a MNC with few employees because its personnel are seconded from national organizations. Multilanguage operations, senior executives with cosmopolitan views, and effective relationships with other types of cooperatives characterize ICIF.
- *C. F. Industries, Inc.* is a large cooperative organization engaged in the manufacture of basic fertilizer products for members in North America. At present, its products are marketed in 42 of the United States, and two provinces of Canada. On the international scale, it has two joint ventures in Canada, and developing facilities in India. Through vertical integration of farmers in local cooperatives this multinational enterprise manufactures three fertilizer components of which two are owned by 15 regional cooperatives in 6,000 local co-ops consisting of 15 million farmers. Although wide volumes of sales in the member organizations, each gets only one vote. Its Indian Farmers Cooperative Ltd. is Indian owned and managed with CFI consultants and U.S. Aid funding.
- *NAF Euro-Coop* and *Inter-Coop* are the major European consumer cooperatives, which employ more than 500,000 people and have a sales volume over

$17 billion. Within countries on this continent are central co-ops which have responsibility for wholesale purchase and distribution of consumer goods, such as food. It is these wholesale societies that take on the multinational character: Nordisk Andelsforbund (NAF) originated in Scandinavian countries and has branches in Brazil, Spain, Argentina, Italy, and the U.S.A. The collaboration extends in the import/export business from purchasing to trade, as well as to other major cooperative organizations. It is owned and controlled by nationals from five countries. The technological knowledge and information regarding the purchasing and handling of food flows freely among the six member organizations. Euro-Coop was set up with the development and framework of the European Economic Community. With head offices in Brussels, it provides the wholesale organization for the European Economic Commission, and coordinates for member co-ops, consumer groups, and trade organizations. It has an information secretariat, standard brands, and takes policy positions within EEC for consumers. Inter-Coop has head offices in Germany and represents an international consortia of cooperatives from both sides of Europe's Iron Curtain, as well as Iceland and Japan. The aim is to increase the competitive power of its 22 central consumer cooperatives. Its major activities are promotion of joint purchases and production collaboration; exchanges of information and experiences in the field of retail trade; exchange of research and product development data. Their share of the retail market demonstrates the potential for collaboration at the multinational level, despite their being loose federations.

Jack Craig cites many other samples of multinational co-ops in the marketing of petroleum products to the development of credit societies and banking. They all demonstrate the synergistic prospects of cooperatives when they become transnational enterprises. A summary of Craig's conceptions about the differences in such enterprises appears on page 328.

Since the structural form of international business does have social impact upon the host country, it would seem that the advantages of the multinational cooperatives are broadened membership and decision-making, as well as the opportunity for greater participation and ownership. Craig concludes that multinational co-ops maximize the advantages and minimize the disadvantages of transnational enterprises. He believes that considerable power can be assembled and delegated through such international cooperatives, while involving the consent of a large segment of the local population. From the viewpoint of the authors the possibilities for synergy through such organizations seem enormous.

SYNERGY THROUGH RELOCATION SERVICES

Organizations may relocate plants or people, or both. When either facilities or personnel are moved from their origins, it involves a transitional experience and

---

Profile of Transnational Enterprises

Organizational Design

From *ethnocentric* with complex organization in home country; centralized decision-making in headquarters; evaluation and control of performance based on home standards; communication flow outward to subsidiaries in host countries which have simpler organizations; ownership and recruitment of key management largely of home nationality.

To *polycentric* with varied and independent organization: less headquarter authority and decision-making; evaluation and control determined locally; wide variations in performance management and standards depending on local cultures; limited communication to/from headquarters and among subsidiaries; ownership, key management and recruitment from host country.

To preferred *geocentric* with increasingly complex, interdependent organization: seeking collaborative approach between and among headquarters/subsidiaries; uses standards for evaluation and control that are both universal and local; international and local executives rewarded for reaching both local and worldwide objectives; ownership, key management and recruitment is cosmopolitan — develop the best person anywhere is the criterion.

Typology or Form of International Business Activity

From *profit-oriented* and investor-owned corporations with direct investments in foreign subsidiaries and joint ventures or consortia, to *mixed orientations* (government-owned to *service-owned* co-operatives.   ∎

---

may cause trauma. Whether the organization moves its operations or its employees from home base domestically or internationally, it may affect employee morale, productivity, customer/national/international relations, profitability or service, financial status and organizational culture. Therefore, it makes sense for the organization to invest in a deployment system that will reduce the premature return rate of transferred personnel and their families, and foster acculturation in the new environment. In *Managing Cultural Differences,* cross-cultural training (Chapters 9 and 11), and a foreign deployment program (Chapter 12) were addressed. The whole thrust of this book has been to suggest ways for promoting synergy in changing cultures and assignments.

Gary M. Wederspahn provides this apt quote from one who has just benefited from intercultural preparation sponsored by his employer:

> This cross-cultural orientation workshop has been very valuable for me and my family, but the one who really needs it is my boss! He has no idea of the cultural obstacles we're facing on this project and little understanding of the adjustment problems my family is up against.[15]

As training director for the Center for Research and Education, Wederspahn has expanded upon the authors' message concerning the need for organizations to develop a system for foreign deployment as part of their overall human resource program. His paradigm, shown in Figure 15-2, offers an overview of the steps to be

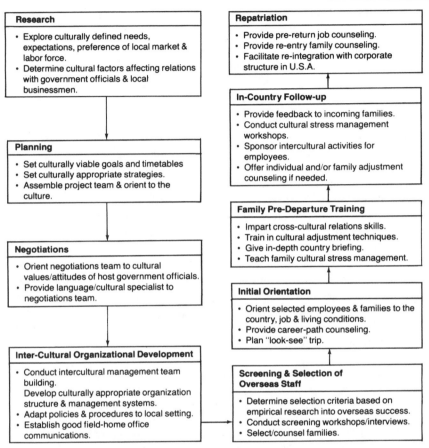

Research
- Explore culturally defined needs, expectations, preference of local market & labor force.
- Determine cultural factors affecting relations with government officials & local businessmen.

Planning
- Set culturally viable goals and timetables
- Set culturally appropriate strategies.
- Assemble project team & orient to the culture.

Negotiations
- Orient negotiations team to cultural values/attitudes of host government officials.
- Provide language/cultural specialist to negotiations team.

Inter-Cultural Organizational Development
- Conduct intercultural management team building.
  Develop culturally appropriate organization structure & management systems.
- Adapt policies & procedures to local setting.
- Establish good field-home office communications.

Repatriation
- Provide pre-return job counseling.
- Provide re-entry family counseling.
- Facilitate re-integration with corporate structure in U.S.A.

In-Country Follow-up
- Provide feedback to incoming families.
- Conduct cultural stress management workshops.
- Sponsor intercultural activities for employees.
- Offer individual and/or family adjustment counseling if needed.

Family Pre-Departure Training
- Impart cross-cultural relations skills.
- Train in cultural adjustment techniques.
- Give in-depth country briefing.
- Teach family cultural stress management.

Initial Orientation
- Orient selected employees & families to the country, job & living conditions.
- Provide career-path counseling.
- Plan "look-see" trip.

Screening & Selection of Overseas Staff
- Determine selection criteria based on empirical research into overseas success.
- Conduct screening workshops/interviews.
- Select/counsel families.

Figure 15-2. Shown here are the major steps in a foreign or major domestic deployment program.

covered in this system by personnel officers, and is equally applicable to major domestic deployment from one geographic area to another.

If necessity requires the reestablishment of either an institution or an individual to a new site, then an enlightened employer does everything feasible to build a bridge between past and future communities. We are all aware of "industrial-age" executives, dictated by only bottom-line considerations, who close a plant with little notice to civic leaders and their own employees, thus causing chaos in the lives of all concerned. Assuming that the decision to relocate the facility is a valid one and that all practical means to keep it in place have been exhausted, a cosmopolitan management group can inaugurate procedures that will promote synergy and cooperation in the major move. These include:

1. Adequate notification to community leaders of the intended close-down, and offers of assistance to deflect the economic impact of the decision to move.

2. Providing employment for those who are willing to transfer to the new site, and relocation services relative to that transition.
3. Working with the new community leaders to facilitate the introduction of the plant and its people into that area.

Such an approach is a demonstration of corporate citizenship and responsibility. We know, for instance, that too many firms suddenly move plants from urban areas to the suburbs, ignoring their impact on the city and its dwellers by such precipitous moves. Now in the 1980s, it is likely many corporations will be returning to the inner cities to build factories because of tax incentives and labor availability. There is not only a challenge to management involved in such reverse relocation regarding the people they bring into the urban environment, but also relative to the locals they will hire. Some civic leaders have begun to establish programs not only to attract industry into deteriorated, blighted areas of their cities, but to facilitate the efforts of industrialists with the change that has enormous implications for urban development. In San Antonio, Texas, the Mexican-American business leaders have organized an Economic Development Foundation to bring in new industry, to undertake research on their community assets, and to communicate that message in such a way as to get both industrial and local support (their initial efforts with EDF brought only protest from the poor). Among the several companies to relocate to San Antonio was Control Data Corporation, which saw the move to inner city as an opportunity, not a charity, and acted accordingly:

> We involved the community people and got their help in doing things like re-designing application blanks because a four-page application intimidates people there. We altered personnel procedures, for many of the unemployed people there could provide no references and had arrest records. The big lesson for Control Data when you put a plant into inner city is to take a position it will be as profitable as any other . . . That's in order to attract good managers and to end up with better employees.

The bottom-line now for San Antonio is that it gets a golden chance to train a cadre of future representatives for expansion into the Latin American market. The future for them is not a problem, but an opportunity. That is synergistic leadership in action.

Another chance for relocation synergy is in the "twin plant" trend. A developed plant in a more affluent area sets up a partner plant in a less developed area, largely for economic advantage. The two facilities may be within one's country of origin, but more often the plant is overseas. Thus, a U.S. plant might be paired with one in Mexico, Korea, or Taiwan. A synergistic leader does not exploit the people in that Third World plant, but takes steps to develop that human resource. Further, such a manager provides cross-cultural training and relocation services for the personnel from the home plant going abroad to interface with their overseas counterparts.

Many consulting firms provide a variety of relocation services to major corporations involved with large numbers of employee transfers. A special section in Appendix C lists some of the more outstanding professionals and publications in this emerging field. The most effective deployment program would include both elements of relocation services and intercultural training.

Dr. R. J. Raymond and Dr. S. V. Eliot are clinical psychologists who operate as Transitions, Inc., offering relocation counseling and consulting to employers, employees and their families, and real estate brokers. Drs. Raymond and Eliot believe that relocations are complex, and transferees seek to protect their emotional and financial well-being when asked to move. They maintain that too many employers are arbitrary and demanding regarding transfer arrangements, instead of recognizing their responsibility to help employees and their families to confront tough personal issues sometimes involved in such relocations. Dr. Eliot cites four factors causing employees to resist corporate requests to uproot themselves and their families:

1. Changing values — away from the work ethic and company loyalty and toward quality of life and family considerations.
2. State of the economy and high interest rates — the cost of housing and living expenses in the new community, and the lack of tax allowances for overseas living.
3. Changing roles of women who are no longer content to concur automatically to a job switch.
4. Dual careers — many families are financially independent because of a second salary, and the spouse resists relocation out of his or her own career considerations.[16]

The last two mentioned issues are so significant that a husband/wife professional team wrote a book, *Making it Together as a Two-Career Couple,* and do psychological research and workshops on that topic. Dr. Morton Shaevitz and his spouse, Marjorie, a mental health consultant, have a practice dealing with this matter (Institute for Family and Work Relationships, 1020 Prospect St., LaJolla, California 92037, USA). Their studies on the two-career phenomenon indicate that the female bears the major strain in such relationships and that overload is the most critical relationship factor — when both or either feel unable to cope with personal or professional problems. When relocation adds to pressures, the effect can be traumatic.

The way in which a company presents the move is key to how the employee views the move, as well as the corporate support provided with the transition, according to Dr. Raymond. As indicated in the chapter on culture shock in *Managing Cultural Differences,* the transitional experience can be perceived in a positive manner as a challenge to personal and professional growth. That should be the focus of relocation services within a personnel deployment program.

Gary L. Cooper, an American professor in Britain, confirms some of the previously mentioned concerns. Although in the past middle managers accepted family uprooting around their country or the world as essential for promotion, today's young executives dissent often on such relocation, according to Cooper, because of changing attitudes and lifestyles. In *Executive Gypsies* Cooper says the stress does not come from the actual physical move or financial considerations, but because in the U.K. the companies give the manager very little notice or assistance with the process.[17]

The problem is complicated because the wives of male managers are now better educated and have their own career involvements. Relocation counseling may have to include aiding that wife to find comparable employment in the new locale. And in overseas assignment within traditional cultures that prevent women from professional activity, the consultation must help that wife find other growth opportunities than work-for-income. Cooper believes companies should first question the assumption that it is good to move people around; then when it is necessary, ask how it can be done effectively for employee and employer with all the organizational support necessary. Professor Cooper asserts that it is more cost effective to provide foreign deployment and relocation services than to ignore the problems that result from no such preparation.

Stephen Gross, president of Merrill Lynch Relocation Management, provides some interesting insights from their studies of 603 U.S. firms. In 1979, 30% of the companies surveyed had an average of 157 employees transferred per year and offered help in finding a new job to the working spouse. This included counseling, resumé preparation, and employment agency referral. The scope of such services includes assistance with home sale, new location counseling, transportation services, property management, international operational assistance, and a turnkey program for group moves.

John Hoffman, president of Family Relocation Services, has developed a network of international resources to assist organizations in this regard. He is concerned about facilitating acculturation either of Americans abroad on assignment, or foreign nationals coming into the United States. Hoffman's experience leads him to seek employees for overseas service who are professionally competent; positive in attitude and can communicate effectively; motivated and adaptable; and supportive of corporate objectives. Hoffman said that his international experience convinced him firsthand that poorly-adjusted personnel contribute to corporate mismanagement:

> If the executive's spouse is lonely, or the children are misplaced in school — in other words, the family is left to sink or swim — then it is bound to reflect in the manager's performance.[18]

FRS, Inc. services include:

1. Screening of proposed transferees and families to determine suitability and adaptability, which are major corporate concerns.
2. Consultation on equitable and reasonable foreign deployment personnel policies.
3. Family assistance services abroad by external consultant to eliminate any family resentment to the organization.
4. A program to improve newcomers' effectiveness in the foreign work and social environment, and improve community relations in the host culture.

The activities of Family Relocation Service for example, begin with predeparture advisement on the realities of corporate transfer policies and the new location. Its main undertaking for a single family begins after they arrive onsite when an escort counselor welcomes them on the first day there. This counselor may also be a successful expatriate from the transferees' country, who becomes a behavior model of effective adjustment. This professional in local acculturation then works for a period of time with the family assisting them in obtaining satisfactory housing, schooling, and language training, as well as in establishing the proper financial and social connections. Thus, the proper home base is set up for the manager or technician and family to operate abroad.

Under the heading of relocation assistance, a wide variety of services are offered, but the aim is the same — preventative "medicine" for stress reduction and facilitating the adjustment to a strange culture. In fact, the missing ingredient in too many relocation efforts is cross-cultural training. Too often the major emphasis is upon the mechanics of transfer with neglect of input on culture generals and specifics to increase awareness and sensitivity while in the host area. Another weakness of such programs is when multinationals bring foreign nationals to their corporate headquarters' country to live. Alison Lanier discusses that phenomenon which has been abetted by foreign firms buying into U.S. companies. Although these people may have worked with Americans abroad, they are subject to severe culture shock when they are suddenly plunged into the full pace, pressure, and impersonality of the U.S.A. The foreign executives' confusion may extend from the organizational culture to the alien ways of Americans regarding driving and driver's licenses, supermarket shopping, income tax preparation, and a host of other strange practices like our non-use of the metric system.[19]

An adequate foreign deployment and relocation system should extend from selection to reentry. Dr. David Freemantle of Britain says that international recruitment is the third dimension of personnnel functions. He cites a 40% growth rate in international recruitment, and gives as one reason: the need of countries with developing industrialization to sustain their rapid growth by foreign managers and technicians from advanced industrialized countries until they can prepare their own local substitutes. Although multinationals may wish to use local talent, reality often forces technology and personnel transfers in tandem. Freemantle recommends these eight rules to facilitate the exchange:

1. Select the highest qualified caliber personnel to be responsible for international recruitment and administration.
2. Develop a dynamic manpower plan in line with the corporation's business plan for overseas development (including action program for recruitment, training, compensation, and relocation services).
3. Utilize an expatriate for foreign assignments only when a competent local national is not available, and then choose someone who can fit well into the total situation.
4. Export your most competent and well-adjusted managers or technicians — it can provide important international development for "high-fliers" and enhance the corporate image abroad.
5. Apply the best personnel practices to international recruitment (such as, relate it to strategic business objectives; provide meaningful job descriptions abroad, as well as job specifications; offer a compensation package that is effective and realistic for overseas; and use skilled selection and induction).
6. International personnel policies and practices should be in writing, clearly understandable, and regularly reviewed.
7. Brief comprehensively each person sent abroad with not only knowledge of your company's operations there, but about the way in which business is done locally and the culture of the people, as well as straight information on living and working conditions in the host country. The counseling of expatriate personnel and their families should demonstrate that the company cares and is sensitive to relocation stress.
8. Terms and conditions for expatriates should never be worse off than they would be at home or with their local counterparts, and should be based on reliable research. Better to be generous with the compensation plan that includes a home-based salary + cost of living allowance + housing and hardship allowance + incentive premium and tax equalization + other specified allowances and foreign labor market adjustments.[20]

Although this expert would recommend that the person be permitted to make a short business trip to the assigned country before accepting the assignment, that is not always possible.

In addition to films and other audio-visuals on the target culture and business practices, Blair Duffy, Jr., vice-president of Asia Pacific Operations for Coldwell-Banker's Previews, Inc. in Honolulu, recommends viewing videotapes of potential home sites abroad. He sits with an executive and spouse to analyze potential house purchases in the host country, and then counsels them on the realities of real estate and living in the new location. (The authors would add to such a procedure videotapes of company expatriates who have successfully adjusted to that specific cultural assignment.)

To complete the deployment cycle, assistance with reentry into the home and corporate cultures should be given to the expatriate. Many multinationals are developing "repatriation agreements" for executives after their overseas service. They are written, general promises that the returning employee will return to a position comparable to the one he or she left, and will receive assistance with outplacement if the post is unacceptable. It has a beneficial psychological effect and relieves anxieties. Organization Resources Counselors, a New York-based consulting firm, reported that in a study of 200 executives regarding considerations of a foreign assignment, career impact and economic factors ranked high in their concerns.[21] Dow Chemical has a "repatriation supervisor" to monitor performance, compensation, and career paths of foreign-based managers; this sponsor begins scouting the right corporate vacancy for the person six months before the individual's return.

V. Lynn Tyler of the Brigham Young University Language Research Center attributes this adjustment challenge to unexpected changes in the home environment, organization, and people, as well as in the self as a result of the experience abroad. Before coming back to the home culture, Tyler advises the expatriate to prepare in the following areas relative to the back-home situation: professionally, financially, socially, linguistically (new business jargon, expressions, etc.), and nationally or politically, as well as educationally (the schools may have changed while you were away and differ markedly from those experienced by children abroad). He indicates the major behavior patterns to confront upon return are: alienation (negative about home culture); reversion (deny that important personal changes have taken place as a result of culture shock); and integration (integrate the changes into the home culture for an expanded identity and lifestyle). Professor Tyler recommends these coping strategies: get the big picture (relate the assignment abroad to one's total career and personal growth); be aware of expectations or anticipate changes; prepare for these changes before departure for home; confirm your foreign experiences with other expatriates who have preceded you home; and plan life-style transitions and integrate the overseas experience with the back-home needs and realities.[22]

If such approaches as described in this section are considered, then synergy will occur between the executive and the organization sponsoring the relocation, between the home and host cultures, between the home corporation and the foreign subsidiary, between the overseas total experience and the new home opportunities.

SYNERGY THROUGH EDUCATIONAL INNOVATION

To capitalize on the synergistic opportunities described in this concluding chapter and many more unmentioned ones, a new way of thinking is required on the part of the would-be leader in *cyberculture*. Our readers may recall that term from *Managing Cultural Differences* — a concept of the late physicist at M.I.T., Norbert Weiner:

> Cyberculture is a description of the emerging society or culture in the post-industrial period of human development. Sometimes referred to as the knowledge

society or technological age, it will be dominated by human creations of cybernated systems in which computers and information processing will be a key feature. The concept is derived from the word "cybernetics" which has been defined as the science of control and communication in man and machines. In other words, a new world culture is coming into being in which cybernation will be a central force — that is, human beings liberated from routine work tasks by their programming of computers to manage machines and automated processes.

The authors have adopted that convenient designation to underscore that the biggest cultural difference with which we must cope in the near future is this phenomenon of universal social change. We have proposed that the promotion of cultural synergy can facilitate our entry into this twenty-first century lifestyle. But all this is an educational challenge and requires much innovation in information exchange and consciousness raising.

To reeducate people in a new mindset that is in harmony with advances in biological sciences and technology, and to control such changes, implies that learning must go beyond the traditional methods and systems of formal education. Mass media capabilities will play a major role in this new nontraditional education. We already witnessed the overstepping of literacy in Third World nations by communication satellites via the transmission of education and training at the village level. Soon we will experience the expansion of home communication centers with their telecommunication potentialities for families to learn a variety of subjects. Television is now being utilized in a variety of ways for college and university education. In the United Kingdom, 200,000 students are enrolled in the Open University, off-campus program through the British Broadcast Corporation. Now sixteen countries throughout the world follow this model, using its videotapes and other learning materials.

An example of synergy in educational innovation occurred when a coalition of eleven Midwestern institutions of higher education in the United States formed the University of Mid-America. It offers college credit courses on public television. Also, ten public television systems and seven collaborating colleges across America have united in the National University Consortium. Aimed at working adults, degrees will be bestowed in humanities, technology, management, and behavioral and social sciences. With such innovations it is possible to raise the awareness, understanding, and intelligence of the whole human family. It is a means of overcoming cultural barriers and provincial ignorance, and promoting cultural synergy and wisdom on a universal scale never dreamed of in human history.

D. L. Hawk of the Center for Creative Leadership in Greensboro, North Carolina, reminds us that we must become life-long students, synthesizing logic and intuition; integrating new knowledge with existing information; seeing relationships, not discrete events. In this effort, he notes this prospect:

> Organizations will play a key role in this learning process. Organizations will
> become arenas for learning. In the future, an organization's effectiveness will

not be measured by just profits and productivity, but its climate for learning, its contribution to society, and its development of the people it employs. In such a future, work and study will become parallel processes in the professional leader's life . . . To those who begin preparation today, the journey into the 21st century will be a phenomenal voyage!

Corporations are already contributing to the delimiting of future shock through information dissemination and learning in diverse ways. Some use media advertising like Exxon's sponsorship of public service documentaries, or Champion International Corporation's periodical advertisements (request their brochure, *Planting Seeds for the Future* from Champion at 1 Landmark Square, Stamford, CT. 06921, USA). Thousands of Americans, for instance, are being reeducated in the basics of reading, writing, and arithmetic by their companies. The National School Public Relations Association in Arlington, Virginia has issued a report on *Education USA,* which confirms this synergy between school and business. Among the happenings it reports are 20 Boston companies or agencies in partnership with 19 secondary schools that not only educate employees, but bring business people into the schools offering courses. Cooperative work programs are on the increase at the high school and college levels so that students work part-time while studying. In Salt Lake City, 1,000 firms and agencies offer services to the schools. The educational involvement of industry includes:

1. Collaborative activities with students aimed at career awareness and skills, such as Junior Achievement.
2. Cooperative efforts that involve managers in school management studies and staff development.
3. Service by corporate leaders on school boards and advisory groups at all levels of education.
4. Corporate training programs and development of instructional materials.

The range extends from corporations running their own degree-granting colleges to Japan's Management Training School in Fujinomiya, which stresses success via suffering — by intensive learning of loyalty, self-sacrifice, and obedience — quite a contrast to the new corporate finishing schools run in the West. Proctor & Gamble is an example of the latter for it runs one of the country's top marketing organizations. It is the "finishing school" for employees in marketing, as General Electric is in management development, or Bell Laboratories in research. Executive recruiters report that talented young performers go to such companies for inservice education, and then pragmatically look to move up or out of the organization as part of career development. They seek "hands-on" experience and profit-loss responsibility as early as possible in this "fast-track" approach to learning.

The increasing synergy between industry and universities on a global basis can be seen in the IBEAR program of the Graduate School of Business Administration, University of Southern California. To meet the challenge of business transactions that cross borders, this International Business Education and Research Program was established. Corporations in the Pacific Basin sponsor middle managers who go back to schools here for one year to earn a Master's degree in business administration. This concentrated study of business techniques and decision-making lacks only one vital component for its international audience — cross-cultural studies. Another example is INSEAD, the international business school at Fontainebleau, France. There the research of Professor André Laurent suggests that managers working for multinational corporations hang on to their national characteristics and resist being incorporated into a "universal" culture. His studies of 772 managers pointed up the similarities and differences in comparative management:

> U.S. and northern European managers tend to define organization in terms of functions, while those in France and Italy take a social approach. The latter emphasis is upon individuality with the use of power sought for its own sake, rather than just to achieve objectives.
>
> West German, French, Belgian, and Swiss managers seek precisely defined roles in their organization, while Dutch, Swedish, and U.S. managers are less concerned.

The findings indicated management of cultural differences regarding conflict, matrix management, management-by-objectives, and other such administrative practices. The educational innovation occurs when transnational managers learn to appreciate and confront the contrasting cultural approaches to the process of management. Companies are learning to capitalize on these differences instead of ignoring them.

Training and education, in or out of industry and formal systems, can promote innovations, cultural awareness, and synergy. To close this section, here are a few other examples of learning innovations:

- In training managers, the Center for Creative Leadership in North Carolina uses these two unique approaches. *Looking Glass* is a simulation exercise of a day in the life of a multimillion dollar corporation. The twenty roles played cover four levels of management and three operating divisions with different product lines and problems. Using real offices and communication systems, the participants go through in-basket exercises for problem-solving in a fast-paced situation containing the usual pressures of managerial life. After the simulations, behavior is analyzed. The Center Information Library has a computer retrieval system to foster organizational innovation by scanning summaries of articles from around the world on the subject of creativity and innovation.
- The American Society for Training and Development in Washington, D.C. notes that its membership has jumped from 8,600 in 1969 to 20,000 members a decade later, now grouped into 119 chapters. ASTD not only promotes professional development for their own members, but conducts R & D that results in publications and better learning aids for the workers trained by their members.

- International meetings of corporations, trade and professional associations are increasingly the means of continuing education for participants. Many of these events now provide audio tapes of their sessions which are made, along with printed conference proceedings, to those employees or members who cannot attend. See Appendix B for further information on the possibilities for intercultural synergy through such meeting encounters.
- A Rand Corporation study was conducted for the President's Commission on Foreign Languages and International Studies. Its report in *Strength Through Wisdom* (1979), concluded that innovative lines of communication must be established between business, the academic community, and government in strengthening the international expertise of business. They pointed to the need for places or programs where the long-term interests of international studies and business come together in a systematic way. Among the Commission recommendations was that business give more priority in selection and recruitment to personnel who have foreign language and international studies training, as well as sophistication for more effective operation in the international business environment.

SYNERGY THROUGH CULTURAL INTERDEPENDENCE

As a conclusion to our two volumes, the authors would like to share a vision of the future with their readers. Our planet is now made up of diverse cultures, and the peoples of those cultures are increasingly dependent on one another. Whether one deals with macrosystems or microsystems, we are realizing their interdependence. To progress, to achieve objectives, to solve problems, we must consciously learn to collaborate, to form coalitions and consortia, to synthesize differences, to seek consensus, to resolve globocentric concerns, and to develop transnational interfaces. In other words, we can no longer manage independently without regard to the impact of our decisions on others and the environment. We need to develop skills of global management that will improve local conditions.

At the 1980 First Global Conference on the Future in Toronto, Paul Rubinyi addressed the need for "wholeness" in leadership, and provided these insights:

> Global management refers to that level of management that exists to direct, integrate, and control a large, complex organization . . . When global management is effective, it liberates, encouraging individualism and self-assertion, while promoting corporate integration of autonomous operating units. Global managers are conceptualizers who think in global rather than local terms, and determine the future direction of the organization as a whole. Using approaches from general system theory, such managers facilitate structural integration of interdependent parts. Global management shifts the center of interest from power to the job of steering and monitoring. For effective global management, the concept must be understood at all levels and there must be agreement about

the identity of the organization as a whole. There needs to be adequate balance between autonomy of operations centers, and the requirements for corporate integration. Global management must be able to communicate well with the organization's various publics, as well as induce internal coordination between organization units and levels of management. Aware of key success and control factors, global management articulates the decision process at all levels of management. It seeks comprehensiveness while interrelating all essential factors. It provides a mechanism for challenging the status quo and introducing change when the opportunity arises. When the degree of complexity is beyond human capacity, it employs management aid systems to assist in informed decisions.

Rubinyi, a consultant with Canada's Ernst & Whinney, has developed such a management aid system framework in his Montreal practice. His observations remind us that in a complex, interdependent world, large systems that span our globe will need a new kind of management. The old industrial age model no longer suffices.

Dr. Jonas Salk maintains that our social systems are replications of biological models. To understand the energy exchanges of our organizational systems, we will have to better comprehend the marvels of the human body and seek clues from it for application to the social body. One scenario from an American Council on Life Insurance report states that by the end of the 20th century:

> Most people believed that physical disease was a symptom of some underlying emotional, mental, social-psychological, or spiritual pathology. It is now realized that the 20th Century emphasis on the individual in ego separateness was a primary cause of many diseases. The stress associated with maximizing profits, survival of the fittest, and other forms of unrestrained competition were triggers that broke down the body's ability to maintain equilibrium.[23]

The ACLI report proposes this interdependent concept for realization in the next two decades: every component of society — the workplace, educational institutions, transportation networks, and the urban environment in general — should be considered part of the health care system. It suggests establishment of a Cooperative Commission on Wellness, and that androgyny, or the realization of both masculine and feminine attributes in every individual, become a cultural goal, especially for management. This remarkable report calls for a

> . . . cultural transformation touching every aspect of Western industrial civilization; new attitudes toward health that go hand-in-hand with the environment, for individual health cannot be separated from social health.[24]

Planning and creating this cultural change on a global basis becomes essential as humankind gets ready to catapult itself out into the universe on a mass scale.

The culture of the 21st century may be as different from prior centuries as the culture that white settlers brought to Australia was from the aboriginal culture, which already existed on that island continent. Rather than the conflict between those two cultures that is gradually destroying the original culture, we hope for some synergy between what our ancestors and we created so far on this planet and what our human successors in the future will develop and take into outer space. One can only speculate upon what other alien cultures tomorrow's children will discover out there in the universe. Will they manage these cultural differences and attain some cultural synergy?

THE BEGINNING, NOT THE END

The old foundations of scientific thought are becoming unintelligible. Time, space, matter, structure, pattern, function, etc. — all require reinterpretation!

Alfred North Whitehead

References

1. Lippitt, G. *Training Today,* October 1980.
2. Drucker, P. *Managing in Turbulent Times.* New York: Harper & Row, 1980.
3. Lifton, R.J. *Home From the War: Vietnam Veterans: Neither Victims Nor Executors.* Touchstone Books, 1974.
4. Rifkin, J. and Howard, T. *Entropy: A New World View.* New York: The Viking Press, 1980.
5. Harman, W. "The Coming Transformation," *The Futurist,* February and April 1977.
6. Ways, M. *The Future of Business: Global Issues of the 80's and 90's.* Elmsford, New York: Pergamon Press, 1979.
7. Cooper, G.L. "Humanizing the European Workplace," *Personnel Journal,* June 1980.
8. Reingold, E. *Time Magazine,* September 8, 1980.
9. Drucker, P. *Wall Street Journal,* June 4, 1980.
10. Morita, A. *Los Angeles Times,,* Octorber 29, 1980.
11. *Los Angeles Times,* October 29, 1980.
12. "Corporate Culture — The Hard-to-Change Values that Spell Success or Failure," *Business Week,* October 27, 1980.
13. Dadzie, K.K.S. *Scientific American,* September 1980, (Vol. 243, No. 1) p. 61.
14. Craig, J. *Multinational Cooperatives: An Alternative for World Development* Saskatoon, Saskatchewan: Western Producers Prairie Books, 1976.
15. Wederspahn, G.M. "Cultural Awareness for Managers," *The Bridge,* Fall 1980.
16. Eliot, S.V. *New York Post,* January 21, 1980.
17. Cooper, G.L. *Executive Gypsies,* London: Macmillan Press, 1980.

18. Hoffman, J. *The New York Times,* January 31, 1980.
19. Lanier, A. *International Business,* September/October 1979.
20. Freemantle, D. *Personnel Management,* October 1978.
21. Organization Resources Counselors. *Business Week,* June 11, 1979.
22. Tyler, V.L. "Coming Home Again: Absorbing Return Shock," *Infogram.* Brigham Young University Language Research Center, 1980.
23. American Council on Life Insurance. "Health Care: Three Reports from 2030 A.D." ACLI, 1850 K Street N.W., Washington, D.C. 20006, U.S.A.

Epilogue

The International Management Productivity Series has attempted to provide global managers with general cultural insights and specific cultural insights. In this second volume, the final unit on "Cultural Specifics and Synergy" attempted to offer helpful information and commentary about major geographic regions. The authors recognize that space and time limitations caused us to omit a number of national cultures and regions. For example, the whole continent of Africa, an area of multi-tribal differences with a great need for synergy was not included. The subject proved too vast for this volume, though the Organization of African States would provide a fascinating case study of synergistic problems and potential. We recognize the importance of Africa in the geopolitical and economic spheres. Many OPEC nations are represented in the Moslem cultures of Northern Africa, while the energy discoveries in Nigeria and Cameroon are again bringing Western business persons into such "Third World" countries.

We hope in future editions or books to correct the imbalance relative to these ancient lands and cultures, many of which formulate the origins and heritages of black people in both North, Central, and South America. Meanwhile, we refer our readers back to our previous book, *Managing Cultural Differences* which has a section on Africa in Chapter 13, "Cultural Themes and Patterns." We urge our readers to focus upon Africa and its talented peoples in any North-South dialogue that is undertaken, because the possibilities for mutually beneficial cooperation are many!

Appendix A
Toward Human Emergence

When men toiled in the primitive interior of Brazil to construct a modern capital for that emerging nation, there were many who must have been appalled by the seeming confusion. Undoubtedly, some could have decried the disunity of ideas on how to build Brasilia. Disagreements over procedures, disruption in schedules, and disparity in priorities took place, for this was a human endeavor.

A North American observer on the scene in its early phases might have been aghast at the impossibility of the task. One might have viewed the lack of many resources, debris scattered everywhere, machinery operating in apparent opposition, construction crews bickering with one another. Yet, Brasilia was a planned city; eventually the architects, engineers, and politicians cooperated with the technicians, craftsmen, and peasants until they wrought a futuristic metropolis that manifests order and beauty. Likewise, the human family struggles to erect the City of Man.

In the long history of our species, progression and regression have been evident. But the perfection of the human endeavor goes forward with ever quickening pace, and better means and materials of construction. Man has evolved into an age of emergence, when we are becoming more mature as a human species.

Expanding Insight

It is a time in the sequence of world events to be excited, to be optimistic, to be involved in the planning and building of the future. Unique opportunities have opened to twentieth-century man to participate in the process of unification, to put

*Reprinted with permission from the *Journal of Human Potential* Vol. 1, No. 4.

together the parts that will bring forth a new order and being. Those planners and doers who expect to form history must look beyond the horizon.

Those who share a vision of the future do not sit on the periphery, bewildered by sudden human advances or set-backs. Since they view human beings in perspective, these people will not be bypassed as the world presses on to its fulfillment. They appreciate that mankind has grown beyond its childhood and comes forth from a state of adolescent confusion. To ascertain present action, these practical visionaries draw insights from man's relatively short past, take an overview of contemporary events, and project this information into the tomorrow. The result of their plausible predictions now are translated into immediate life modifications and contributions.

World Shaping — Choices

For those who aspire to be world shapers, rather than earth squatters, it is necessary to take an orbital view of this planet and its activities. Like the astronauts who took a global fix in space to photograph this planet's land and water masses, so we must focus on human development in terms of long-range history and existential situation. Then, it may become clear that we are emerging into a new state of being and are at a major turning point in our existence.

With the help of imagination, one's mental pictures of the human experience and condition might be viewed from three perspectives. First, there is the fact of continuous *change* in us and our environment. The startling reality of the moment is that the rate of this change is accelerating astronomically. Secondly, we are in the position of constant *choice,* with freedom to determine what course of action we will take. But today's choices have a collective impact that now go beyond earth into the universe. Will we, for example, extend a reign of unity or disunity beyond this planet which served as our place of habitation until now? Finally, we exercise increasing *control* over ourselves and our external environment. But will we regulate the amazing new technology and discoveries about life itself, or will we be controlled by the forces of our own making?

Prospects for the future are both challenging and terrifying. The moral imperative of this century hinges on human choices in controlling changes. In this process we are aided by recent breakthroughs in communication, and we contribute to the accomplishment of numerous convergences which hasten world development. However, the fundamental problem affecting human survival and universal emergence is our ability to formulate a set of values upon which we act for the benefit of *all* mankind. Individual welfare in this time of the world depends upon the common good. In other words, we must develop an all-or-none guidance system that directs our course into the future. Perhaps a brief analysis of these factors in human emergence will provide some insight into the search for meaning.

Transformation

To live, to be, is to *change*. The whole universe demonstrates dynamic and continuous movement from potentiality to fulfillment. The reality of this is readily verified in mankind, the magnification of all creation. But such change is not merely relative or cyclical, it is either spurious or purposeful. If it is meaningless, there can be no concept as human emergence. But if man's life is like a river flowing to a merger, then two more alternatives present themselves. Does man's purposefulness flow inexorably toward destruction and disintegration? Or rather, does mature man innately strive toward good, toward unity, despite the fact that he follows a course marked by progression and regression? The writer accepts the premises of perfectability of mankind and our ability to develop human potential. Should the reader agree, then we are in a position to explore together the many faceted potentialities for man's emergence into a new, improved being.

The challenge, of course, is also to consider one's personal contribution to the acceleration of this goal individually and for the species.

Self Visualization

Man is the encapsulation of the beginning to the end of time. Thus in probing for the answer to "who am I," we tend to project ourselves beyond time itself. Generally, we assume that we had a beginning and that we would end, or be fulfilled. Our speculations on this reality have been expressed in many ways as we have attempted to understand, or relate to our span of existence.

For centuries we have reasoned and speculated about our physical existence, while discovering ways to extend life. We have also been aware of our social being, as a member of a human family. Presently, we appreciate more forcefully the interdependence of the human family. Furthermore, as spiritual beings, we are predisposed to contemplate a personal and corporate meaning.

We are witness to the profound transformation within ourselves of the mineral, vegetable, animal and spiritual elements that also surround us. However, we are not only influenced by our changing physical and social environment, but we are *agents of change*. We not only adapt to our environment. We change it and, in the process, we change ourselves.

The staggering difference about this time of the world is that the *rate and means of change* have vastly and dramatically increased. The changes in tomorrow's technopolis not only affect how we live, but our very view of ourselves, our neighbors, and the cosmos.

Decision-Making

Man is not a victim of fate; he can create history. In an epoch of nuclear power, technology, cybernetics and bio-chemical advances, the opportunities to plot and navigate human evolution have never been greater. The *choices* that we make will largely determine the degree of control we exercise over changes, and in turn, the beneficial effects of them.

We can *decide* to increase our alienation from technological society, to waste genius on trivialities, to use increased leisure for self destruction, to leave our great gifts unused. Or we can build a bridge from the present anguish over the abyss that seems to loom ahead to the accomplishment of our highest ideals. We can choose to use freedom to develop our intellectual, cultural, and spiritual qualities. We can choose to channel the new powers which we have unleashed into the improvement of the human condition. We can choose to humanize urban areas and social institutions. We can take steps to further our own emergence that range from the intelligent, universal use of mass media to the expansion of education for all peoples. We can choose to do such things, or we can sit by, allowing history to accumulate and science to run away with itself.

Self Regulation

These choices become more pressing for the whole race because of the extent of control man has been privileged to gain over his surroundings, his own being, his destiny. The first major indication of this ability to control the circumstance of life came some millenia ago. The event-in-time has been designated as the agricultural revolution.

Man applied his brawn to newly invented tools and turned the earth from jungles into gardens and farms. As man learned to till the soil, he moved progressively away from the survival-of-the-fittest mode of life. Mastering the hostile forces of nature which enslaved him during this primitive period of existence, man improved the means for self-preservation, thereby providing for future needs. Thus, he obtained time to develop family life and *culture*. Along with this socialization came increased leisure, organization, and communication. In the process, the very manifestation of his nature changed — man became an abstract thinker, a creator of beauty, a searcher after truth, a being more capable of expressing love and compassion for fellow humans.

The culmination of this phase in fashioning civilization — a specifically human task — was another event-in-time, called the Industrial Revolution. Now man was using his brain, and not merely brawn, to apply power to more sophisticated tools called machines.

Since then we have more rapidly extended control over our external environment. Having almost subdued the earth, we now seek to conquer space.

Within the last four centuries, mankind has added astoundingly to the accumulated wisdom of the ages. New professional fields like history, archeology, anthropology, sociology, and psychology have piled knowledge upon knowledge. Tremendous breakthroughs occurred in the natural sciences, and they have interlocked to form new learning, such as bio-engineering, bio-chemistry, and atomic physics. At the same time man advanced in the area of electronics and technology. The fantastic result has been that the swift compilation of information, interacting and compounding, producing an explosion of knowledge. History and time are constantly being compressed; larger and more startling intellectual explosions may be expected.

Cybernation — Freedom To Be

The principal means of control to unfold in the twentieth century was the automation of human skills and machines. By harnessing the computer to the automated machines, a whole new system of control and communication came into being — cybernetics. Through it we not only extend minds but provide a mechanical electronic substitute for our brains. The knowledge worker engaged in information processing and research will predominate in the post-industrial age.

Since the work of the new technology is supervised without the necessity of someone's presence, reduction of laborers will not only occur on the assembly line but at the managerial and executive levels. Thus, the dawn of cyberculture signifies a fundamental shift in our society from the ethic of work to that of leisure.

Humans no longer need to be slaves to work, or to enslave others for that purpose. Machines, computers and robots can now serve in this capacity. Further, a person will no longer be measured in the future by what he or she does jobwise, but what he or she is as an individual human being.

Man is freeing himself to be — but to be what? Again, the element of choice appears. We can permit ourselves to become slaves of technology and other scientific advances, or we can control the totality of these changes so that we can become more human. The time formerly devoted to production in farm, factory, or office can be used to bring forth latent human potential. Therefore, careers of thinking, research, exploration, and service should predominate in the future. Voluntary jobs, such as in the Peace Corps, should increase sharply.

Directed Destiny

Furthermore, the next fifty years will be marked by a series of significant "linkups" or integrations. Computers and electronics have already invaded farms, libraries, laboratories, hospitals and universities with results that stagger the imagination. Cybernetics coupled with human engineering or nuclear energy unleashes enormous knowledge and power. This permits us not only to control our surroundings, but the process of life itself. With these new insights, we can choose to feed, clothe, and house the world. We can decide to extend our own life. We can determine the size, amount, and type of terrestrial life, and perhaps that of other planets.

Man has the knowhow, for instance, in the area of genetic surgery and control, to improve life on earth and possibly to colonize the universe. Yet, with all these fantastic prospects, will we become more alienated because we cannot control our inner disharmony and external expressions of it? Will we become an interplanetary destructive force?

We hope we will use conscience to control this genius and such dire forebodings will not be realized. Instead, man may transform and transcend the world through a positive, peaceful influence.

Communication

Another marvel interwoven in the process of human emergence is *communication*. It is used to effect changes, to inform of choices, and to exercise control. It enables us to be intensely sensitive to the interplay of forces and factors around us. Our communication is multidimensional — with the divine, with all animal life, and with our own species.

Two related trends may be noted which have fostered the process. First, there is astonishing progress in transportation which allows for high-speed travel by the masses. The impact caused ranges from radar and superhighways to atomic ships, jets, and satellites. Second, there is the move toward urbanization on the part of the bulk of the earth's population. Mass media, computer, and satellite communication in this century really cracked the barriers among humans, bringing the walls that separate nations, races, and cultures tumbling down.

Through mass media, we further extend ourselves and our vision. Thus, we spectacularly contribute to the development of a truly planetary civilization. Whether it is educational or intercontinental television, radio or advertising, movies or magazines, we have consistently perfected our means for communicating. The synergy of media and technology opens unprecedented opportunities for human association.

Predictions for the future in communication amaze the average person — worldwide television; a common computer language; videophones for instant contact anywhere with anyone; perfected mental telepathy. In fact, it appears that any means we can consciously conceive, can in time be invented and made practical.

In education, the impact of this revolution in communication is brought into sharp focus. It goes beyond the replacement of blackboards and textbooks by electronic classrooms and pocket video receivers for home study. It challenges the need, scope, and purpose of the "institutions" of learning. It engenders the possibilities for paid learners, the restructuring and interrelating of academic curricula, the developing of wholly new areas of knowledge to be studied, the actual programming of education and culture.

Extension of Self

As we solve the problem of *how* to communicate through technological media, we are confronted with *what* to communicate. We have such difficulty communicating within ourselves (meditation, introspection), and with the source of our essence, that we are confounded with this prospect. Modern man is more concerned with *meaning* rather than *effect*. Although we surge ahead in our ability to extend ourselves everywhere instantaneously, we are confronted with the absolute need to turn in upon ourselves for answers and to communicate in depth with other persons. Simultaneously, we are becoming more feeling animals, more sensitive to life and persons around us.

Again, we face a choice. Will we permit media and technology merely to be an extension into numbness, or a means for the improvement of human welfare and deeper personal enrichment?

Homogenized Society

Fortunately, at a time of essential change in sense perception and awareness, we have also discovered ways of sensitivity training. We have methods for acquiring skills in human relations and capitalizing on the dynamics of groups. We have learned how to change organizational behavior and to develop leadership.

As we analyze our behavior, we painfully attain wisdom on how to communicate love and control hatred. As the divisions that separate humans disappear and tension lessens, we learn to get along with others, regardless of beliefs, origins, or appearances. We are creating, instead, a homogenized society. With this growth in awareness toward fellow humans, there is reason to hope that the intercommunicating human mass will interchange constructive information, useful knowledge, and positive values.

Extremes of individualism and collectivism may be counteracted by this increased social consciousness.

Emergence Through Convergence

There is a point of view that perceives human emergence as further advanced by a series of *convergences*. Instead of these apparent opposite positions polarizing, synergy occurs.

Actually what appeared to be divergent viewpoints may turn out to be two complementary faces of the same phenomenon. This perspective may become more understandable when one analyzes in some depth the concepts of space/time, matter/spirit, individual/community rights, national/international interests, and poverty/plenty. For example, the common roots of the Judeo-Christian and humanistic traditions are being explored and experienced as we face up to social problems like racism, illiteracy, and human want. Or, the old division between East and West is giving way to cultural gaps based on "have" and "have not." In the more sophisticated society of the future, ideologies and systems like communism and capitalism will forge new relationships through improved knowledge and technology. Our choices now will contribute to the harmonization in the centuries ahead of today's seemingly contrary positions.

Optimistically, this view contemplates mankind making the right choices for the furtherance of convergent consciousness. The emergence of man into a state of thought will then promote union among humans. Meanwhile, until that time, the major gulf separating us may be an attitude of mobility and immobility; those with a vision of the future versus those with their minds in a rut of the status quo.

Moral Being

Obviously, the evolutions and revolutions within the human family until now have made us more social beings. The question of this day, and decades to come, is whether we will become more *moral* beings in the technological age?

The substitution of human muscle and nervous system with automatic controls demands even greater moral responsibility on our part. "Cyberculture" or "technopolis" will require new ethics, social principles, and value judgments. By practicing cooperation and collaboration we can produce a new spirit among humans, that of service. We can choose good — that which promotes and improves human life — and reject or diminish evil — that which degrades, endangers and destroys human life.

Catalysts

There are steps that must be taken now to insure individual and collective emergence. Those who address themselves to these issues and promote synergy will be the catalysts of the future. There are many leaders in training now for this purpose. They are the ones who will use cybernation and bio-engineering to provide a better global socio-economic order. They are characterized by openness and tolerance, flexibility and adaptability, competency and sensitivity.

By the year 2000, these leaders of the cybernated generation may have contributed to the emergence of a person who is as different from present-day humans as twentieth-century dwellers are from primitives. *During the next fifty years our contemporaries may make the most decisive choices and utilize the most influential controls in the whole process of human evolution.* As such men and women push back the frontiers of the future, there will be no shock for them. They have been involved in the dynamic movements of our times and are cognizant of what lies ahead.

Vitalized Aspiration and Action

As we cope with the challenges of the cybercultural revolution, we will be enriched by the exciting experience of living at a most generative moment in history. Time-past and time-present will pass smoothly into time-future. The men and women of tomorrow will be concerned especially with the sacredness of living. Knowing the true meaning of man's being and acts, they will seek the perfection of human endeavor. These determiners of the future will vitalize human aspiration and action. Their energy will be used to transform creation. Such leaders may well result from synergistic efforts that develop human resources.

Appendix B
Synergy Through
International Meetings

During the past quarter century there has been a phenomenal growth in international meetings conducted by trade and professional associations, multinational corporations, as well as by government agencies. Generally, the purpose is information exchange and professional development, and the size ranges from small-group continuing education events to conventions of thousands. What is different about such endeavors is that the participants leave their home culture to convene in another host culture. Advances in mass communication and transportation have made this mass world travel and exchange feasible. However, rising inflation, energy costs, and hotel expenses abroad may restrict these intercultural seminars, workshops, and conferences overseas. The next twenty-five years, instead, may see a dramatic increase in international teleconferencing, which will combine satellites, computers, and television. Thus, the expectation should be for multicultural interchange on a scale unprecedented in human history — instead of thousands moving their bodies across borders, it is likely that millions will transfer the thoughts from their minds in global interface.

The implications of such mass information exchanges are staggering, raising problems and challenges. The AT & T Corporate Planning Emerging Issues Group has already identified one concern relative to transborder data flows. In their report *Labor Issues of the '80s,* (October 1980 — AT & T, Room 7211 N2, Basking Ridge, N.J. 07920, USA) they point up that the electronic transfer of information, or TDF, across national borders has prompted many governments to establish controls. These approaches seek to regulate the types of information on individuals that public and private organizations can collect, use, and disseminate. Such privacy protection concerns are understandable, as long as it does not curb legitimate human search for wisdom and understanding by sharing knowledge.

Electronic technology can be used on a universal scale to raise the educational level of the world's population. The United Nations, for example, estimates that almost one third of the human family is illiterate. UNESCO sees this deplorable condition as a challenge to teach literacy to these 814 million humans via educational television, and their teachers will have a need for information exchanges among themselves as to the best methods for accomplishing such a vast goal. In any event, whether the purpose is basic or professional learning achieved through an onsite meeting or teleconferencing, cultural awareness and sensitivity is called for if synergy is to occur in these exchanges.

Meeting planning today is a professional field requiring expertise and skill. Two of the leading publications in this emerging field have annual issues that concentrate on conducting international meetings and the sites available: *Successful Meetings* (1422 Chestnut St., Philadelphia, Pa. 19102, USA) and *Meetings & Conventions* (One Park Ave., New York, N.Y. 10016, USA). Each offers special books to improve meeting management. For example *SM* publishes *Professional Manager's Handbook,* while *MC* has an annual *Official Meeting Facilities Guide*.

The Conference Book by Leonard and Zeace Nadler (Houston, Texas: Gulf Publishing Company, 1977) is also an excellent source of international conference planning and implementation information.

To give readers some insight into the scope of international meetings, it is worth noting that when the American Society of Association Management (1101 16th St., N.W., Washington, D.C. 20036, USA) reported that more than half of its 4,000 members hold meetings, conventions, and trade missions outside the continental U.S. each year. Foreign sites are chosen sometimes for employee reward, as part of an incentive travel plan, or because the transnational organization is bringing together personnel or members from around the globe. Group transportation rates and promotability are often cited as reasons for such decisions. As part of global marketing, meetings near foreign operations permit visits to be scheduled to local plants, subsidiaries, distributors. Meeting with foreign counterparts can be both stimulating and insightful, as well as profitable. The trend toward regional economic development and operations also warrants leaving one's own country for a neighboring nation for mutual professional growth.

Perhaps a few examples of the variety and scope of such events will underscore the significance of international business meetings. In the past decade Bestline Products, Inc. brought 2,000 sales people to Paris. Although an American company, it used this opportunity for its worldwide distributors to either attend training sessions or benefit from an incentive contest. Culligan International Company combined business and pleasure in a dealers' convention in Brussels. Despite complicated logistics, the corporation conducted a 13-day convention trip to 4 countries, supplemented by optional pre- or post-tours to additional nations. Coca Cola Company wanted privacy and pleasure, as well as exclusive use of meeting facilities, so they rented an entire island in the Bahamas for 70 plant managers and their spouses. Diebold Europe, an American-owned management consulting firm, annually conducts a number of small regional seminars throughout that continent, and then a major conference of several hundred management information specialists from both sides of the "Iron Curtain."

In a knowledge society dominated by information processing, keeping up on the state of the art of one's field is an important ingredient in career development. The International Federation of Training and Development Organization annually attracts to various world sites thousands of human resource specialists to advance their own skills, as well as the millions of personnel they serve. Most international conferences now offer simultaneous translation equipment, audio-visuals in several languages, as well as handouts and post-conference reports in the major languages of the participants. For those who wish to review the contents of a session or make up for one they missed, there are audio and video-tapes available of the speaker's presentations. When the First Global Conference on the Future was held in Toronto, Canada, in 1980, Conference Tape (8 Woodburn Drive, Ottawa, Ontario K1B 3A7) not only offered such recordings to attendees, but also to members who could not attend.

Many meeting planners are providing more sophisticated arrangements for couples who attend. Instead of the old-fashioned shows and travel tours for the wives, special conference rates are for the two-career professional couple, as well as sessions exclusively for spouses that foster both personal and professional growth and insight into local culture.

Many organizations use the group travel arrangements as a time for further information exchange and learning. This may include a seminar enroute, if the means of transportation is a ship or train; or closed-circuit television or movies for data on language, culture, and sightseeing, if an air plane or bus is utilized. In any event, international meetings are wonderful means for promoting synergy and intercultural goodwill, as well as learning, if they are very carefully planned and managed. Such events certainly should not be left to amateurs, and even trainers who are familiar with conducting meetings in their own country need professional assistance when planning a conference abroad. The following insights are gleaned from one of the authors' (Harris) association with *Successful Meetings* magazine:

Planning Tips for International Meetings

- *Personally inspect the overseas facility, and negotiate with suppliers abroad.* Develop rapport with suppliers, discuss needs and problems, but never issue orders or be demanding. All visits to intended hotel sites should be by appointment and not unannounced. Let the hotel manager treat you as is customary, and avoid being overly business-like while getting to know the hotel staff.
- *Intercultural communication requires sensitivity to local customs and traditions.* For example, unlike Americans who prefer first names, in Europe, Africa, and

Asia, the last name is used until you are invited to use a first or nickname. Titles are often very important and to be respected. Business cards in both the local and your own language are to be encouraged. Speak more slowly as you give instructions or requests. If your native language is American English, for instance, be prepared for different versions of English abroad, especially in Commonwealth nations.

- Interpreters may be supplied by the hotel or through local commercial outlets to facilitate the planning and implementation of the meeting. Headphones, which are portable and allow translation simultaneously in several languages, are usual for international meetings, along with printed meeting outlines in the language of the participant. The same resource can also arrange for published translations of the conference proceedings. All such costs should be included in planning.

- *Fully utilize international resources.* Beginning with a professional travel agent, there are many specialists available, including airline or transport agencies, government tourist boards, and the hotel itself, who can assist in the meeting planning, as well as link you with reliable local suppliers. Since meeting space worldwide is scarce, reserve early — sometimes a year or even two years ahead of the actual event. Also consider the new conference centers that are being developed overseas, especially on large estates. Be prepared to pay for meeting space, and consider using a government convention facility conveniently located near hotels. Abroad, it is typical to pay for reservations in advance and to expect a 48-hour guarantee period; equipment rental companies also often anticipate prepayment. Check out all differences in equipment compatibility and electric currents/voltages. Request written bids for all services rendered.

- *Observe protocol overseas regarding the hierarchy of command in various countries.* Using titles, and dealing directly with a supervisor is important. It is improper to bypass that person to communicate needs with a hotel manager's subordinates. When planning a meeting abroad, make sure the facilities' manager and all relevant department heads are included in the process and decisions. Work with and through the existing system without appearing to take responsibility from the locals.

- *Food negotiations are critical,* before arrival and just prior to the event. Let your own members know what is included in a continental breakfast, and that they must pay for extras. Encourage them to experiment with the local cuisine, and not insist for unique dishes from your own nation, which may be costly additions. Discuss, then sample, meals selected with the catering manager. Talk brands when you order liquor or wine, and discover price relationships. Consider taking your participants to outside restaurants one or two evenings of the conference, either in small or large groups. European stately homes and mansions are often available for banquets and provide a nice touch to an international meeting. Buses can be used for local transportation if chartered in advance.

- *Customs regulations differ by country* and can be difficult unless planned for in advance. Canada, for example, is likely to charge on slides and AV equipment brought into the country, unless prior arrangements are made. The easy way to clear meeting materials across borders is by filing a customs document in advance — a list of all materials you pledge to take in and out temporarily. This "carnet system" facilitates the transfer of equipment and conference materials into the foreign country for the meeting, and eliminates many of the usual customs delays. The U.S. Council of the International Chamber of Commerce is the official American agent for the forms and program.
- *Currency issues are important* considerations because of the rapid fluctuations in international exchange rates. If a fixed rate is agreed upon beforehand, often the hotel will accept the difference in costs. Sometimes it is possible to negotiate in dollars to avoid changes in exchange rates. Others open up a bank account in the foreign country the moment negotiations get underway for the site, and pay from then on in local currency. In any event, it is not wise to try and impose "unfair" terms on overseas' suppliers regarding exchange rates, or the services received may suffer as a result. Your local banker can be of great assistance in your dealing with foreign bankers; the latter can even be a mine of information on local facilities. (Also check with your insurance agent on various coverages for equipment and people.) Money conversion charts are available from Universal Currency Converter (1 News Plaza, Peoria, Ill 61601, USA) and will be appreciated by your participants. The U.S. Customs Service can also provide for attendees a small brochure on the amount of money and goods a citizen may bring coming or going.
- *Conference materials,* in addition to technical handouts, might include prior to time of departure: (a) travel cards with information on the foreign place in terms of suitable clothing, language and meal terms, transportation systems, and other useful data (available from Travelcards, 833 North Merican St., Indianapolis, Ind. 46204, USA); (b) brightly colored group-identifiable luggage tags, printed company sheets on tips, hotel payments, registration fees, dress recommendations, health and immigration requirements, and other corporate expectations of personnel; (c) arrangements for a hospitality or information desk for participants when they arrive onsite that gives details on local tours, events, and opportunities.
- *Group dynamics should be considered* in planning so that the participants experience at the international level a variety of meeting techniques and approaches. This would involve different types of participation from lectures and small group problem-solving to field trips and simulations. The first evening of arrival should be open with an informal reception if possible; and time should be built into the schedule for local shopping and sightseeing — all part of the intercultural educational experience. Alternative plans should be ready in case luggage is delayed, room assignments are changed, or "O'Toole's Law" is in operation. Murphy's Law is that regardless of planning, if anything can go

wrong, it will; O'Toole's dictum is that Murphy is an optimist. Some cultures are not yet comfortable with participatory meetings. So, if one experiments abroad with group process, involve local professionals in the planning and execution, allow more time for implementation, and be prepared for the unexpected.

As one *SM* staff member counseled, "keep an open mind, and most differences in customs and culture which affect international meetings will be easily resolved. Accept the emphasis on formality and protocol as a cultural difference and handle it accordingly." International meeting managers should also "hang loose" and anticipate minor disasters as par for the course. Many foreigners, for example, wish to so please the visitor and make a good impression for their country that they say what they think the foreign planner wishes to hear often promising what they cannot possibly deliver, because they think it will make you happy. Thus, it may be wiser to bring all essential learning materials and equipment with you, and then hire local technicians for the support services necessary to use them. When electronic equipment is involved, be prepared to use local contractors because of differences in AC/DC power. Also be prepared that semantic differences in meaning for communication symbols might cause the foreign host to provide something entirely different from what you thought you requested months prior.

Clues with Multicultural Audiences

Cultural synergy is more likely to be attained at international meetings if planners and presenters take audience diversity into consideration. Dr. Ernest Dichter, distinguished motivational psychologist, in an interview in *SM* magazine offers these insights for improved intercultural communication:

- Avoid national *stereotypes* either in your presentation, or as assumptions in planning your speech (e.g., "Germans are industrious, overlooking that French and Italians may be more so, and that Germans are easy-going people").
- *Deference* should be given to some participants because of their positions in the organization, especially in Europe and the Orient. (A managing director expects certain respect to be shown in many small ways, including seating.)
- Intercultural *behavior* requires one to avoid brashness and seek to do what is appropriate in the situation (e.g., use of titles like "Herr Doctor Engineer" or the avoidance of familiarity such as "back-slapping"). Political and off-color jokes and stories are out.
- *Attitude* toward foreign nations should avoid condescension and ethnocentricity (e.g., a superiority complex can cause defensiveness in the host nationals, and exclusions from the social benefits of being abroad. Their attitude toward certain occupations should also be appreciated. For example, in Europe a real

gentleman would never be a salesman, so Americans might refer to such persons as "customer service representatives or consultants." Since Europeans have a special appreciation of "culture," cultural events (e.g., music and dance) might be scheduled into the renamed sales meeting. Some sessions might be held in a castle or royal estate to take the selling stigma away, and what selling is actually done through the meeting should be less direct and more subtle.

* *Meeting dynamics* range from planning as many small sessions as feasible to provisions for sports and relaxation, especially after lunch (American compulsion for work, time use and "getting your money's worth" from employees is not appreciated in many civilized societies). A myth to be avoided is the belief that Americans are more organized than Europeans; for instance, many foreigners might be most concerned with administrative details. Incentive travel should be a motivator, especially with sales persons, who want personal and professional development to result from a trip abroad. People who go away for a meeting should have an enjoyable and different experience from back at the home work place.

International meetings when well-organized, well-executed, and culturally sensitive can be the means for intercultural cooperation and collaboration, as well as promoting international goodwill.

Appendix C
Resources for
Synergistic Effectiveness

This is a directory of publishing sources useful to managers and trainers who seek to improve their own and others' effectiveness in promoting synergistic actions. Many of the entries include books and other learning aids that are related to the themes of our book *Managing Cultural Synergy.* Readers are urged to write to the addresses given for catalogs and other information.

This listing supplements the reference sections in the previous fifteen chapters. It should be used in conjunction with our companion volume, *Managing Cultural Differences,* Appendix D, "Resources for Intercultural Effectiveness." We have avoided repeating the same citations here, unless the source has publications which are relevant to the synergy theme. The authors (Harris/Moran) welcome feedback of information that should be included in future editions of both volumes.

ORGANIZATIONS AND SERVICES

Adult Education Association, 810 18th Street, N.W., Washington, DC 20006, USA. Promotes mutual cooperation among adult educators through special studies and meetings which are published along with a newsletter, books, and pamphlets.

AFS International, 313 East 43rd Street, New York, NY 10017, USA. In addition to international exchanges of secondary school students, it publishes bulletins, *Facilitator's Handbook,* and newsletter.

American Council on Teaching of Foreign Languages, Inc., 2 Park Ave., Rm. 1814, New York, NY 10016, USA. Besides being a materials resource center, it publishes the *Foreign Language Annals,* a journal; *Annual Bibliography of Books and Arti-*

cles on Foreign Language Pedagogy; Foreign Language Education Series, annually, thematic focus. Also available are AV learning materials such as *Along the Pan-American Highway, Building Support for Foreign Languages;* printed materials such as *101 Ways to Stimulate a Conversation in a Foreign Language,* and *Directory of Foreign Language Service Organizations.*

American Management Associations (AMACOM), 135 West 50th Street, New York, NY 10020, USA. A membership organization for managers, it has a Human Resource Division, International Division, affiliated management centers around the world, and subsidiaries such as the International Management Association. AMACOM does its own book publishing and media productions, including titles such as: *How to Be an Effective Supervisor, Winning with Leadership Skills, Creative Problem Solving, Successful Team Work, Tough-Minded Team Building.*

American Society for Health Manpower Education and Training, 840 N. Lake Shore Dr., Chicago, IL 60611, USA. Affiliated with the American Hospital Association, this organization of health HRD specialists not only conducts meetings and surveys, but offers numerous books, publications, newsletter and journal.

American Society for Information Sciences, 1155 16th St., N.W., Suite 210, Washington, DC 20036, USA. Among publications: *Computer-Readable Bibliographic Data Bases: A Directory and Sourcebook* by M. E. Williams and S. H. Rouse, 1978.

American Society for Personnel Administration, 19 Church St., Berea, OH 44017, USA. A professional association for personnel and industrial relations managers, it acts as an information clearing house. Publishes *The Personnel Administrator,* newsletters, and research reports.

American Society for Training and Development, 600 Maryland Ave., S.W., Washington, DC 20024, USA. Largest organization of HRD specialists with 100 chapters around the world, and divisions for international, organization development, and other interest groups. It publishes *Training and Development Journal, The National Report,* and monographs, such as *Speakers Bureau Directory.* Among their many books: *Training and Development Handbook, Developing Media for Instruction,* and *Evaluation of Training,* and a newsletter, *International Dateline.*

Asian Productivity Organization, 4-14 Akasaka 8-Chome, Minato-ku, Tokyo 107 Japan. Inter-governmental, regional organization concerned with increasing productivity and economic development in specific areas. In addition to conferences and symposia, it conducts research and surveys which are then published. It also develops training manuals, AV aids, and cooperates with other international/regional/national organizations and institutions. Over 300 titles of general and technical publications.

Association for Systems Management, 24587 Bagley Road, Cleveland, OH 44138, USA. Professional society with journals and books, such as, *Business Systems* and *Information Resource Management.*

Bilingual Education Service Center, 500 S. Dwyer Ave., Arlington Heights, IL 60005, USA. Clearinghouse on bilingual and multi-cultural education which publishes *BESC Newsletter* and other educational materials.

Business Council for International Understanding, The American University, Washington, DC 20016, USA. In addition to its varied foreign deployment services, it publishes brochures and catalogs.

Canadian Association for Future Studies, #302, 100 Glouster St., Ottawa, Ontario K2P OA4, Canada. Co-sponsor of the First Global Conference on the Future, it publishes *Futures Canada,* a bulletin, as well as book reviews of futures publications.

Canadian International Development Agency, 122 Bank Street, Ottawa, Ontario Canada. In addition to its Briefing Centre programs for overseas services, it publishes reports and bulletins on cross-cultural training. For a catalog contact Communications Branch, P.O. Box 1430, Postal Station B, Hull, Quebec, J8X 3Y3 Canada.

Center for International Business, Suite 105, 4600 Post Oak Place Drive, Houston, TX 77027 or Suite 184, World Trade Center, Dallas, TX 75258, USA. In addition to international trade conference and special briefings for members, the center publishes the issues discussed at their meetings. Four volume series available on *The International Essays for Business Decision Makers,* and other titles, such as, *Regaining Leadership in the Multinational Arena.*

Center for Research and Education, 1800 Pontiac, Denver, CO 80220, USA. A division of Systran Corporation, the center conducts cross-cultural training and briefing. The *Bridge* Bookstore and international school, also divisions of Systran, are located at the same address.

Clearinghouse for Adult Education and Lifelong Learning Informatics, 6011 Executive Blvd., Rockville, MD 20852, USA. An information exchange for those in the field of continuing education.

Didactic Systems, Inc., Box 457, Cranford, NJ 07016, USA. Issues an annual free catalog of ideas and publications for action-oriented training and communicating. In addition to listing titles of other publishers, it publishes books, such as *The Linking Elements Concept;* self-study units, such as *Effective Communications;* management simulation games, such as *Effective Delegation, Leading Groups to Better Decisions, Productivity,* and *Women in Management.*

East-West Center Publications, 1777 East-West Center Road, Honolulu, HI 96848, USA. Issues reports and papers of their scholars' research, as well as conference proceedings from this prestigious federal center in the field of international and intercultural relations. In conjunction with University Press of Hawaii, their book titles include: *Mass Communication and the Press in the Pacific Island: A Bibliography; Popular Media in China; Shaping New Cultural Patterns; Modern Communi-*

cations Technology in a Changing Society: A Bibliography; Popular Images of America; Communication and Change; Communication for Group Transformation in Development; Bridging the Managerial Skills Gap Through Modular Instruction; Counseling Across Cultures; Culture Learning; Concepts, Applications and Research; Intercultural Education in the Community of Man; Bonds Without Bondage; Entrepreneur-Manager Training Manual; and many others.

Education Research, P.O. Box 4205, Warren, NJ 07060 U.S.A. Request catalog of business games and other management training aids.

Educational Resources Information Center, U.S. Office of Education, Washington, DC 20202, USA; **Eric Clearinghouse on Adult, Career, and Vocation Education,** Ohio State University, 1960 Kenny Rd., Columbus, OH 43210, USA. National information system for obtaining documents on microfiche or hard copy with clearinghouses in languages, educational media and technology, etc.

Experiment in International Living, Brattleboro, VT 05301, USA. Facilitates international exchanges of students and professionals.

F.A. Niles Communication Centers, Inc., 1058 West Washington Blvd., Chicago, IL 60607, USA. International media production services, including films on change and motivation.

Family Relocation Services, Inc. P.O. Box 10797, Stamford, CT 06904, USA. Selection, preparation, and orientation of employees and families for domestic and foreign transfers.

Farnham Castle Centre for International Briefing, The Castle Farnham, Surrey, GU9 OAG, England. In conjunction with European foreign deployment services, it produces videotapes and culture specific publications.

General Cassette Corp., 2311 N. 35th Avenue, Phoenix, AZ 85009, USA. Request catalog of audio cassettes for self-learning and directory of national speakers association.

Gulf Publishing Company, P.O. Box 2608, Houston, TX 77001, USA. In addition to technical and energy publications, as well as our *Managing Cultural Differences/ Managing Cultural Synergy* books and videotapes, other related titles from annual catalog: *Modern Personnel Management; Communication and the Technical Professional; Putting Management Theories to Work; Technology Transfers — A Realistic Approach; Practical Protocol — A Guide to International Courtesies; Managing Intergroup Conflict in Industry; Diary of an OD Man; The New Managerial Grid; The Conference Book, The Small Meeting Planner; The Client-Consultant Handbook; Handbook of Creative Learning Exercises; Creative Worklife; The Adult Educator; Human Resource Development: The European Approach; The NOW Employee,* etc. This company also has a division called **International Training Company** which provides specific training services worldwide to energy-related industries.

Harris International, Box 2321, LaJolla, CA 92038, USA. Publications and instructional systems resulting from customized training programs. Titles include *Manag-*

ing Organizational Dynamics, Performance Management Handbook, Effective Management of Change, Improving Management Communications Skills, Leadership Effectiveness with People, A Day-to-Day Key to Successful Employee Negotiations. Sponsored client-research reports not available to public.

HRA Publications, 5 Sandyford Rd., Paisley, PA3 4HW, Scotland. Publishes quarterly *HRD International Journal* on human resource development.

Human Synergistics, 39819 Plymouth Rd., Plymouth, MI 48170, USA. Instrumentation for human data-gathering, inventories on lifestyles and organization development.

Info World, 530 Lytton Ave., Palo Alto, CA 94301. A newspaper for the microcomputing community and network.

INSEAD, European Institute of Business Administration, Boulevard de Constance, 77305 Fontainbleau Cedex, France. Management education programs and publications for Europeans.

Institute International de la Communication de Montreal, 5255 Avenue Becelles, Montreal, Quebec, Canada H3T 1V6. Family orientation and education in language and intercultural relations worldwide.

Institute of International Education, 809 United Nations Plaza, New York, NY 10017, USA. Arranges for international exchange of students and scholars; has computer-based referral services on universities, research centers, government ministries, and international agencies worldwide for job placement purposes.

Intercom, American Graduate School of International Management, Glendale, AZ 85306, USA. Offers key-manager language programs for executives and spouses, international business programs, and cross-cultural training and preparation programs.

Intercultural Communication, Inc., P.O. Box 14358, University Station, Minneapolis, MN 55414. ICI offers training and culture specific orientation programs for families and managers. Language training and preselection assessment counseling are also offered.

Intercultural Press, 70 W. Hubbard St., Chicago, IL 60601, USA (a joint venture between Intercultural Network, Inc. and Systran Corp.) In addition to carrying the intercultural texts of other publishers (such as SIETAR, ICA, and Gulf), they issue their own works such as: *The Evaluation Handbook for Cross-cultural Training and Multicultural Education; Country Orientation Series* (e.g. *Interact: Mexico/U.S.); Survival Kit for Overseas Living; The American in Saudi Arabia,* etc.

Intercultural Relations Institute, P.O. Box A-B, Stanford, CA 94305, USA. Consulting group on intercultural resources and services, especially related to Japan and teacher exchanges. Cosponsor of annual Stanford Institute for Intercultural Communication.

International Communication Association, Balcones Research Center, 10, 100 Burnet Road, Austin, TX 78758, USA. Among the eight divisions of this professional organization is one on Intercultural Communication. Publishes *Journal of Communication,* and *International and Intercultural Communication Annual.*

International Consultants Foundation, 5605 Lamar Road, Washington, DC 20016, USA. Publishes *Annual International Consultants Registry;* newsletter, *International Consultants News;* monographs, such as, *The Consulting Process in Action;* annual proceedings, such as, *Helping Across Cultures; Innovation in Global Consultation; Systems Implications for International Consultants,* etc. (Also source of Development Publications' *Multimedia Resources Catalogue.)*

International Council on Education for Teaching, One Dupont Circle, N.W. Suite 616, Washington, D.C. 20036. International nongovernment network of educators. Exchange and cross-cultural orientation programs.

International Federation of Training and Development Organizations, Box 5307, Madison, WI 53705, USA. A coordinating association of international training and human resource development organizations. Cassettes and proceedings of annual meetings, and publications in various languages, of national member organizations available, plus newsletter; *International Resource Directory* of consultants/ suppliers.

International Institute for Organizational and Social Development, Predikheren-berg 55, B-3200 Leuven, Belgium. Social science research and consulting group operating in six languages and which publishes learning materials in conjunction with program offerings. These range from the ERGOM exercises or inventories to member papers to action research on high achieving personnel and accompanying manual.

International Management Development Institute, #905, 2600 Virginia Ave. N.W., Washington, DC 20037. Publishes *International Corporate Citizenship,* a publications and program review; significant Top Management Reports on *Interde-pendence and the International Corporation; Government-Business Cooperation in the Field of International Public Affairs; Corporate Citizenship in the Global Community; The Management of International Corporate Citizenship,* etc.

International Publications Limited, Melbourne House, Parliament St., Hamilton 5-31, Bermuda. Distributor of Canadian Organizational Tests Ltd. instruments for data collection and training. Titles include: *Management Style Diagnosis Test, Communication Sensitivity Inventory, Culture Shock Inventory, Management Change Inventory, Management Coaching Relations, Values Inventory, Supervisory Human Relations,* etc.

ISIS, Via della Pelliccia 31, 00153, Rome, Italy or Case Postale 301, 1227, Ca-roughe, Geneva, Switzerland. It is a resource and documentation center for the international women's liberation movement, which coordinates feminist networks and publishes a quarterly bulletin.

Klemmer International Training Memorandum, 666 E. Ocean Blvd., Suite 2608, Long Beach, CA 90802, USA. Produces a bimonthly newsletter for trainers.

Knowledge Industry Publications, 2 Corporate Park Dr., White Plains, NY 10604, USA. Publishes *Overseas Assignment Directory Services,* regularly with monthly supplements, for business travels/operations.

Language and Intercultural Research Center, Brigham Young University, 240 B-34, Provo, UT 84602, USA. Helpful *Culturgrams* are culture specific pamphlets on 69 countries and the USA; *Intercultural Communicator Resources,* annotated collection of learning materials; Infogram Series on return shock, jet lag and decision-making, family success abroad; *Communication Learning Aids,* booklets on various peoples of the same language groups (e.g., French/Spanish/German-speaking), etc.

Lisle Center for Intercultural Studies, 145 College Rd., Suffern, NY 10901, USA. Promotes summer foreign exchanges/scholarships.

Moran, Stahl, and Boyer International Division, 355 Lexington Ave., New York, NY 10016, USA (formerly Overseas Briefing Associates). In addition to relocation services, this division is the source of Alison Lanier's Update Series on country specifics (now being distributed by Intercultural Press above), the latest of which is *The People's Republic of China; Living in the U.S.A.*

MCB Human Resource Ltd, 198/200 Keighley Rd., Bradford, West Yorkshire BB9 4JQ, England. Publishes *Journal of European Industrial Training, Journal of Human Resource Development, Leadership and Organization Development Journal.*

National Association for Multiracial Education, 23 Doles Lane, Findern, Berby DE6 6AX, England. Publishes multiracial education journal and annual volume.

Newbury House Publishers, 58 Warehouse Lane, Rowley, MA 01969, USA. Bilingual, multicultural brochure useful in education and training. Catalog emphasis on learning aids for teaching English as a second language.

Nightingale-Conant Corp., 3700 W. Devon Ave., Chicago, IL 60659, USA. Request catalog of audio cassettes for human resource development.

Noonmark Corporation, 511 Second Street, N.E., Washington, DC 20002, USA. In conjunction with its cross-cultural seminars, these AV training packages are available: *An Introduction to Issues in Cultural Interaction; Cultures in Contrast; An Intercultural Awareness Survey.*

NTL Institute, 1815 N. Fort Meyer Drive, Arlington, VI 22209, USA. Publishes annual catalog of human relations/sensitivity training laboratories and accompanying learning materials; *Journal of Applied Behavioral Science;* directory of International Association of Applied Social Scientists (see University Associates catalog also).

Organization Development Network, 1011 Park Ave., Plainfield, NJ 10017, USA. An outgrowth of networks in ASTD/NTL, these professionals in OD meet annually and publish proceedings/newsletter for members.

Participation Publishers and Linkage, Inc., 4221 W. Yucca, Phoenix, AZ 85029. Pamphlets and network for futurists of varied disciplines in the communications field.

Pergamon Press, Maxwell House, Fairview Park, Elmsford, NY 10523, USA (offices in Oxford, Toronto, Paris, Frankfurt and Sydney, etc.) Among important books and journals, they feature publications in science and technology for development, planning and management, new international economic order. Titles include variety of Club of Rome publications; *Transnational Corporations, Technology Transfer and Development: A Bibliography Sourcebook; Integration of Science and Technology with Development; The Education Dilemma; The State of the Planet; The Global 2000 Report to the President of the U.S.: Entering the Twenty-first Century; The Future Is in Our Hands; Policy Reform in Developing Countries; Multinational Cooperation in Africa; The Obstacles to the New International Economic Order; An International Redistribution of Wealth and Power; Technology and Science in the People's Republic of China.*

Price Waterhouse Information Guide, 1251 Avenue of the Americas, New York, NY, USA. Provides free brochures on financial/tax information for over 90 countries, including one for foreign nationals in the United States.

Sage Publications, 275 South Beverly Drive, Beverly Hills, CA 90212, USA. Publishers of professional social science journals and proceedings in such specialized fields as cross-cultural psychology, simulations, etc.

Simile II, Box 910, Del Mar, CA 92014, USA. Publishes annual catalog and simulation games for all levels of education and on cross-cultural issues, such as *Bafá, Bafá; Napoli, Relocation, Crisis,* etc.

Society for International Development, 1346 Connecticut Ave., N.W., Washington, DC 20036, USA. In addition to newsletter, journal, and proceedings, they periodically publish *Films in a Changing World/Critical International Guide.*

Society for Intercultural Educational, Training and Research, 1414 Twenty-second St., N.W., Washington, DC 20037, USA. For professionals, they publish a newsletter, *Communiqué;* a quarterly, *International Journal of Intercultural Relations,* and helpful reports. The latter include: *American Cultural Patterns; Manual of Structured Experiences for Cross-Cultural Learning; Intercultural Sourcebook; Overview of Intercultural Education, Training and Research* (now 3 vols.); *Intercultural Theory and Practice.*

Syracuse University, International Management Development Department, 105 Roney Lane, Syracuse, NY 13210, USA. Short-term, intensive management education, especially for foreign nationals.

Transcultural Services, 59 Rogers Street, San Francisco, CA 94103, USA. Employee assistance program, especially relative to family foreign deployment services.

University Associates, 8517 Production Ave., San Diego, CA 92121, USA. Publish *Annual Handbook for Group Facilitators, Behavioral Science and the Manager's Role, Gellerman on Motivation and Productivity, Handbook of Structured Experiences for Human Relations Training, The Consulting Process in Action; Developing Support Groups; The Critical Incident in Growth Groups; Exploring Contemporary Male/Female Roles; Making Meetings Work; Conference Planning; Role Playing,* etc.

University Microfilms International, 300 North Zeeb Road, Ann Arbor, MI 48106, USA. Dissertation information services on more than 600,000 graduate research publications, with 35,000 new titles added yearly. Distribute *American Dissertation Bibliography* without cost, which notes subject areas of unpublished dissertations, such as Latin America, Black Studies, Japan, Korea, PRC, and Soviet Union. Those interested can purchase microfilms of such dissertations. For example, the United States International University has available doctorate dissertations from this source on *The Effectiveness of Classroom Instruction of Attitudes Toward Overseas Culture Shock Issues; Analysis of Selected Top Performers' Success Experiences; An Empirical Study of the Influences of Foreign Culture on the Performance of Managers in the International Banking Industry,* etc.

U.S. Department of Commerce, 14th St. and Constitution Ave., N.W., Washington, DC 20230, USA. In addition to field offices around the U.S., they have country consultants (East Coast South America — DOC Room 4039, Tel. 202/377-5427; Andean Countries — DOC Room 4036, Tel. 202/377-5427; Caribbean Countries — DOC Room 4036 above; Mexico/Central America — DOC Room 4031, Tel. 202/ 377-2313; Export Information Division, DOC Room 1033; Overseas Business Opportunities — DOC Room 2323; Information Library, 7th Floor, Main Commerce Bldg.)

U.S. Department of State, 2101 C Street, N.W., Washington, DC 20520, USA. Desk Officers/Bureau of Inter-American Affairs: Tel. 202/655-4000; Office of Commercial Affairs/Bureau of Economic & Business Affairs: Tel. 202/632-0669; U.S. Embassies in Latin America and Canada (see directory, *Key Officers of Foreign Service Posts: Guide for Business Representatives.*)

U.S. Superintendent of Documents, Government Printing Office, Washington, DC 20402, USA. Their catalog will reveal many useful publications from various government agencies ranging from the Peace Corps, Department of State/ICA, Department of Commerce, Department of Education to special reports like, The President's Commission on Foreign Language and International Studies. For example, the Department of Labor issues country labor profiles on such countries as Brazil, Canada, Chile, Ghana, Ireland, and Kenya, while the Department of Commerce issues comparable ones on doing business in such nations. For further information also contact The Federal Clearinghouse, 4040 N. Fairfax Drive, Suite 110, Arlington, VA 22209, USA.

World Future Society, 4916 St. Elmo Ave., Washington, DC 20014, USA. A multi-disciplinary society with various divisions that publish newsletters, such as *Future Survey, Education Tomorrow;* also *The Futurist,* Journal of Forecasts, Trends and Ideas about the future; special occasional books, such as, *The Study of the Future.*

World Information Sources, 130 North Road Vershire, Vt. 05079 USA. Publishes *Global Guide Series.*

World Press Review, 230 Park Avenue, New York, NY 10169, USA. Monthly extracts from newspapers around the world for international coverage.

BOOKS AND PUBLICATIONS

These references are divided into three sections, which correspond to the three units of the book. The references within each of these sections are then subdivided into chapter groupings so the reader can more easily obtain further information on material that is addressed in specific chapters.

Unit 1 Themes — International Management; Comparative Management; Motivation, Decision-making, Power, and Conflict; Communication and Negotiation.

Chapter 1

Cole, R.E. *Work, Mobility and Participation.* Los Angeles: University of California Press, 1979.

Coulter, N.A. Jr. *Synergetics: An Adventure in Human Development.* Englewood Cliffs, NJ: Prentice-Hall, Inc. 1976.

Connor, Patrick E. *Dimensions in Modern Management.* Boston: Houghton Mifflin Company, 1977.

Doctoroff, M. *Synergistic Management.* New York: AMACOM, 1977.

Drucker, Peter F. *An Introductory View of Management.* New York: Harper's College Press, 1978.

Drucker, Peter F. *People and Performance: The Best of Peter Drucker on Management.* New York: Harper & Row, 1977.

Ebert, Ronald J. and Mitchell, Terence R. *Organizational Decision Processes.* New York: Crane, Russak & Co., Inc., 1975.

England, George. *The Manager and His Values: An International Perspective from the U.S., Japan, Korea, India and Australia.* MA: Ballinger Publishing Co., 1976.

Lasker, G.E. (ed.) *Applied Systems and Cybernetics.* Six volumes, New York: Pergamon Press, 1981.

Ouchi, W. *Theory Z: How American Business Can Meet the Japanese Challenge.* Redding, MA: Addison-Wesley Publishing Company, 1981.

Pascale, R.T. and Athos, A.G. *The Art of Japanese Management: Applications for American Executives.* New York: Simon & Shuster, 1981.

Webber, Ross A. *Management: Basic Elements of Managing Organizations.* Homewood, IL: Irwin Publishers, 1979.

Chapter 2

Bass, Bernard M. et al. *Assessment of Managers: An International Comparison.* New York: Macmillan Publishing Company, Inc., 1979.

Dolman, A.J. *Global Planning and Resource Management.* New York: Pergamon Press, 1980.

England, George W., Anant R. Negandhi, and Bernhard Wipert, *Organizational Functioning in a Cross-Cultural Perspective.* Kent, OH: Kent State University Press, 1979.

Fillol, Tomas Roberto. *Social Factors in Economic Development: The Argentine Case.* Westport, CT: Greenwood Press, 1961.

Stopford, J. M., Dunning, J. H. and Haberich, K. O. *The World Directory of Multinational Enterprises.* New York: Facts on File, Inc. 1981.

Weinshall, Theodore D. (ed.) *Culture and Management.* New York: Penguin Books, Ltd., 1977.

Chapter 3

Adams, S. and Griffin, A. *Modern Personnel Management.* Houston, TX: Gulf Publishing, 1981.

Arnold, John D. "Six Steps to Effective Decision Making," *Nations' Business.* November 1976.

Connor, Patrick E. *Dimensions in Modern Management.* Boston: Houghton Mifflin Company, 1977.

Darling, F. C. *The Westernization of Asia.* Cambridge, MA: Schenkman Publishing Co., 1979.

Dickerman, Allen, *Training Japanese Managers.* New York, NY: Praeger Publishers, Inc, 1974.

Dowling, W. F. *How Managers Motivate: The Imperative of Supervision.* New York: McGraw-Hill, 1978.

Drucker, Peter F. *An Introductory View of Management.* New York: Harper's College Press, 1978.

Drucker, Peter F. *People and Performance: The Best of Peter Drucker on Management.* New York: Harper & Row, 1977.

Ebert, Ronald J. and Mitchell, Terence R. *Organizational Decision Processes.* New York: Crane, Russak & Co., Inc., 1975.

England, George, *The Manager and His Values: An International Perspective from the U.S., Japan, Korea, India and Australia.* MA: Ballinger Publishing Co., 1976.

Exton, W. *Motivational Leverage: A New Approach to Managing People.* West Nyack, New York: Parker Publishing, 1975.

Gellerman, S. W. *Management by Motivation.* New York: AMACOM, 1978.

Harrison, E. Frank. *The Managerial Decision-Making Process.* Boston, MA: Houghton Mifflin Co., 1977.

Hill, Roy. "How Effective are Works Councils?" *International Management.* October 1977.

Jain, Hem C. "Worker Participation: Lessons from the European Experience." *Management Review.* May 1980.

Kast, Fremont E. and Rosenzweig, James E. *Organization and Management: A Systems Contingency Approach.* New York, 1979.

Morton, Michael S. Scott. *Management Decision Systems: Computer-Based Support for Decision Making.* Cambridge, MA: Harvard College, 1971.

Patz, Alan and Rowe, Alan. *Management Control and Decision Systems: Text, Cases, and Readings.* New York: John Wiley and Sons, 1977.

Radford, K. J. *Managerial Decision-Making.* Reston, VA: Prentice-Hall Co., 1975.

Reischauer, E. O. *The Japanese.* Cambridge, MA: Harvard University Press, 1977.

Rohan, Thomas M. "Europeans in America Practice 'Foreign' Management," *Industry Week.* January 22, 1979.

Steers, Richard and Porter, Lyman. *Motivation and Work Behavior.* New York: McGraw-Hill, 1979.

Tubbs, Stewart L. and Widgery, Robin N. "When Productivity Lags . . . Are Key Managers Really Communicating?" *Management Review.* November 1978.

Vogel, Ezra F. *Modern Japanese Organization and Decision-Making.* Berkeley, CA: University of California Press, 1975.

Winchester, M. B. *The International Essay for Business Decision-Makers.* Volume 2, Houston: Gulf Publishing, 1971. Volumes 3, 4, and 5, New York: AMACOM, 1978-80.

Yoshino, M. Y. *Japan's Managerial System: Tradition and Innovation.* Cambridge, MA: The MIT Press, 1969.

Zartman, William. *The 50% Solution.* New York: Anchor Books, Anchor Press/Doubleday, 1976.

Chapter 4

Burns, James M. *Leadership.* New York: Harper & Row, 1978.

Bennis, Warren G. *The Unconscious Conspiracy: Why Leaders Can't Lead.* New York: AMACOM, 1976.

Christie, Richard. *Machiavellian Attitude Inventory in the 1978 Handbook for Group Facilitors.* La Jolla, CA: University Associates, 1978.

Christie, Richard et al. *Studies in Machiavellianism.* New York: Academic Press, 1970.

Clarke, John R. *Executive Power: How to Use it Effectively.* Englewood Cliffs, NJ: Prentice-Hall, 1979.

Deutsch, Morton. *The Resolution of Conflict: Constructive and Destructive Processes.* New Haven: Yale University Press, 1979.

Doolittle, Richard J. *Orientations to Communication and Conflict.* Chicago: Science Research Associates, Inc., 1976.

Duncan, Jack. *Organizational Behavior.* Boston: Houghton-Mifflin Company, 1978.

Goldstein, Leonard P., Lubin, Bernard and Lubin, Alice W. (eds.) *Organizational Change, Source Book II: Cases in Conflict: Management.* La Jolla, CA: University Associates, 1979.

Hofstede, G. *Culture's Consequences: International Differences in Work-Related Values.* Beverly Hills: Sage Publications, 1980.

Kotter, John P. *Power in Management.* New York: AMACOM, 1979.

Lumsden, George J. *Impact Management: Personal Power Strategies for Success,* New York: AMACOM, 1979.

Nightingale, Donald. "Conflict and Conflict Resolution." In: *Organizational Behavior Research and Issues* edited by George Strauss et al. Belmont, CA: Wadsworth Publishing Company, Inc., 1976.

Savage, Dean. *Founders, Heirs, and Managers: French Industrial Leadership in Transition.* London: Sage Publications, 1979.

Suleiman, Ezra N. *Elites in French Society: The Politics of Survival.* Princeton: Princeton University Press, 1978.

Chapter 5

Allen, Richard K. *Organizational Management Through Communication.* New York: Harper & Row, 1977.

Coffin, R. A. *The Negotiator: A Manual for Winners.* New York: AMACOM, 1973.

Fischer, H-D and Merrill, J.C. *International and Intercultural Communication.* New York: Hastings House, 1980.

Greenbaum, H.H. and Falcione, R.L. *Organizational Communication.* Beverly Hills, Calif.: Sage Publications, vol. 5-1980, vol. 6-1981

Ilich, J. *The Art and Skill of Successful Negotiation.* NJ: Prentice-Hall, 1973.

Jervis, Robert. *Perception and Misperception in International Politics.* Princeton, NJ: Princeton University Press, 1976.

Kapoor, Ashok. *Planning For International Business Negotiations.* Cambridge, MA: Ballinger Publishing Company, 1975.

Kessler, S. Multicultural Management. Fountain Valley, CA: National Institute for Professional Training, 1981.

Kochman, T. (ed.) *Rappin and Stylin Out. Communication in Urban Black America.* Chicago, IL: University of Illinois Press, 1977.

Kochman, T. (ed.) *Black and White Styles in Conflict.* Chicago, IL: University of Chicago Press, 1981.

Lehman, M. and Burke, T.J. (eds.) *Communication Technologies and Information Flow.* New York: Pergamon Press, 1981.

Lockhart, Charles. *Bargaining in International Conflicts.* New York: Columbia University Press, 1979.

Long, William A. and Seo, K. K. *Management in Japan and India, With Reference to the United States.* New York: Praeger Publishers, 1977.

Louden, J. Keith. *Managing at the Top: Roles and Responsibility of the Chief Executive Officer.* New York: AMACOM, 1977.

Marshall, E. and Kuntz, P. D. (eds.) *Interpersonal Helping Skills, Models, and Training Methods.* Nashville, TN: Human Resource Development Press, 1981.

Samovar, L.A., Porter, R.E. and Jain, N.C. *Understanding Intercultural Communication.* Belmont, CA: Wadsworth Pub., 1980.

Scanlan, Burt and Keys, J. Bernard. *Management and Organizational Behavior.* New York: John Wiley & Sons, Inc., 1979.

U.S. Department of Labor. *Industrial Democracy in 12 Nations.* Washington, DC: Bureau of International Affairs, January, 1979.

Walsh, John. "Cultural Aspects of Treaty Negotiation: A Project of the East-West Culture Learning Institute," *Culture Learning Institute Report,* Volume 5, No. 2, January, 1978.

Webber, Ross A. *Management: Basic Elements of Managing Organizations.* Homewood, IL: Irwin Publishers, 1979.

Zartmen, I. William (ed.) *The Negotiation Process: Theories and Applications.* Beverly Hills: Sage Publications, 1978.

Unit 2 Themes — Organizational Cultures; Team Management; Professional Synergy; Education and Training; Synergistic Leadership.

Chapter 6

Bennis, W. *Collaboration in Organizations.* New York: Human Sciences Press, 1981.

Benton, L. (ed.) *Management for the Future.* New York: McGraw-Hill, 1978.

Bing, G. *Corporate Acquisitions.* Houston: Gulf Publishing Company, 1980.

Burke, W. W. and Goodstein (eds.) *Trends and Issues in OD.* San Diego: University Associates, 1981.

Capelle, R. G. *Changing Human Systems.* Toronto: International Human Systems Institute, 1979.

Eddy, W. B. and Burke, W. W. (eds.) *Behavioral Science and the Manager's Role.* San Diego: University Associates, 1981.

Evans, C. *The Micro Millennium.* New York: Viking Press, 1979.

Hall, J. *The Competence Process: Managing Commitment and Creativity.* Woodlands, TX: Teleometrics International, 1981.

Harris, P. R. and Malin, G. H. *Innovations in Global Consultation.* Washington, DC 20016: International Consultants Foundation, 1980.

Klatt, L. A. *Human Resource Management: The Behavioral Systems Approach.* Homewood, IL: Richard D. Irwin, 1978.

Kumar, K. *Transnational Corporations: Their Impact on Third World Societies and Cultures.* Honolulu: Westview Press, 1980.

Scobel, D. *Creative Worklife.* Houston: Gulf Publishing Company, 1980.

Tavel, C. H. *The Third Industrial Age: Strategy for Business Service.* Homewood, IL: Dow Jones-Irwin, 1975.

Sheppard, C. S. and Carroll, D. C. (eds.) *Working in the Twenty-first Century.* New York: Wiley-Interscience, 1980.

Ways, M. (ed.) *The Future of Business: Global Issues in the '80s & '90s.* New York: Pergamon Press, 1979.

Chapter 7

Bradford, L. P. *Making Meetings Work.* San Diego, CA: Learning Resources Corp., 1976.

Dyer, W. G. *Team Building.* Reading, MA: Addison-Wesley, 1977.

Francis, B. and Young, B. *Improving Work Groups.* San Diego: University Associates, 1980.

Harris, P. R. *Managing Organizational Dynamics.* La Jolla, CA: Harris International, 1980.

Heenan, D. A. and Perlmutter, H. V. *Multinational Organizational Development.* Reading, MA: Addison-Wesley, 1979.

Jones, J. E. and Pfeiffer, J. W. *The 1981 Annual Handbook for Group Facilitators.* San Diego: University Associates, 1981.

Kraus, W. A. *Collaboration in Organizations.* Human Services Press, 1981.

Lau, J. P. *Behavior in Organizations.* Homewood, IL: Richard D. Irwin, Inc., 1979.

McNulty, N. (ed.) *Management Development Programs: The World's Best.* Washington, D.C.: American Society for Training and Development, 1981.

Merry, U. and Allerhand, M. E. *Developing Teams and Organizations.* San Diego: Learning Resources Corp., 1976.

Nadler, D. A. *Feedback and Organization Development.* Reading, MA: Addison-Wesley, 1977.

Rubin, I. M., Plounick, M. S. and Fry, R. E. *Task-Oriented Team Development.* New York: McGraw-Hill, 1978.

Woodstock, M. *Team Development Manual.* New York: John Wiley & Sons, 1979.

Chapter 8

Ayres, R.U. *Uncertain Future: Challenges for Decision-Makers.* New York: John Wiley & Sons, 1979.

Brislin, R.W. (ed.) *Culture Learning: Concepts, Applications, and Research.* University of Hawaii Press, 1977.

Bullock, A. and Stallybrass, O. (eds.) *The Harper Dictionary of Modern Thought.* New York: Harper & Row, Publishers, 1977.

Coelho, G., Hamburg, D. A. and Adams, J. E. *Coping and Adaptation.* New York: Basic Books, 1974.

Coelho, G. *Coping and Adaptation: Annotated Bibliography.* Washington, DC: Government Printing Office, 1980. (Contract #PLD, NIMH 14543-76: DHEW Pub. N080-863.)

Coulter, N. A. *Synergistics: An Adventure in Human Development.* New York: Behavioral Book Institute, 1980.

Feather, F. (ed.) *Through the '80s: Thinking Globally, Acting Locally.* Washington, DC: World Future Society, 1980.

Goodman, L. J. and Love, R. N. *Management of Development Projects.* Vol. 1 (1979) and *Integrated Project Planning & Management.* Vol. 2 (1980). New York: Pergamon Press, Inc.

Kumar, K. (ed.) *Bonds Without Bondage: Explorations in Transcultural Interactions.* Honolulu: University Press of Hawaii, 1979.

Lippitt, R. and G. *Systems Thinking: A Resource for Organization Diagnosis and Intervention.* Washington, DC: International Consultants Foundation, 1981.

Harris, P. and Malin, G. (eds.) *Innovation in Global Consultation.* Washington, DC: International Consultants Foundation, 1980.

Hiltz, R. and Turoff, M. *The Network Nation: Human Communication via Computer.* Reading, MA: Addison-Wesley, 1978.

Senger, J. *Individuals, Groups and the Organization.* West Nyack, NY: Winthrop Publishers, 1980.

Snyder, C. R. and Fromkin, H. *Uniqueness: The Human Pursuit of Difference.* New York: Plenum Press, 1980.

Chapter 9

Aslanian, C. B. and Brickell, H. M. *Americans in Transition: Life Changes as Reasons for Adult Learning.* New York: College Entrance Examination Board, 1980.

American Field Services International, *Facilitator's Handbook.* New York: AFS International, 1980.

Black, G.J. *Trends in Management Development and Education: An Economic Study.* Washington, D.C.: American Society for Training and Development, 1981.

Bochner, S., Brislin, R. W. and Lonner, W. J. *Cross-Cultural Perspectives on Learning.* New York: John Wiley/Halsted Division, 1975.

Boshier, R. *Towards A Learning Society.* Vancouver, BC: Learningpress Ltd. (370 W. 10th Ave), 1980.

Botkin, J. W. (ed.) *No Limits to Learning: Bridging the Human Gap.* Elmsford, NY: Pergamon Press, 1979.

Coehlo, G. and Ahmed, P. *Toward a New Definition of Health.* New York: Plenum Publishers, 1979.

Dickson, P. *The Future: A Guide for People with One Foot in the 21st Century.* New York: Rowson Associates Publishers, 1977.

Ferguson, H. *Manual for Multicultural and Ethnic Studies.* Chicago, IL: Intercultural Press, 1977.

Frank, H. E. *Human Resource Development: The European Approach.* Houston: Gulf Publishing Company, 1974.

Griffin, W. H. "International Educational Cooperation and the World's Future," Vol. 3, *Topics in Culture Learning Annual.* Honolulu: East-West Learning Center, 1975.

Grove, N. *Survival Kit for Classroom Teaching.* Chicago: Intercultural Press, 1981.

International Labor Office. *Impact of Micro-electronics.* New York: UNIPUB, 1980.

Kinlaw, D. C. *Helping Skills for Human Resources Development.* San Diego, CA: University Associates, 1981.

Klatt, L. A., Murdick, R. C. and Schuster, F. E. *Human Resources Management: A Behavioral Systems Approach.* Homewood, IL: Richard D. Irwin, 1978.

Lafayette, R. C. (ed.) *Teaching Culture: Strategies and Techniques.* Arlington, VA: Center for Applied Linguistics, 1978.

Marsella, A.J. and Pedersen, P.B. (eds.) *Cross-Cultural Counseling and Psychotherapy.* Elmsford, N.Y.: Pergamon Press, 1981.

Mill, C. R. *Activities for Trainers.* San Diego: University Associates, 1981.

Nadler, L. (ed.) *The Training Resource: A Comprehensive Guide to Packaged Learning Programs.* Amherst, MA: Human Resource Development Press, 1981.

Nadler, L. *Developing Human Resources.* San Diego, CA: Learning Concepts/University Associates, 1979.

Newman, J. W. and Scannell, E. *Games Trainers Play: Experimental Learning Exercises.* New York: McGraw-Hill Book, 1980.

Renwick, G. W. *Evaluation Handbook: For Cross-Cultural Training.* Chicago: Intercultural Press, 1978.

Shane, H. G. *The Educational Significance of the Future.* Bloomington, IN: Phi Delta Kappa, 1973.

Springer, J. W. (ed.) *Issues in Career and Human Resource Development.* ASTD Research Series No. 5, 1980.

Triandis, H. C. and Lambert, W. W. (eds.) *Handbook of Cross-Cultural Psychology — Perspectives.* Vol. 1, *Methodology.* Vol. 2, *Social Psychology.* Vol. 8. Boston: Allyn and Bacon, 1980.

Walker, J. W. *Human Resource Planning.* New York: McGraw-Hill, 1980.

Chapter 10

Brandt, Willy (ed.) *North-South: A Programme for Survival.* Cambridge, MA: MIT Press, 1980

Christopher, W. F. *Management for the 1980s.* Englewood Cliffs, NJ: Prentice Hall, 1980.

Harris, P. and D. *Leadership Effectiveness With People.* Phoenix, AZ: General Cassette, 1978. (Six audio cassette presentations to accompany author's manual, *Organizational Dynamics,* 1980. Both available through Harris International, Box 2321, La Jolla, CA 92038, USA).

Hawrylyshyn, B. *Road Maps to the Future: Toward More Effective Societies.* New York: Pergamon Press, 1980.

Heath, D. H. *Maturity and Competence: A Transcultural View.* New York: Garden Publishers, 1977.

Henderson, H. *The Politics of Reconceptualization.* New York: Anchor/Doubleday, 1980.

Illman, P. E. *Developing Overseas Managers — And Managers Overseas.* New York: AMACOM, 1980.

Lasch, C. *Culture of Narcissism: American Life in an Age of Diminishing Expectations.* New York: Warner Books, 1980.

Lassey, W. R. and Fernandez, R. F. (eds.) *Leadership and Social Change.* San Diego: University Associates, 1980.

Lippitt, R. and Lindaman, E. *Choosing the Future You Prefer.* Washington, DC (5605 Lamar Road): Development Publications, 1980.

Oshry, B. *Power and Position.* Boston, MA (Box 388): Power & Systems Training Inc., 1977.

Sheppard, C. S. and Carroll, D. C. (eds.) *Working in the Twenty-first Century.* New York: Wiley-Interscience, 1980.

Sirkin, A. M. *Living with Interdependence: The Decade Ahead in America.* Princeton, NJ: Aspen Institute of Humanistic Studies, 1975.

Stanley, C. M. *Managing Global Problems.* Iowa City, IA: Univ. of Iowa Press, 1980.

Tavel, C. *The Third Industrial Age: Strategy for Business Survival.* Homewood, IL: Dow Jones-Irwin, Inc., 1975.

The Conference Board (E. C. Bursk, ed.) *Challenge to Leadership: Managing in a Changing World.* New York: The Free Press, 1973.

Winchester, M., (ed.) *The International Essays for Business Decision Makers.* Vol. IV. New York: AMACOM, 1979.

Work in America Institute, *Studies in Productivity* (17 volumes published in 1979 on such topics as *Productivity and the Quality of Work Life; Managerial Productivity; Redesigning Work: A Strategy for Change; Changing Attitudes Toward Work; Women in Management; Performance Evaluation for Professional Personnel.*) Work in America Institute, 700 White Plains Road, Scarsdale, NY 10583, USA.

Unit 3 Themes — Asian Management; Middle Eastern Management; European Management; Pan American Management; Transnational Management Synergizers.

Chapter 11

Darling, F. C. *The Westernization of Asia.* Cambridge, MA: Schenkman Publishing Co., 1979.

Fersch, F. *Asia: Teaching About/Learning From.* Denver, CO: Teachers College/Columbia/The Bridge, 1977.

Lebra, W.P. *Transcultural Research in Mental Health: Vol. 2, Asia and Pacific.* University of Hawaii Press, 1972.

Rosenfeld, E. and Geller, H. *Afro-Asian Studies.* Denver, CO: Barons/*The Bridge,* 1979.

Smith, G. R. and Otero, G. P. *Images of China.* Denver, CO: CTIR/*The Bridge,* 1977.

Australia

Area Handbook on Australia. Washington, DC: U.S. Government Printing Office, 1976.

Background Notes on the Commonwealth of Australia. Washington, DC: U.S. Government Printing Office.

Culturgram: Australia. Provo, UT: Language Research Center, Brigham Young University, 1977.

Horne, Donald. *The Australian People: Biography of a Nation.* Angus and Robertson, 1972.

Learmouth, Nancy. *The Australians: How They Live and Work.* New York: Praeger Publishers, 1973.

Renwick, George. *Australia/U.S. Interact Series.* Chicago: Intercultural Press, Inc., 1981.

Hong Kong

Language Research Center. *Building Bridges of Understanding — People of Hong Kong.* Provo, UT: Brigham Young University, 1977.

Language Research Center. *Culturgram: Hong Kong,* Provo, UT: Brigham Young University, 1977.
Seybolt, Peter. *Through Chinese Eyes.* New York: Praeger, 1974.
U.S. State Department. *Background Notes: Hong Kong.* Washington, DC: U.S. Government Printing Office.
Yuan-li, Wu (ed.) *China, A Handbook.* New York: Praeger, 1973.

India

Cormack, Margaret and Skagen, Kiki (eds.) *Voices From India.* New York: Praeger, 1972.
Johnson, D. J. and Johnson, J. E. (eds.) *Through Indian Eyes.* New York: Praeger, 1974.
Lamb, Beatrice P. *India, A World in Transition.* New York: Praeger, 1975.
Language Research Center. *Culturgram: India.* Provo, UT: Brigham Young University, 1977.
Roy, G. C. *Indian Culture.* New Delhi, India: Ajanta Publications, 1976.
U.S. State Department. *Area Handbook for the Republic of India.* Washington, DC: U.S. Government Printing Office, 1975.

Indonesia

Indonesia Development News, Hill and Knowlton, Inc. 633 Third Avenue, New York, NY, 10017.
Lanier, Alison. *Update: Indonesia.* New York: Overseas Briefing Associates, 1976.
Language Research Center. *Culturgram: Indonesia.* Provo, UT: Brigham Young University, 1977.
U.S. State Department. *Background Notes on the Republic of Indonesia.* Washington, DC: U.S. Government Printing Office.

Japan

Aoki, M.Y. and Dandess, M.B. *As the Japanese See It: Past and Present.* University of Hawaii Press, 1981.
Asumi, K., Hickson, D., Horvath, D. and McMillan, C. "Japanese Organizations: Are They Really So Different". Working paper, University of California, Berkeley, 1978.
Clark, Rodney. *The Japanese Company.* New Haven: Yale University Press, 1979.
Dickerman, Allen, *Training Japanese Managers.* New York: Praeger Publishers, Inc., 1974.
Gibney, Frank. *Japan: The Fragile Superpower.* Tokyo: Tuttle, 1979.
Lebra, Takie S. *Japanese Patterns of Behavior.* Honolulu: The University Press of Hawaii, 1976.
Marsh, R. M. and Mannari, H. *Modernization and Japanese Factory.* Princeton University Press, 1976.

Norbury, Paul and Bownas, J. (eds.) *Business in Japan*. Boulder, CO: Westview Press, 1980.

Ouchi, W. H. and Jaeger, A. M. "Type Z Organization: A Better Match for a Mobile Society," *Academy of Management Review*. July 1978.

Ouchi, W. H. and Johnson, Jerry B. "Type of Organizational Control and Their Relationship to Emotional Well-Being," *Administrative Science Quarterly*. June 1978.

Pascale, R. T. "Zen and the Art of Management", *Harvard Business Review*, March-April 1978, pp.153-162.

Pascale, R. T. "Communications and Decision-Making Across Cultures: Japanese and American Comparisons," *Administrative Science Quarterly*. March 1978.

Reischauer, E. O. *The Japanese*. Cambridge, MA: Harvard University Press, 1977.

Vogel, Ezra F. *Japan as No. One: Lessons for America*. Cambridge, MA: Harvard University Press, 1979.

Vogel, E. F. *Modern Japanese Organization and Decision-Making*. University of California Press, 1975.

Yoshino, M. Y. *Japan's Multinational Enterprises*. Harvard University Press, 1976.

Korea

Hamilton, Angus. *Korea: Cultural Interpretations*. New York: C. Schribner's Sons Publishing, 1974.

Korean Overseas Information Service. *Facts About Korea*. Seoul, Korea, 1979.

Language Research Center. *Building Bridges of Understanding — Koreans*. Provo, UT: Brigham Young University, 1976.

Language Research Center. *Culturgram: Korea*. Provo, UT: Brigham Young University, 1977.

Stanley, John W. *Foreign Businessmen in Korea*. Seoul: Kyumoon Publishing Company, 1972.

U.S. State Department. *Area Handbook for the Republic of Korea*. Washington, DC: U.S. Government Printing Office, 1975

Malaysia

Hirschman, C. *Ethnic and Social Stratification in Peninsular Malaysia*. Washington, DC: American Sociological Association, 1975.

Language Research Center. *Culturgram: Malaysia*. Provo, UT: Brigham Young University, 1977.

Pedersen, Paul. *Malay-Chinese Relations: Background and Guidelines for Americans in Malaysia*. Scottsdale, AZ: Intercultural Network Inc., 1978.

Renwick, George W. *Malays and Americans: Definite Differences, Unique Opportunities*. Intercultural Management Series, No. 2, Scottsdale, AZ: Intercultural Network Inc., 1977.

Vreeland, Nena. *Area Handbook for Malaysia*. 3rd Edition, Washington, DC: U.S. Government Printing Office, 1977.

Chapter 12

Algeria

Gillespie, J. *Algeria, Rebellion and Revolution.* Greenwood Press, 1976.

Ottaway, D. and M. *Algeria: The Politics of a Socialist Revolution.* Berkeley, CA: University of California Press, 1970.

Stevens, J. and V. *Algeria and The Sahara: A Handbook for Travelers.* New York: International Publications Service, 1977.

Egypt

Area Handbook on Egypt. Washington, DC: U.S. Government Printing Office, 1976.

Farah, Caesar. *Islamic Beliefs and Observances.* Woodbury, NY: Barrons, 1970.

Hussein, Taha. *The Future of Culture in Egypt.* Translated by Sidney Glazer. New York: Octogan Books, 1975.

Jordan, Paul. *Egypt: The Black Land.* New York: Dutton, 1976.

Lanier, Alison. *Update: Egypt.* Chicago: Intercultural Press, 1978.

Murrell, K. L. "A Cultural Analysis of Egyptian Management Environment." In: *Innovations in Global Consultation,* edited by P. R. Harris and G. H. Malin for International Consultants Foundation Washington, DC 20016, USA.

Nelson, Nina. *Egypt.* London, 1976.

Richmond, John. *Egypt in Modern Times.* New York: Columbia University Press, 1977.

Iran

Benny, R. *Iran: Elements of Destiny.* Everest House, 1978.

Holliday, F. *Iran: Dictatorship and Development.* New York: Penguin Press, 1979.

Kedourie, E., and Halm, S. G. *Iran: Toward Modernity Studies in Thought, Politics, and Society.* New York: Biblio. Distr., 1979.

Lenczowski, G. C. *Iran Under the Pahlavis.* Hoover Inst. Press, 1978.

Sterling, M. and R. *Iran Diary.* New York: Berkley Publications, 1980.

Iraq

Penrose, E. and E. F. *Iraq: Economics, Oil, and Politics.* New York: Westview Publications, 1978.

Fichter, G. *Iraq.* New York: Watts Publication, 1978.

Ismail, M. (editor in chief) *Iraq Today,* a continuing bi-monthly publication. Baghdad, Iraq, Ministry of Culture and Information.

Jordan

Patai, R. *Jordan, Lebanon, and Syria, An Annotated Bibliography.* New York: Greenwood Press, 1973.

Barakat, A. Z. (publisher) *Jordan,* a quarterly published by the Jordan Information Bureau in Washington, DC.

Morocco

Ashford, D. E. *Morocco Tunisia: Politics and Planning.* New York: Syracuse University Press, 1965.
Aubin, E. *Morocco of Today.* New York: Gordon Press, 1977.
Birdwell, R. *Morocco Under Colonial Rule: French Administration of Tribal Areas.* New York: Biblio. Distr., 1973.

Oman

Hawley, D. *Oman and its Renaissance.* London: 1977.
Peterson, J. E. *Oman in the Twentieth Century.* New York: 1978.
Skeet, I. *Muscat and Oman: The End of an Era.* London: 1974.
Townsend, J. *Oman: The Making of the Modern State.* 1977.

Saudi Arabia

Al-Farsy, Fouad Abdelsalam. *Saudi Arabia: A Case Study In Development.* Ann Arbor: University Microfilms International, 1979.
Allanheld, O. *Trading with Saudi Arabia: A Guide to Shipping, Trade, Investment, and Tax Laws.* New York: UNIPUB, 1980.
American University. *Area Handbook for Saudi Arabia.* Washington, DC: U.S. Government Printing Office, 1976.
Bidwell, R. and Seargent, R. *Arabian Studies.* London: Hurst, 1976.
Fleming, Q.W. *A Guide to Doing Business on the Arabian Peninsula.* New York: AMACOM, 1981.
Haddad, Hassan S. and Nijim, Basheer K. *The Arab World: A Handbook.* Wilmette: Medina Press, 1978.
Lee, Eve. *The American in Saudi Arabia.* Chicago: Intercultural Press, 1980.
Long, David E. *Saudi Arabia. The Washington Papers.* Vol. 4, no. 39. Beverly Hills and London: Sage Publications, 1976.
Mansfield, Peter. *The Arabs.* London: Allen Lane, 1977.
Otero, G. G. *Teaching About Perceptions: The Arabs.* CITR. Denver, CO: University of Denver, 1977.
Patai, Raphael. *The Arab Mind.* New York: Charles Scribner's Sons, 1976.
Successful Transition into Saudi Arabia. Saudi Arabian Airlines, Kansas City, MO and the Center for Research and Education, Denver CO, 1978.

Chapter 13

Boddewyn, J. J. (ed.) *European Managers: West and East.* White Plains, NY: International Arts and Sciences Press, Inc., 1976.

Burmeister, Irmgard. *Meeting German Business: A Practical Guide for American and Other English-Speaking Businessmen in Germany.* Hamburg, Germany: Atlantik-Brucke, 1977.

Burmeister, I. *Co-Determination: Worker Participation in German Industry.* New York, NY: German Information Center, 1977.

Davidson, David S. "Employee Participation Can Mean Increased Employee Satisfaction," *Supervisory Management.* February 1979.

Heller, Robert and Willatt, Norris. *The European Revenge.* London, England: Barrie and Jenkins, Ltd., 1975.

Hilton, Lynn M. (ed.) *France, Its People and Culture.* Skokie, IL: National Textbook Company, 1977.

Laurent, A. *Cultural Dimensions Managerial Ideologies: National vs. Multinational Cultures.* Unpublished address at Fountainebleau, France: INSEAD, 1979.

Padover, Saulik. *French Institutions,* Westport, CT: Greenwood Press, 1978.

Romer, Karl. *Facts About Germany.* Gutersloh, Germany: Bertelsmann Lexikon-Verlag, 1979.

Suleiman, Ezra N. *Elites in French Society.* Princeton, New Jersey: Princeton University Press, 1979.

Teakfield. *Sources of European Economic Information.* New York:UNIPUB, 1980.

Weiner, M. J. *English Culture and the Decline of the Industrial Spirit — 1850-1980.* Cambridge, England: Cambridge University Press, 1981.

Woodgate, Roger. "Participation in West Germany: Another Side of the Story," *Personnel Management.* February 1979.

Chapter 14

Asante, M. K. and Vandi, A. S. *Contemporary Black Thought.* Beverly Hills, CA: Sage Publications, 1980.

Bottin International: International Business Register. Published annually by Annuaire du Commerce Didot-Bottin, Paris, France. (Directory of world industry, including Latin America, USA, Canada).

Business and Legal Aspects of Latin American Trade and Investment, edited by D. R. Shea and F. W. Swacker. Center for Latin America, University of Wisconsin, Milwaukee, WI 53201, USA, 1976.

Canada Handbook, Publishing Section Information Division Statistics, Ottawa, Canada KIA OT6.

Canadian Council for International Cooperation, *Directory of Canadian Non-Government Organizations Engaged in International Development.* (CCIC, 75 Sparks St., Ottawa, Canada KIP 5A5), 1980.

Colombo, J. R. *Canadian References.* Toronto: John Deyell Co., 1976.

Daedalus. *American Indians, Blacks, Chicanos, and Puerto Ricans.* Vol. 110, Spring 1981. American Academy of Arts and Sciences, Cambridge Mass. 02138.

Duignan, P. and Rabushka, A. (eds.) *The United States in the 1980s.* Stanford, CA: Hoover Institution/Stanford University, 1980.

Economic and Social Progress in Latin America: Annual Report. Inter-American Development Bank, Washington, DC 20557, USA. (Also monthly newsletter and useful library).

Economic Survey of Latin America. United Nations Economic Commission for Latin America, 1801 K. St., N.W., Washington, DC 20005, USA. Annual.

Gold, M. J. *In Praise of Diversity: A Resource Book for Multicultural Education (America's Pluralism).* (Teacher's Corps/Association for Teacher Educators, 1701 K Street, N.W., Washington, DC 20006, USA), 1980.

Guide to Latin American Business Information Sources. Organization of American States, Washington, DC 20006, USA. 1977. (Request Publications Catalog).

International Market Guide: Latin America. Dun & Bradstreet International, New York, NY 10019, USA. Annual and supplements.

Lanier, A. R. *Living in the U.S.A.* Chicago: Intercultural Press, 1979.

Latin America 1980. Facts on File, Inc., 119 West 57th St., New York, NY 10019, USA. Annual.

Laurent, A. *Matrix Organization and Latin Cultures.* Fountainebleu, France: IN-SEAD, 1979.

Levine, D. H. *Churches and Politics in Latin America.* Beverly Hills, CA: Sage Publications, 1980.

Mayers, M. K. *A Look At Latin American Lifestyles.* Dallas, TX: SIL Museum of Anthropology, 1976.

Operating in Latin America's Integral Markets: ANCOM/CACM/CARICOM/ LAFTA. Business International Corp., One Dag Hammarskjold Plaza, New York, NY 10017, USA. 1977. (Also publishes a weekly periodical, *Business Latin America*).

Sewell, J. W. et al. *The United States and World Development: Agenda 1980.* Washington, DC: Overseas Development Council, 1980.

Sigmund, P. E. *Multinationals in Latin America: The Politics of Nationalization.* Madison, WI: The University of Wisconsin Press, 1980.

Stewart, E. C. *American Cultural Patterns: A Cross-Cultural Perspective.* Washington, DC: SIETAR/Intercultural Press, 1976.

Theberge, J. O. and R. W. Fontaaine. *Latin America: Struggle for Progress.* Lexington, MA: The Third Century Corp./Lexington Books, 1977.

White, E. "The International Projection of Firms from Latin American Countries" In: *Multinationals from Developing Countries,* edited by K. Kumar and M. McLeod. New York: Lexington Books/D. C. Heath, 1980.

Chapter 15

Agmon, T. and Kindleberger, C. P. *Multinationals from Small Countries.* Cambridge, MA: MIT Press, 1977.

Bass, B. M. and Burger, P. G. *Assessment of Managers: an International Comparison.* New York, NY: The Free Press/Macmillan, 1980.

Beer, S. *The Heart of Enterprise.* London: John Wiley & Sons Ltd., 1979.

Bergsten, F. C., Horst, T. and Moran, T. H. *American Multinationals and American Interests.* Washington, DC: Brookings Institution, 1978.

Brown, H. *Learning How to Live in a Technological Society.* Tokyo: The Simul Press, 1979.

Brown, H. *The Human Future Revisited: The World Predicament and Possible Solutions.* New York: W. W. Norton, Co., 1978. (Both available from East-West Center Publications, 1777 East-West Road, Honolulu, Hawaii, 96848, USA).

Casmir, F. L. (ed.) *Intercultural and International Communications.* Washington, DC: University Press of America, 1978.

Christopher. W. F. *Management for the 1980s.* Englewood Cliffs, NJ: Prentice-Hall, 1980.

Clague, L. and Krupp, N. *International Personnel: The Repatriation Problem.* Denver: The Center for Research and Education, 1980. Available from The Bridge Bookstore, 1800 Pontiac St., Denver, CO.

Coleman, E. (ed.) *Information and Society.* Basking Ridge, N.J.: A.T.&T./Corporate Planning & Emerging Issues Group, 1981.

Dordick, H.S., Bradley, H.G., and Nanus B. *The Emerging Network Marketplace.* Norwood, N.J.: Ablex Pub. Corp., 1981.

England, G. W., Negandhi, A. R. and Wilpert, B. (eds.) *Organizational Functioning in a Cross-Cultural Perspective.* Kent, OH: Kent State University Press, 1980.

Hamnett, M.P. and Brislin, R.W. (eds.) *Language and Conceptual Studies.* University of Hawaii Press, 1980.

Hofstede, G. *Culture Consequences: International Variations of in Organizations.* Beverly Hills, CA: Sage Publications, 1980.

Kasterns, M. L. *Redefining the Manager's Job.* New York: AMACOM, 1980.

Kerr, C. and Rosow, J. M. (eds.) *Work in America: The Decade Ahead.* New York: Van Nostrand Reinhold, 1979.

King, A. (ed.) *The State of the Planet.* Elmsford, NY: Pergamon Press, 1980.

Kumar, K. *Technology Transfer from Developing Countries.* Elmsford, NY: Pergamon Press, 1981.

Kumar, K. (ed.) *Transnational Enterprises: Their Impact on Third World Societies and Cultures.* Boulder, CO: Westview Press, 1980.

Kumar, K. and McLeod, S. (eds.) *Multinationals from Developing Countries.* New York: D. C. Heath, 1980.

Laszlo, E. and Bierman, J., (eds.) *Goals in the Global Community.* Elmsford, NY: Pergamon Press, Vol. 1-1977; Vol. II, 1978.

Marshall, E. and Kutz, P. D. (eds.) *Interpersonal Helping Skills: Models and Training Methods.* Memphis, TN: Human Resource Development Press, 1981.

McNeill, W. H. and Adams, R. S. (eds.) *Human Migration: Patterns and Policies.* Bloomington, IN: Indiana University Press, 1978.

Mulvihill, D. F. *An Annotated Bibliography of Business Articles in The Futurist.* Kent, OH: Institute for 21st Century Business/Kent State University, 1977.

Peccei, A. *The Human Quality.* Elmsford, NY: Pergamon Press, 1977.

Rifkin, J. and Howard, T. *Entropy: A New World View.* New York: The Viking Press, 1980.

Seurat, S. *Technology Transfer: A Realistic Approach.* Houston: Gulf Publishing Company, 1979.

Sheppard, C. S. and Carroll, D. C. (eds.) *Working in the Twenty-first Century.* New York: John Wiley & Sons, 1980.

Sunkel, O. and Fuenzalida, E. *The Effects of Transnational Corporations on Culture.* Paris: UNESCO, 1976.

Tavel, C. *The Third Industrial Age: Strategy for Business Survival.* Homewood, IL: Dow Jones-Irwin, 1975.

Ways, M. (ed.) *The Future of Business: Global Issues in the '80s and '90s.* Elmsford, NY: Pergamon Press, 1979.

Relocation Services

A Study of Employee Relocation Policies Among Major U.S. Corporations, 1980; *Relocation Management '80 Proceedings.* Merrill Lynch Relocation Management, Inc. (4 Corporate Park Drive, White Plains, NY 10604, USA).

Brasch, R. *Relocation Guide.* Executive Publications, Ltd. 19080 West Ten-Mile Road, South Field, MO 48075, USA.

Directory of International Business Travel and Relocation. 1980, Gale Research Co., Book Tower Bldg., Detroit, MI 48226, USA.

Kohls, L. R. *Survival Kit for Overseas Living.* Chicago: Intercultural Press, 1980.

Lanier, Alison R. *The UPDATE Series.* Culture specifics about foreign countries and their peoples, Intercultural Press, Inc. (70 West Hubbard St., Chicago, IL 60610, USA).

Lanier, Alison R. *Your City: Handbook for International Trainers.* International Division/Moran, Stahel, and Boyer (355 Lexington Ave., New York, NY 10016, USA), 1976.

Percival, S. *Transfer Training Manual.* USO Orientation, 151 Slater Street, Ottawa, Ontario K1P 5H5 Canada.

Raymond, R. J. and Eliot, S. V. *Grow Your Roots Anywhere Anytime.* Peter A. Wyden Publishers (Box 151 Ridgefield, CT. 06877, USA), 1980.

Steen, E. and Russell, D. *Moving Overseas.* International Transfer Consultants (P.O. Box 73133, Houston, TX 77090, USA), 1980.

Subject Index

A

Abu Dhabi, 243
Accomplishments, 40
Accountability, 165
Acculturation, 189
Acquisition, 112-113, 115
Action learning, 175 ff.
Active listening, 87 ff.
Adab, 212
Adat, 213-214
Ad hocracies, 123
Adult Education Association, 359
Aerospace industry, 129
Africa, culture, 26
  Portuguese in, 192
AFS International, 359
Age, in Korea, 232-233
  in Malaysia, 216
Airbus Industrie, 117-118
Ajman, 243
Alliance for Progress, 275
AMACOM, 360
American Council on Education, 182
American Council on Teaching of
    Foreign Languages, 359
American Management Associations
(AMACOM), 360
American Motors—Canada, 173
American Society for Health
    Manpower Education and
    Training, 360

American Society for Information
    Sciences, 360
American Society for Personnel
    Administration, 360
American Society for Training and
    Development, 182, 338, 360
American Telephone and
    Telegraph, 318
Andean Pact, 297
Angola, 192
Anticipatory learning, 168
Anticipatory management, 173
Arab culture. *See* Middle East
Aramco, 242
Argentina, 18, 297
  leadership style, analysis, 58, 59
ASEAN, 211
Asian management, synergy
    with, 210-236
Asian Productivity Organization, 360
Association of Southeast Asian
    Nations, 211
Association for Systems
    Management, 360
Atlantic Richfield Company, 318
Australia, 58, 59, 377
Austria, 58, 59
Authoritarianism, German
    business, 254
Authority, French business,
    259, 261 ff.
Automation, 348

Author Index